DISNEY MASTERS

MICKEY MOUSE:
THE RIVER OF TIME

by Corrado Mastantuono

Publisher: GARY GROTH
Editor: DAVID GERSTEIN
Production: PAUL BARESH and BEN HORAK
Design: DAVID GERSTEIN AND C HWANG
Associate Publisher: ERIC REYNOLDS

Mickey Mouse: The River of Time is copyright © 2024 Disney Enterprises, Inc.
All contents copyright © 2024 Disney Enterprises, Inc. unless otherwise noted. All rights reserved.

Disney Masters showcases the work of internationally acclaimed Disney artists. Many of the stories presented in the
Disney Masters series appear in English for the first time. This is *Disney Masters* Volume 25. Permission to quote or
reproduce material for reviews must be obtained from the publisher.

Fantagraphics Books, Inc. | 7563 Lake City Way NE | Seattle WA 98115 | (800) 657-1100

Visit us at fantagraphics.com. Follow us on Twitter at @fantagraphics and on Facebook at facebook.com/fantagraphics.

Cover art by Corrado Mastantuono; color by Disney Italia, restoration by Fábio Figueiredo (IC SPD 32).

Special thanks to Francesco Artibani, Fábio Figueiredo, Aki Hyyppä, Francesco Spreafico, and Fernando Ventura.

First printing: May 2024 | ISBN 978-1-68396-940-2 | Printed in China | Library of Congress Control Number: 2017956971

"Boomer Buff's Big Boost," "Birthday Bad Guys," "The Explorers of Tomorrow," "Mouse in the Mirror," and "Once Upon a Pastry"
appear here for the first time in North America.

The stories in this volume were originally published in the following magazines:

"The River of Time" ("Topolino e il fiume del tempo") in Italian *Topolino* #2243 and 2244, November 24 and December 1, 1998,
translated in American *Mickey Mouse Adventures* [series II] #2, February 2005 (I TL 2243-1)
"Boomer Buff's Big Boost" ("Paperino e la macchina della conoscenza") in Italian *Topolino* #2172, July 15, 1997 (I TL 2172-1)
"Birthday Bad Guys" ("Buon compleanno Mickey") in Italian *Topolino* #3286, November 14, 2018 (I TL 3286-4A)
"The Explorers of Tomorrow" ("Topolino e gli esploratori dei domani") in Italian *Topolino* #2979, January 1, 2013 (I TL 2979-1)
"Mouse in the Mirror" ("Topolino allo specchio") in Italian *Topolino* #2388, September 4, 2001 (I TL 2388-1)
"Once Upon a Pastry" ("Paperino e Bum Bum pasticcieri pasticcioni") in Italian *Topolino* #2206, March 10, 1998 (I TL 2206-1)

TITLES IN THIS SERIES
Mickey Mouse: The Delta Dimension (Romano Scarpa; Vol. 1)
Donald Duck: Uncle Scrooge's Money Rocket (Luciano Bottaro; Vol. 2)
Mickey Mouse: The Case of the Vanishing Bandit (Paul Murry; Vol. 3)
Donald Duck: The Great Survival Test
(Daan Jippes and Freddy Milton; Vol. 4)
Mickey Mouse: The Phantom Blot's Double Mystery
(Romano Scarpa; Vol. 5)
Uncle Scrooge: King of the Golden River
(Giovan Battista Carpi; Vol. 6)
Mickey Mouse: The Pirates of Tabasco Bay (Paul Murry; Vol. 7)
Donald Duck: Duck Avenger Strikes Again (Romano Scarpa; Vol. 8)
Mickey Mouse: The Ice Sword Saga Book 1 (Massimo De Vita; Vol. 9)
Donald Duck: Scandal on the Epoch Express
(Mau and Bas Heymans; Vol. 10)
Mickey Mouse: The Ice Sword Saga Book 2 (Massimo De Vita; Vol. 11)
Donald Duck: The Forgetful Hero (Giorgio Cavazzano; Vol. 12)
Mickey Mouse: The Sunken City (Paul Murry; Vol. 13)
Donald Duck: Follow the Fearless Leader
(Dick Kinney and Al Hubbard; Vol. 14)
Mickey Mouse: New Adventures of the Phantom Blot
(Paul Murry; Vol. 15)
Donald Duck: Jumpin' Jupiter! (Luciano Bottaro; Vol. 16)
Mickey Mouse: The Man From Altacraz (Romano Scarpa; Vol. 17)
Uncle Scrooge: Pie in the Sky (William Van Horn; Vol. 18)
Mickey Mouse: Trapped in the Shadow Dimension
(Andrea "Casty" Castellan; Vol. 19)
Donald Duck: 20,000 Leaks Under the Sea
(Dick Kinney and Al Hubbard; Vol. 20)
Mickey Mouse: The Monster of Sawtooth Mountain
(Paul Murry; Vol. 21)

Uncle Scrooge: Operation Galleon Grab (Giorgio Cavazzano; Vol. 22)
Mickey Mouse: The Riddle of Brigaboom (Romano Scarpa; Vol. 23)
Uncle Scrooge: World Wide Witch (Daniel Branca; Vol. 24)
Mickey Mouse: The River of Time (Corrado Mastantuono; Vol. 25)

COMING SOON
Donald Duck: Tales of Andold Wild Duck (Marco Rota; Vol. 26)

ALSO AVAILABLE
Adventures of the Gummi Bears: A New Beginning
(Bobbi JG Weiss, Doug Gray, Anibal Uzál, and others;
The Disney Afternoon Adventures Vol. 4)
Disney One Saturday Morning Adventures
(40+ creators including Daan Jippes, Laura McCreary,
and Scott Gimple)
Donald Duck: The 90th Anniversary Collection
(35 creators including Carl Barks, Giorgio Cavazzano, Daan Jippes,
Don Rosa, Marco Rota, Romano Scarpa, and William Van Horn)
Mickey and Donald Fantastic Futures
(15 creators including Mirka Andolfo, Francesco Artibani,
and Lorenzo Pastrovicchio)
Mickey and Donald: Mickey's Craziest Adventures
(Lewis Trondheim and Nicolas Keramidas)
Scrooge McDuck: The Dragon of Glasgow
(Joris Chamblain and Fabrizio Petrossi)
Uncle Scrooge and Donald Duck in Les Misérables and War and Peace
(Giovan Battista Carpi)
Walt Disney's Donald Duck: "Mystery of the Swamp"
(Carl Barks; *The Complete Carl Barks Disney Library* Vol. 3)
*Walt Disney's Silly Symphonies 1935-1939 Starring Donald Duck
and the Big Bad Wolf* (Al Taliaferro with Carl Barks,
Merrill De Maris, and Ted Osborne)

Walt Disney

Mickey Mouse

The River of Time

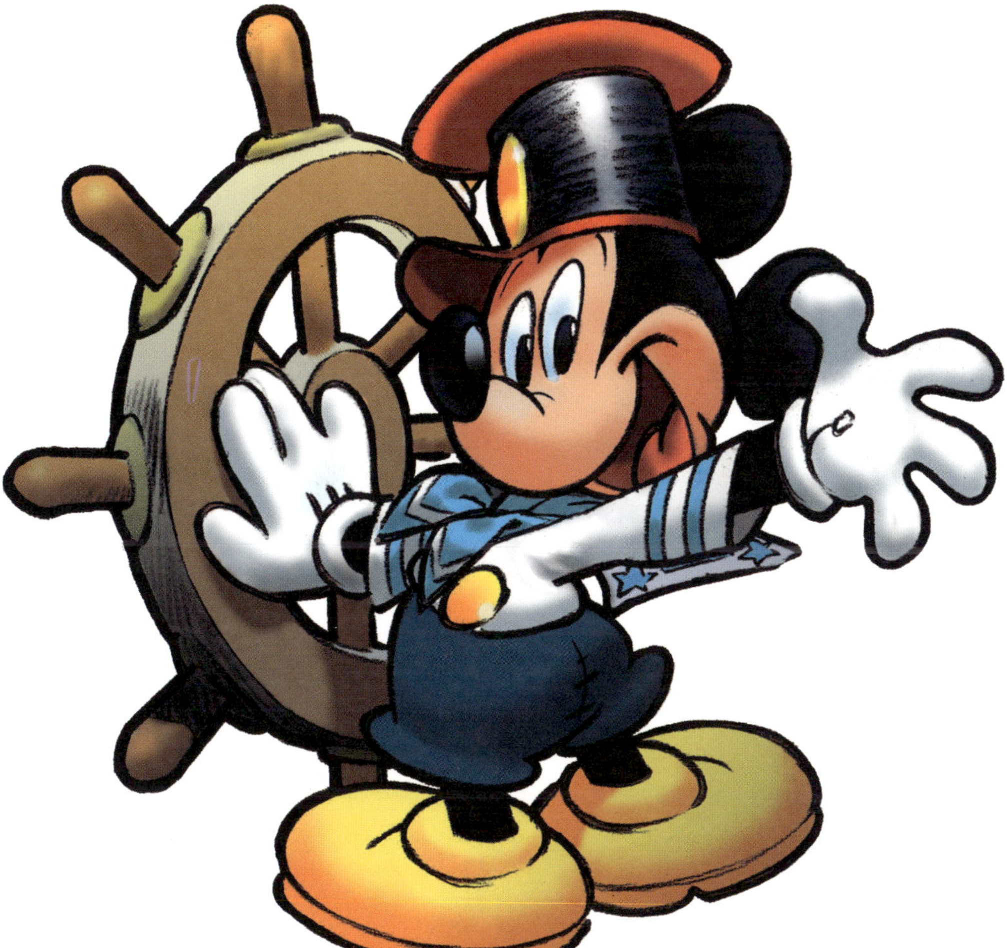

CONTENTS

The River of Time 1
Story: Francesco Artibani and Tito Faraci • Art: Corrado Mastantuono
Translation and Dialogue: Dwight Decker • Color: Disney Italia
Lettering: Paul Baresh and Ben Horak

Boomer Buff's Big Boost 51
Story and Art: Corrado Mastantuono • Translation and Dialogue:
Joe Torcivia • Color: Disney Italia • Lettering: Paul Baresh and Ben Horak

Birthday Bad Guys 82
Story: Tito Faraci • Art: Corrado Mastantuono • Translation, Dialogue and
Lettering: David Gerstein • Color: Disney Italia

The Explorers of Tomorrow 83
Story: Francesco Artibani • Art: Corrado Mastantuono
Translation and Dialogue: Jim Fanning and David Gerstein
Color: Disney Italia • Lettering: Paul Baresh, Ben Horak and C Hwang

Illustration 118
Art: Corrado Mastantuono • Color: Disney Italia

Mouse in the Mirror................................119
Story and Art: Corrado Mastantuono • Translation and Dialogue: Jonathan H. Gray • Color: Disney Italia • Lettering: Paul Baresh and Ben Horak

Illustration 154
Art: Stefano Intini • Color: Sanoma

Once Upon a Pastry...............................155
Story and Art: Corrado Mastantuono • Translation and Dialogue: Joe Torcivia • Color: Disney Italia • Lettering: Paul Baresh and Ben Horak

Corrado Mastantuono 185
Alberto Becattini

Illustration 186
Art and Color: Corrado Mastantuono

This content was first created from 1998-2018.

Some stories were produced during an earlier time and may include cartoon violence, historically dated material, or gags that depict smoking and gunplay. We present them here with a caution to the reader that they reflect the era in which they were made.

This title includes negative depictions and mistreatment of people or cultures. These stereotypes were wrong then and are wrong now. Rather than remove this content, we want to acknowledge its harmful impact, learn from it and spark conversation to create a more inclusive future together. Disney is committed to creating stories with inspirational and aspirational themes that reflect the rich diversity of the human experience around the globe. To learn more about how stories have impacted society, please visit www.disney.com/StoriesMatter.

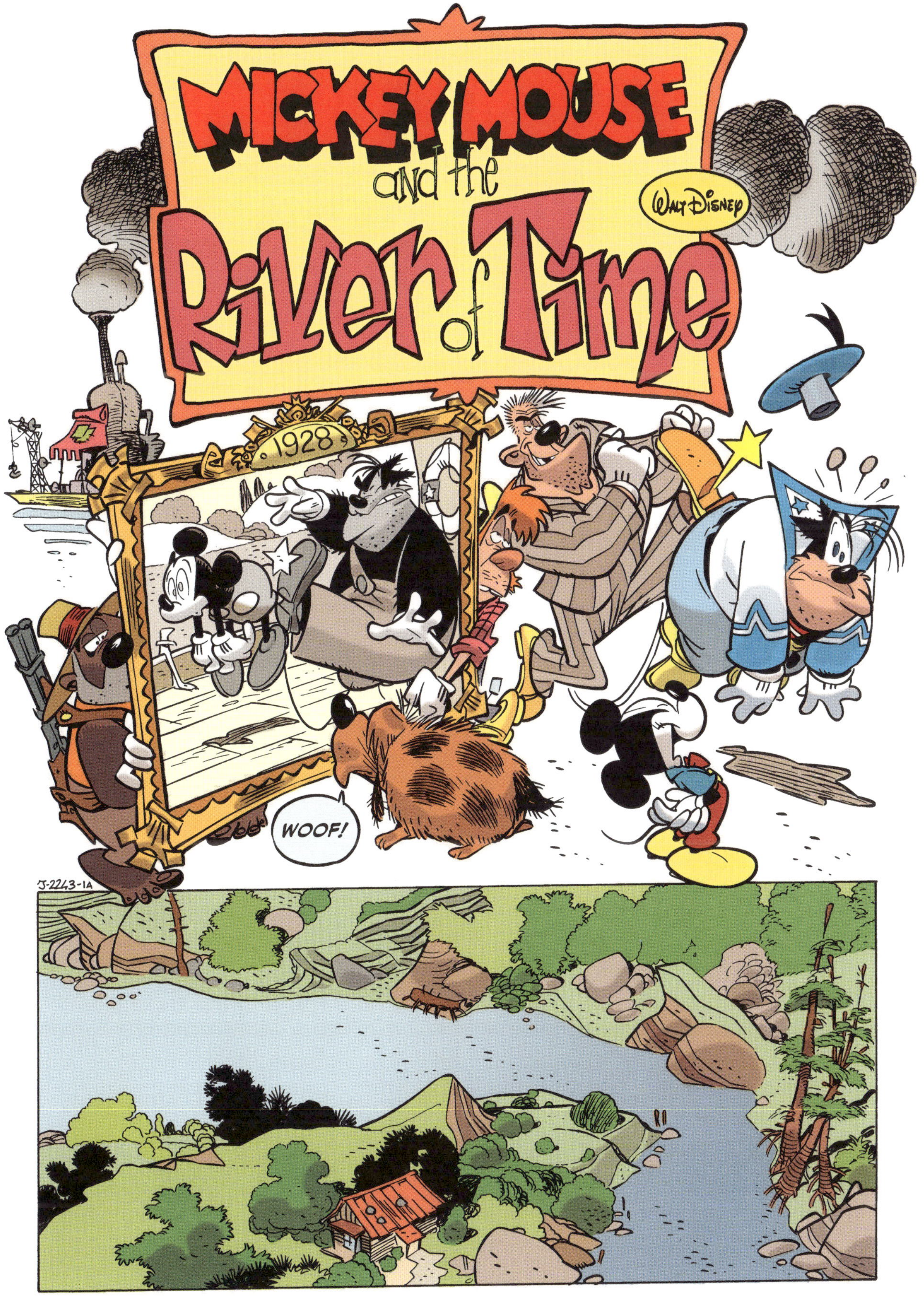
MICKEY MOUSE
and the
River of Time
WALT DISNEY
1928
WOOF!
J-2243-1A

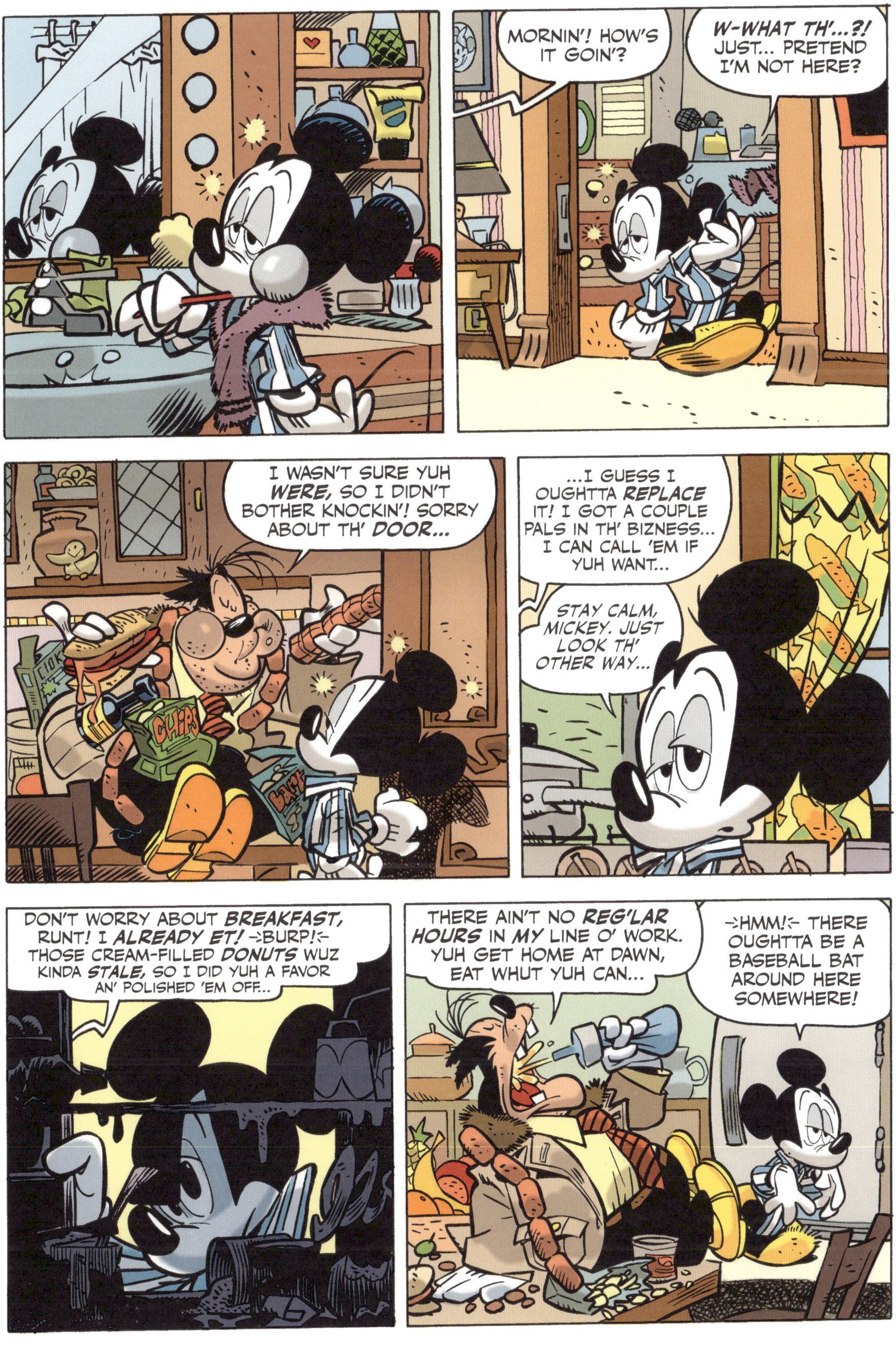
MORNIN'! HOW'S IT GOIN'?
W-WHAT TH'...?! JUST... PRETEND I'M NOT HERE?
I WASN'T SURE YUH WERE, SO I DIDN'T BOTHER KNOCKIN'! SORRY ABOUT TH' DOOR...
CHIPS
...I GUESS I OUGHTTA REPLACE IT! I GOT A COUPLE PALS IN TH' BIZNESS... I CAN CALL 'EM IF YUH WANT...
STAY CALM, MICKEY. JUST LOOK TH' OTHER WAY...
DON'T WORRY ABOUT BREAKFAST, RUNT! I ALREADY ET! -BURP!- THOSE CREAM-FILLED DONUTS WUZ KINDA STALE, SO I DID YUH A FAVOR AN' POLISHED 'EM OFF...
THERE AIN'T NO REG'LAR HOURS IN MY LINE O' WORK. YUH GET HOME AT DAWN, EAT WHUT YUH CAN...
-HMM!- THERE OUGHTTA BE A BASEBALL BAT AROUND HERE SOMEWHERE!

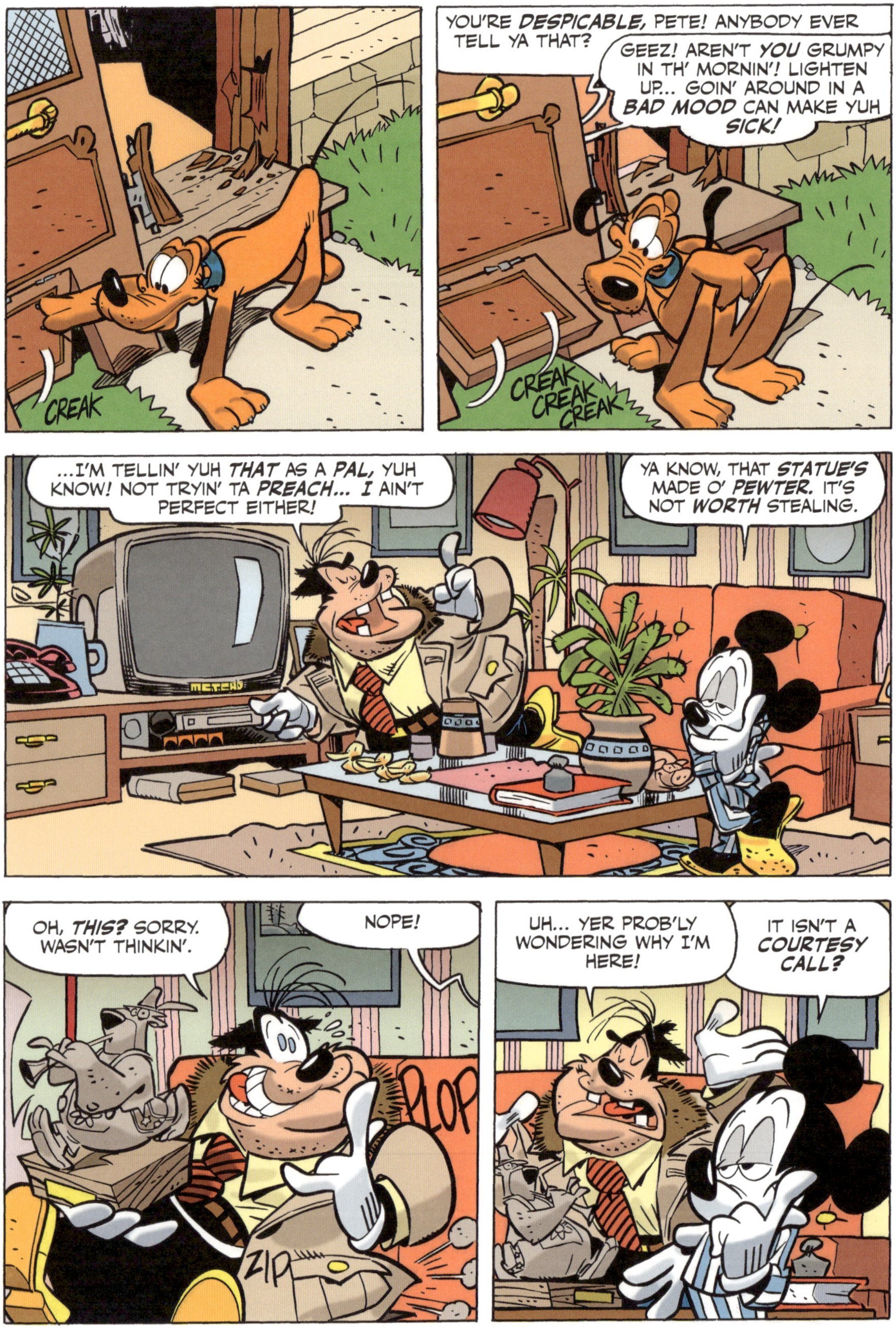
CREAK
YOU'RE DESPICABLE, PETE! ANYBODY EVER TELL YA THAT?
GEEZ! AREN'T YOU GRUMPY IN TH' MORNIN'! LIGHTEN UP... GOIN' AROUND IN A BAD MOOD CAN MAKE YUH SICK!
CREAK CREAK CREAK
...I'M TELLIN' YUH THAT AS A PAL, YUH KNOW! NOT TRYIN' TA PREACH... I AIN'T PERFECT EITHER!
YA KNOW, THAT STATUE'S MADE O' PEWTER. IT'S NOT WORTH STEALING.
OH, THIS? SORRY. WASN'T THINKIN'.
NOPE!
PLOP
ZIP
UH... YER PROB'LY WONDERING WHY I'M HERE!
IT ISN'T A COURTESY CALL?

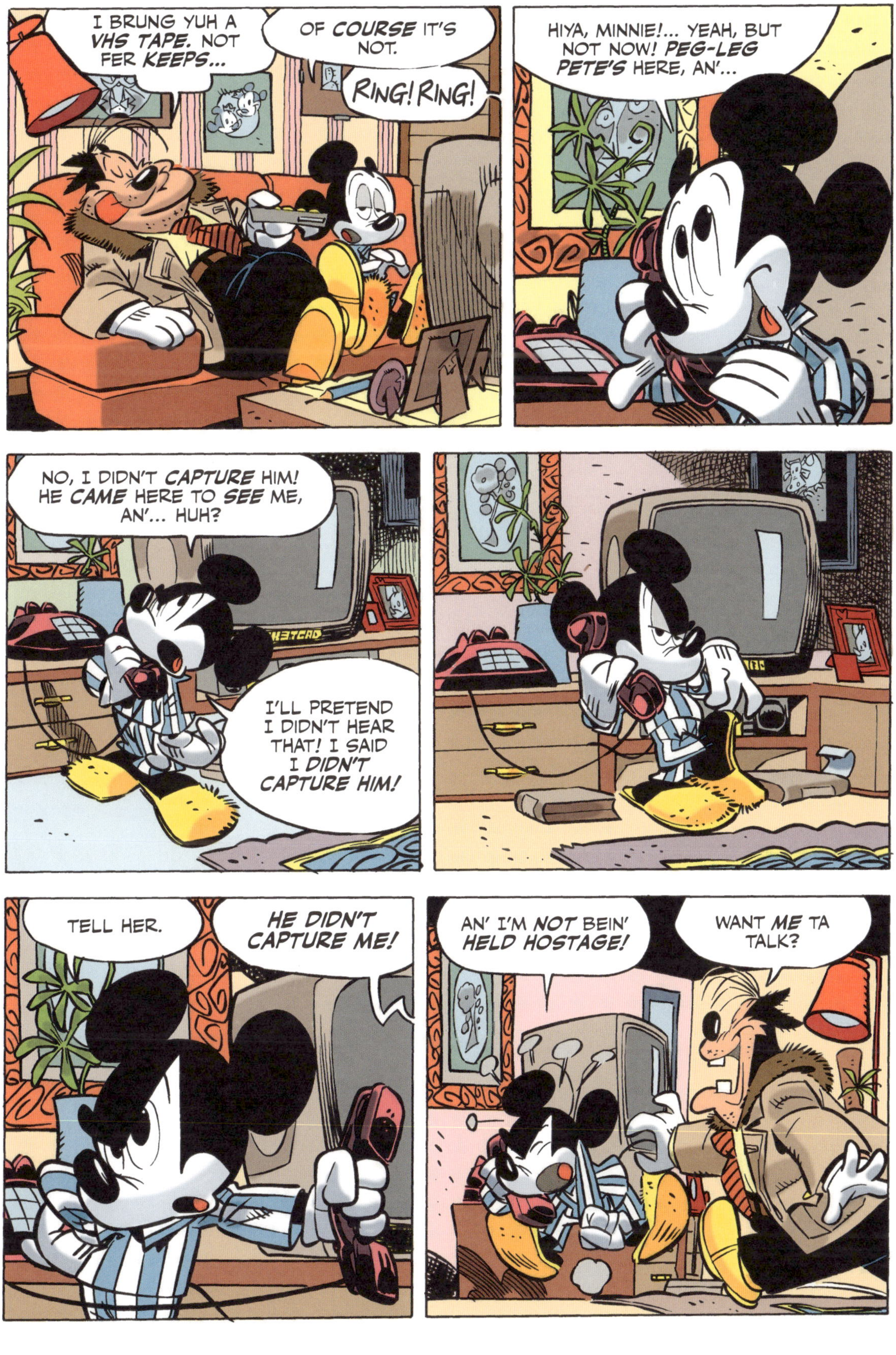

I BRUNG YUH A VHS TAPE. NOT FER KEEPS...
OF COURSE IT'S NOT.
RING! RING!
HIYA, MINNIE!... YEAH, BUT NOT NOW! PEG-LEG PETE'S HERE, AN'...
NO, I DIDN'T CAPTURE HIM! HE CAME HERE TO SEE ME, AN'... HUH?
I'LL PRETEND I DIDN'T HEAR THAT! I SAID I DIDN'T CAPTURE HIM!
TELL HER.
HE DIDN'T CAPTURE ME!
AN' I'M NOT BEIN' HELD HOSTAGE!
WANT ME TA TALK?

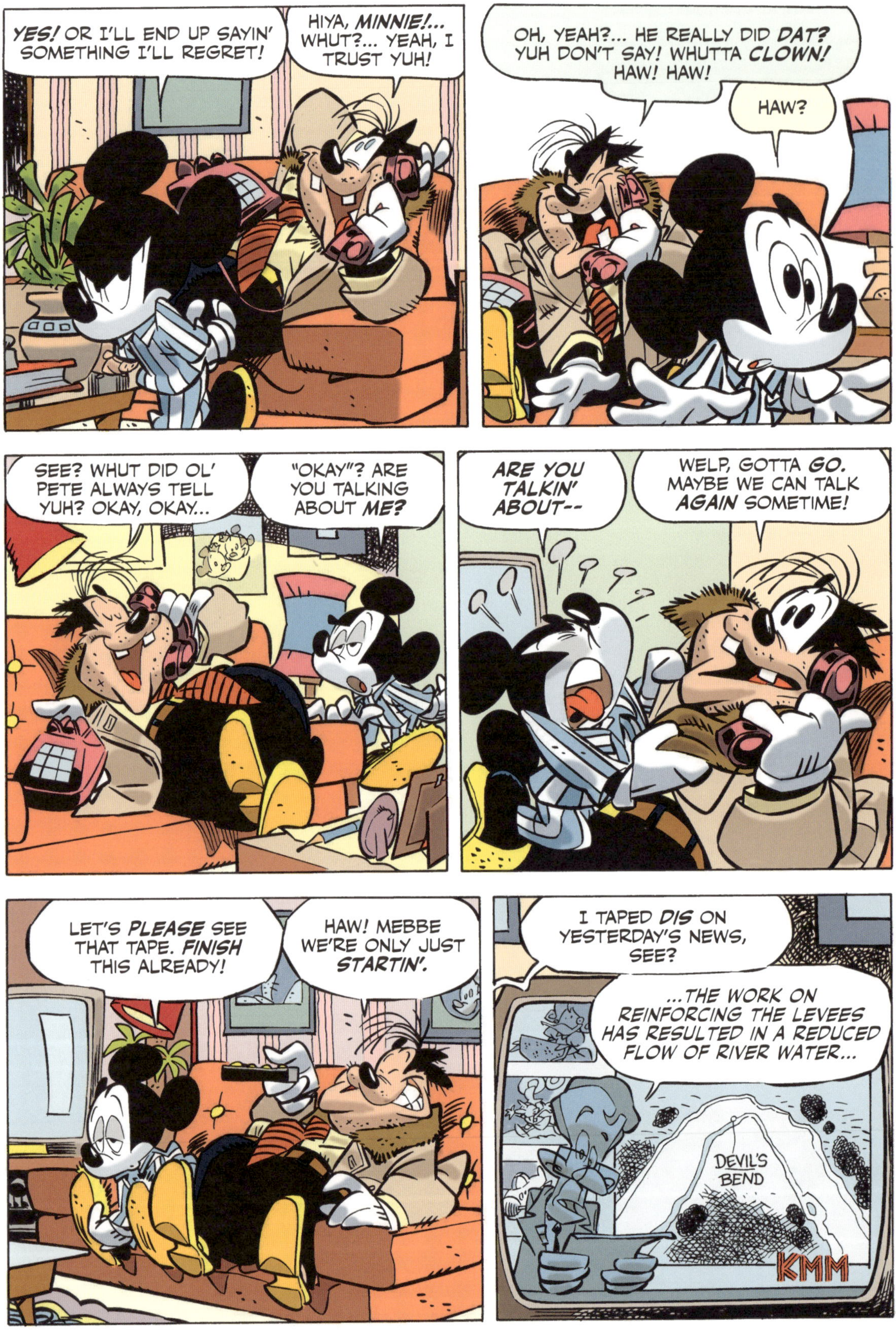
YES! OR I'LL END UP SAYIN' SOMETHING I'LL REGRET!
HIYA, MINNIE!... WHUT?... YEAH, I TRUST YUH!
OH, YEAH?... HE REALLY DID DAT? YUH DON'T SAY! WHUTTA CLOWN! HAW! HAW!
HAW?
SEE? WHUT DID OL' PETE ALWAYS TELL YUH? OKAY, OKAY...
"OKAY"? ARE YOU TALKING ABOUT ME?
ARE YOU TALKIN' ABOUT--
WELP, GOTTA GO. MAYBE WE CAN TALK AGAIN SOMETIME!
LET'S PLEASE SEE THAT TAPE. FINISH THIS ALREADY!
HAW! MEBBE WE'RE ONLY JUST STARTIN'.
I TAPED DIS ON YESTERDAY'S NEWS, SEE?
...THE WORK ON REINFORCING THE LEVEES HAS RESULTED IN A REDUCED FLOW OF RIVER WATER...
DEVIL'S BEND
KMM

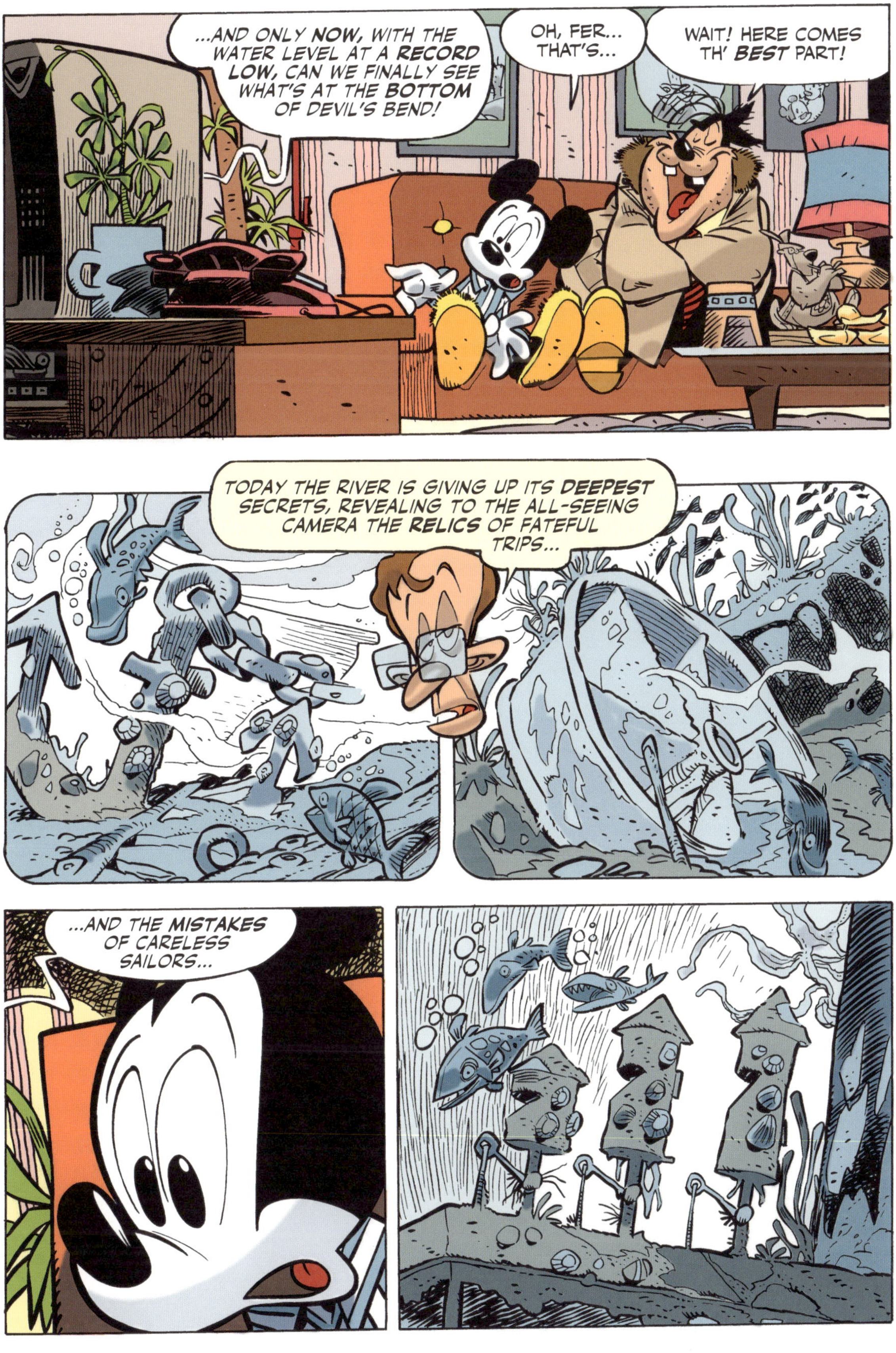
...AND ONLY NOW, WITH THE WATER LEVEL AT A RECORD LOW, CAN WE FINALLY SEE WHAT'S AT THE BOTTOM OF DEVIL'S BEND!
OH, FER... THAT'S...
WAIT! HERE COMES TH' BEST PART!
TODAY THE RIVER IS GIVING UP ITS DEEPEST SECRETS, REVEALING TO THE ALL-SEEING CAMERA THE RELICS OF FATEFUL TRIPS...
...AND THE MISTAKES OF CARELESS SAILORS...

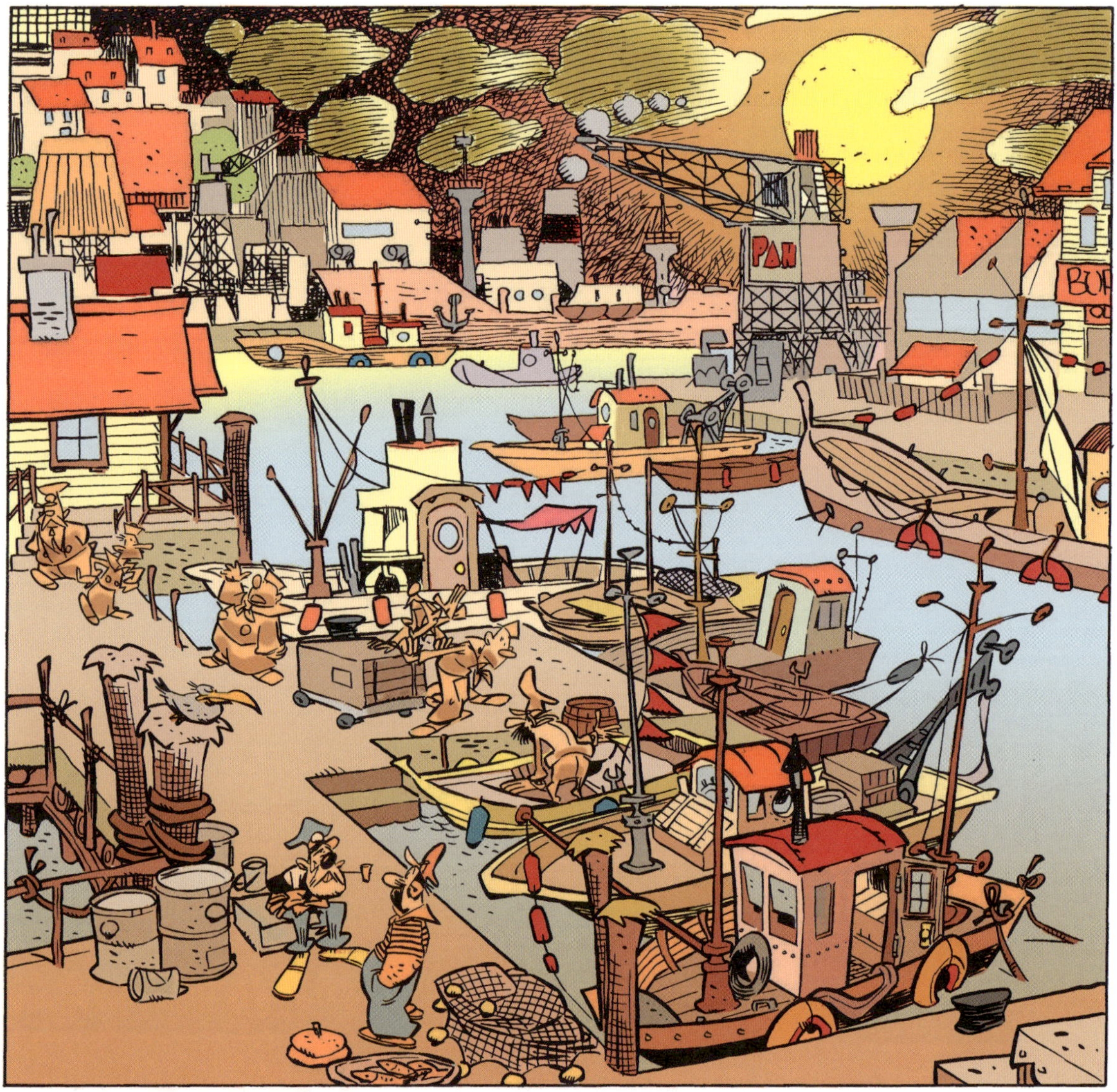
PAN

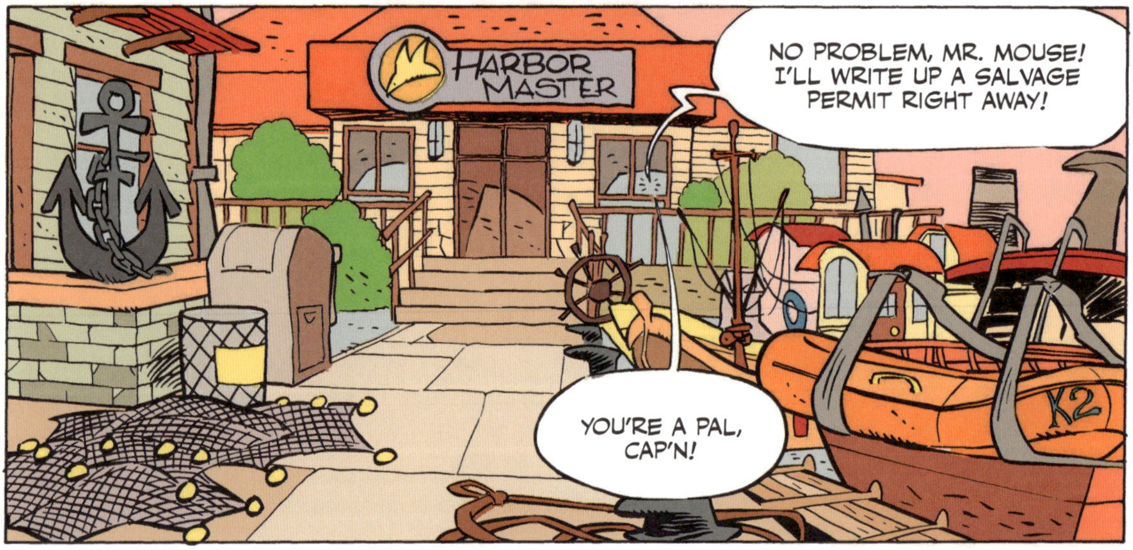
HARBOR MASTER
NO PROBLEM, MR. MOUSE! I'LL WRITE UP A SALVAGE PERMIT RIGHT AWAY!
YOU'RE A PAL, CAP'N!
K2

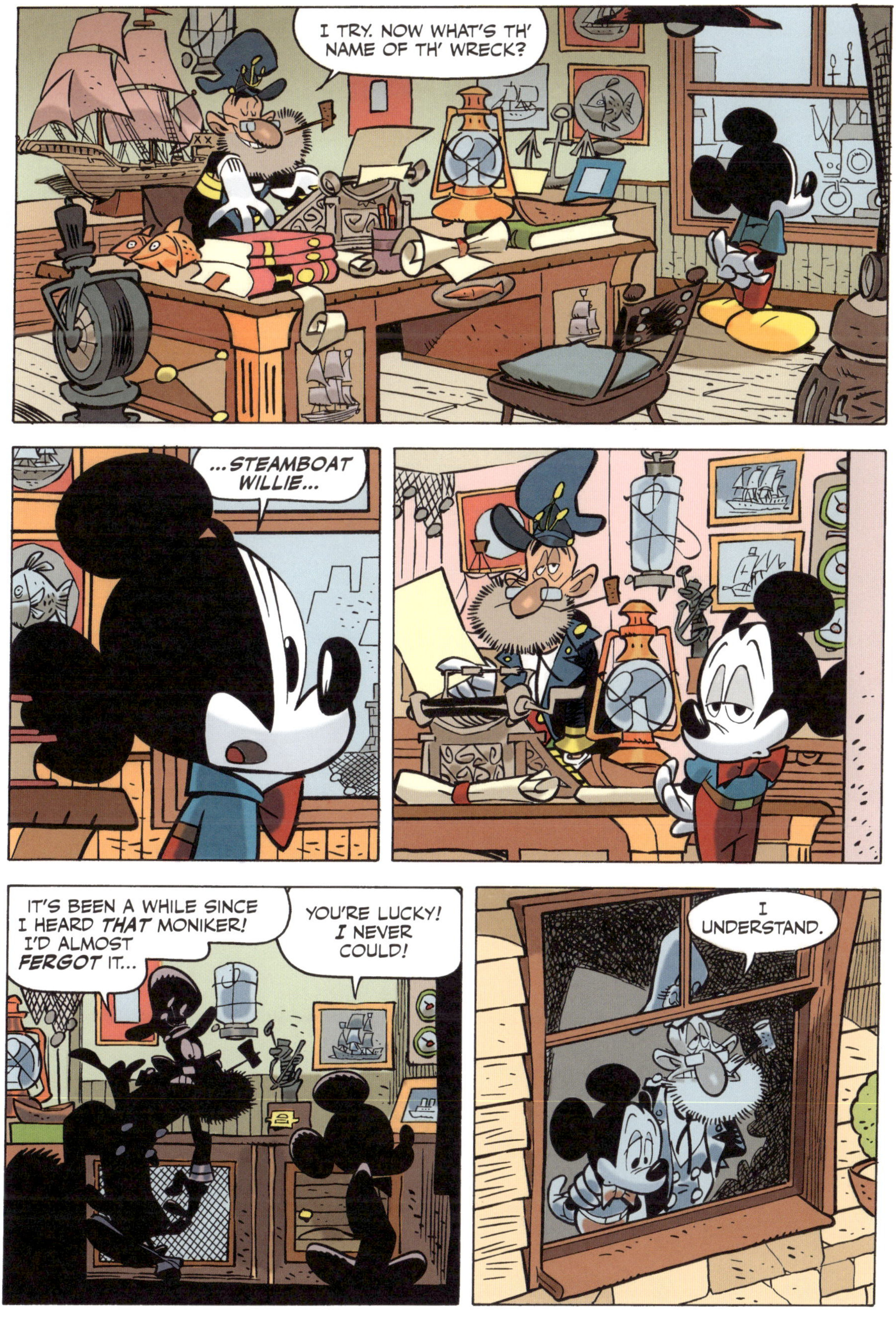

I TRY. NOW WHAT'S TH' NAME OF TH' WRECK?
...STEAMBOAT WILLIE...
IT'S BEEN A WHILE SINCE I HEARD *THAT* MONIKER! I'D ALMOST *FERGOT* IT...
YOU'RE LUCKY! *I* NEVER COULD!
I UNDERSTAND.

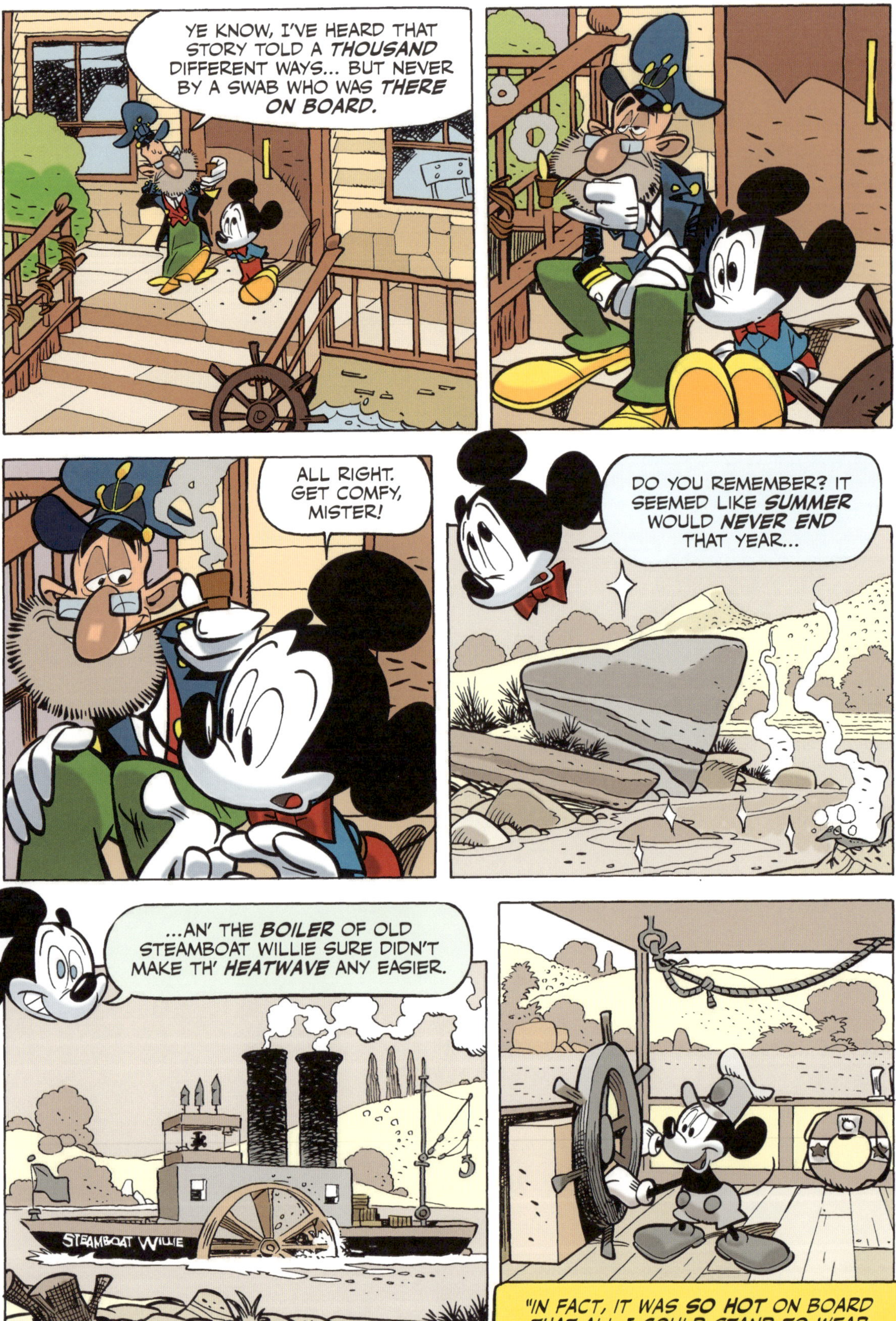

YE KNOW, I'VE HEARD THAT STORY TOLD A THOUSAND DIFFERENT WAYS... BUT NEVER BY A SWAB WHO WAS THERE ON BOARD.
ALL RIGHT. GET COMFY, MISTER!
DO YOU REMEMBER? IT SEEMED LIKE SUMMER WOULD NEVER END THAT YEAR...
...AN' THE BOILER OF OLD STEAMBOAT WILLIE SURE DIDN'T MAKE TH' HEATWAVE ANY EASIER.
STEAMBOAT WILLIE
"IN FACT, IT WAS SO HOT ON BOARD THAT ALL I COULD STAND TO WEAR WAS MY SHORTS!"

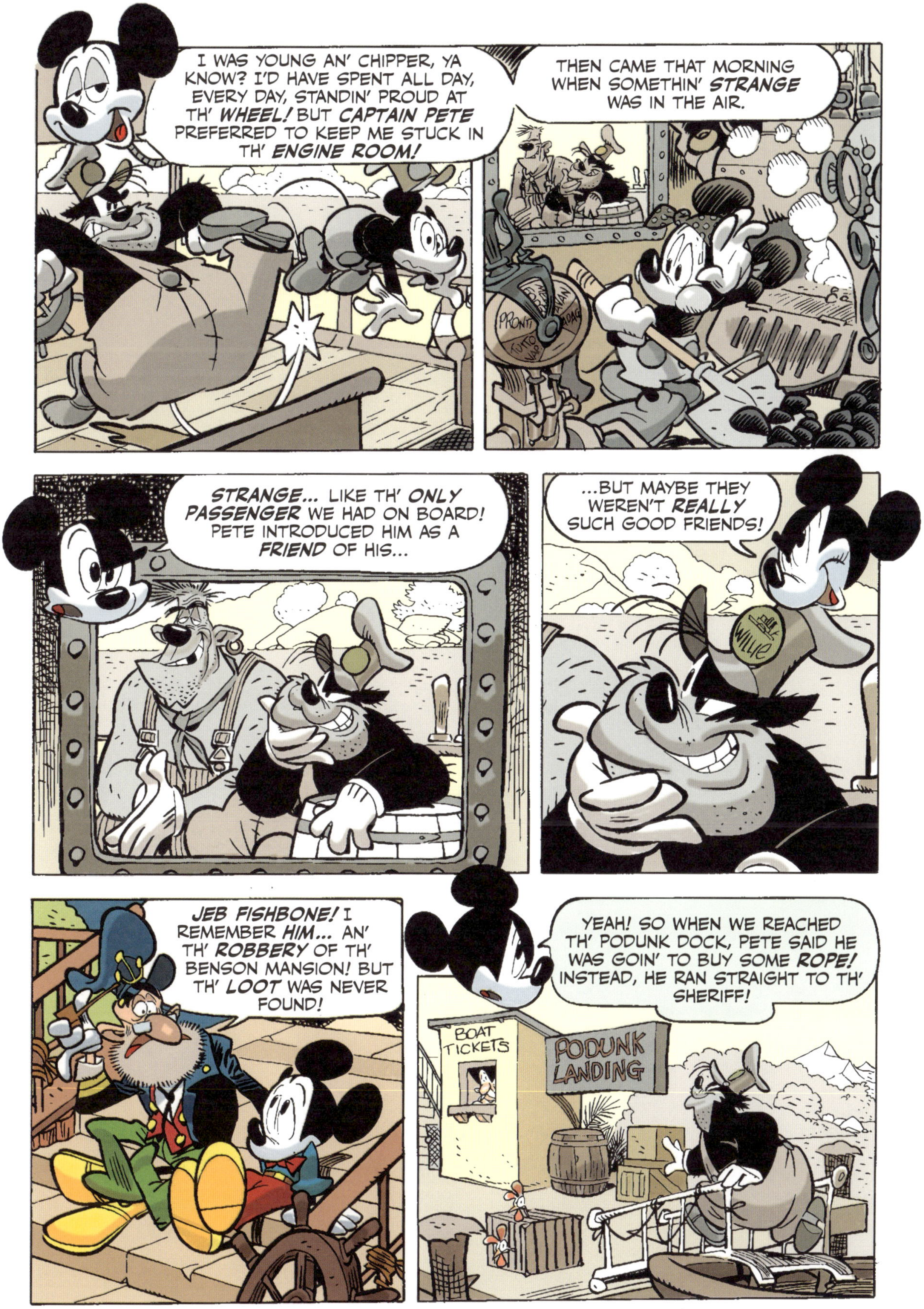
I WAS YOUNG AN' CHIPPER, YA KNOW? I'D HAVE SPENT ALL DAY, EVERY DAY, STANDIN' PROUD AT TH' WHEEL! BUT CAPTAIN PETE PREFERRED TO KEEP ME STUCK IN TH' ENGINE ROOM!
THEN CAME THAT MORNING WHEN SOMETHIN' STRANGE WAS IN THE AIR.
STRANGE... LIKE TH' ONLY PASSENGER WE HAD ON BOARD! PETE INTRODUCED HIM AS A FRIEND OF HIS...
...BUT MAYBE THEY WEREN'T REALLY SUCH GOOD FRIENDS!
WILLIE
JEB FISHBONE! I REMEMBER HIM... AN' TH' ROBBERY OF TH' BENSON MANSION! BUT TH' LOOT WAS NEVER FOUND!
YEAH! SO WHEN WE REACHED TH' PODUNK DOCK, PETE SAID HE WAS GOIN' TO BUY SOME ROPE! INSTEAD, HE RAN STRAIGHT TO TH' SHERIFF!
BOAT TICKETS
PODUNK LANDING

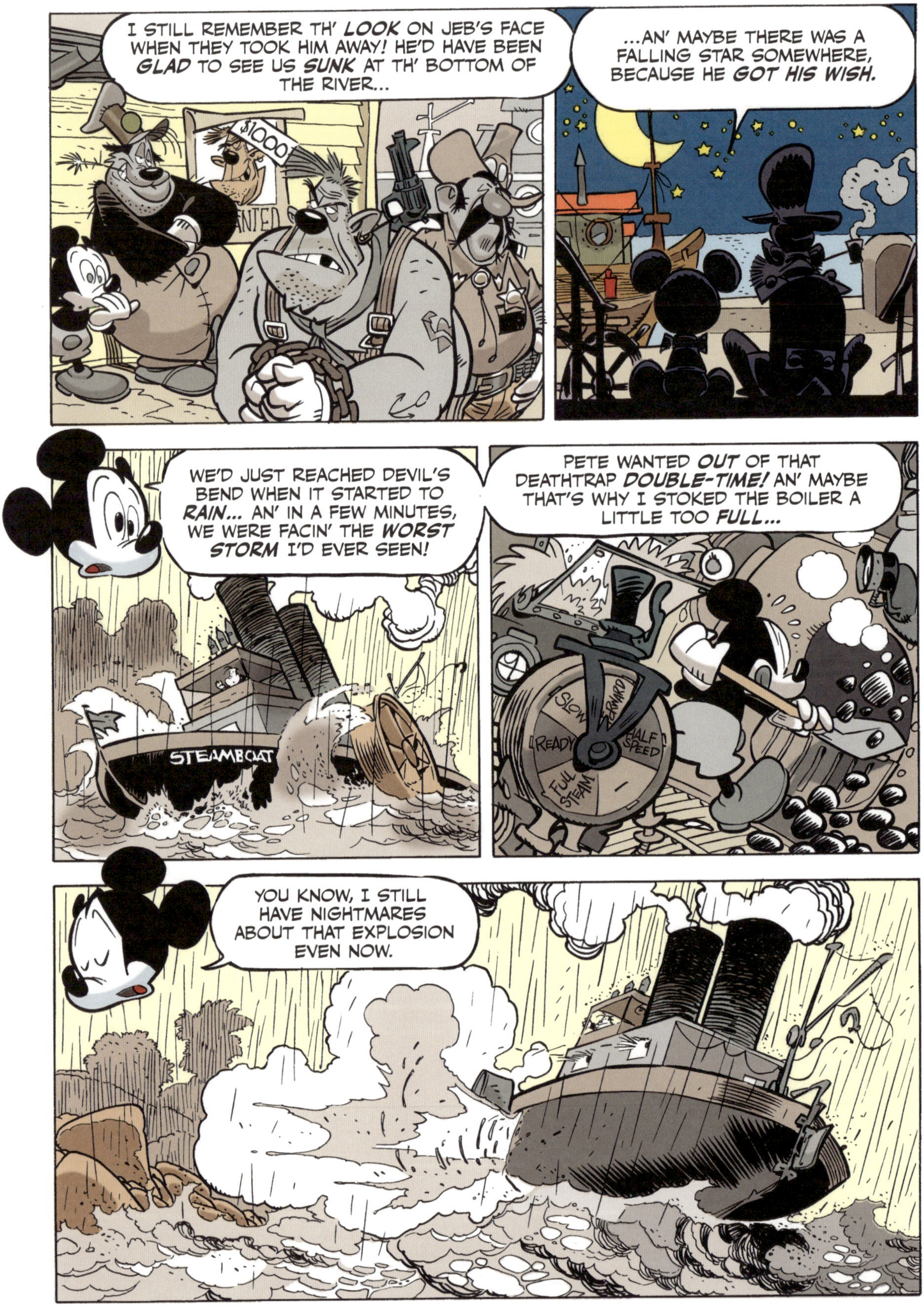
I STILL REMEMBER TH' LOOK ON JEB'S FACE WHEN THEY TOOK HIM AWAY! HE'D HAVE BEEN GLAD TO SEE US SUNK AT TH' BOTTOM OF THE RIVER...
$1000
...AN' MAYBE THERE WAS A FALLING STAR SOMEWHERE, BECAUSE HE GOT HIS WISH.
WE'D JUST REACHED DEVIL'S BEND WHEN IT STARTED TO RAIN... AN' IN A FEW MINUTES, WE WERE FACIN' THE WORST STORM I'D EVER SEEN!
STEAMBOAT
PETE WANTED OUT OF THAT DEATHTRAP DOUBLE-TIME! AN' MAYBE THAT'S WHY I STOKED THE BOILER A LITTLE TOO FULL...
SLOW
FORWARD
READY
HALF SPEED
FULL STEAM
YOU KNOW, I STILL HAVE NIGHTMARES ABOUT THAT EXPLOSION EVEN NOW.

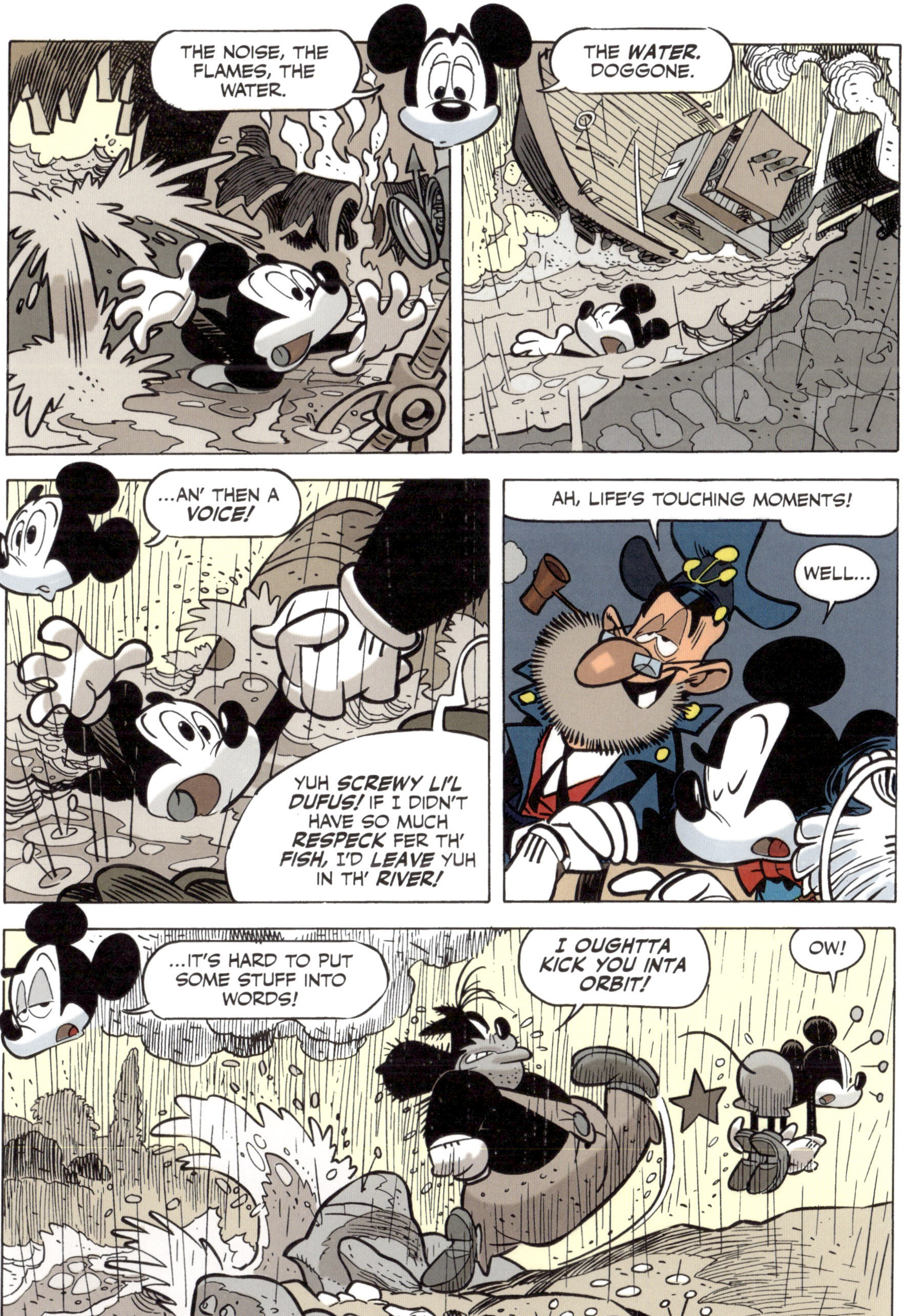

THE NOISE, THE FLAMES, THE WATER.
THE WATER. DOGGONE.
...AN' THEN A VOICE!
YUH SCREWY LI'L DUFUS! IF I DIDN'T HAVE SO MUCH RESPECK FER TH' FISH, I'D LEAVE YUH IN TH' RIVER!
AH, LIFE'S TOUCHING MOMENTS!
WELL...
...IT'S HARD TO PUT SOME STUFF INTO WORDS!
I OUGHTTA KICK YOU INTA ORBIT!
OW!

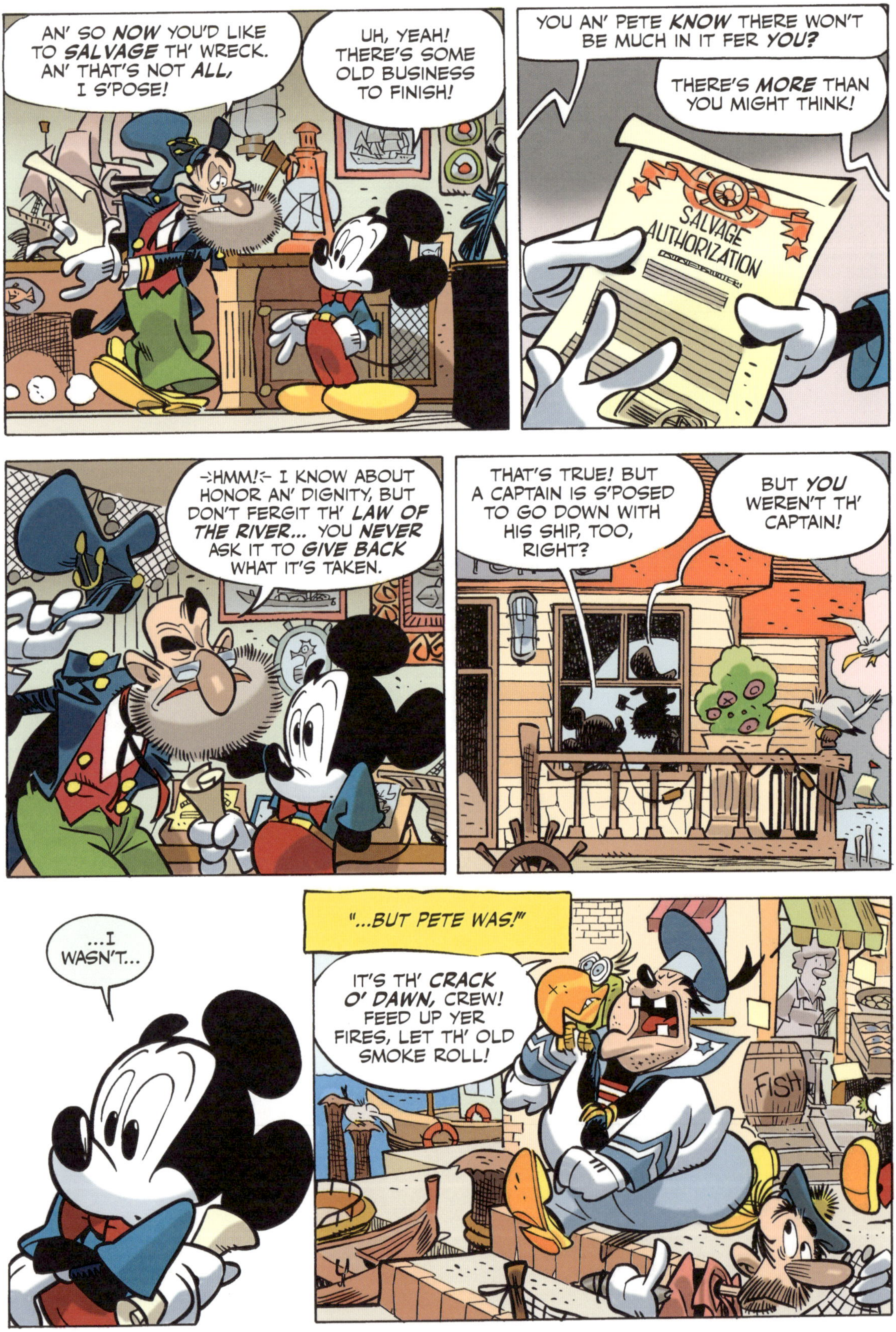
AN' SO NOW YOU'D LIKE TO SALVAGE TH' WRECK. AN' THAT'S NOT ALL, I S'POSE!
UH, YEAH! THERE'S SOME OLD BUSINESS TO FINISH!
YOU AN' PETE KNOW THERE WON'T BE MUCH IN IT FER YOU?
THERE'S MORE THAN YOU MIGHT THINK!
SALVAGE AUTHORIZATION
-HMM!- I KNOW ABOUT HONOR AN' DIGNITY, BUT DON'T FERGIT TH' LAW OF THE RIVER... YOU NEVER ASK IT TO GIVE BACK WHAT IT'S TAKEN.
THAT'S TRUE! BUT A CAPTAIN IS S'POSED TO GO DOWN WITH HIS SHIP, TOO, RIGHT?
BUT YOU WEREN'T TH' CAPTAIN!
...I WASN'T...
"...BUT PETE WAS!"
IT'S TH' CRACK O' DAWN, CREW! FEED UP YER FIRES, LET TH' OLD SMOKE ROLL!
FISH

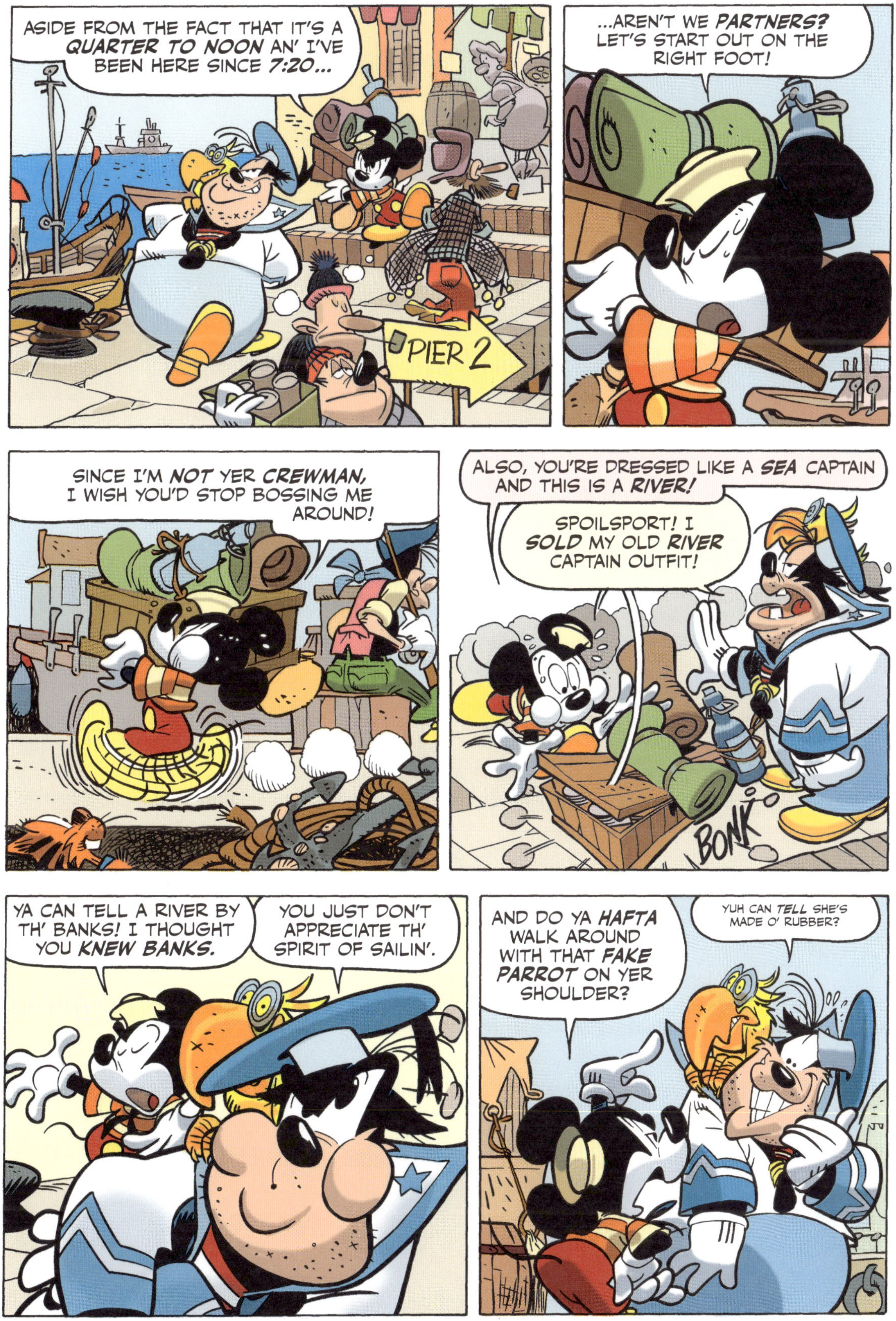
ASIDE FROM THE FACT THAT IT'S A QUARTER TO NOON AN' I'VE BEEN HERE SINCE 7:20...
PIER 2
...AREN'T WE PARTNERS? LET'S START OUT ON THE RIGHT FOOT!
SINCE I'M NOT YER CREWMAN, I WISH YOU'D STOP BOSSING ME AROUND!
ALSO, YOU'RE DRESSED LIKE A SEA CAPTAIN AND THIS IS A RIVER!
SPOILSPORT! I SOLD MY OLD RIVER CAPTAIN OUTFIT!
BONK
YA CAN TELL A RIVER BY TH' BANKS! I THOUGHT YOU KNEW BANKS.
YOU JUST DON'T APPRECIATE TH' SPIRIT OF SAILIN'.
AND DO YA HAFTA WALK AROUND WITH THAT FAKE PARROT ON YER SHOULDER?
YUH CAN TELL SHE'S MADE O' RUBBER?

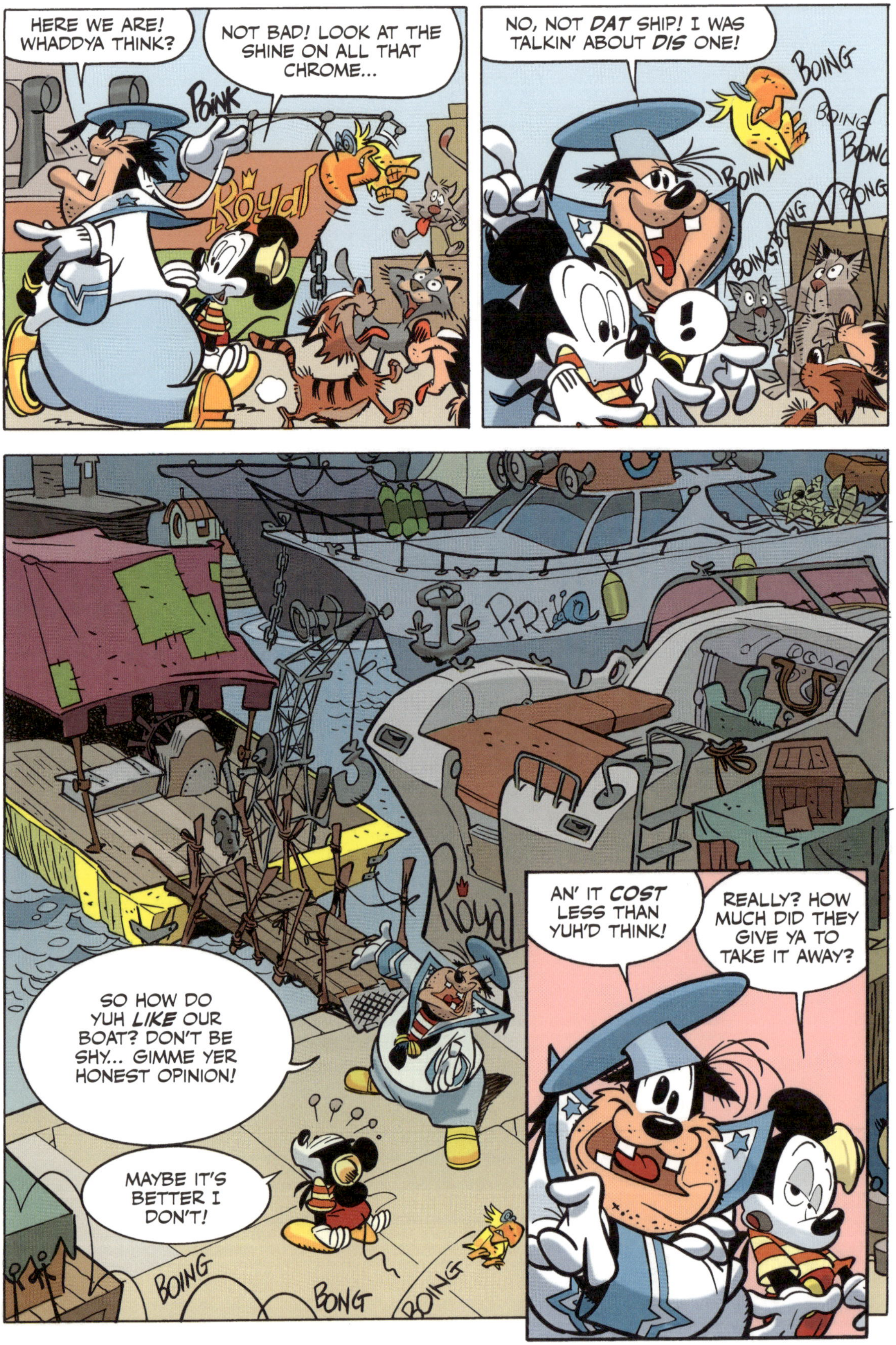

HERE WE ARE! WHADDYA THINK?
NOT BAD! LOOK AT THE SHINE ON ALL THAT CHROME...
POINK
Royal
NO, NOT DAT SHIP! I WAS TALKIN' ABOUT DIS ONE!
BOING
BOING
BONG
BOING
BONG
BONG
BOING
!
PIRI
Royal
SO HOW DO YUH LIKE OUR BOAT? DON'T BE SHY... GIMME YER HONEST OPINION!
MAYBE IT'S BETTER I DON'T!
BOING
BONG
BOING
AN' IT COST LESS THAN YUH'D THINK!
REALLY? HOW MUCH DID THEY GIVE YA TO TAKE IT AWAY?

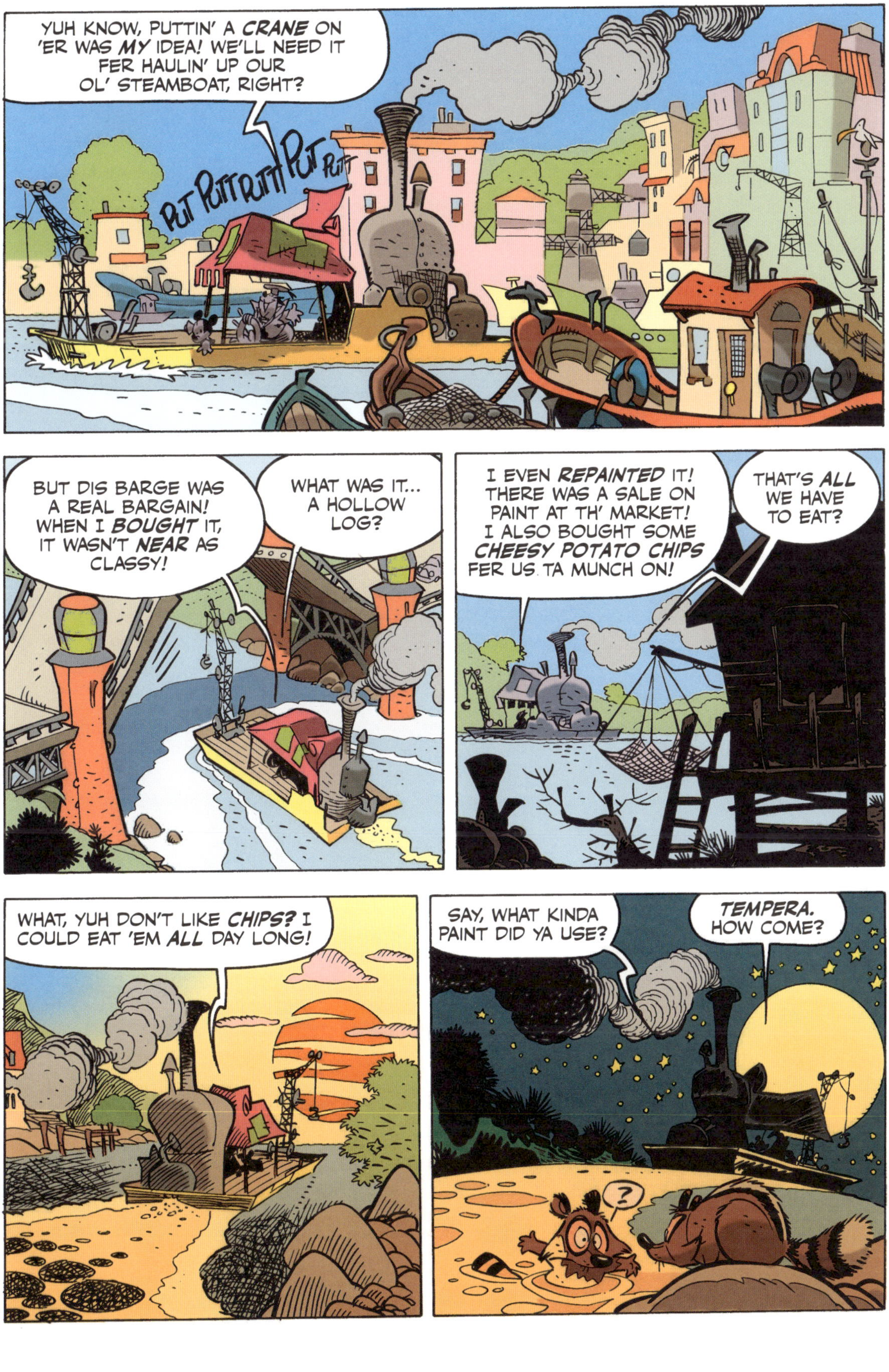

YUH KNOW, PUTTIN' A CRANE ON 'ER WAS MY IDEA! WE'LL NEED IT FER HAULIN' UP OUR OL' STEAMBOAT, RIGHT?
PUT PUTT PUTT PUTT PUT PUTT
BUT DIS BARGE WAS A REAL BARGAIN! WHEN I BOUGHT IT, IT WASN'T NEAR AS CLASSY!
WHAT WAS IT... A HOLLOW LOG?
I EVEN REPAINTED IT! THERE WAS A SALE ON PAINT AT TH' MARKET! I ALSO BOUGHT SOME CHEESY POTATO CHIPS FER US TA MUNCH ON!
THAT'S ALL WE HAVE TO EAT?
WHAT, YUH DON'T LIKE CHIPS? I COULD EAT 'EM ALL DAY LONG!
SAY, WHAT KINDA PAINT DID YA USE?
TEMPERA. HOW COME?
?

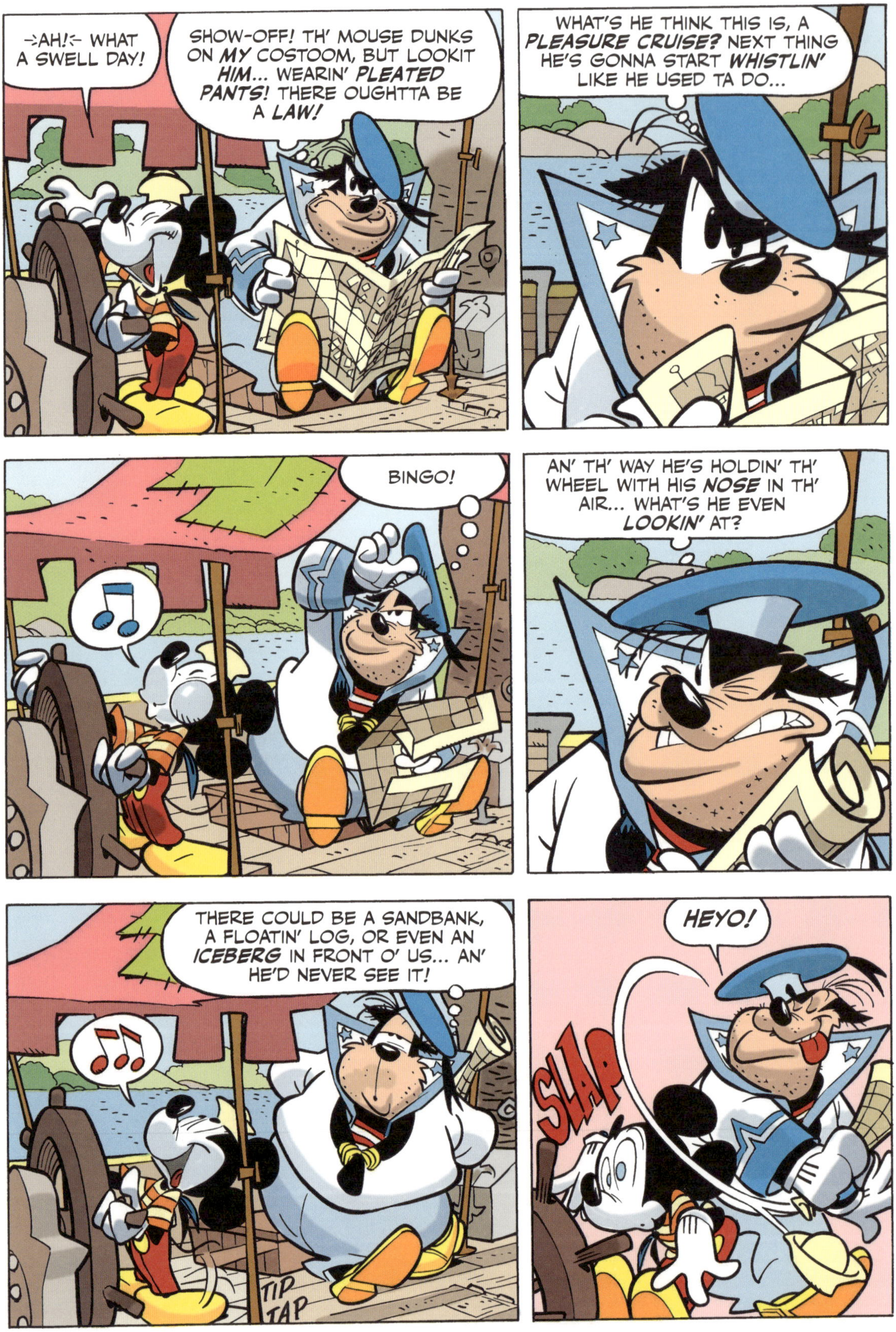

-AH!- WHAT A SWELL DAY!
SHOW-OFF! TH' MOUSE DUNKS ON *MY* COSTOOM, BUT LOOKIT *HIM*... WEARIN' *PLEATED PANTS!* THERE OUGHTTA BE A *LAW!*
WHAT'S HE THINK THIS IS, A *PLEASURE CRUISE?* NEXT THING HE'S GONNA START *WHISTLIN'* LIKE HE USED TA DO...
BINGO!
AN' TH' WAY HE'S HOLDIN' TH' WHEEL WITH HIS *NOSE* IN TH' AIR... WHAT'S HE EVEN *LOOKIN'* AT?
THERE COULD BE A SANDBANK, A FLOATIN' LOG, OR EVEN AN *ICEBERG* IN FRONT O' US... AN' HE'D NEVER SEE IT!
TIP TAP
HEYO!
SLAP

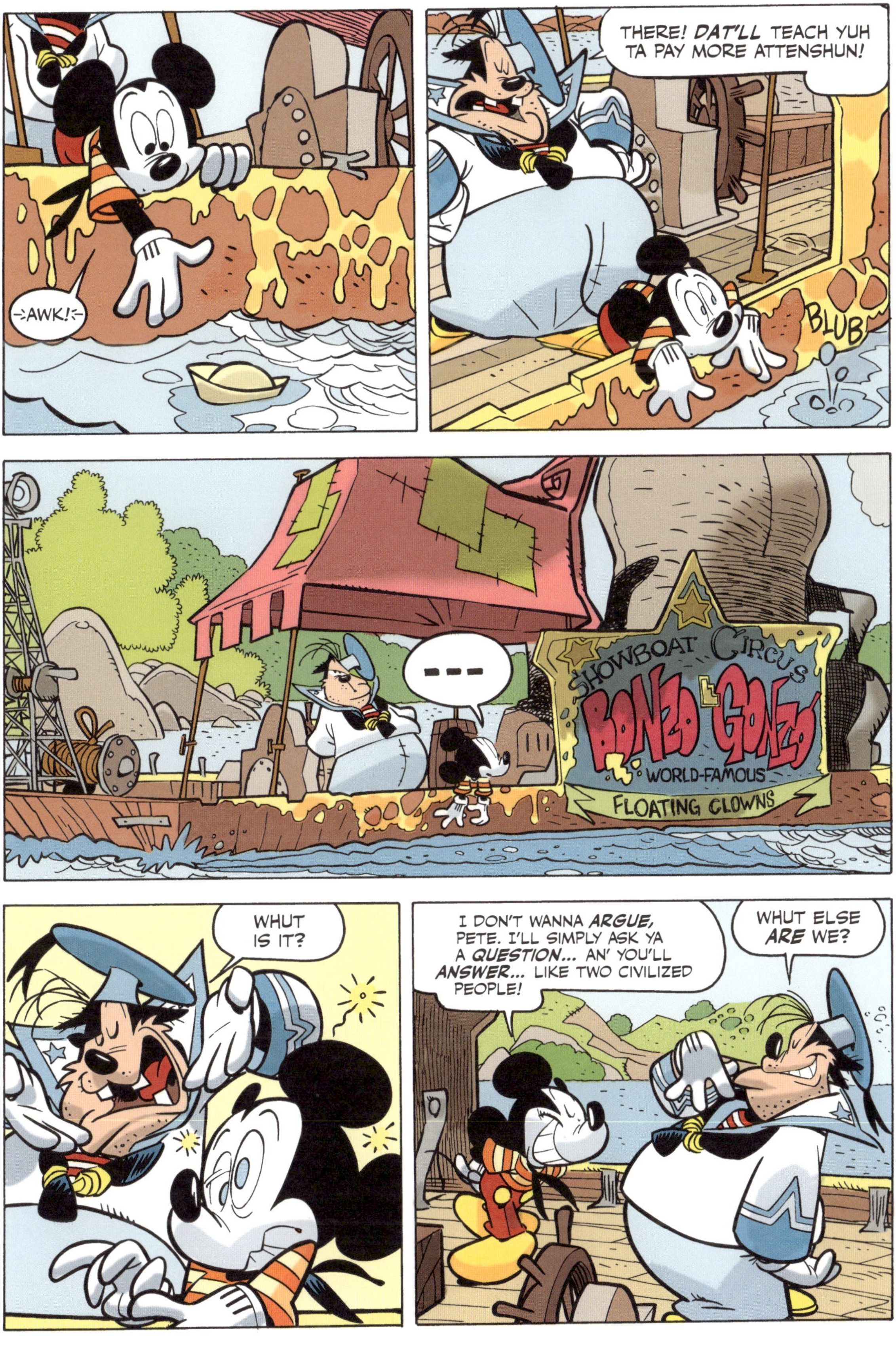

AWK!
THERE! DAT'LL TEACH YUH TA PAY MORE ATTENSHUN!
BLUB
SHOWBOAT CIRCUS
BONZO 'L' GONZO
WORLD-FAMOUS
FLOATING CLOWNS
- - -
WHUT IS IT?
I DON'T WANNA ARGUE, PETE. I'LL SIMPLY ASK YA A QUESTION... AN' YOU'LL ANSWER... LIKE TWO CIVILIZED PEOPLE!
WHUT ELSE ARE WE?

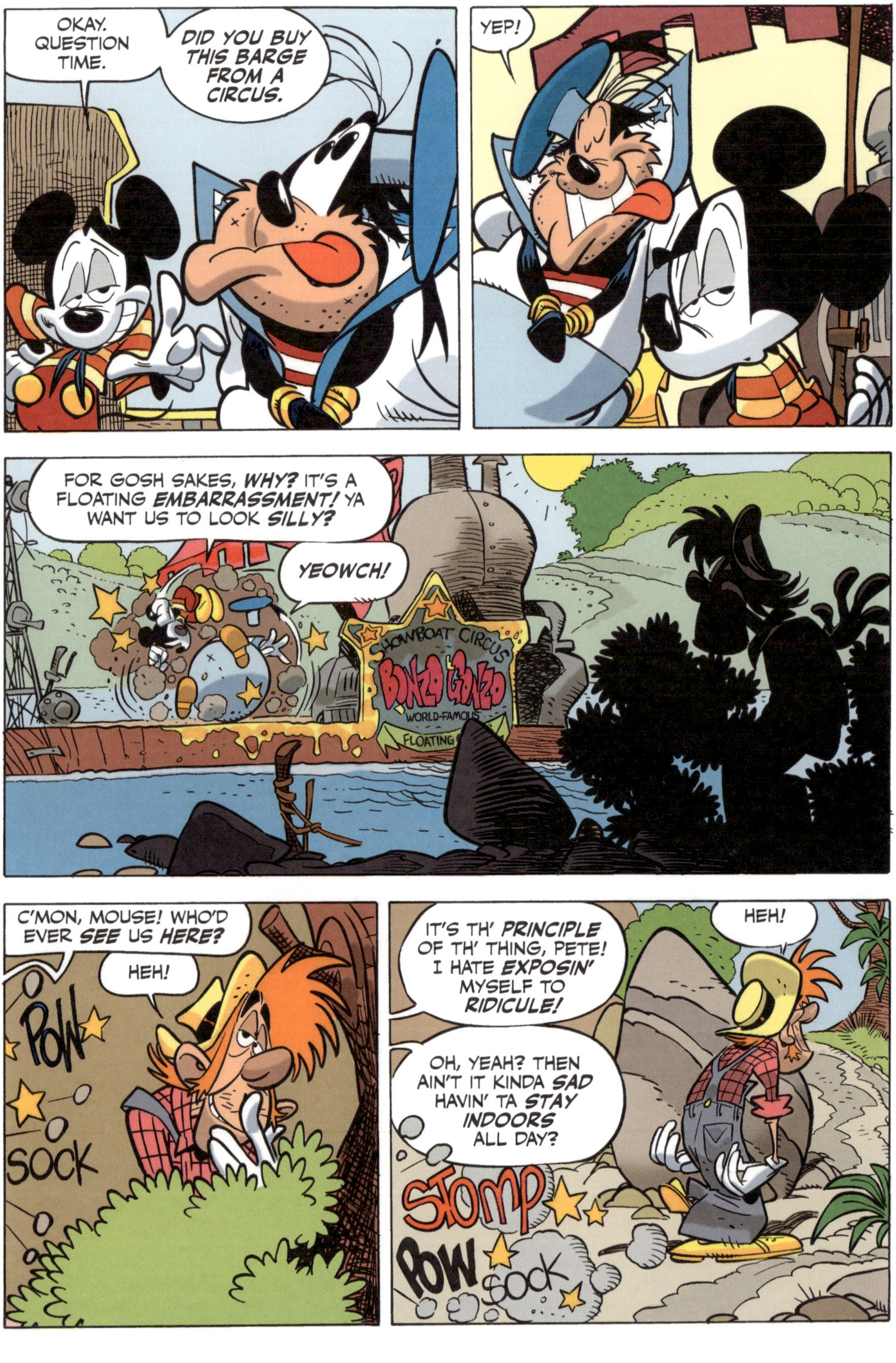
OKAY. QUESTION TIME.
DID YOU BUY THIS BARGE FROM A CIRCUS.
YEP!
FOR GOSH SAKES, WHY? IT'S A FLOATING EMBARRASSMENT! YA WANT US TO LOOK SILLY?
YEOWCH!
SHOWBOAT CIRCUS
BONZO L. GONZO
WORLD-FAMOUS
FLOATING
C'MON, MOUSE! WHO'D EVER SEE US HERE?
HEH!
POW
SOCK
IT'S TH' PRINCIPLE OF TH' THING, PETE! I HATE EXPOSIN' MYSELF TO RIDICULE!
HEH!
OH, YEAH? THEN AIN'T IT KINDA SAD HAVIN' TA STAY INDOORS ALL DAY?
STOMP
POW
SOCK

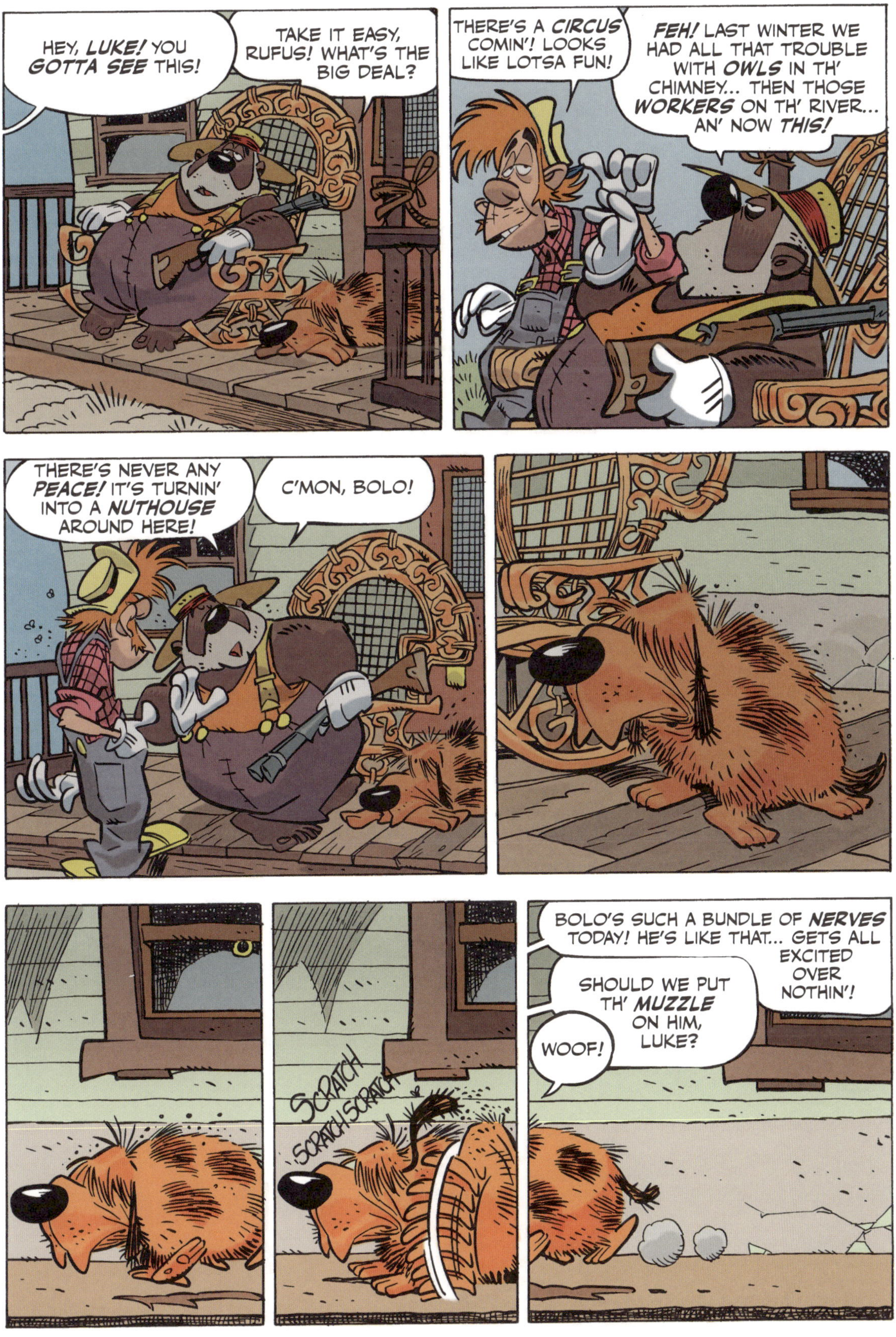
HEY, LUKE! YOU GOTTA SEE THIS!
TAKE IT EASY, RUFUS! WHAT'S THE BIG DEAL?
THERE'S A CIRCUS COMIN'! LOOKS LIKE LOTSA FUN!
FEH! LAST WINTER WE HAD ALL THAT TROUBLE WITH OWLS IN TH' CHIMNEY... THEN THOSE WORKERS ON TH' RIVER... AN' NOW THIS!
THERE'S NEVER ANY PEACE! IT'S TURNIN' INTO A NUTHOUSE AROUND HERE!
C'MON, BOLO!
SCRATCH
SCRATCH SCRATCH
BOLO'S SUCH A BUNDLE OF NERVES TODAY! HE'S LIKE THAT... GETS ALL EXCITED OVER NOTHIN'!
SHOULD WE PUT TH' MUZZLE ON HIM, LUKE?
WOOF!

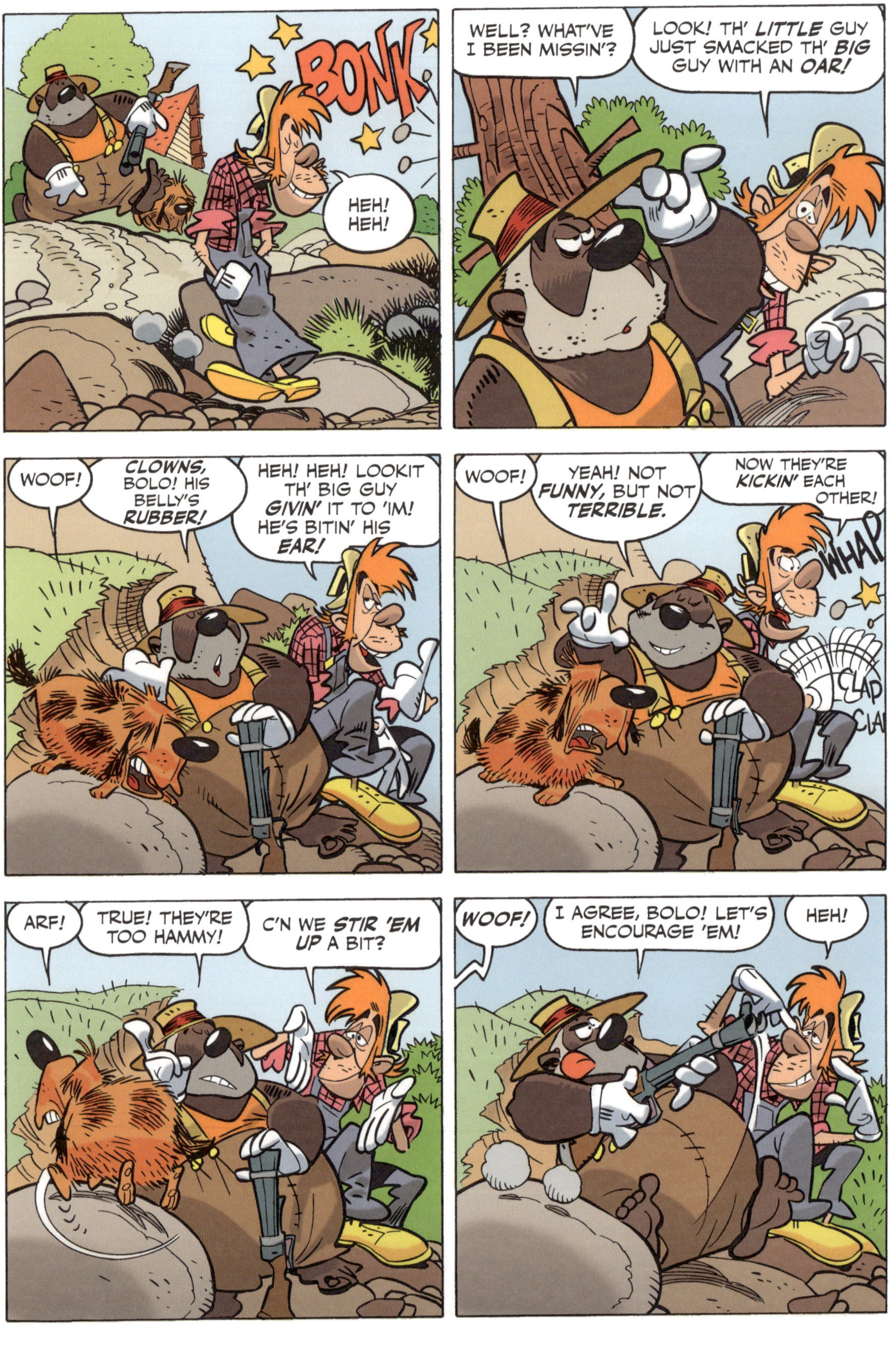
BONK
HEH! HEH!
WELL? WHAT'VE I BEEN MISSIN'?
LOOK! TH' *LITTLE* GUY JUST SMACKED TH' *BIG* GUY WITH AN *OAR!*
WOOF!
CLOWNS, BOLO! HIS BELLY'S *RUBBER!*
HEH! HEH! LOOKIT TH' BIG GUY *GIVIN'* IT TO 'IM! HE'S BITIN' HIS *EAR!*
WOOF!
YEAH! NOT *FUNNY,* BUT NOT *TERRIBLE.*
NOW THEY'RE *KICKIN'* EACH OTHER!
WHAP
CLAP
ARF!
TRUE! THEY'RE TOO HAMMY!
C'N WE *STIR 'EM UP* A BIT?
WOOF!
I AGREE, BOLO! LET'S ENCOURAGE 'EM!
HEH!

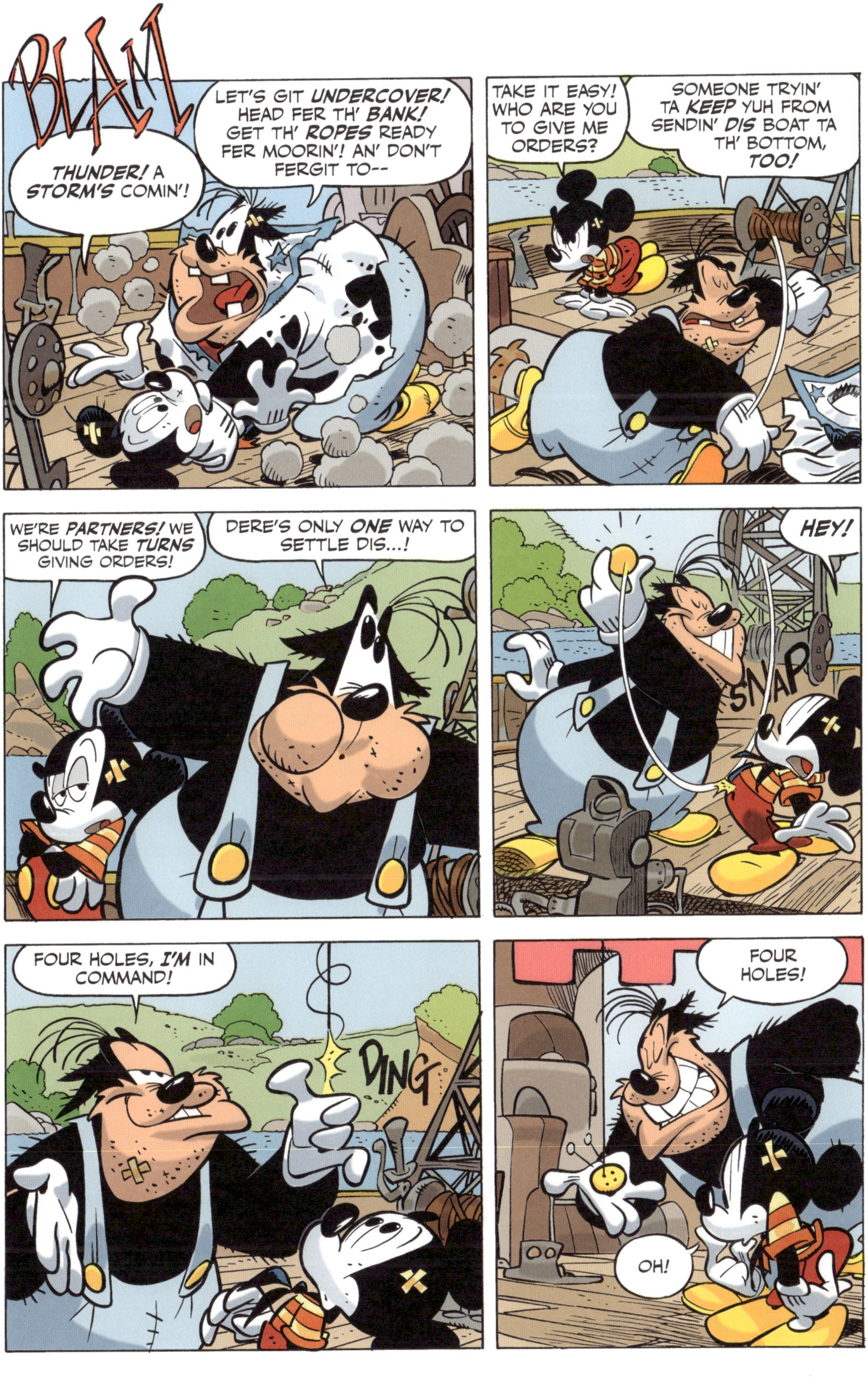

BLAM
THUNDER! A STORM'S COMIN'!
LET'S GIT UNDERCOVER! HEAD FER TH' BANK! GET TH' ROPES READY FER MOORIN'! AN' DON'T FERGIT TO--
TAKE IT EASY! WHO ARE YOU TO GIVE ME ORDERS?
SOMEONE TRYIN' TA KEEP YUH FROM SENDIN' DIS BOAT TA TH' BOTTOM, TOO!
WE'RE PARTNERS! WE SHOULD TAKE TURNS GIVING ORDERS!
DERE'S ONLY ONE WAY TO SETTLE DIS...!
HEY!
SNAP
FOUR HOLES, I'M IN COMMAND!
DING
FOUR HOLES!
OH!

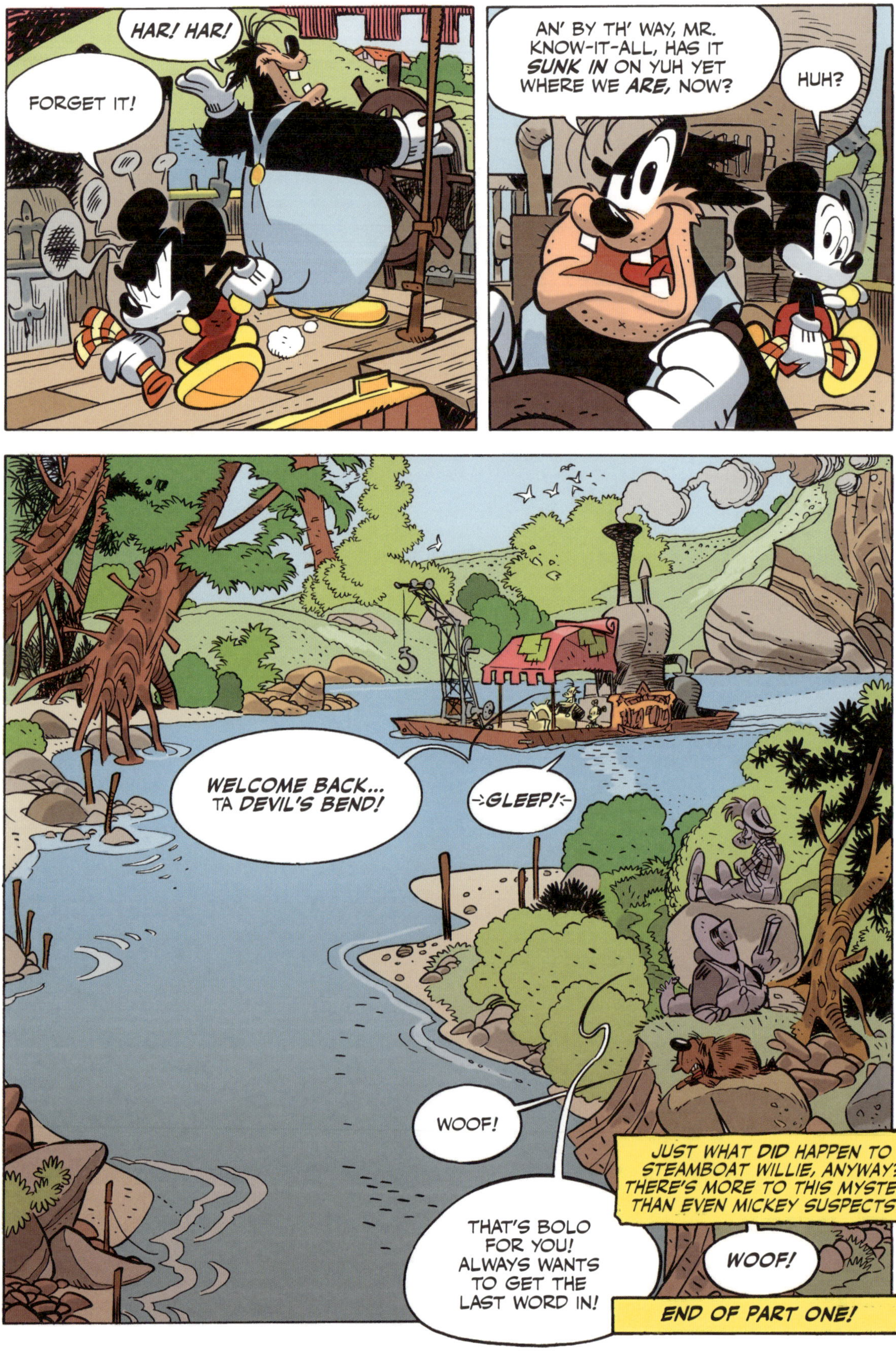
FORGET IT!
HAR! HAR!
AN' BY TH' WAY, MR. KNOW-IT-ALL, HAS IT SUNK IN ON YUH YET WHERE WE ARE, NOW?
HUH?
WELCOME BACK... TA DEVIL'S BEND!
GLEEP!
WOOF!
THAT'S BOLO FOR YOU! ALWAYS WANTS TO GET THE LAST WORD IN!
JUST WHAT DID HAPPEN TO STEAMBOAT WILLIE, ANYWAY? THERE'S MORE TO THIS MYSTERY THAN EVEN MICKEY SUSPECTS...
WOOF!
END OF PART ONE!

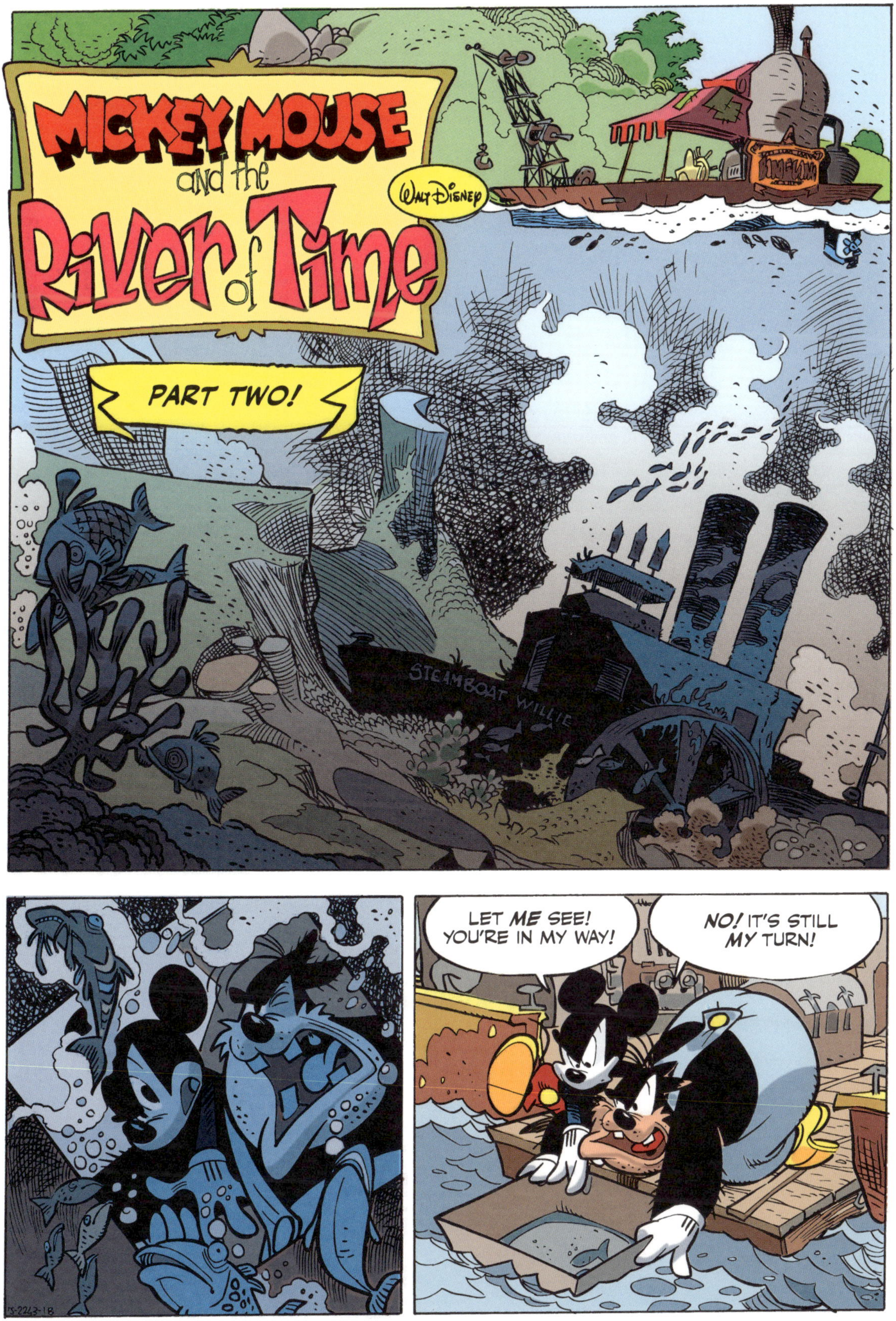
MICKEY MOUSE
and the
River of Time
WALT DISNEY
PART TWO!
STEAMBOAT WILLIE
LET ME SEE! YOU'RE IN MY WAY!
NO! IT'S STILL MY TURN!

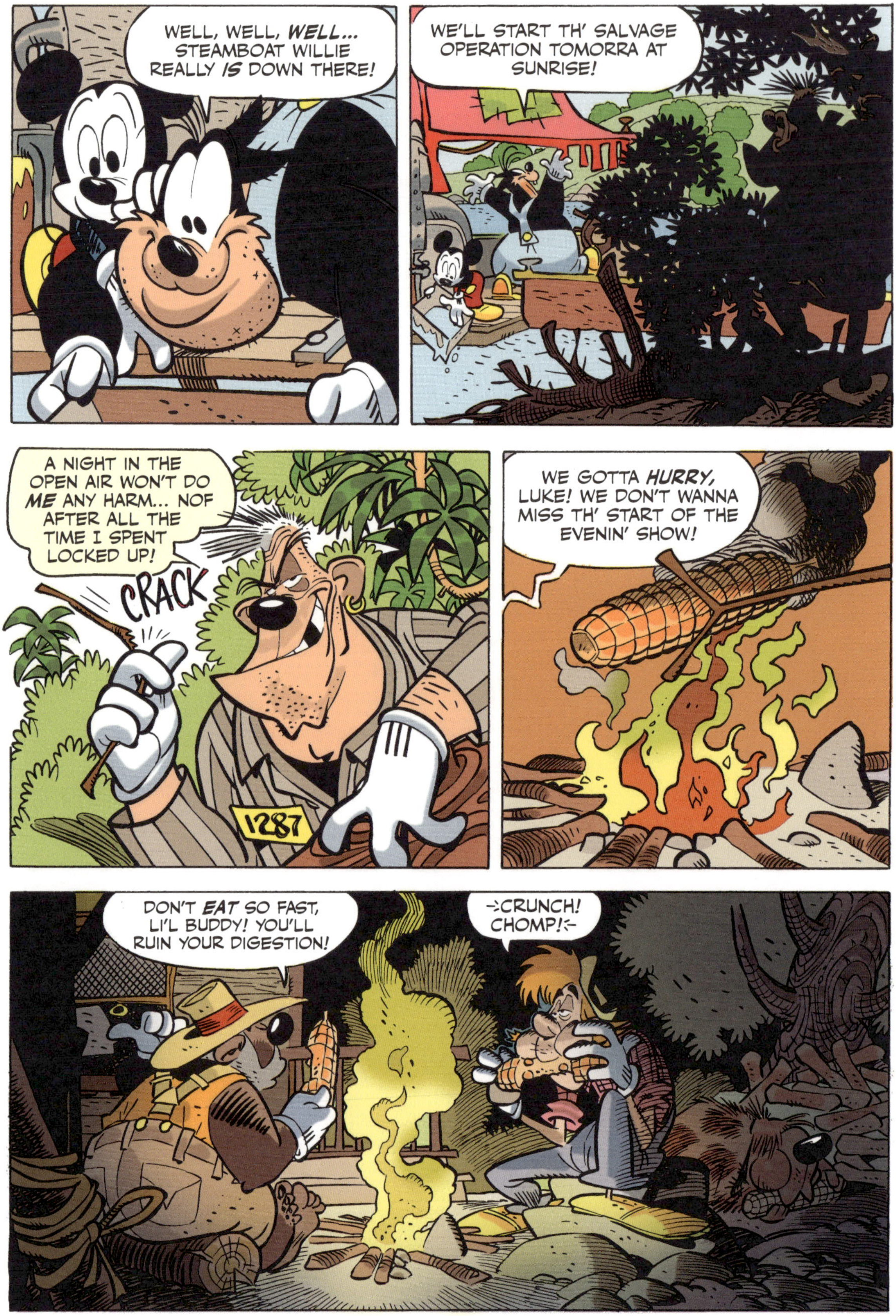
WELL, WELL, WELL... STEAMBOAT WILLIE REALLY IS DOWN THERE!
WE'LL START TH' SALVAGE OPERATION TOMORRA AT SUNRISE!
A NIGHT IN THE OPEN AIR WON'T DO ME ANY HARM... NOF AFTER ALL THE TIME I SPENT LOCKED UP!
CRACK
1287
WE GOTTA HURRY, LUKE! WE DON'T WANNA MISS TH' START OF THE EVENIN' SHOW!
DON'T EAT SO FAST, LI'L BUDDY! YOU'LL RUIN YOUR DIGESTION!
CRUNCH! CHOMP!

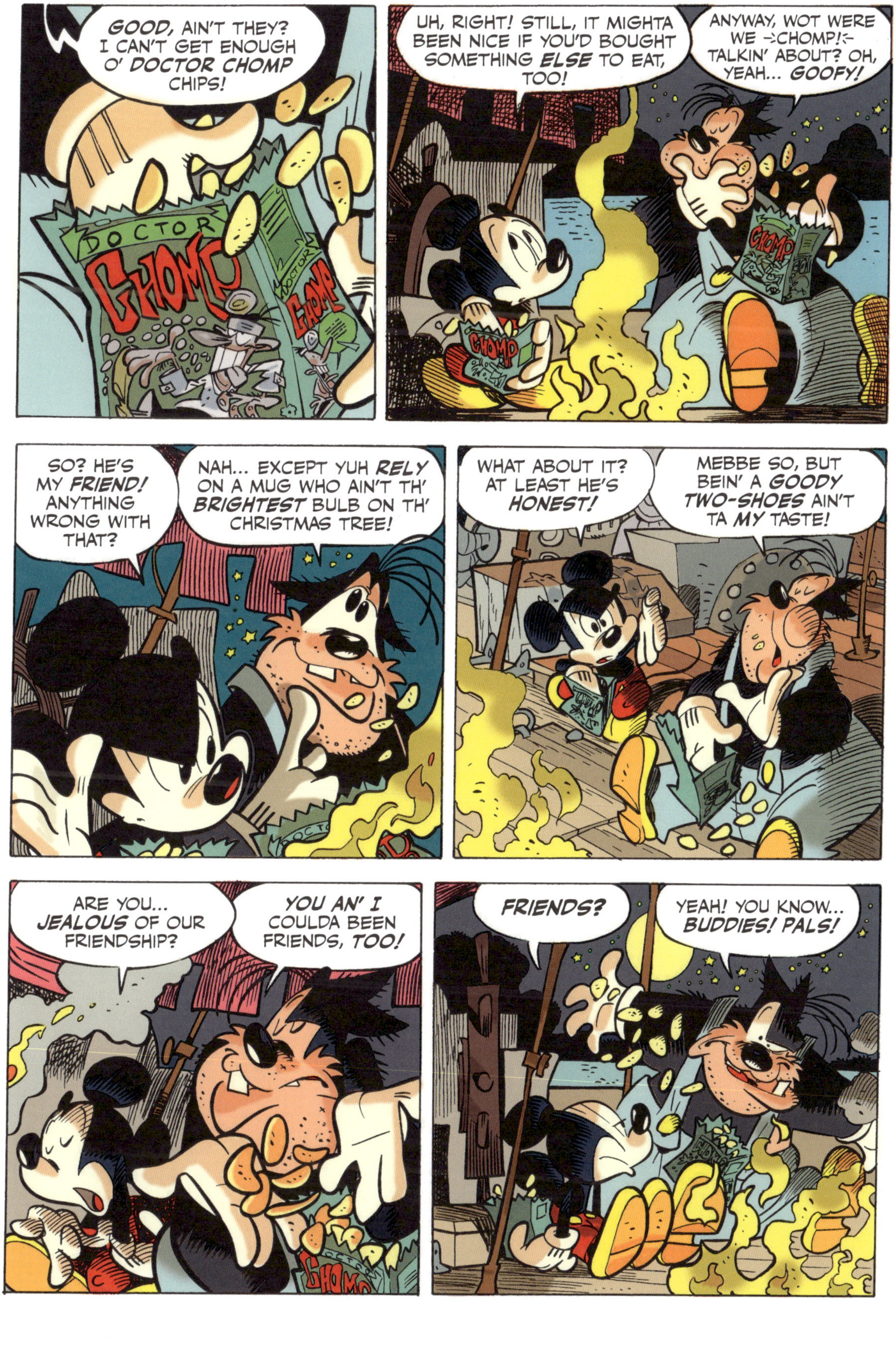
GOOD, AIN'T THEY? I CAN'T GET ENOUGH O' DOCTOR CHOMP CHIPS!
DOCTOR CHOMP
UH, RIGHT! STILL, IT MIGHTA BEEN NICE IF YOU'D BOUGHT SOMETHING ELSE TO EAT, TOO!
ANYWAY, WOT WERE WE -CHOMP!- TALKIN' ABOUT? OH, YEAH... GOOFY!
SO? HE'S MY FRIEND! ANYTHING WRONG WITH THAT?
NAH... EXCEPT YUH RELY ON A MUG WHO AIN'T TH' BRIGHTEST BULB ON TH' CHRISTMAS TREE!
WHAT ABOUT IT? AT LEAST HE'S HONEST!
MEBBE SO, BUT BEIN' A GOODY TWO-SHOES AIN'T TA MY TASTE!
ARE YOU... JEALOUS OF OUR FRIENDSHIP?
YOU AN' I COULDA BEEN FRIENDS, TOO!
FRIENDS?
YEAH! YOU KNOW... BUDDIES! PALS!

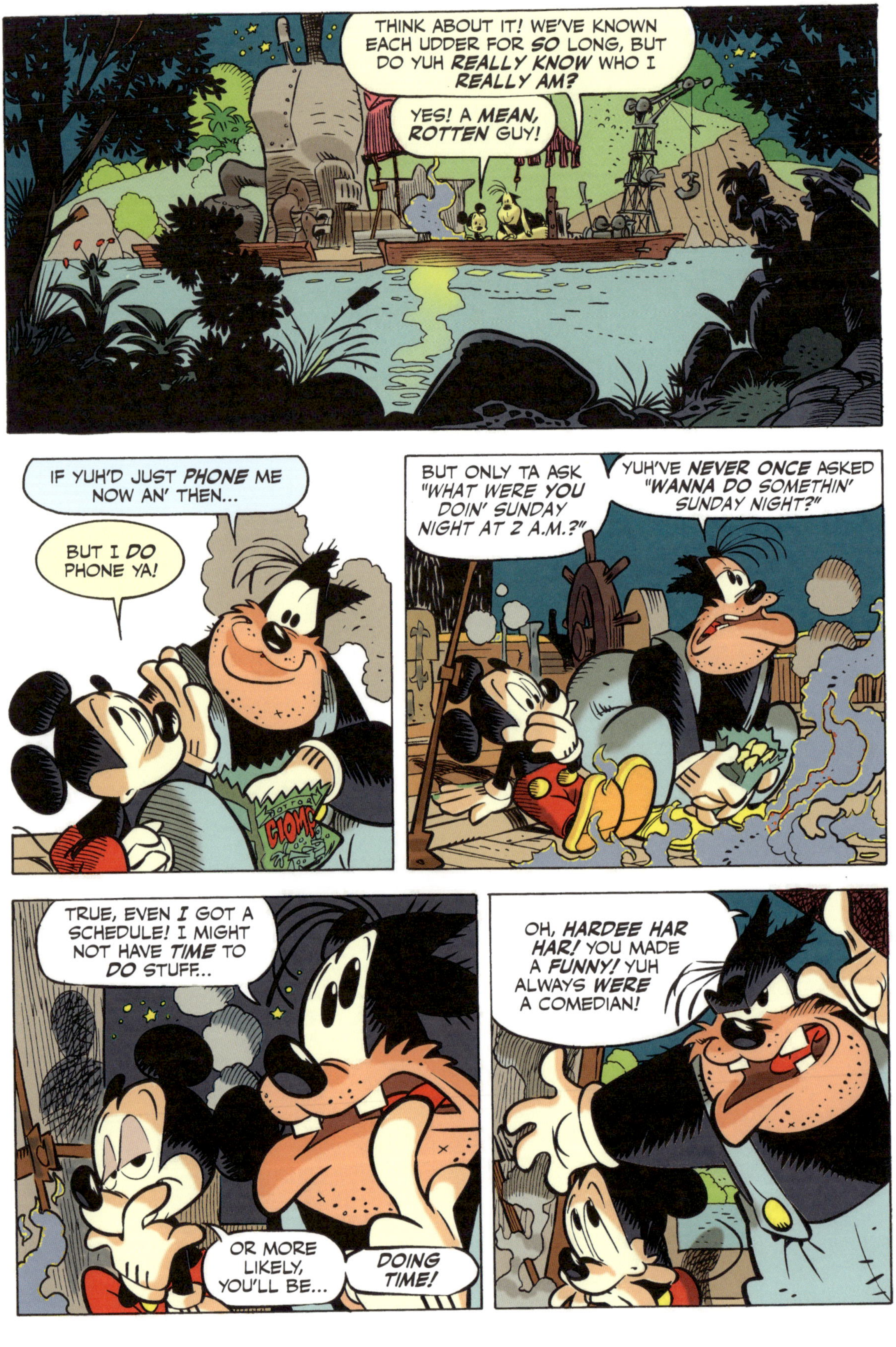

THINK ABOUT IT! WE'VE KNOWN EACH UDDER FOR SO LONG, BUT DO YUH REALLY KNOW WHO I REALLY AM?
YES! A MEAN, ROTTEN GUY!
IF YUH'D JUST PHONE ME NOW AN' THEN...
BUT I DO PHONE YA!
CIOMP
BUT ONLY TA ASK "WHAT WERE YOU DOIN' SUNDAY NIGHT AT 2 A.M.?"
YUH'VE NEVER ONCE ASKED "WANNA DO SOMETHIN' SUNDAY NIGHT?"
TRUE, EVEN I GOT A SCHEDULE! I MIGHT NOT HAVE TIME TO DO STUFF...
OR MORE LIKELY, YOU'LL BE...
DOING TIME!
OH, HARDEE HAR HAR! YOU MADE A FUNNY! YUH ALWAYS WERE A COMEDIAN!

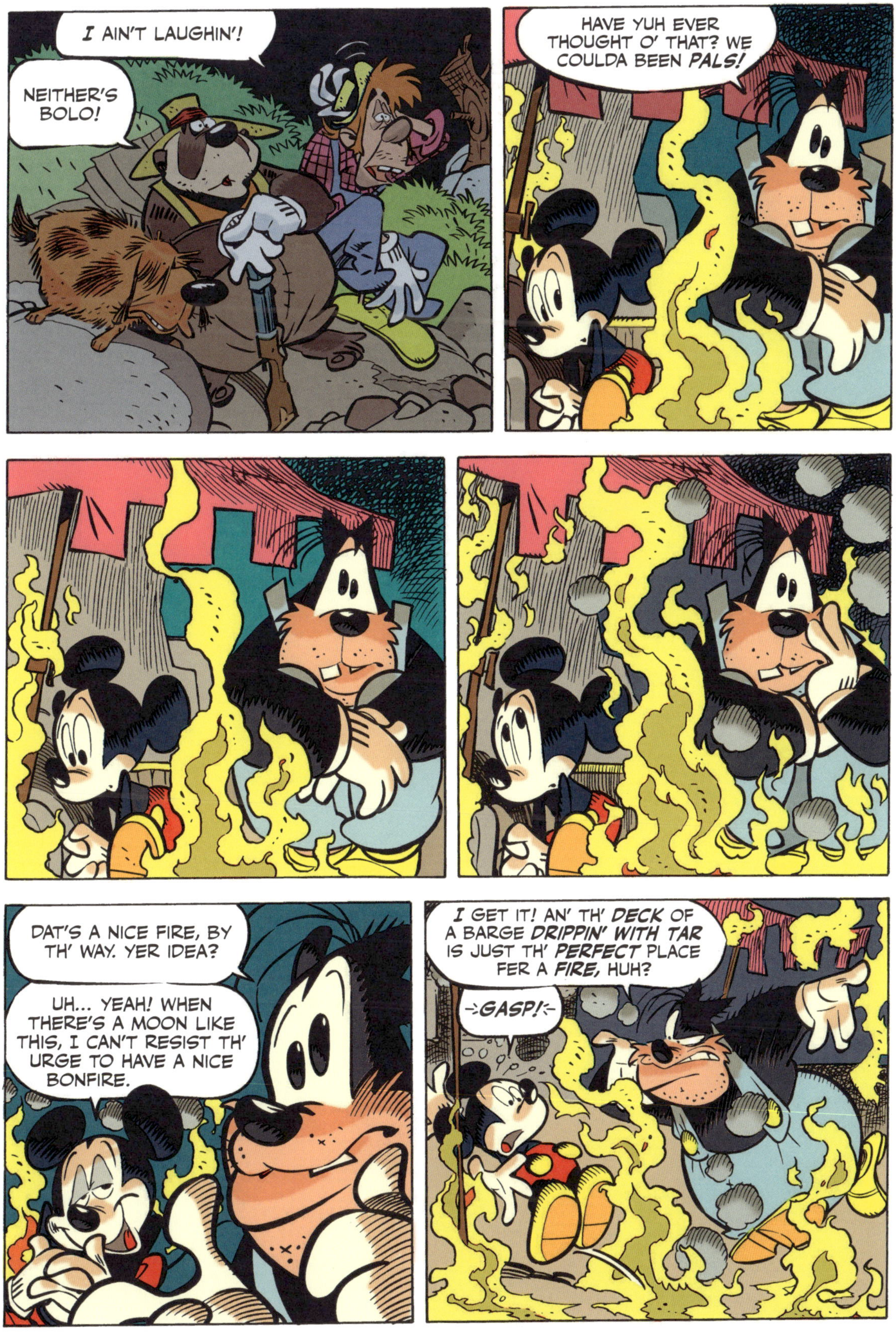
I AIN'T LAUGHIN'!
NEITHER'S BOLO!
HAVE YUH EVER THOUGHT O' THAT? WE COULDA BEEN PALS!
DAT'S A NICE FIRE, BY TH' WAY. YER IDEA?
UH... YEAH! WHEN THERE'S A MOON LIKE THIS, I CAN'T RESIST TH' URGE TO HAVE A NICE BONFIRE.
I GET IT! AN' TH' DECK OF A BARGE DRIPPIN' WITH TAR IS JUST TH' PERFECT PLACE FER A FIRE, HUH?
GASP!

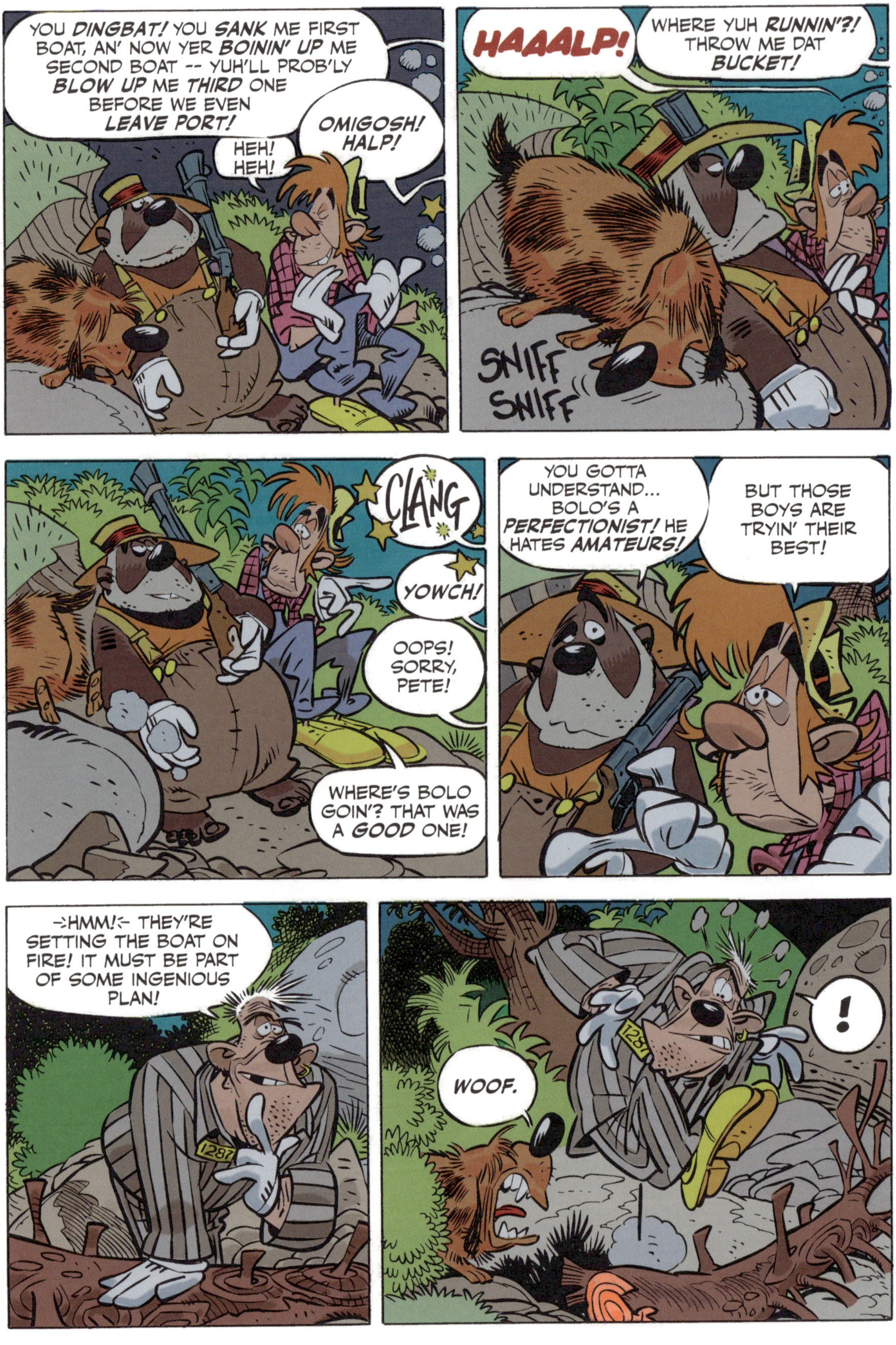
YOU DINGBAT! YOU SANK ME FIRST BOAT, AN' NOW YER BOININ' UP ME SECOND BOAT -- YUH'LL PROB'LY BLOW UP ME THIRD ONE BEFORE WE EVEN LEAVE PORT!
HEH! HEH!
OMIGOSH! HALP!
HAAALP!
WHERE YUH RUNNIN'?! THROW ME DAT BUCKET!
SNIFF SNIFF
CLANG
YOWCH!
OOPS! SORRY, PETE!
WHERE'S BOLO GOIN'? THAT WAS A GOOD ONE!
YOU GOTTA UNDERSTAND... BOLO'S A PERFECTIONIST! HE HATES AMATEURS!
BUT THOSE BOYS ARE TRYIN' THEIR BEST!
-HMM!- THEY'RE SETTING THE BOAT ON FIRE! IT MUST BE PART OF SOME INGENIOUS PLAN!
WOOF.
!

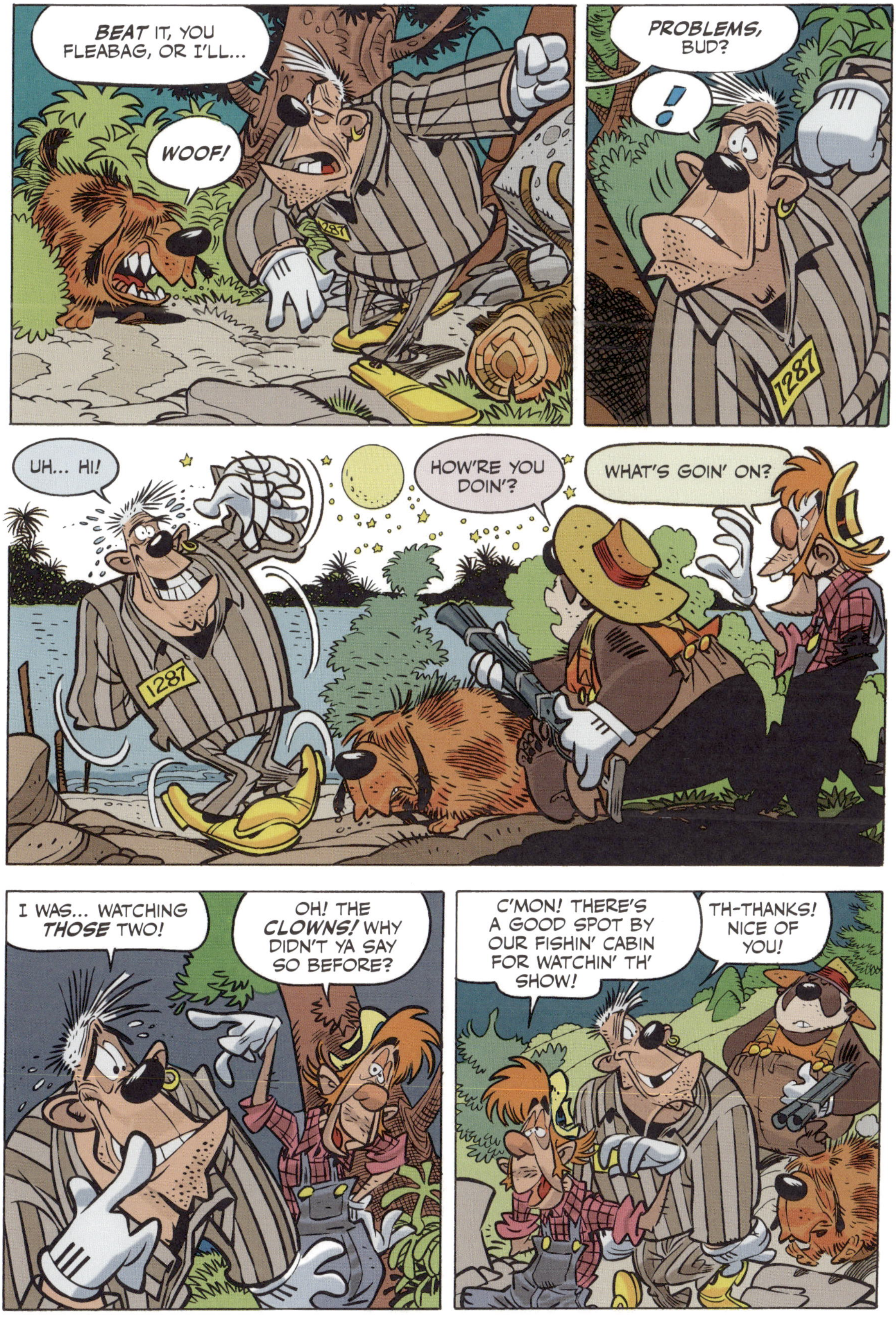

BEAT IT, YOU FLEABAG, OR I'LL...
WOOF!
PROBLEMS, BUD?
!
1287
UH... HI!
HOW'RE YOU DOIN'?
WHAT'S GOIN' ON?
1287
I WAS... WATCHING *THOSE* TWO!
OH! THE *CLOWNS!* WHY DIDN'T YA SAY SO BEFORE?
C'MON! THERE'S A GOOD SPOT BY OUR FISHIN' CABIN FOR WATCHIN' TH' SHOW!
TH-THANKS! NICE OF YOU!

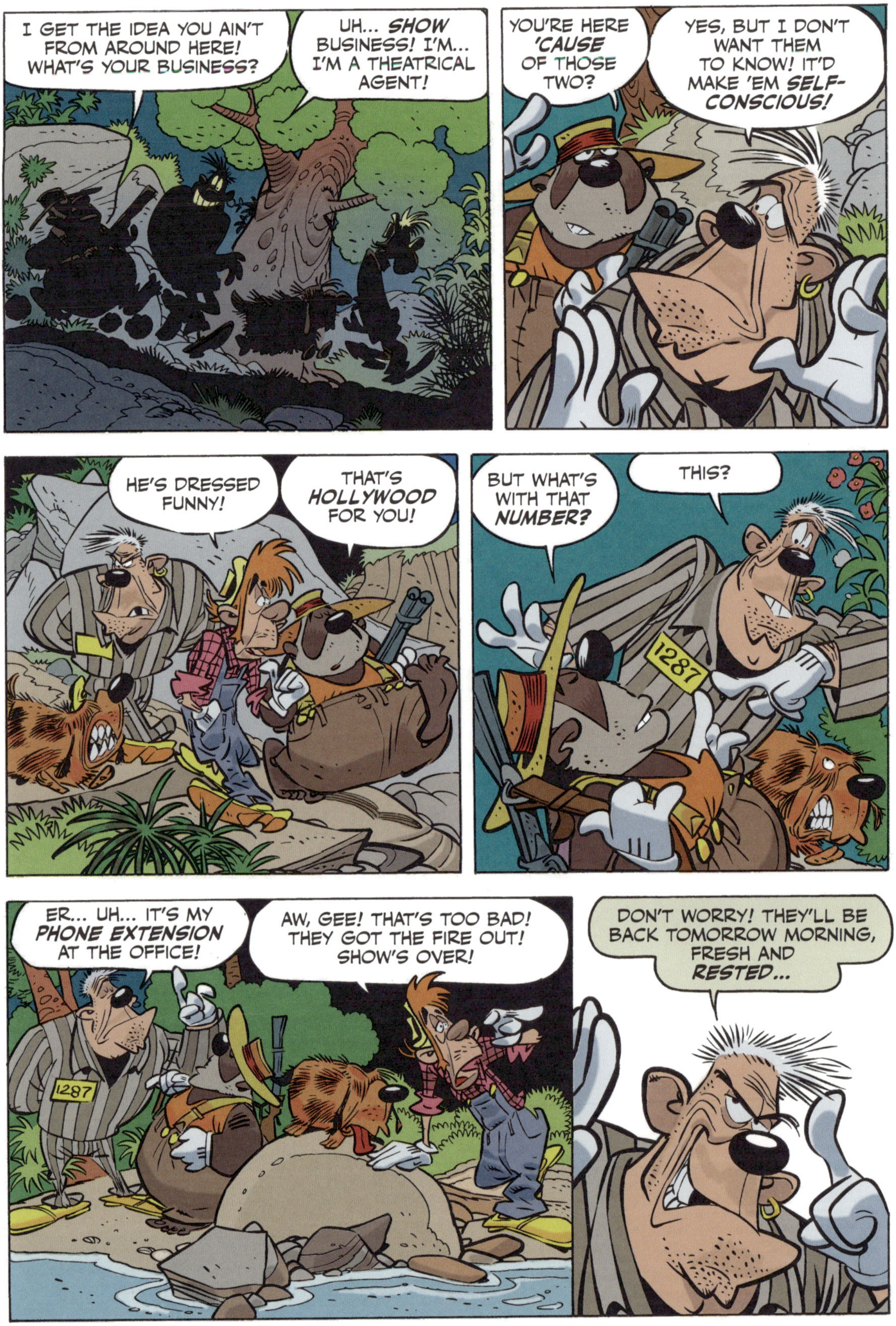
I GET THE IDEA YOU AIN'T FROM AROUND HERE! WHAT'S YOUR BUSINESS?
UH... SHOW BUSINESS! I'M... I'M A THEATRICAL AGENT!
YOU'RE HERE 'CAUSE OF THOSE TWO?
YES, BUT I DON'T WANT THEM TO KNOW! IT'D MAKE 'EM SELF-CONSCIOUS!
HE'S DRESSED FUNNY!
THAT'S HOLLYWOOD FOR YOU!
BUT WHAT'S WITH THAT NUMBER?
THIS?
1287
ER... UH... IT'S MY PHONE EXTENSION AT THE OFFICE!
1287
AW, GEE! THAT'S TOO BAD! THEY GOT THE FIRE OUT! SHOW'S OVER!
DON'T WORRY! THEY'LL BE BACK TOMORROW MORNING, FRESH AND RESTED...

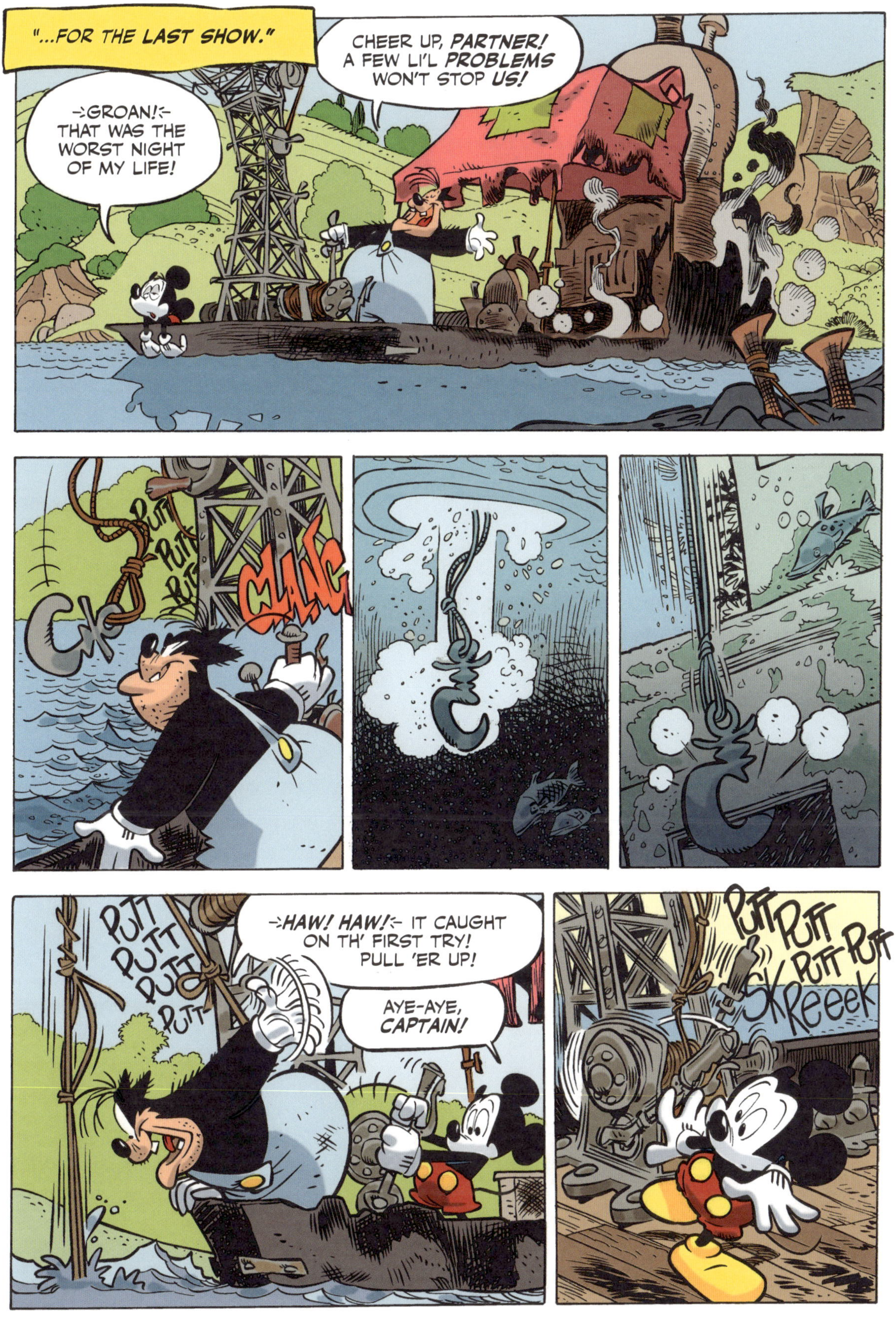
"...FOR THE LAST SHOW."
-GROAN!- THAT WAS THE WORST NIGHT OF MY LIFE!
CHEER UP, PARTNER! A FEW LI'L PROBLEMS WON'T STOP US!
PUTT PUTT PUTT
CLANG
-HAW! HAW!- IT CAUGHT ON TH' FIRST TRY! PULL 'ER UP!
AYE-AYE, CAPTAIN!
PUTT PUTT PUTT PUTT
PUFF PUFF PUFF PUFF
SKREEEK

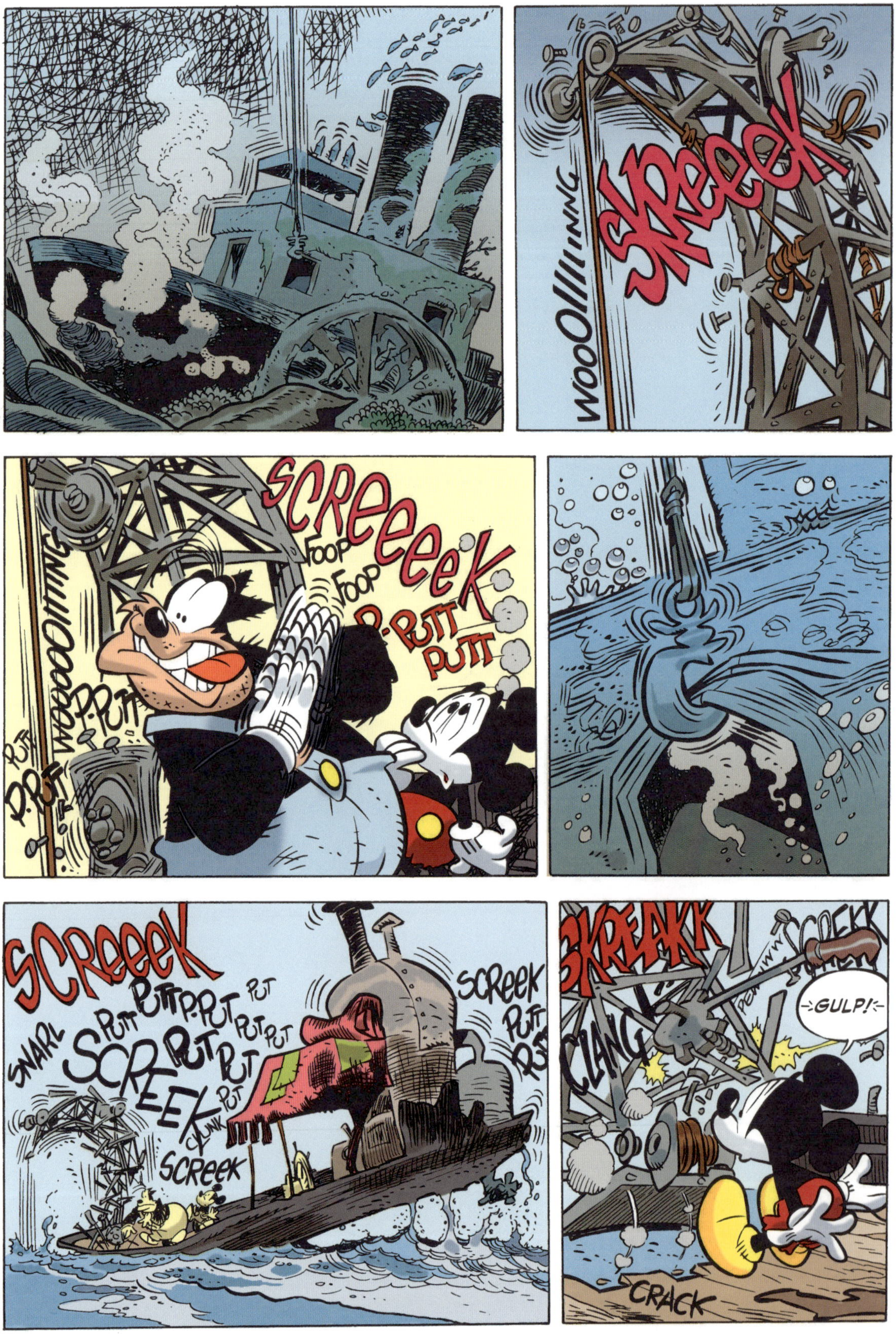

WOOOOIIIIIINNNG
SKREEEK
SCREEEEEK
FOOP
FOOP
P-PUTT
PUTT
WOOOOOIIIING
P-PUTT
P-PUTT
PUTT
SCREEEK
SNARL
PUTT
PUTT
P-PUT
PUT
PUT PUT
PUT PUT
SCREEEK
PUT
PUT
CLUNK
SCREEK
SCREEK
PUTT
SKREAKK
SCREKK
CLANG
-GULP!-
CRACK

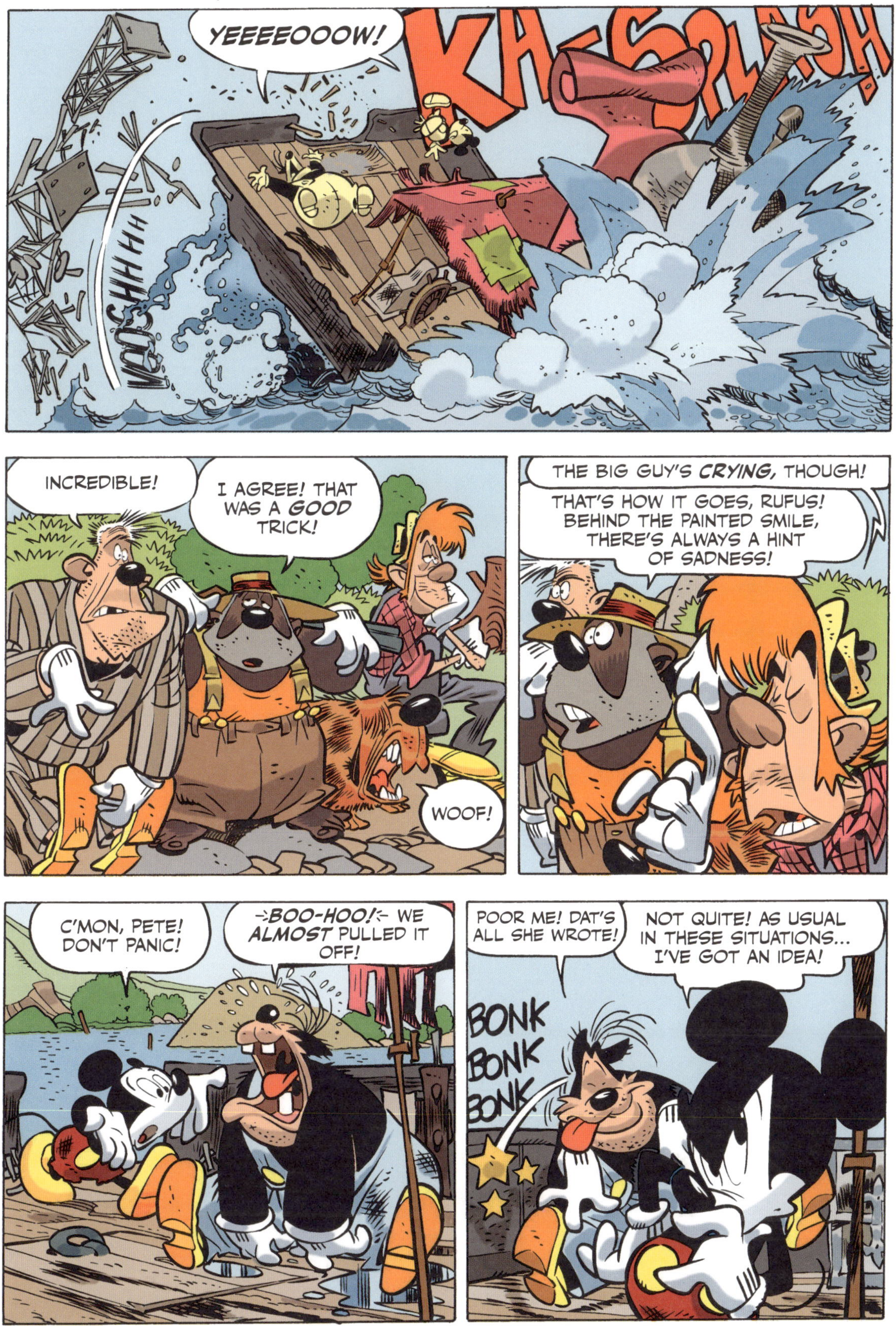
YEEEEOOOW!
KA-SPLASH
VOOSHHHH
INCREDIBLE!
I AGREE! THAT WAS A GOOD TRICK!
WOOF!
THE BIG GUY'S CRYING, THOUGH!
THAT'S HOW IT GOES, RUFUS! BEHIND THE PAINTED SMILE, THERE'S ALWAYS A HINT OF SADNESS!
C'MON, PETE! DON'T PANIC!
BOO-HOO! WE ALMOST PULLED IT OFF!
POOR ME! DAT'S ALL SHE WROTE!
NOT QUITE! AS USUAL IN THESE SITUATIONS... I'VE GOT AN IDEA!
BONK
BONK
BONK

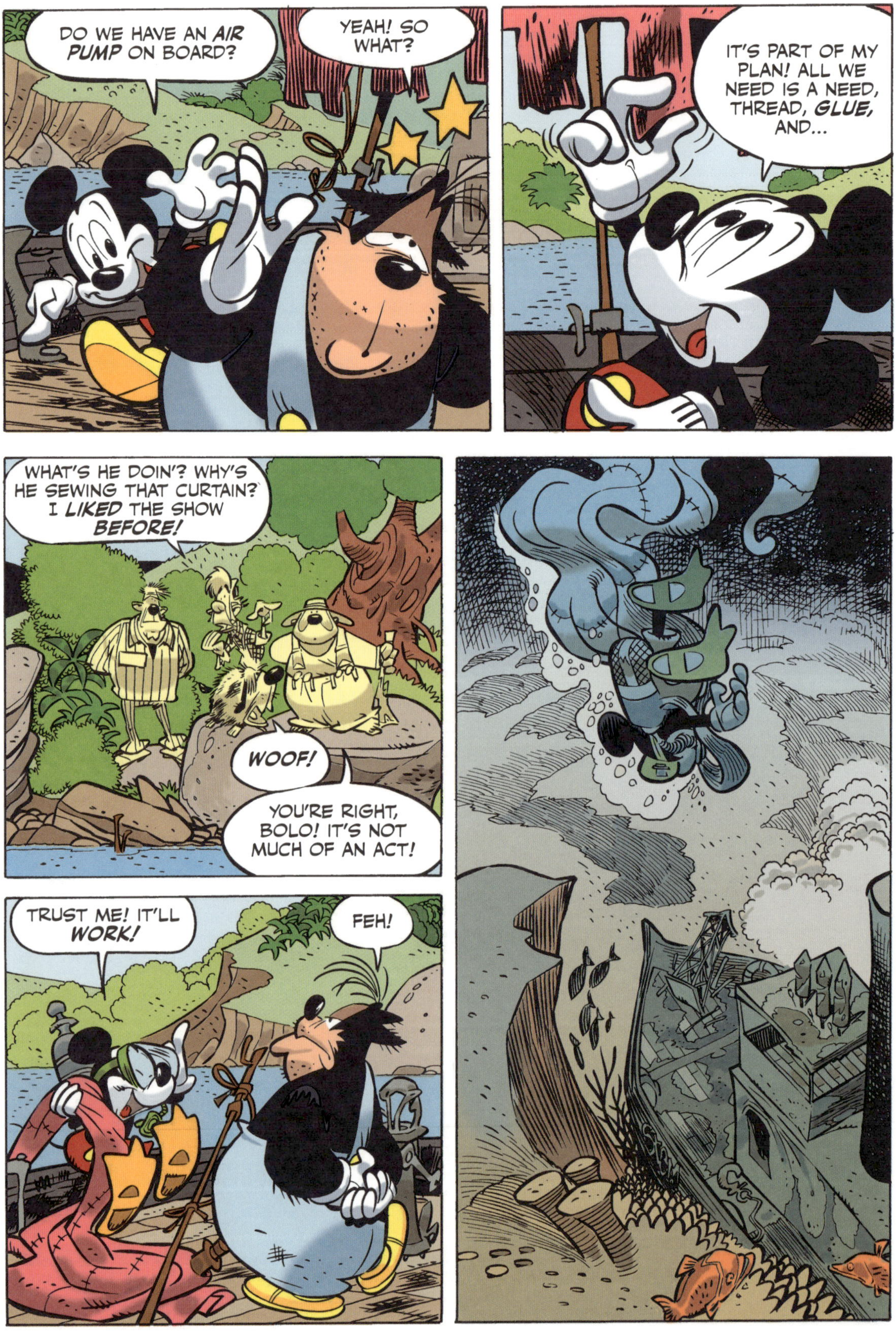

DO WE HAVE AN *AIR PUMP* ON BOARD?
YEAH! SO WHAT?
IT'S PART OF MY PLAN! ALL WE NEED IS A NEED, THREAD, *GLUE,* AND...
WHAT'S HE DOIN'? WHY'S HE SEWING THAT CURTAIN? I *LIKED* THE SHOW *BEFORE!*
WOOF!
YOU'RE RIGHT, BOLO! IT'S NOT MUCH OF AN ACT!
TRUST ME! IT'LL *WORK!*
FEH!

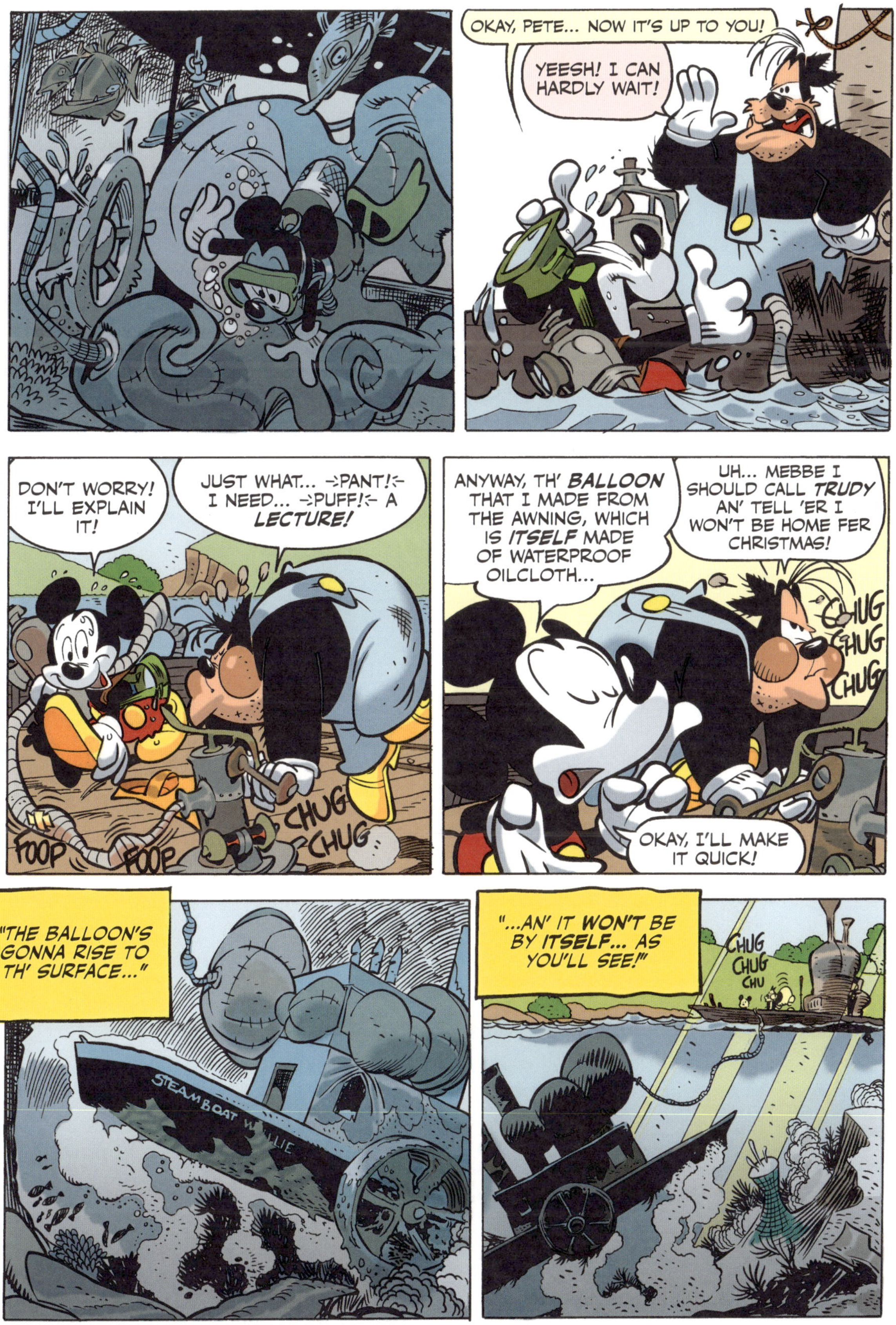

OKAY, PETE... NOW IT'S UP TO YOU!
YEESH! I CAN HARDLY WAIT!
DON'T WORRY! I'LL EXPLAIN IT!
JUST WHAT... -PANT!- I NEED... -PUFF!- A LECTURE!
CHUG CHUG
FOOP FOOP
ANYWAY, TH' BALLOON THAT I MADE FROM THE AWNING, WHICH IS ITSELF MADE OF WATERPROOF OILCLOTH...
UH... MEBBE I SHOULD CALL TRUDY AN' TELL 'ER I WON'T BE HOME FER CHRISTMAS!
CHUG CHUG CHUG
OKAY, I'LL MAKE IT QUICK!
"THE BALLOON'S GONNA RISE TO TH' SURFACE..."
STEAMBOAT WILLIE
"...AN' IT WON'T BE BY ITSELF... AS YOU'LL SEE!"
CHUG CHUG CHU

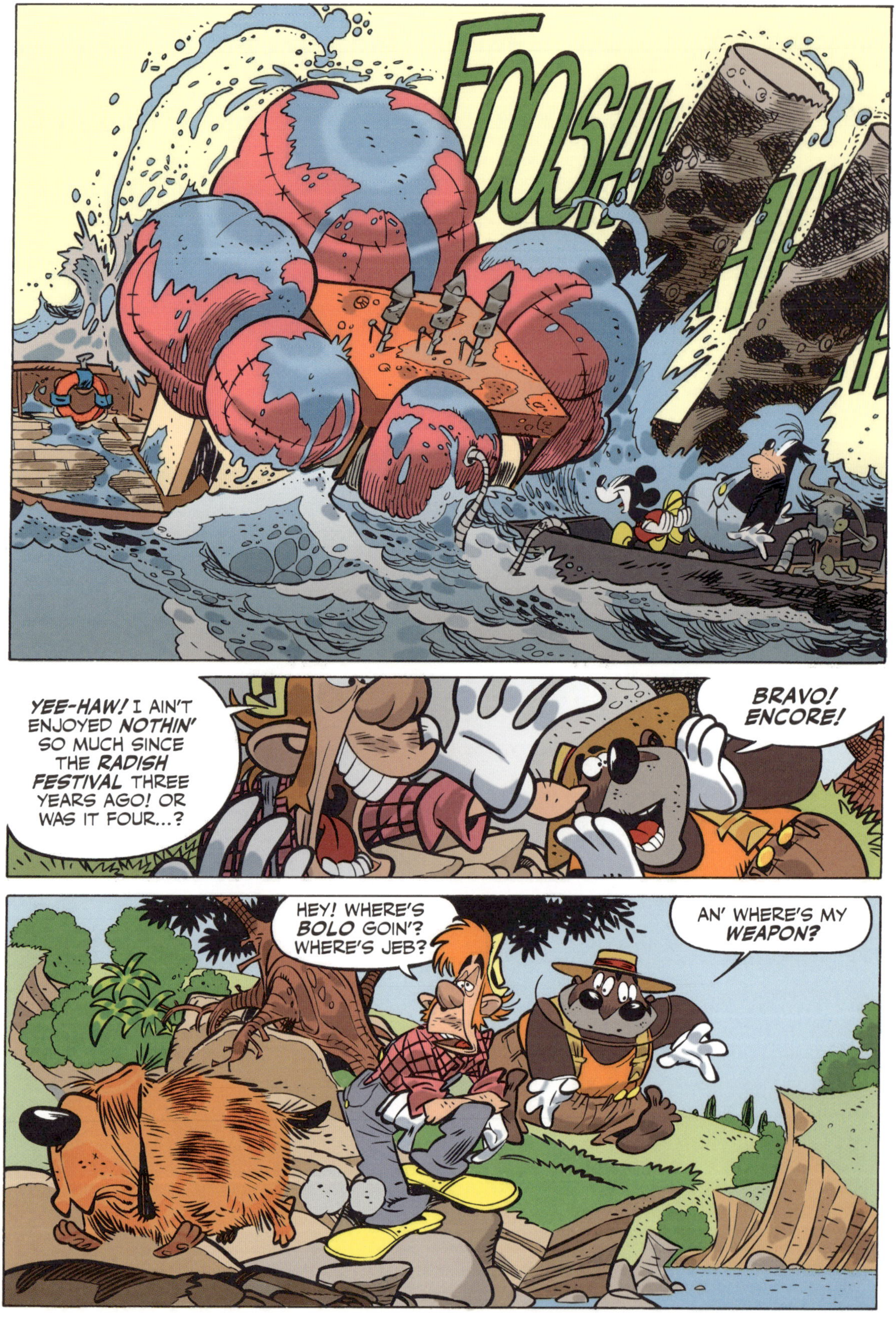
FOOSHH
YEE-HAW! I AIN'T ENJOYED NOTHIN' SO MUCH SINCE THE RADISH FESTIVAL THREE YEARS AGO! OR WAS IT FOUR...?
BRAVO! ENCORE!
HEY! WHERE'S BOLO GOIN'? WHERE'S JEB?
AN' WHERE'S MY WEAPON?

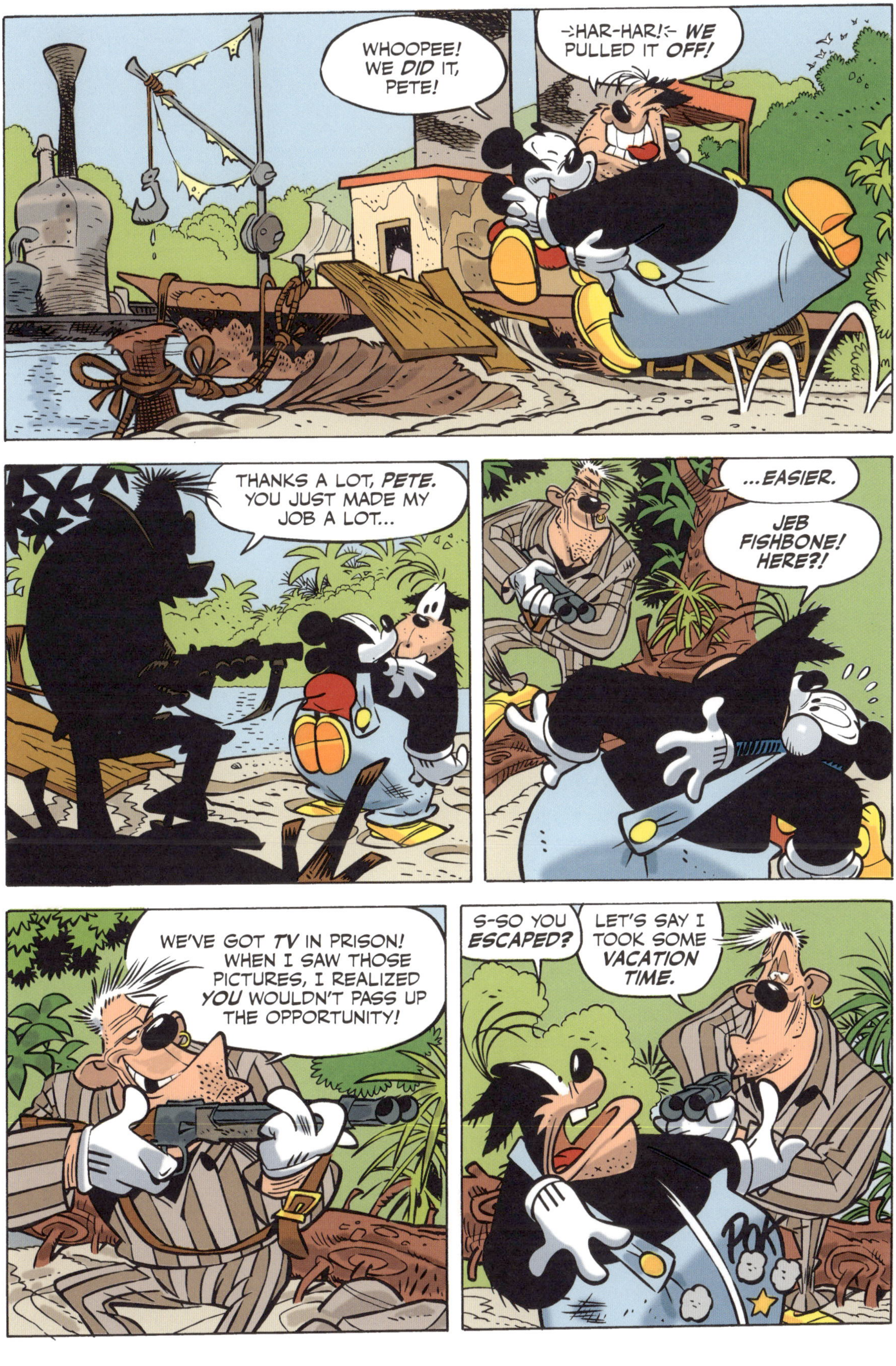
WHOOPEE! WE DID IT, PETE!
-HAR-HAR!- WE PULLED IT OFF!
THANKS A LOT, PETE. YOU JUST MADE MY JOB A LOT...
...EASIER.
JEB FISHBONE! HERE?!
WE'VE GOT TV IN PRISON! WHEN I SAW THOSE PICTURES, I REALIZED YOU WOULDN'T PASS UP THE OPPORTUNITY!
S-SO YOU ESCAPED?
LET'S SAY I TOOK SOME VACATION TIME.
POK

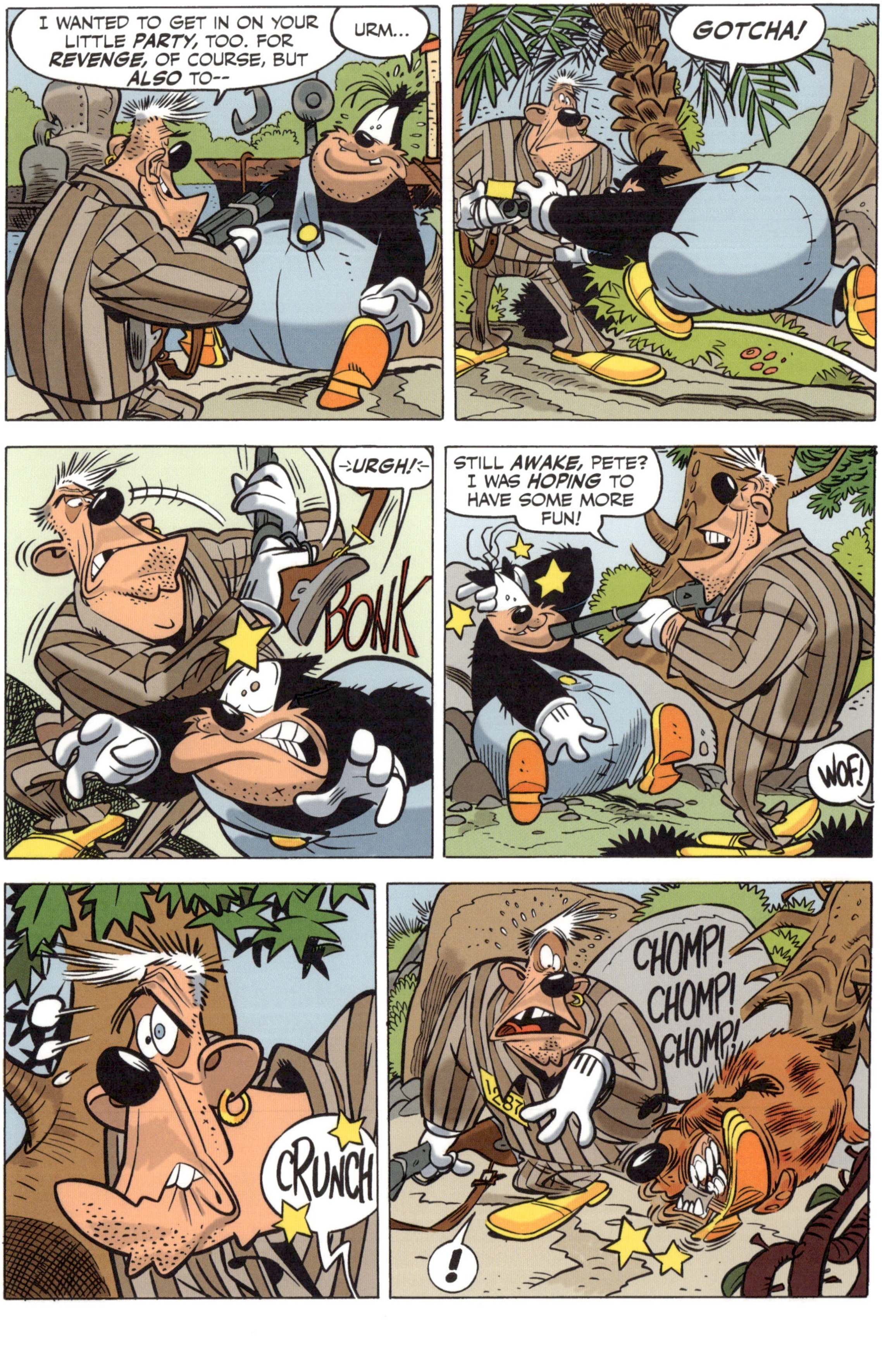

I WANTED TO GET IN ON YOUR LITTLE PARTY, TOO. FOR REVENGE, OF COURSE, BUT ALSO TO--
URM...
GOTCHA!
-URGH!-
BONK
STILL AWAKE, PETE? I WAS HOPING TO HAVE SOME MORE FUN!
WOF!
CRUNCH
CHOMP! CHOMP! CHOMP!
!

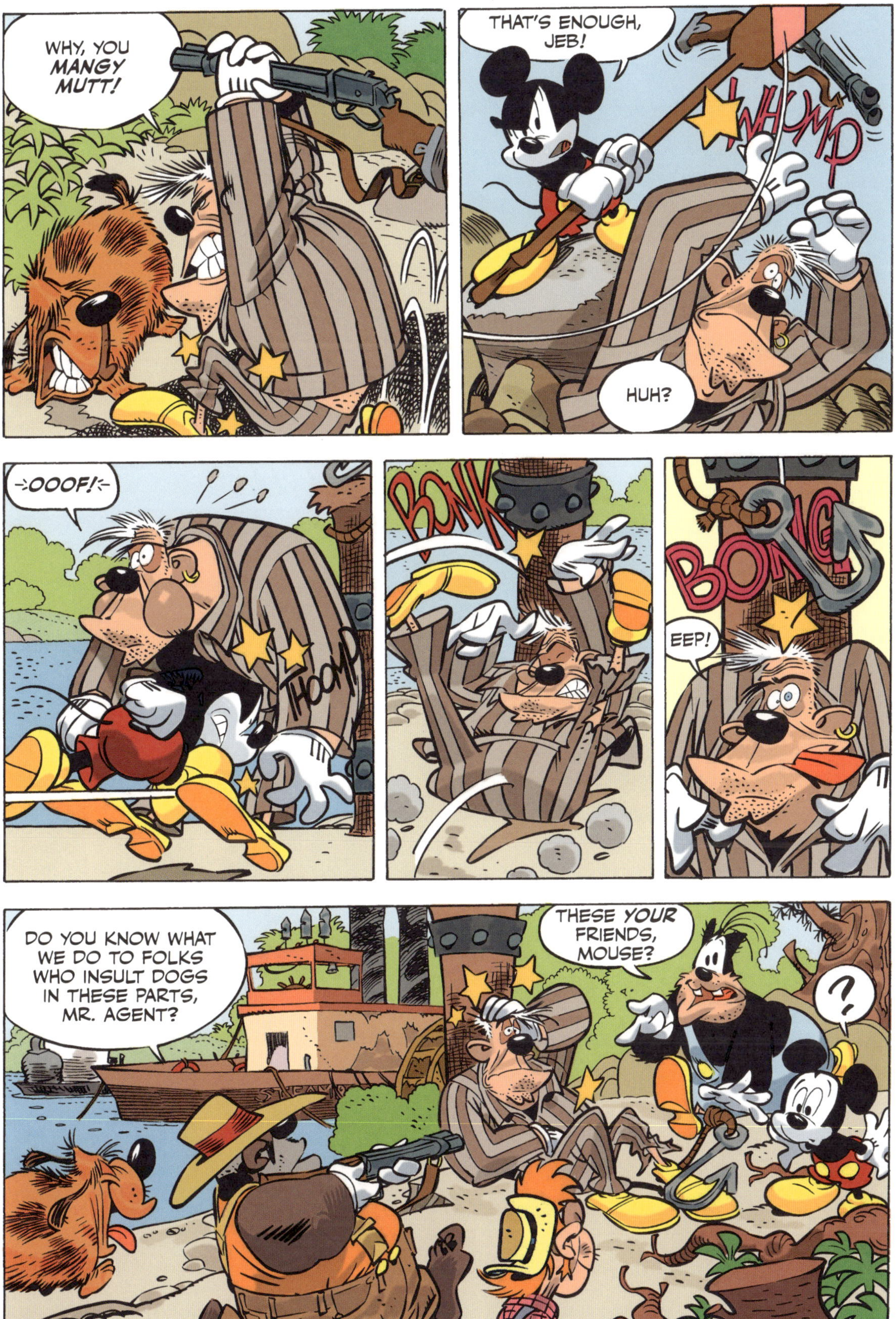
WHY, YOU *MANGY MUTT!*
THAT'S ENOUGH, JEB!
WHOMP
HUH?
OOOF!
THOOMP
BONK
EEP!
DO YOU KNOW WHAT WE DO TO FOLKS WHO INSULT DOGS IN THESE PARTS, MR. AGENT?
THESE *YOUR* FRIENDS, MOUSE?
?

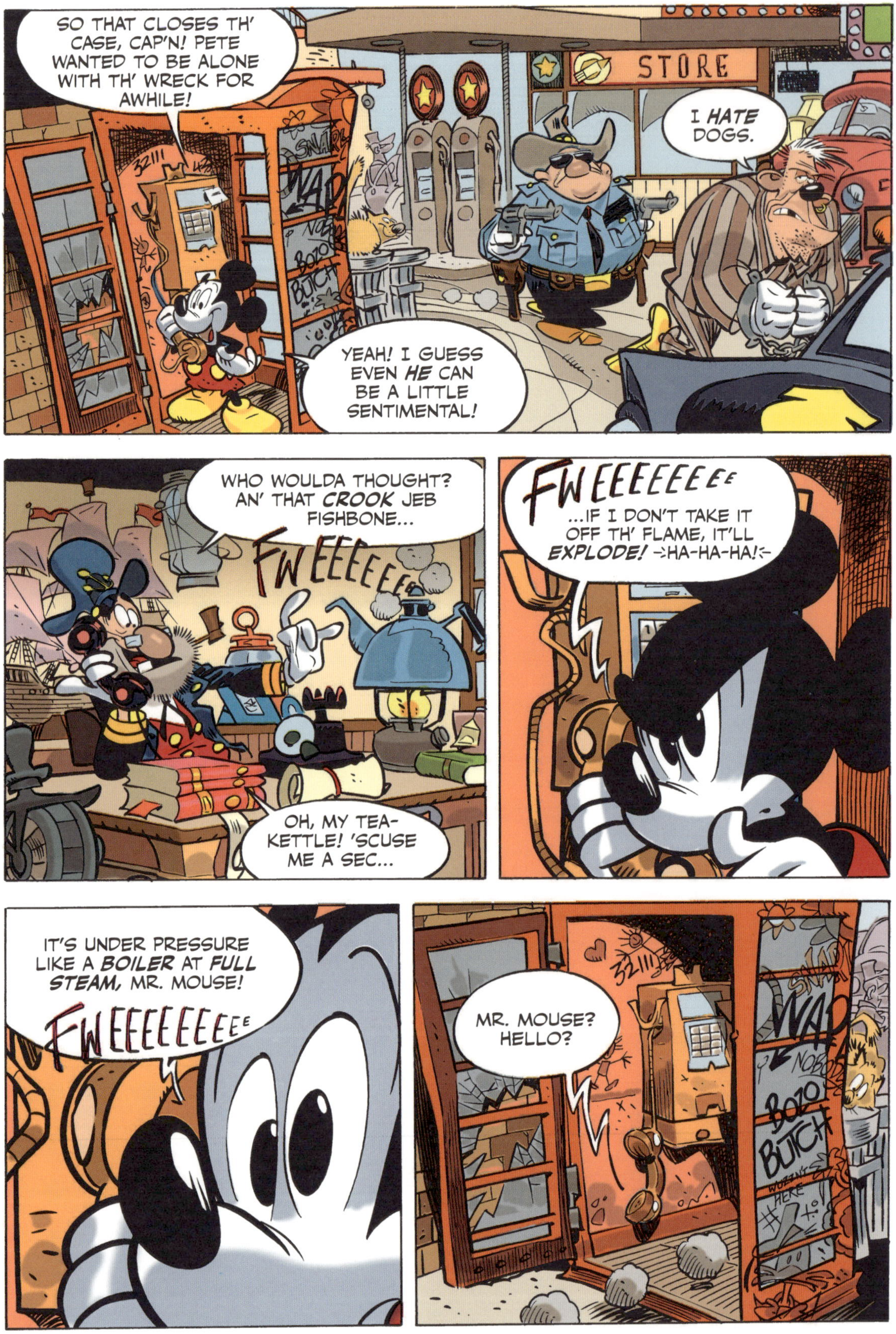
SO THAT CLOSES TH' CASE, CAP'N! PETE WANTED TO BE ALONE WITH TH' WRECK FOR AWHILE!
STORE
I *HATE* DOGS.
YEAH! I GUESS EVEN *HE* CAN BE A LITTLE SENTIMENTAL!
WHO WOULDA THOUGHT? AN' THAT *CROOK* JEB FISHBONE...
FWEEEEEEE
OH, MY TEA-KETTLE! 'SCUSE ME A SEC...
FWEEEEEEEE
...IF I DON'T TAKE IT OFF TH' FLAME, IT'LL *EXPLODE!* -HA-HA-HA!-
IT'S UNDER PRESSURE LIKE A *BOILER* AT *FULL STEAM,* MR. MOUSE!
FWEEEEEEEEE
MR. MOUSE? HELLO?

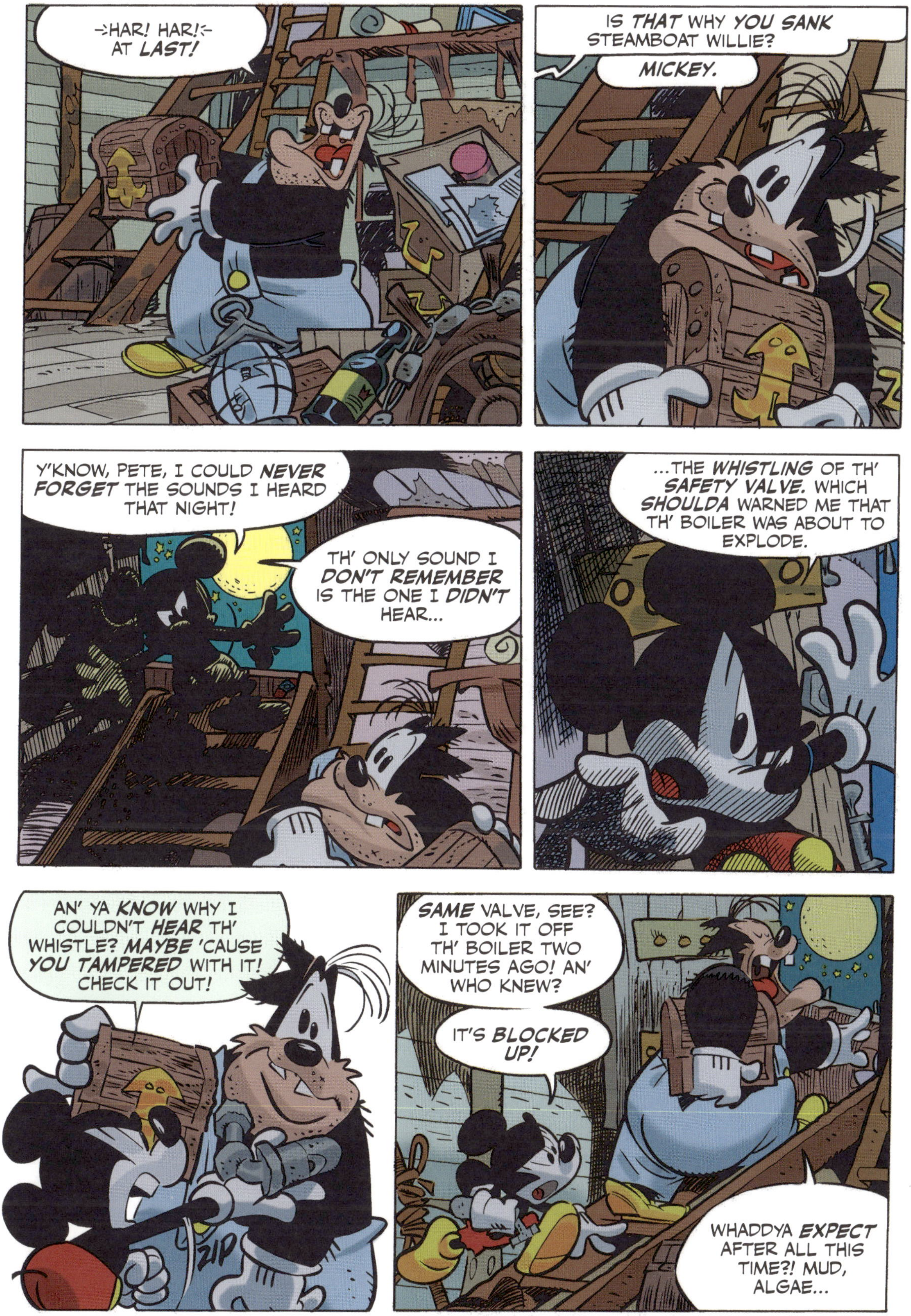

HAR! HAR! AT LAST!
IS THAT WHY YOU SANK STEAMBOAT WILLIE?
MICKEY.
Y'KNOW, PETE, I COULD NEVER FORGET THE SOUNDS I HEARD THAT NIGHT!
TH' ONLY SOUND I DON'T REMEMBER IS THE ONE I DIDN'T HEAR...
...THE WHISTLING OF TH' SAFETY VALVE. WHICH SHOULDA WARNED ME THAT TH' BOILER WAS ABOUT TO EXPLODE.
AN' YA KNOW WHY I COULDN'T HEAR TH' WHISTLE? MAYBE 'CAUSE YOU TAMPERED WITH IT! CHECK IT OUT!
ZIP
SAME VALVE, SEE? I TOOK IT OFF TH' BOILER TWO MINUTES AGO! AN' WHO KNEW?
IT'S BLOCKED UP!
WHADDYA EXPECT AFTER ALL THIS TIME?! MUD, ALGAE...

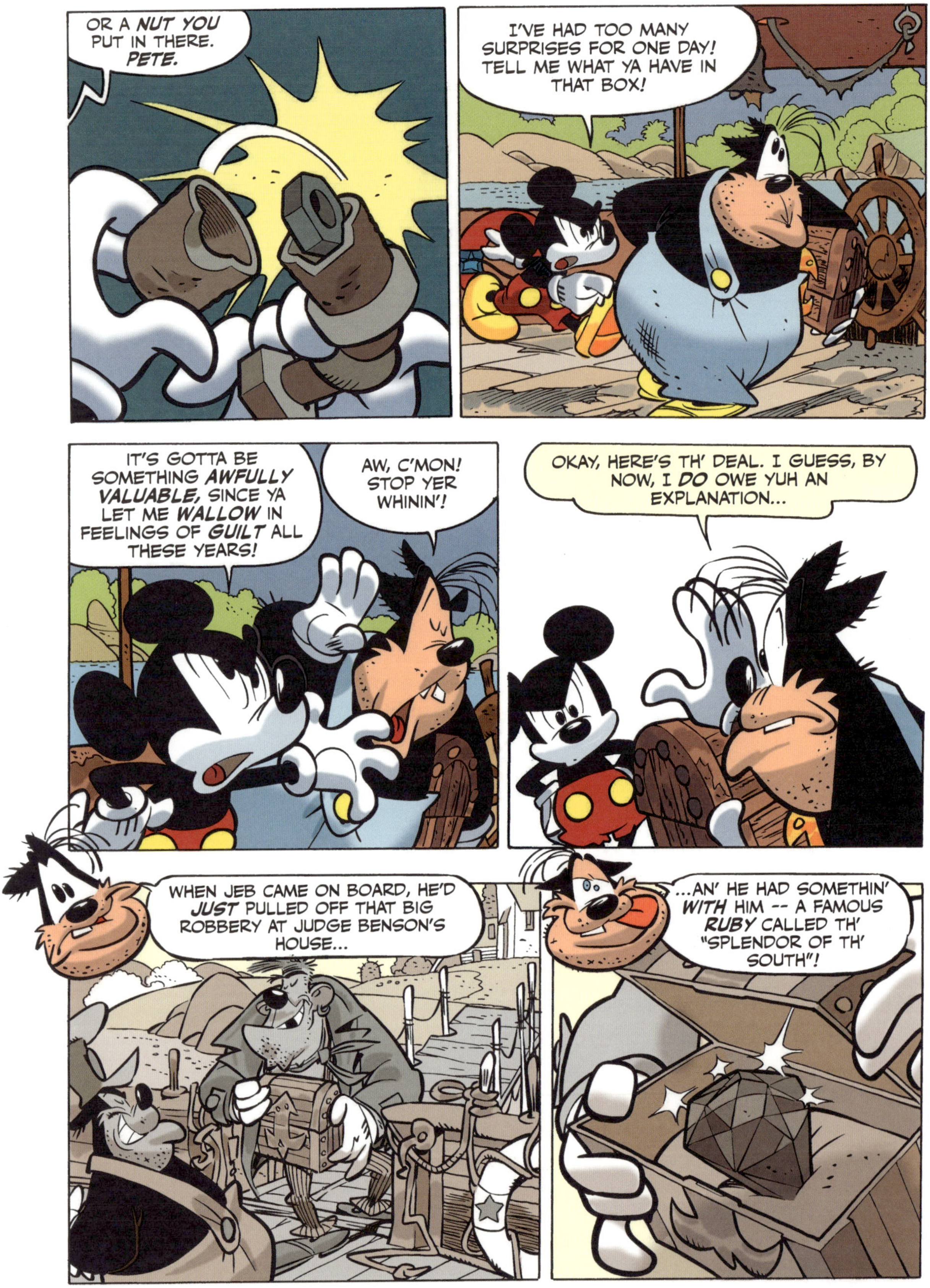

OR A NUT YOU PUT IN THERE. PETE.
I'VE HAD TOO MANY SURPRISES FOR ONE DAY! TELL ME WHAT YA HAVE IN THAT BOX!
IT'S GOTTA BE SOMETHING AWFULLY VALUABLE, SINCE YA LET ME WALLOW IN FEELINGS OF GUILT ALL THESE YEARS!
AW, C'MON! STOP YER WHININ'!
OKAY, HERE'S TH' DEAL. I GUESS, BY NOW, I DO OWE YUH AN EXPLANATION...
WHEN JEB CAME ON BOARD, HE'D JUST PULLED OFF THAT BIG ROBBERY AT JUDGE BENSON'S HOUSE...
...AN' HE HAD SOMETHIN' WITH HIM -- A FAMOUS RUBY CALLED TH' "SPLENDOR OF TH' SOUTH"!

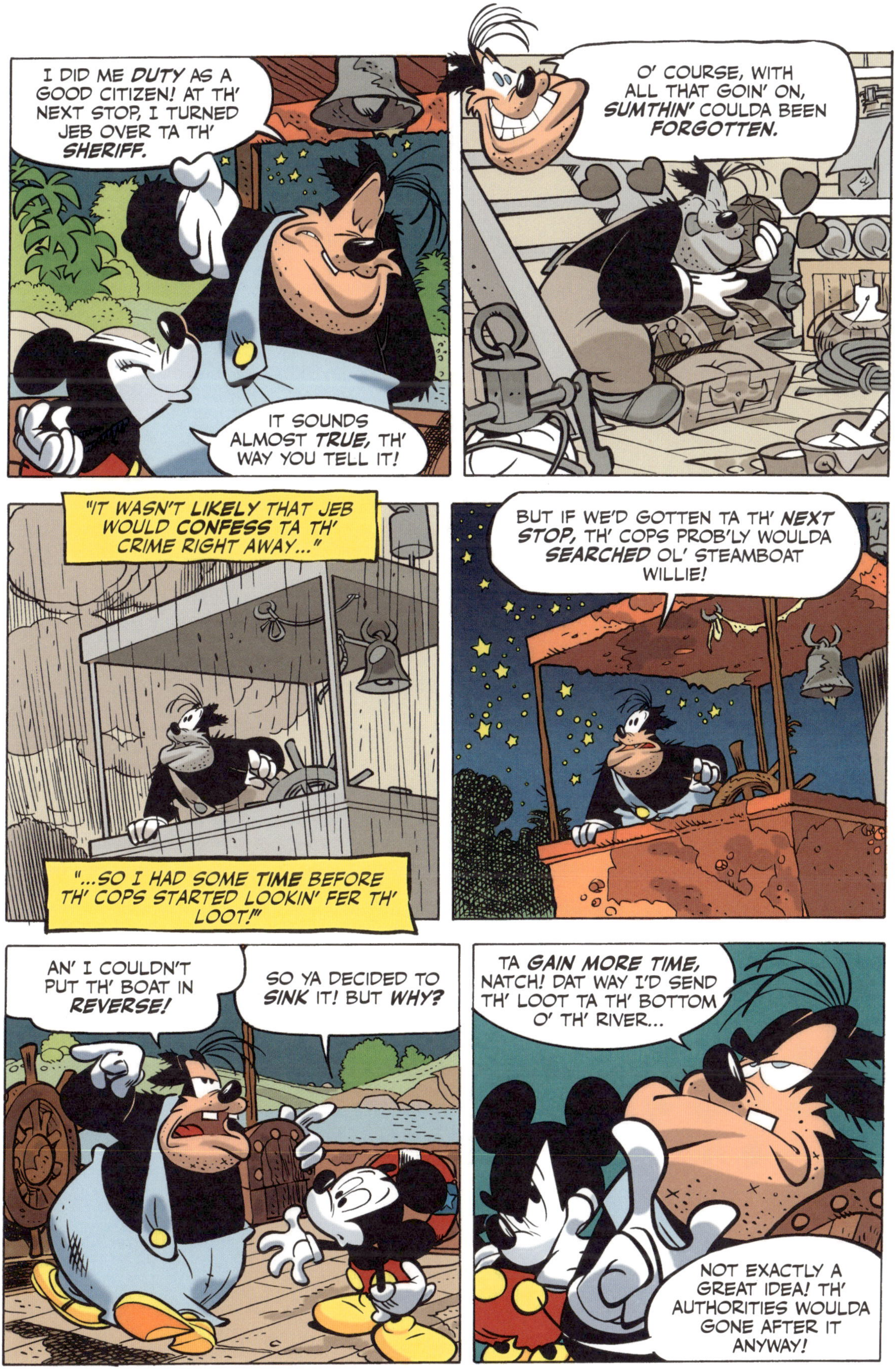
I DID ME DUTY AS A GOOD CITIZEN! AT TH' NEXT STOP, I TURNED JEB OVER TA TH' SHERIFF.
IT SOUNDS ALMOST TRUE, TH' WAY YOU TELL IT!
O' COURSE, WITH ALL THAT GOIN' ON, SUMTHIN' COULDA BEEN FORGOTTEN.
"IT WASN'T LIKELY THAT JEB WOULD CONFESS TA TH' CRIME RIGHT AWAY..."
"...SO I HAD SOME TIME BEFORE TH' COPS STARTED LOOKIN' FER TH' LOOT!"
BUT IF WE'D GOTTEN TA TH' NEXT STOP, TH' COPS PROB'LY WOULDA SEARCHED OL' STEAMBOAT WILLIE!
AN' I COULDN'T PUT TH' BOAT IN REVERSE!
SO YA DECIDED TO SINK IT! BUT WHY?
TA GAIN MORE TIME, NATCH! DAT WAY I'D SEND TH' LOOT TA TH' BOTTOM O' TH' RIVER...
NOT EXACTLY A GREAT IDEA! TH' AUTHORITIES WOULDA GONE AFTER IT ANYWAY!

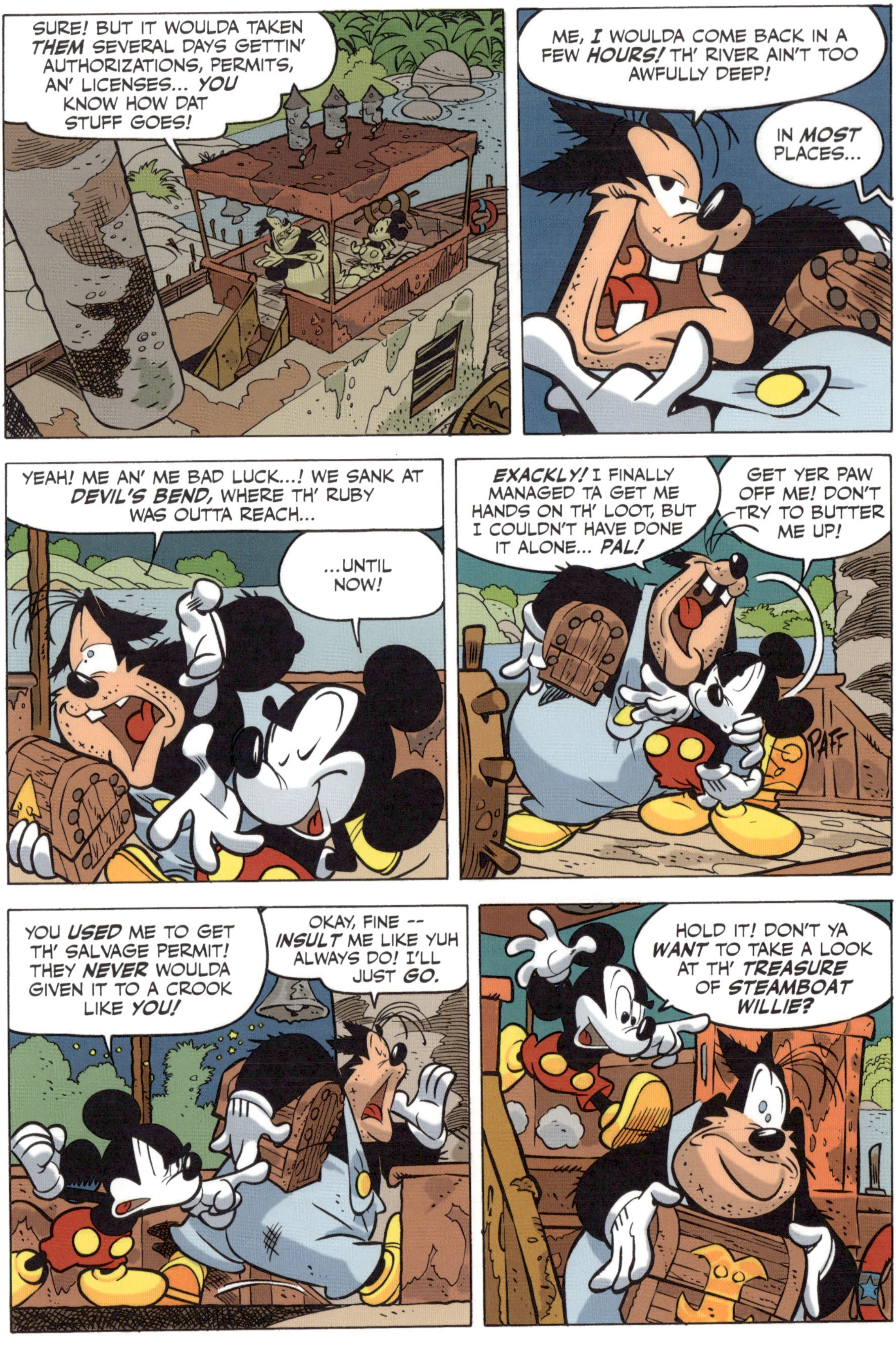
SURE! BUT IT WOULDA TAKEN THEM SEVERAL DAYS GETTIN' AUTHORIZATIONS, PERMITS, AN' LICENSES... YOU KNOW HOW DAT STUFF GOES!
ME, I WOULDA COME BACK IN A FEW HOURS! TH' RIVER AIN'T TOO AWFULLY DEEP!
IN MOST PLACES...
YEAH! ME AN' ME BAD LUCK...! WE SANK AT DEVIL'S BEND, WHERE TH' RUBY WAS OUTTA REACH...
...UNTIL NOW!
EXACKLY! I FINALLY MANAGED TA GET ME HANDS ON TH' LOOT, BUT I COULDN'T HAVE DONE IT ALONE... PAL!
GET YER PAW OFF ME! DON'T TRY TO BUTTER ME UP!
PAFF
YOU USED ME TO GET TH' SALVAGE PERMIT! THEY NEVER WOULDA GIVEN IT TO A CROOK LIKE YOU!
OKAY, FINE -- INSULT ME LIKE YUH ALWAYS DO! I'LL JUST GO.
HOLD IT! DON'T YA WANT TO TAKE A LOOK AT TH' TREASURE OF STEAMBOAT WILLIE?

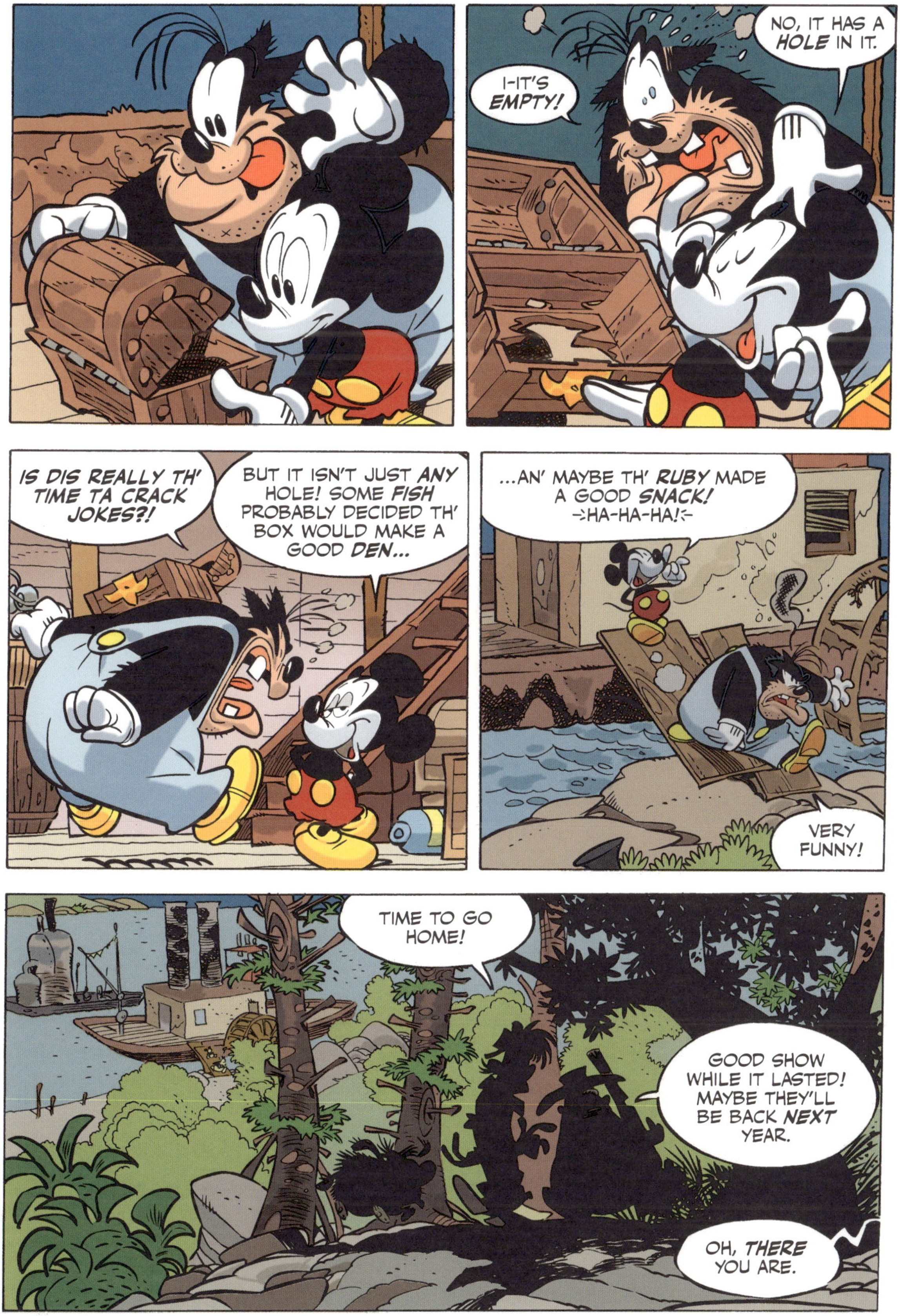
I-IT'S EMPTY!
NO, IT HAS A HOLE IN IT.
IS DIS REALLY TH' TIME TA CRACK JOKES?!
BUT IT ISN'T JUST ANY HOLE! SOME FISH PROBABLY DECIDED TH' BOX WOULD MAKE A GOOD DEN...
...AN' MAYBE TH' RUBY MADE A GOOD SNACK!
HA-HA-HA!
VERY FUNNY!
TIME TO GO HOME!
GOOD SHOW WHILE IT LASTED! MAYBE THEY'LL BE BACK NEXT YEAR.
OH, THERE YOU ARE.

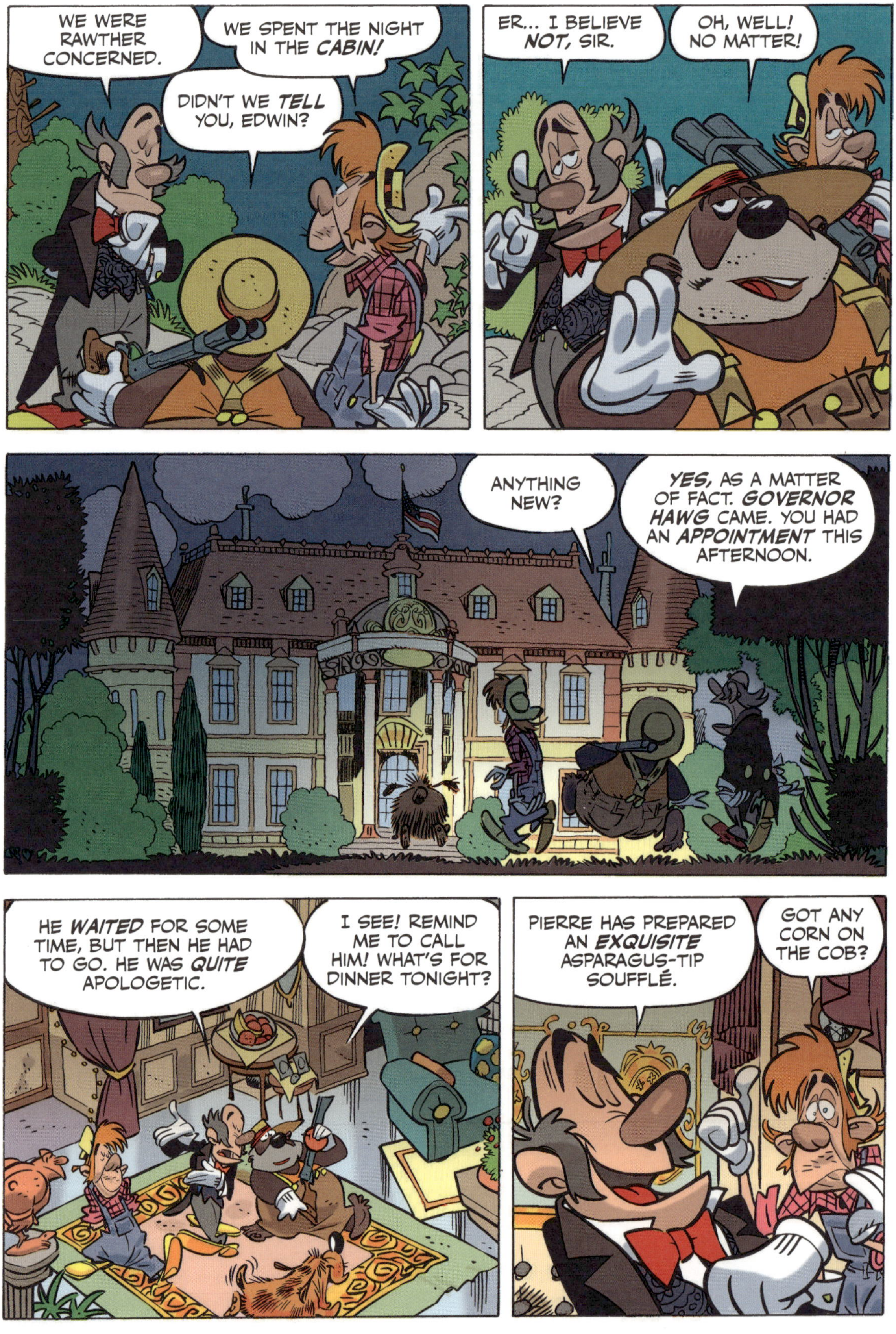
WE WERE RAWTHER CONCERNED.
WE SPENT THE NIGHT IN THE CABIN!
DIDN'T WE TELL YOU, EDWIN?
ER... I BELIEVE NOT, SIR.
OH, WELL! NO MATTER!
ANYTHING NEW?
YES, AS A MATTER OF FACT. GOVERNOR HAWG CAME. YOU HAD AN APPOINTMENT THIS AFTERNOON.
HE WAITED FOR SOME TIME, BUT THEN HE HAD TO GO. HE WAS QUITE APOLOGETIC.
I SEE! REMIND ME TO CALL HIM! WHAT'S FOR DINNER TONIGHT?
PIERRE HAS PREPARED AN EXQUISITE ASPARAGUS-TIP SOUFFLÉ.
GOT ANY CORN ON THE COB?

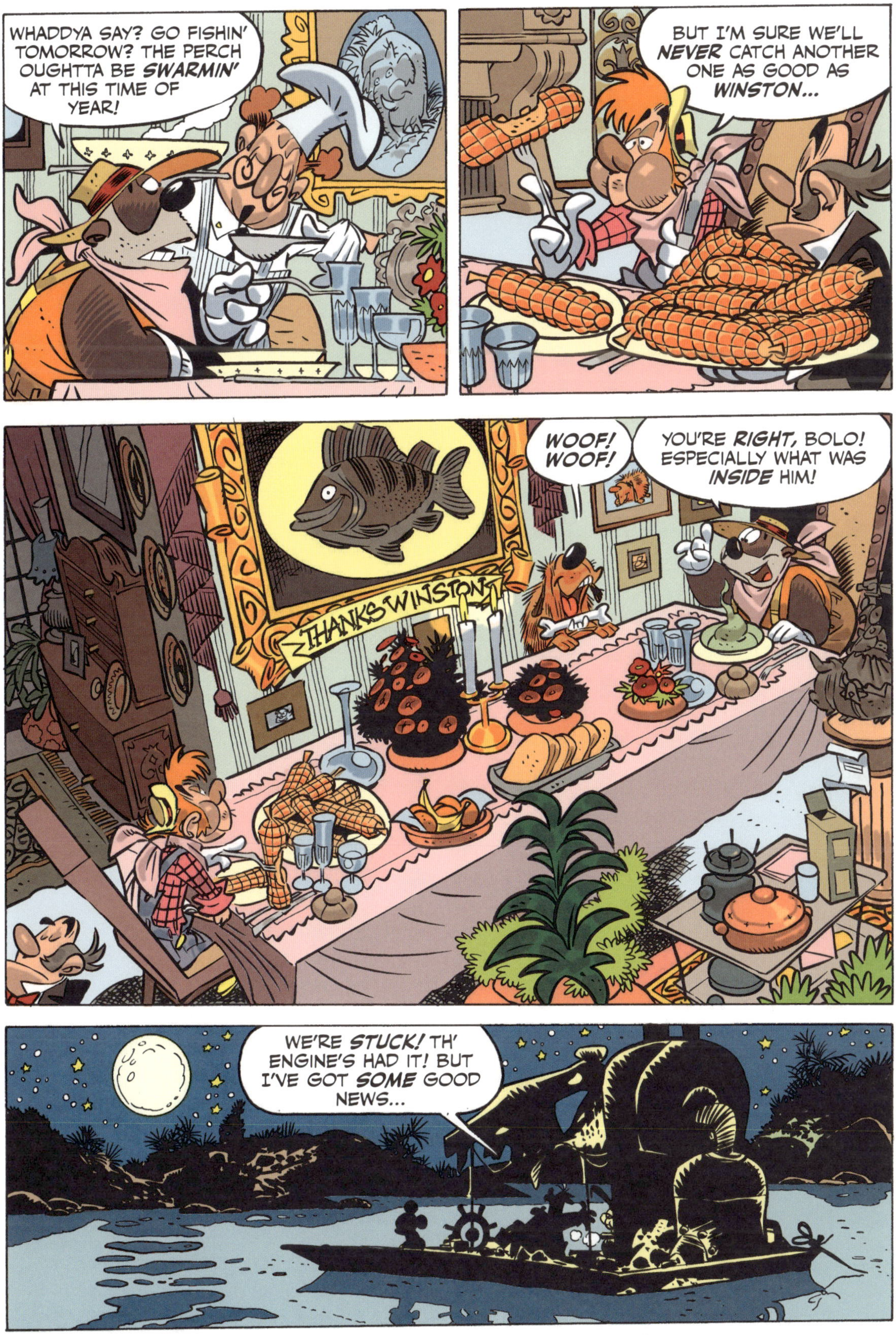
WHADDYA SAY? GO FISHIN' TOMORROW? THE PERCH OUGHTTA BE SWARMIN' AT THIS TIME OF YEAR!
BUT I'M SURE WE'LL NEVER CATCH ANOTHER ONE AS GOOD AS WINSTON...
THANKS WINSTON
WOOF! WOOF!
YOU'RE RIGHT, BOLO! ESPECIALLY WHAT WAS INSIDE HIM!
WE'RE STUCK! TH' ENGINE'S HAD IT! BUT I'VE GOT SOME GOOD NEWS...

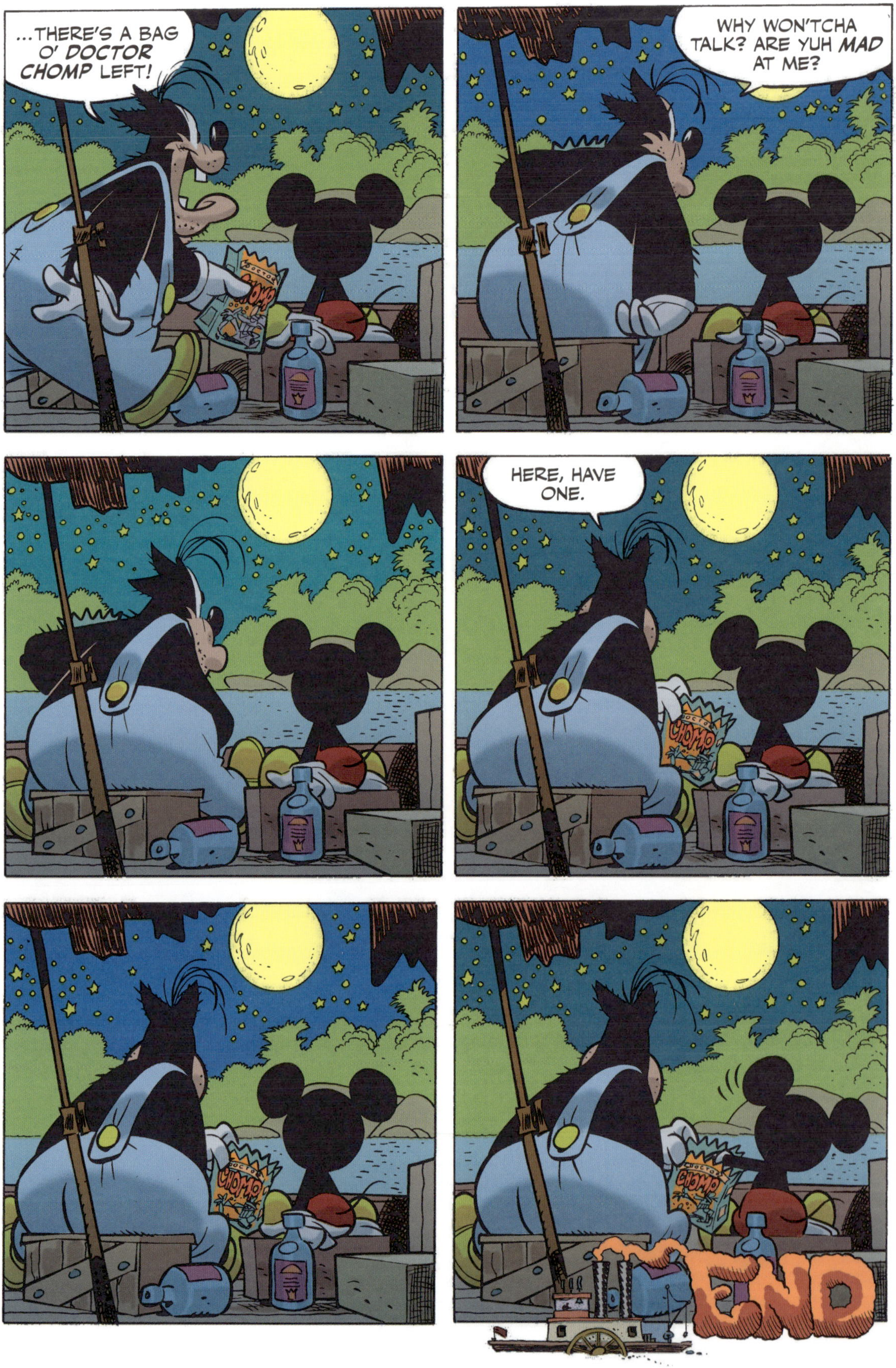
...THERE'S A BAG O' DOCTOR CHOMP LEFT!
DOCTOR CHOMP
WHY WON'TCHA TALK? ARE YUH MAD AT ME?
HERE, HAVE ONE.
DOCTOR CHOMP
DOCTOR CHOMP
DOCTOR CHOMP
END

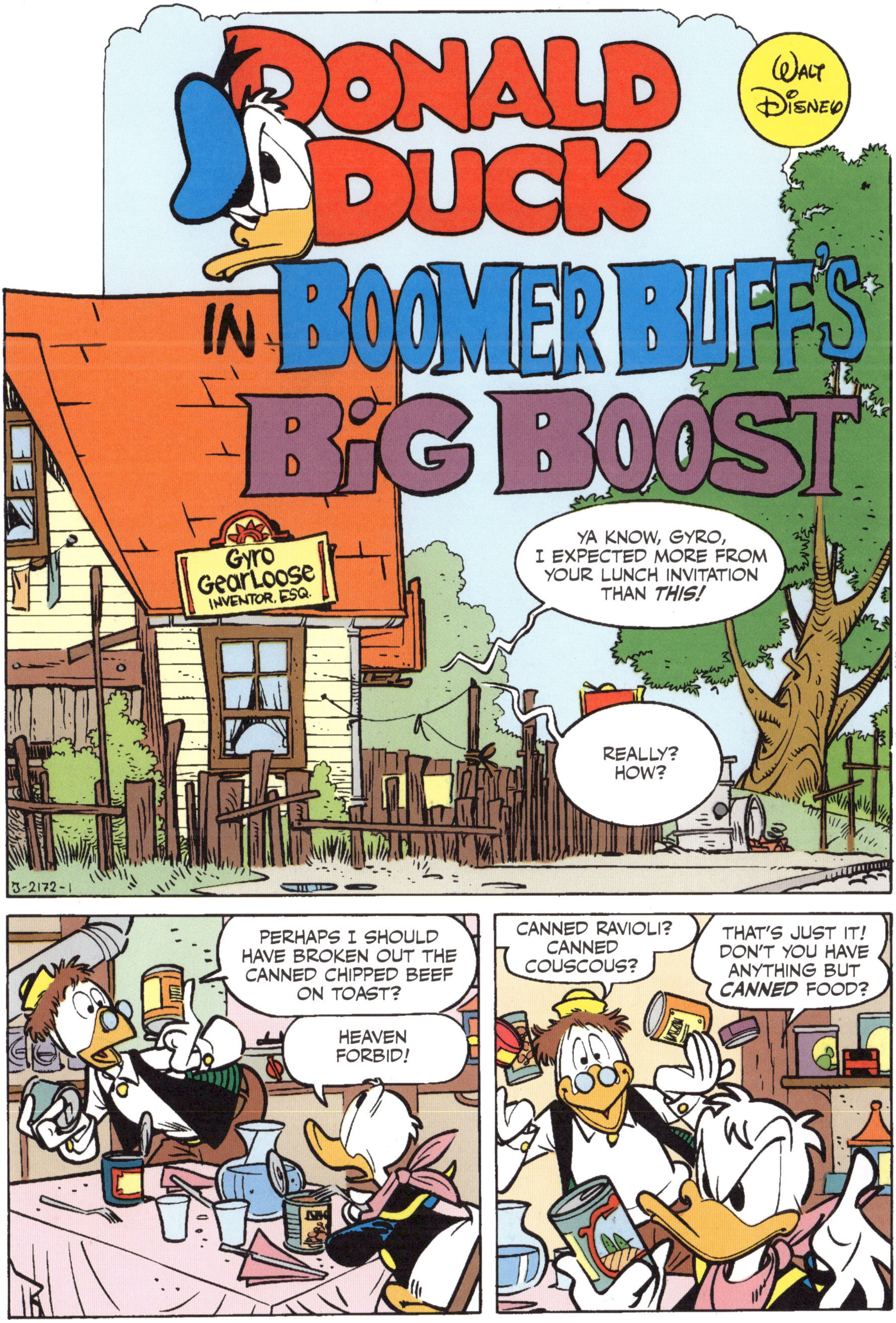
WALT DISNEY
DONALD DUCK
IN BOOMER BUFF'S BIG BOOST
Gyro GearLoose INVENTOR, ESQ.
YA KNOW, GYRO, I EXPECTED MORE FROM YOUR LUNCH INVITATION THAN *THIS!*
REALLY? HOW?
J-2172-1
PERHAPS I SHOULD HAVE BROKEN OUT THE CANNED CHIPPED BEEF ON TOAST?
HEAVEN FORBID!
CANNED RAVIOLI? CANNED COUSCOUS?
THAT'S JUST IT! DON'T YOU HAVE ANYTHING BUT *CANNED* FOOD?

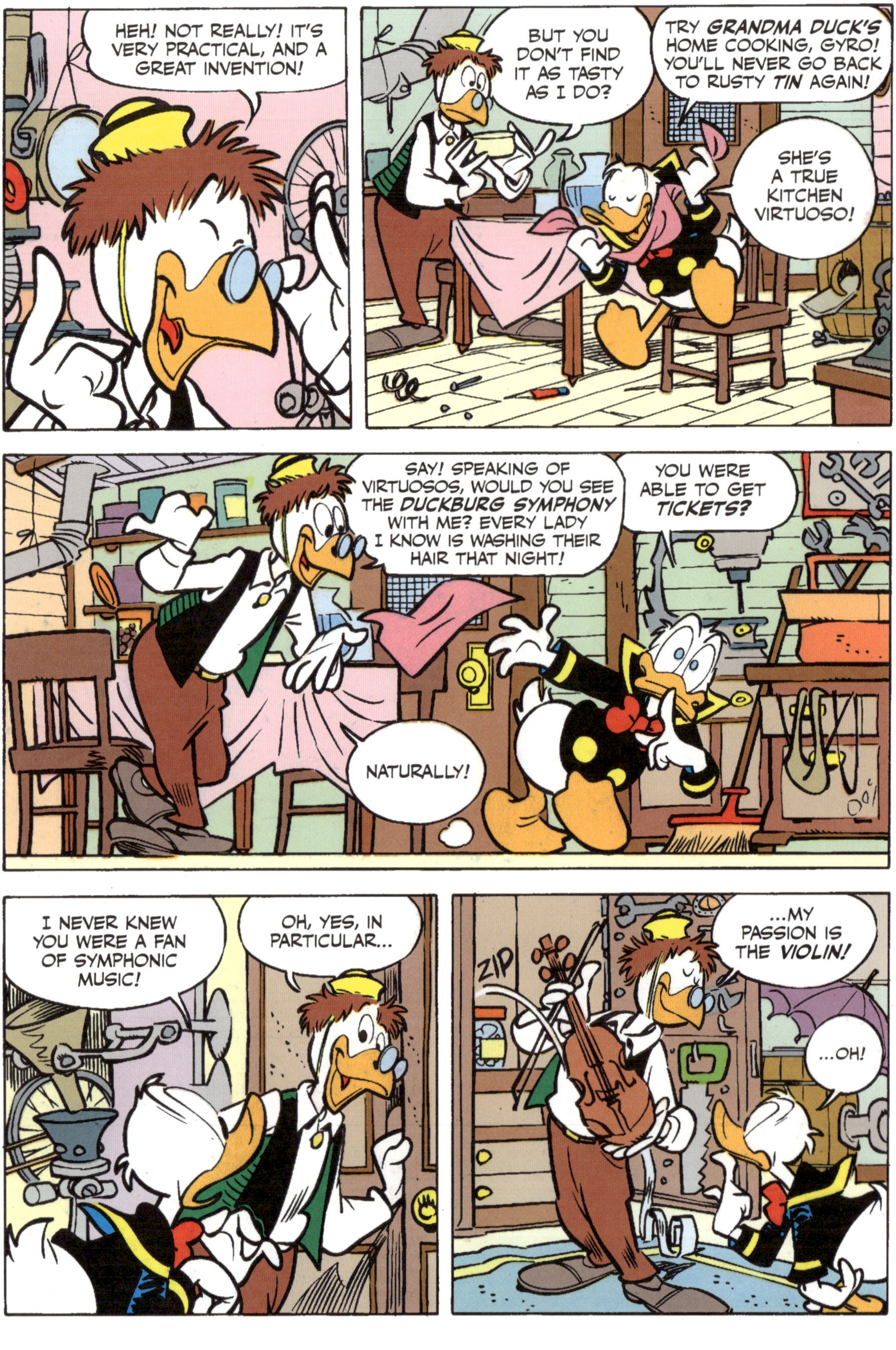

HEH! NOT REALLY! IT'S VERY PRACTICAL, AND A GREAT INVENTION!
BUT YOU DON'T FIND IT AS TASTY AS I DO?
TRY GRANDMA DUCK'S HOME COOKING, GYRO! YOU'LL NEVER GO BACK TO RUSTY TIN AGAIN!
SHE'S A TRUE KITCHEN VIRTUOSO!
SAY! SPEAKING OF VIRTUOSOS, WOULD YOU SEE THE DUCKBURG SYMPHONY WITH ME? EVERY LADY I KNOW IS WASHING THEIR HAIR THAT NIGHT!
YOU WERE ABLE TO GET TICKETS?
NATURALLY!
I NEVER KNEW YOU WERE A FAN OF SYMPHONIC MUSIC!
OH, YES, IN PARTICULAR...
ZIP
...MY PASSION IS THE VIOLIN!
...OH!

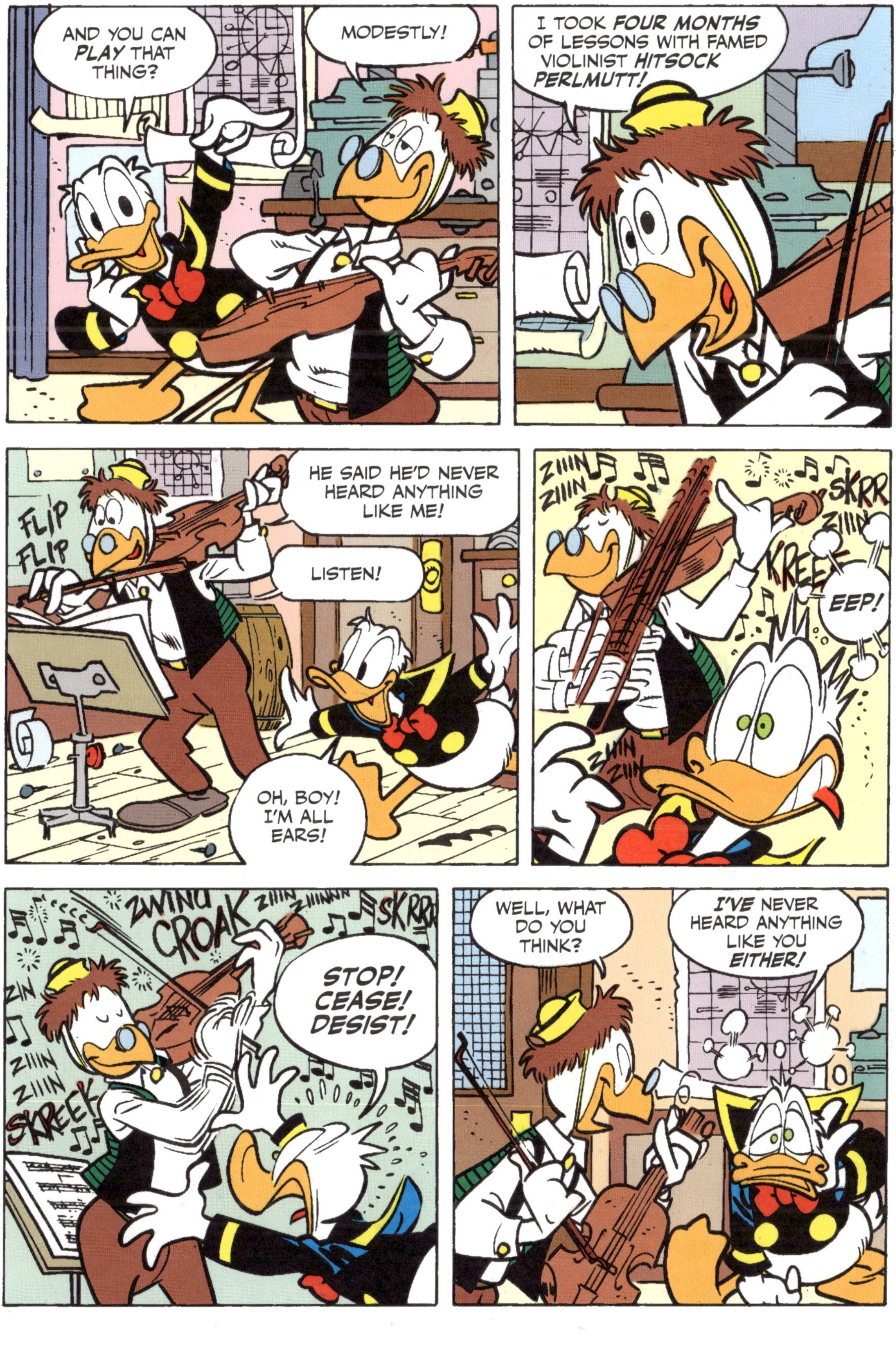
AND YOU CAN PLAY THAT THING?
MODESTLY!
I TOOK FOUR MONTHS OF LESSONS WITH FAMED VIOLINIST HITSOCK PERLMUTT!
FLIP FLIP
HE SAID HE'D NEVER HEARD ANYTHING LIKE ME!
LISTEN!
OH, BOY! I'M ALL EARS!
ZIIIN ZIIIN
SKRR
KREEE
EEP!
ZWING
CROAK
SKRRR
ZIIIN ZIIIN
SKREEK
STOP! CEASE! DESIST!
WELL, WHAT DO YOU THINK?
I'VE NEVER HEARD ANYTHING LIKE YOU EITHER!

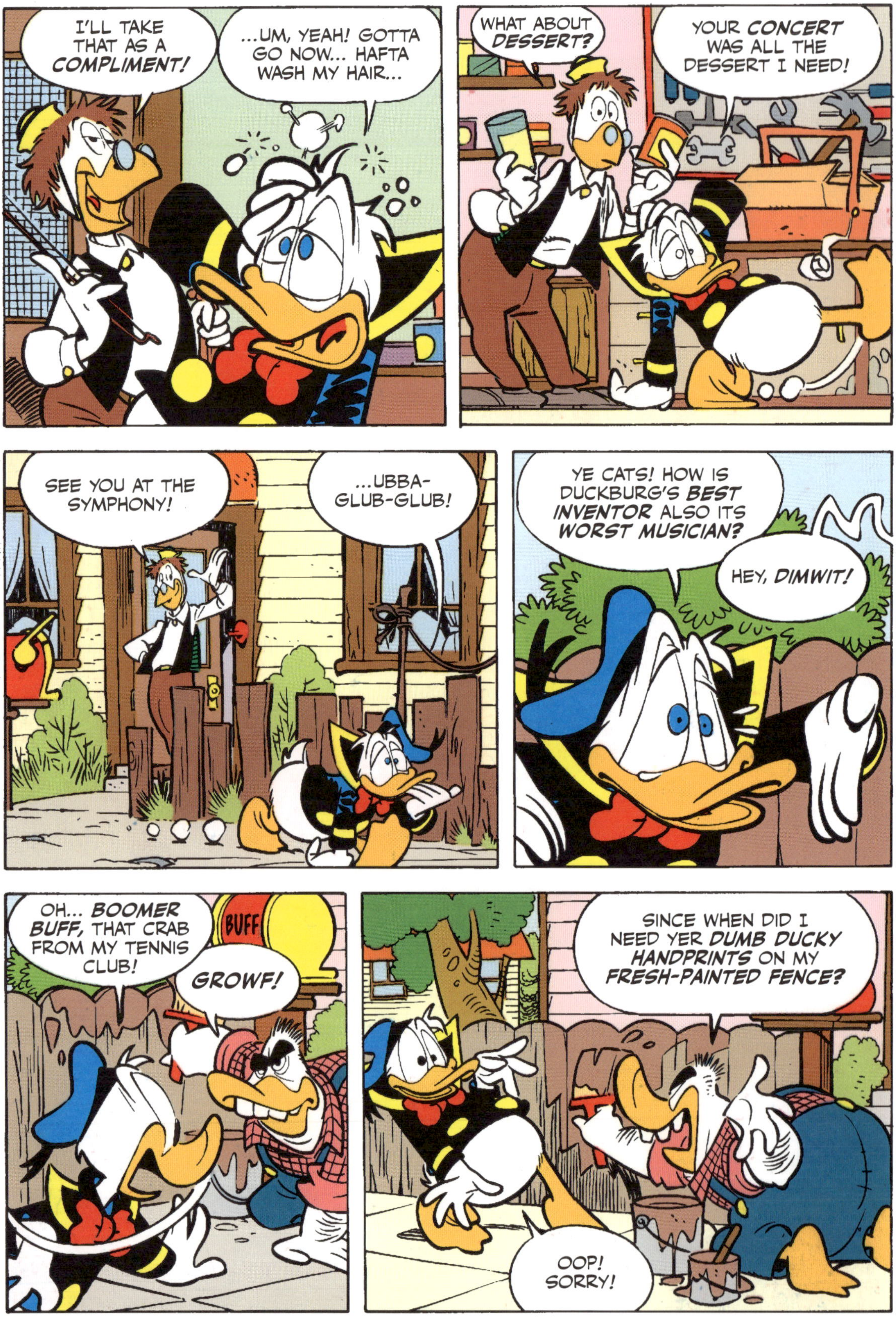
I'LL TAKE THAT AS A *COMPLIMENT!*
...UM, YEAH! GOTTA GO NOW... HAFTA WASH MY HAIR...
WHAT ABOUT *DESSERT?*
YOUR *CONCERT* WAS ALL THE DESSERT I NEED!
SEE YOU AT THE SYMPHONY!
...UBBA-GLUB-GLUB!
YE CATS! HOW IS DUCKBURG'S *BEST INVENTOR* ALSO ITS *WORST MUSICIAN?*
HEY, *DIMWIT!*
OH... *BOOMER BUFF,* THAT CRAB FROM MY TENNIS CLUB!
BUFF
GROWF!
SINCE WHEN DID I NEED YER *DUMB DUCKY HANDPRINTS* ON MY *FRESH-PAINTED FENCE?*
OOP! SORRY!

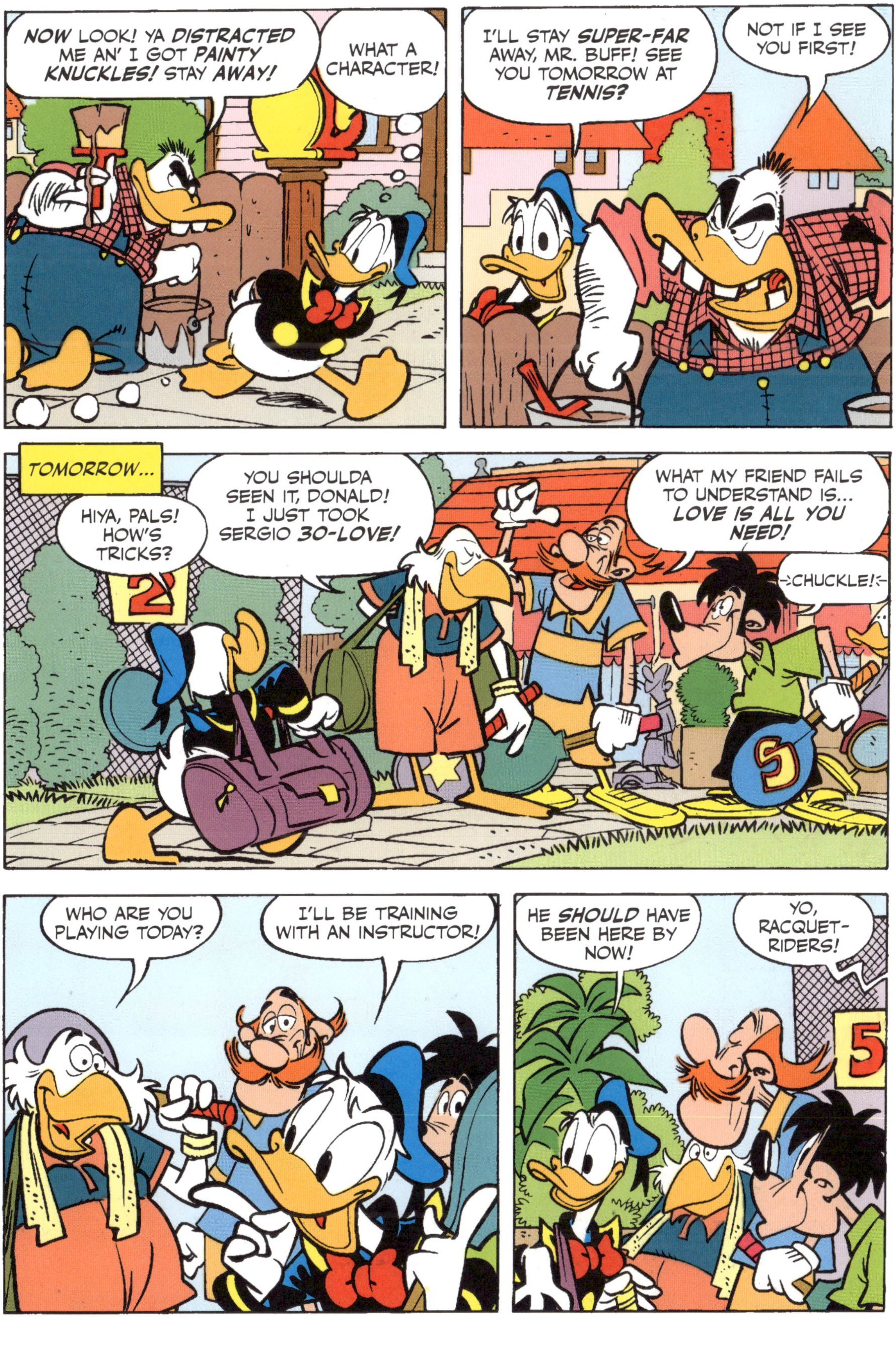
NOW LOOK! YA DISTRACTED ME AN' I GOT PAINTY KNUCKLES! STAY AWAY!
WHAT A CHARACTER!
I'LL STAY SUPER-FAR AWAY, MR. BUFF! SEE YOU TOMORROW AT TENNIS?
NOT IF I SEE YOU FIRST!
TOMORROW...
HIYA, PALS! HOW'S TRICKS?
YOU SHOULDA SEEN IT, DONALD! I JUST TOOK SERGIO 30-LOVE!
WHAT MY FRIEND FAILS TO UNDERSTAND IS... LOVE IS ALL YOU NEED!
CHUCKLE!
2
WHO ARE YOU PLAYING TODAY?
I'LL BE TRAINING WITH AN INSTRUCTOR!
HE SHOULD HAVE BEEN HERE BY NOW!
YO, RACQUET-RIDERS!
5

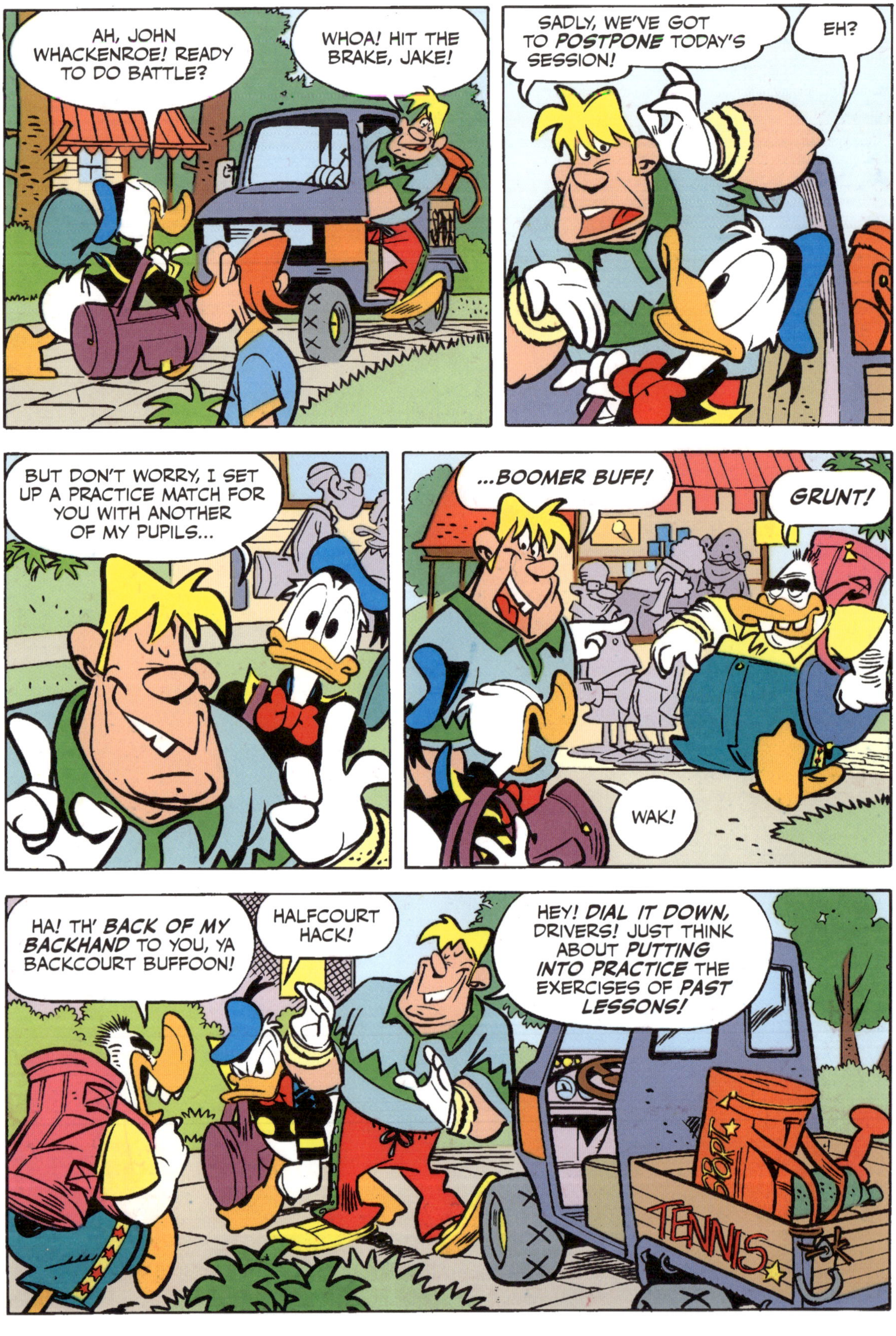
AH, JOHN WHACKENROE! READY TO DO BATTLE?
WHOA! HIT THE BRAKE, JAKE!
SADLY, WE'VE GOT TO POSTPONE TODAY'S SESSION!
EH?
BUT DON'T WORRY, I SET UP A PRACTICE MATCH FOR YOU WITH ANOTHER OF MY PUPILS...
...BOOMER BUFF!
GRUNT!
WAK!
HA! TH' BACK OF MY BACKHAND TO YOU, YA BACKCOURT BUFFOON!
HALFCOURT HACK!
HEY! DIAL IT DOWN, DRIVERS! JUST THINK ABOUT PUTTING INTO PRACTICE THE EXERCISES OF PAST LESSONS!
SPORT
TENNIS

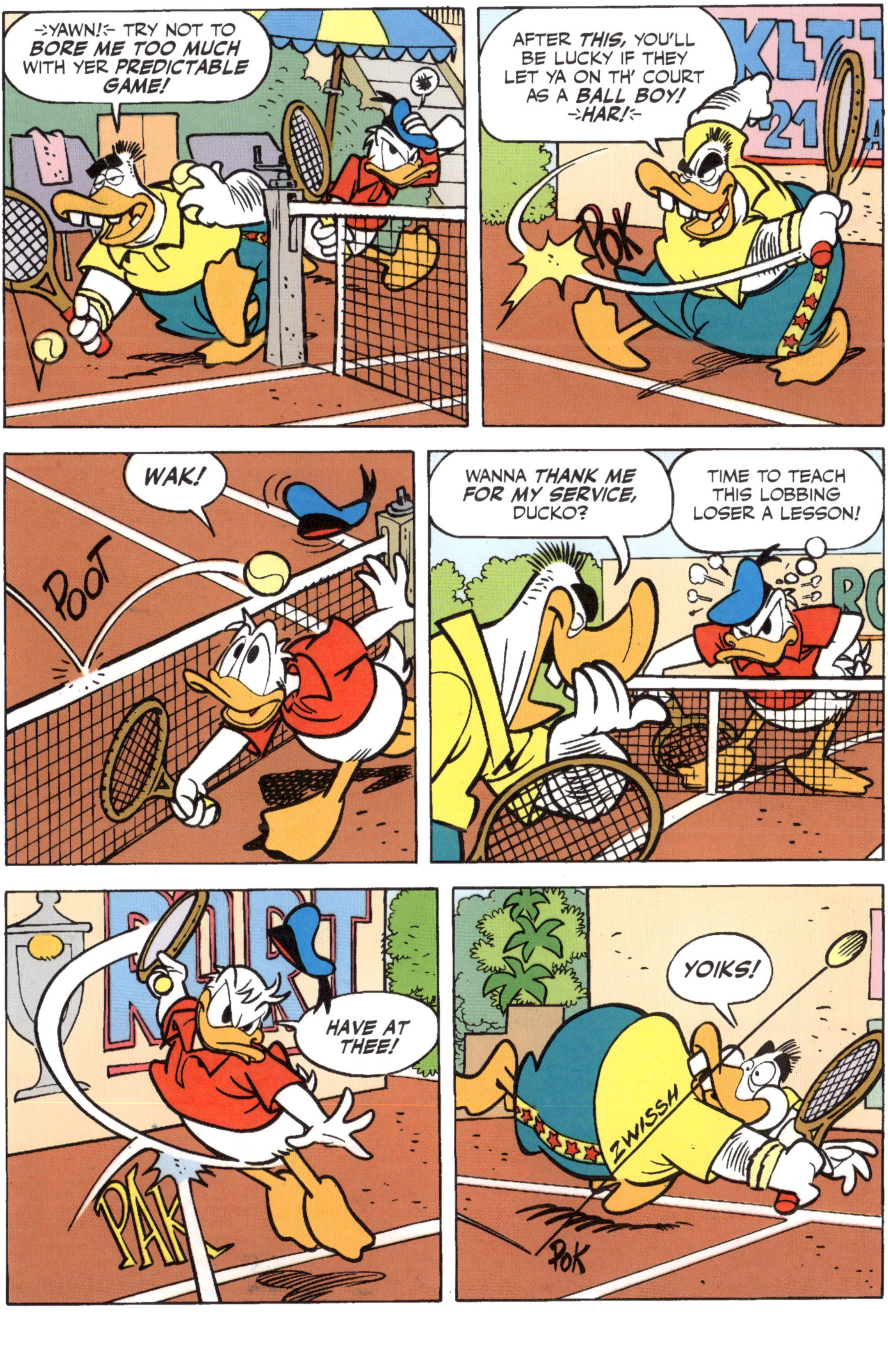
-YAWN!- TRY NOT TO BORE ME TOO MUCH WITH YER PREDICTABLE GAME!
AFTER THIS, YOU'LL BE LUCKY IF THEY LET YA ON TH' COURT AS A BALL BOY! -HAR!-
POK
WAK!
POOT
WANNA THANK ME FOR MY SERVICE, DUCKO?
TIME TO TEACH THIS LOBBING LOSER A LESSON!
HAVE AT THEE!
PAK
YOIKS!
ZWISSH
POK

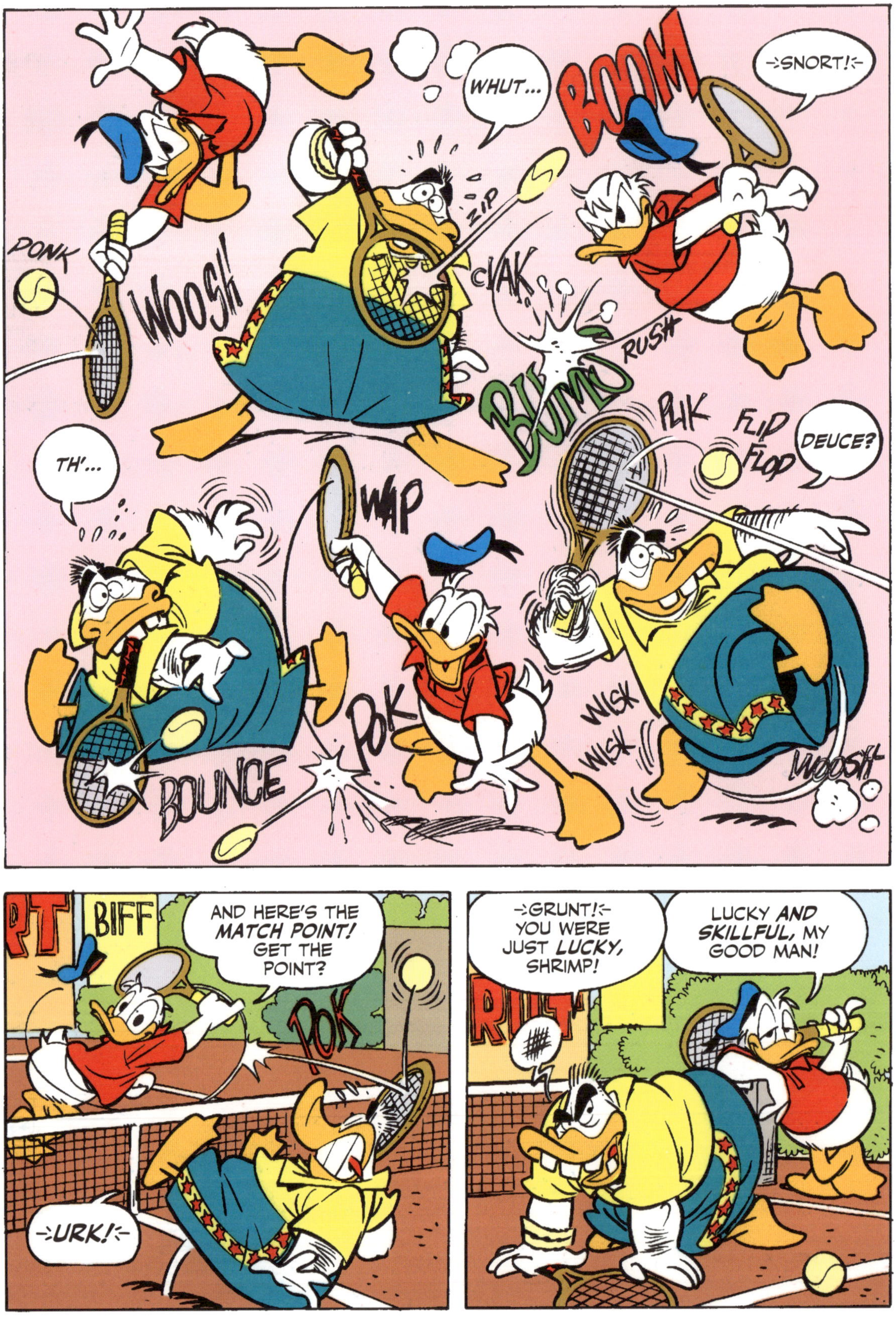
WHUT...
-SNORT!-
BOOM
PONK
WOOSH
ZIP
CIAK
RUSH
BUMP
PLIK
FLIP
FLOP
DEUCE?
TH'...
WAP
POK
WISK
WISK
WOOSH
BOUNCE
BIFF
AND HERE'S THE *MATCH POINT!* GET THE POINT?
POK
-URK!-
-GRUNT!- YOU WERE JUST *LUCKY,* SHRIMP!
LUCKY *AND SKILLFUL,* MY GOOD MAN!

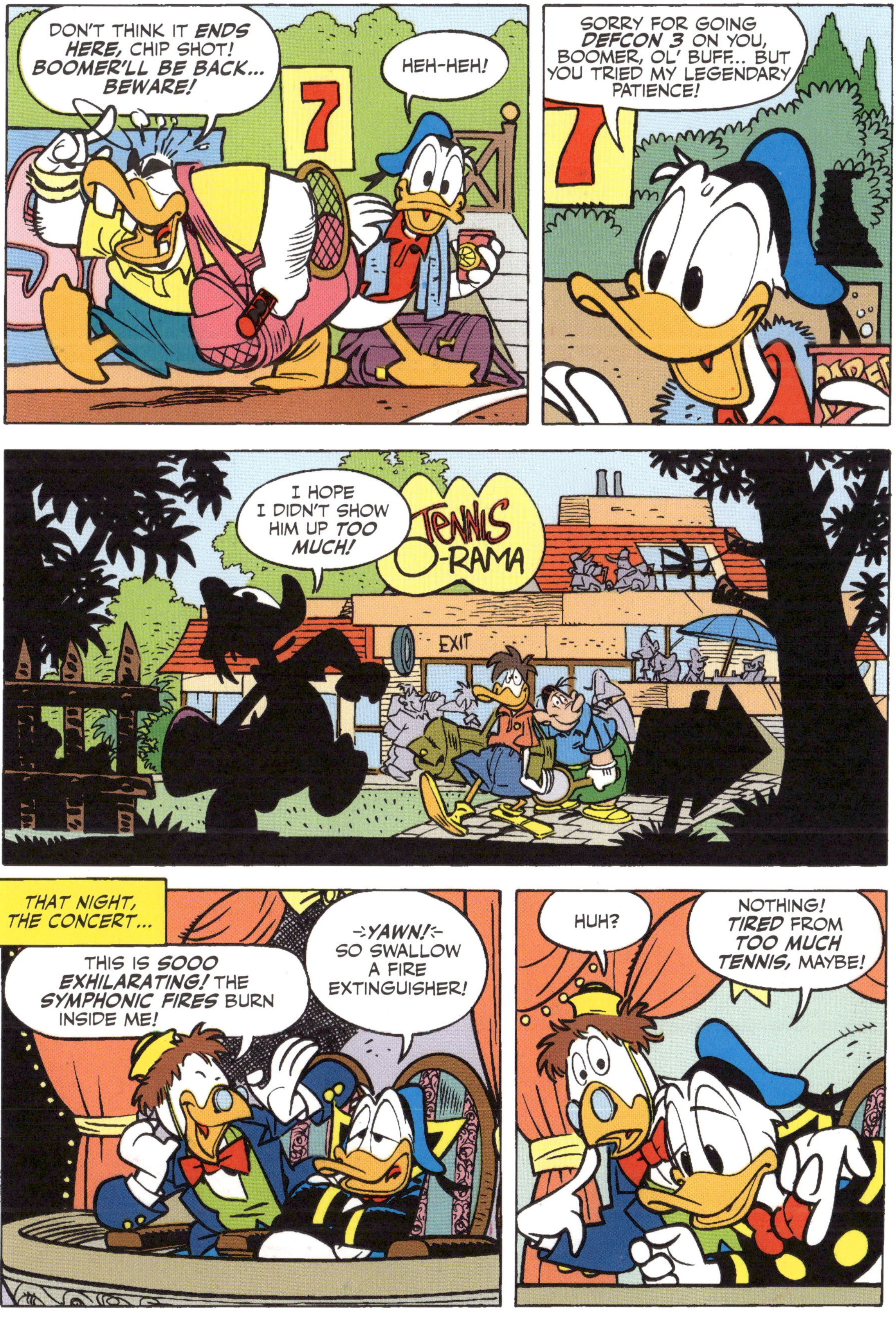
DON'T THINK IT ENDS HERE, CHIP SHOT! BOOMER'LL BE BACK... BEWARE!
HEH-HEH!
7
SORRY FOR GOING DEFCON 3 ON YOU, BOOMER, OL' BUFF.. BUT YOU TRIED MY LEGENDARY PATIENCE!
I HOPE I DIDN'T SHOW HIM UP TOO MUCH!
TENNIS-O-RAMA
EXIT
THAT NIGHT, THE CONCERT...
THIS IS SOOO EXHILARATING! THE SYMPHONIC FIRES BURN INSIDE ME!
YAWN! SO SWALLOW A FIRE EXTINGUISHER!
HUH?
NOTHING! TIRED FROM TOO MUCH TENNIS, MAYBE!

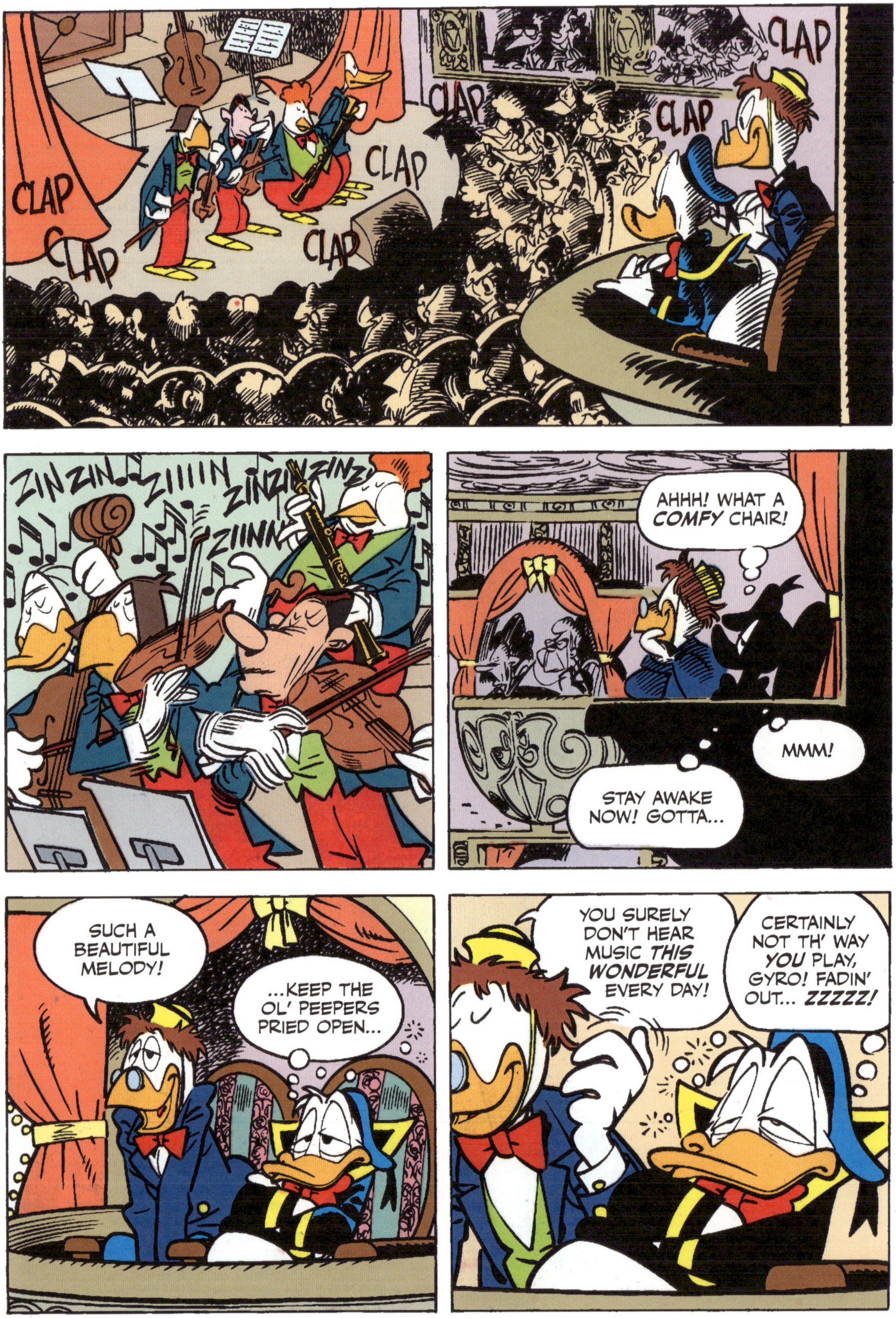
CLAP
CLAP
CLAP
CLAP
CLAP
CLAP
CLAP
ZIN ZIN ZIIIIN ZINZIN ZINZ ZIINN
AHHH! WHAT A COMFY CHAIR!
STAY AWAKE NOW! GOTTA...
MMM!
SUCH A BEAUTIFUL MELODY!
...KEEP THE OL' PEEPERS PRIED OPEN...
YOU SURELY DON'T HEAR MUSIC THIS WONDERFUL EVERY DAY!
CERTAINLY NOT TH' WAY YOU PLAY, GYRO! FADIN' OUT... ZZZZZ!

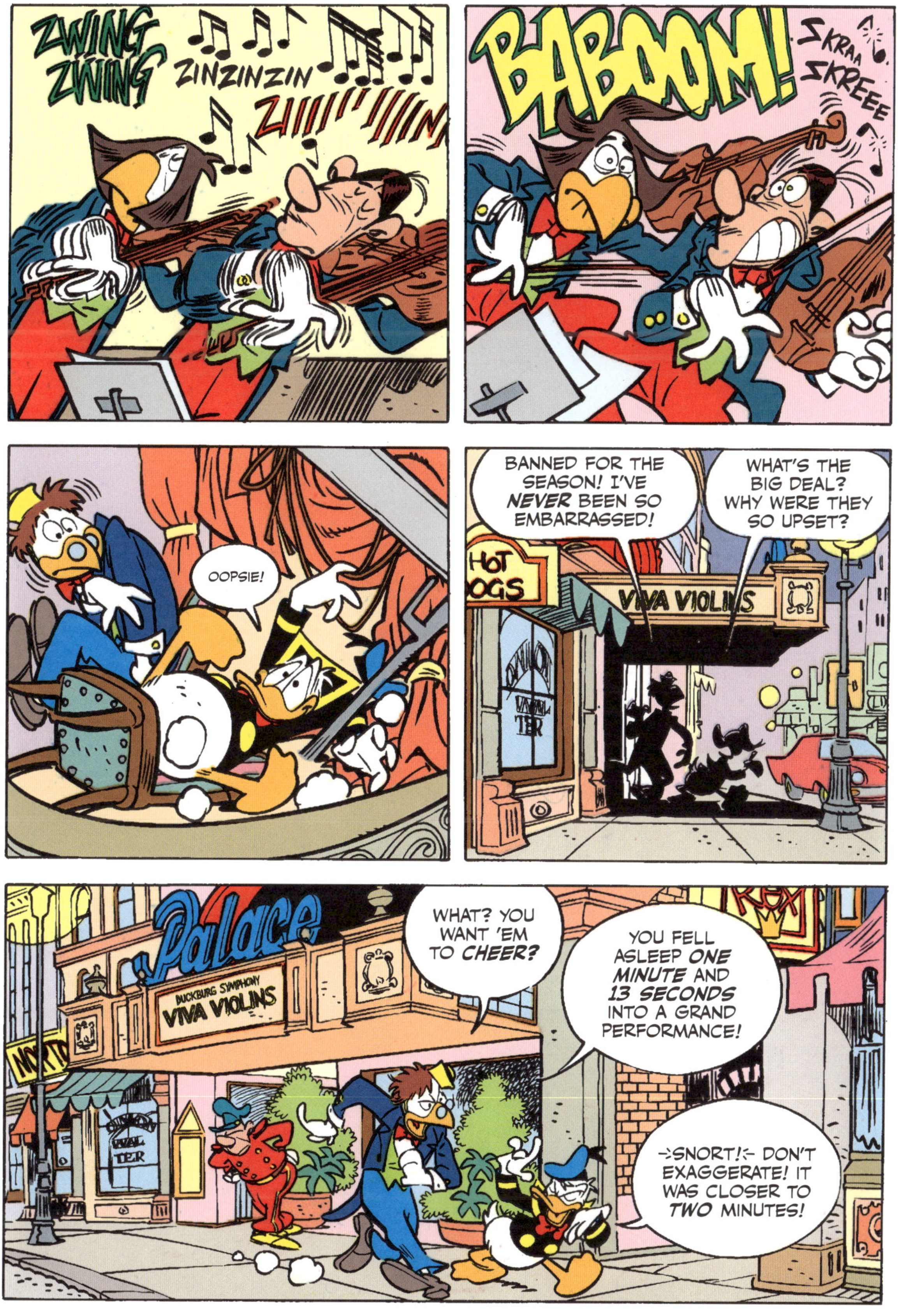
ZWING ZWING
ZINZINZIN
ZIIIIIIIN
BABOOM!
SKRAA
SKREEEE
OOPSIE!
BANNED FOR THE SEASON! I'VE *NEVER* BEEN SO EMBARRASSED!
WHAT'S THE BIG DEAL? WHY WERE THEY SO UPSET?
HOT DOGS
VIVA VIOLINS
Palace
DUCKBURG SYMPHONY
VIVA VIOLINS
WHAT? YOU WANT 'EM TO *CHEER?*
YOU FELL ASLEEP *ONE MINUTE* AND *13 SECONDS* INTO A GRAND PERFORMANCE!
-SNORT!- DON'T EXAGGERATE! IT WAS CLOSER TO *TWO* MINUTES!

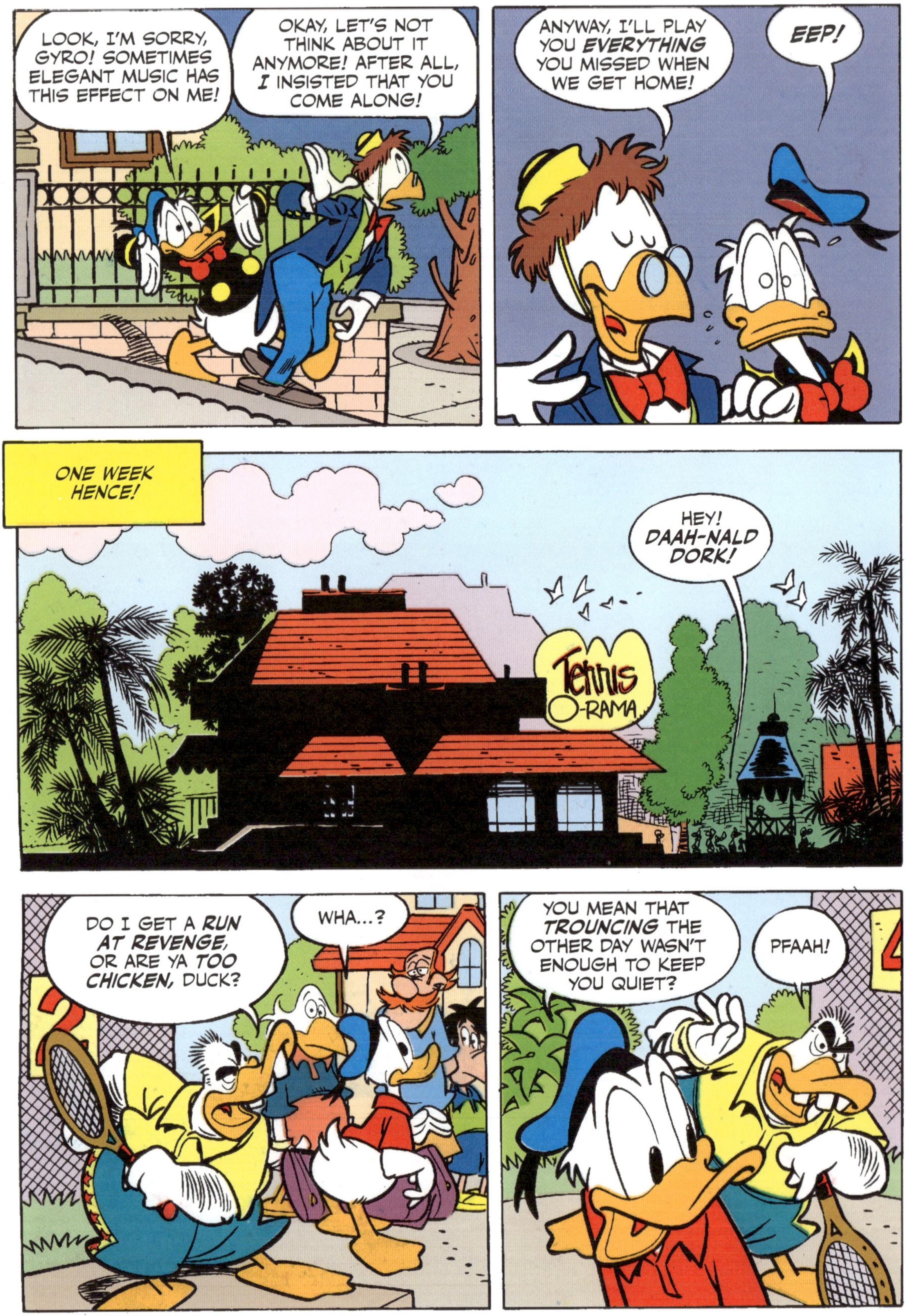
LOOK, I'M SORRY, GYRO! SOMETIMES ELEGANT MUSIC HAS THIS EFFECT ON ME!
OKAY, LET'S NOT THINK ABOUT IT ANYMORE! AFTER ALL, *I* INSISTED THAT YOU COME ALONG!
ANYWAY, I'LL PLAY YOU *EVERYTHING* YOU MISSED WHEN WE GET HOME!
EEP!
ONE WEEK HENCE!
TENNIS O-RAMA
HEY! *DAAH-NALD DORK!*
DO I GET A *RUN AT REVENGE*, OR ARE YA *TOO CHICKEN,* DUCK?
WHA...?
YOU MEAN THAT *TROUNCING* THE OTHER DAY WASN'T ENOUGH TO KEEP YOU QUIET?
PFAAH!

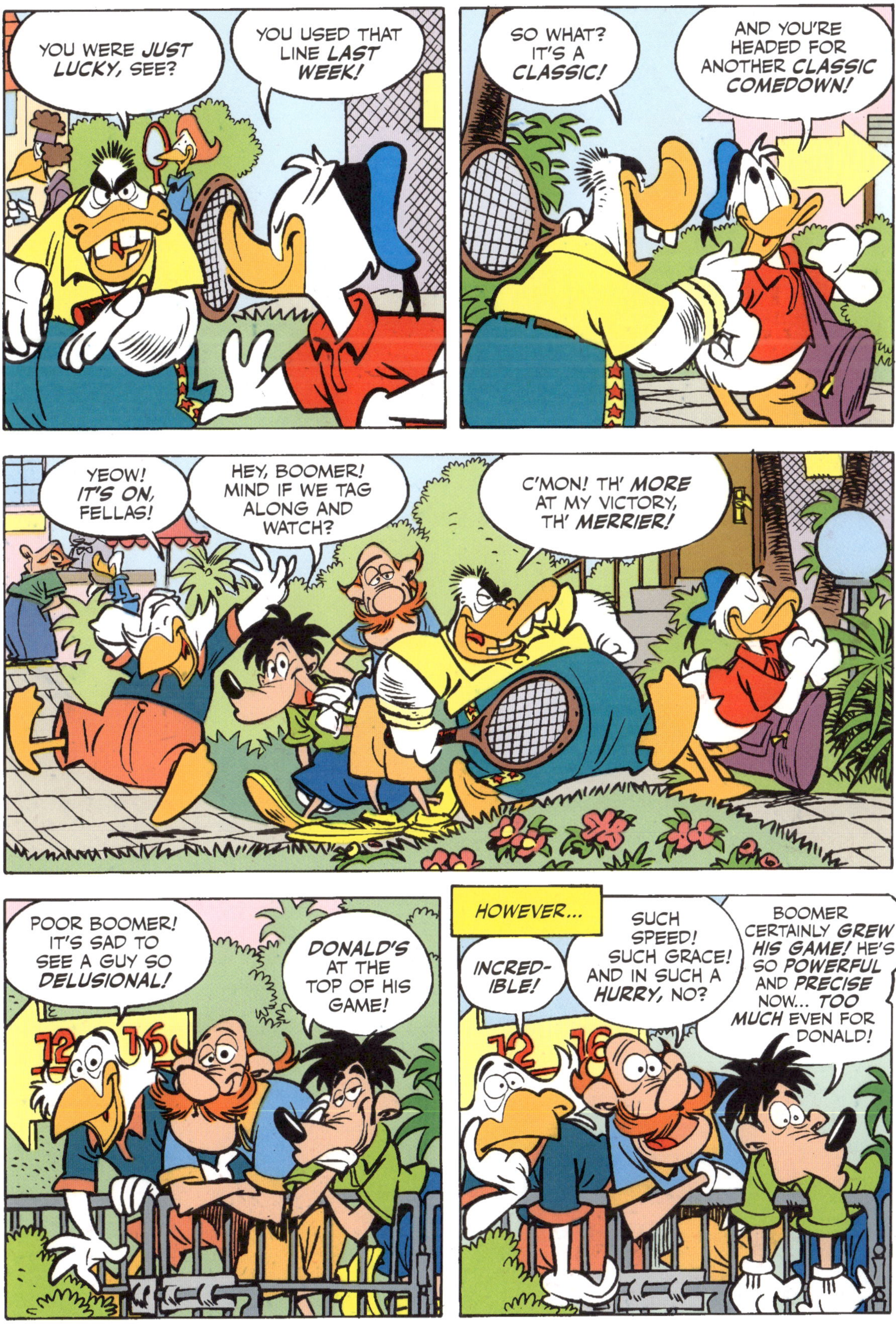

YOU WERE JUST LUCKY, SEE?
YOU USED THAT LINE LAST WEEK!
SO WHAT? IT'S A CLASSIC!
AND YOU'RE HEADED FOR ANOTHER CLASSIC COMEDOWN!
YEOW! IT'S ON, FELLAS!
HEY, BOOMER! MIND IF WE TAG ALONG AND WATCH?
C'MON! TH' MORE AT MY VICTORY, TH' MERRIER!
POOR BOOMER! IT'S SAD TO SEE A GUY SO DELUSIONAL!
DONALD'S AT THE TOP OF HIS GAME!
HOWEVER...
INCRED-IBLE!
SUCH SPEED! SUCH GRACE! AND IN SUCH A HURRY, NO?
BOOMER CERTAINLY GREW HIS GAME! HE'S SO POWERFUL AND PRECISE NOW... TOO MUCH EVEN FOR DONALD!

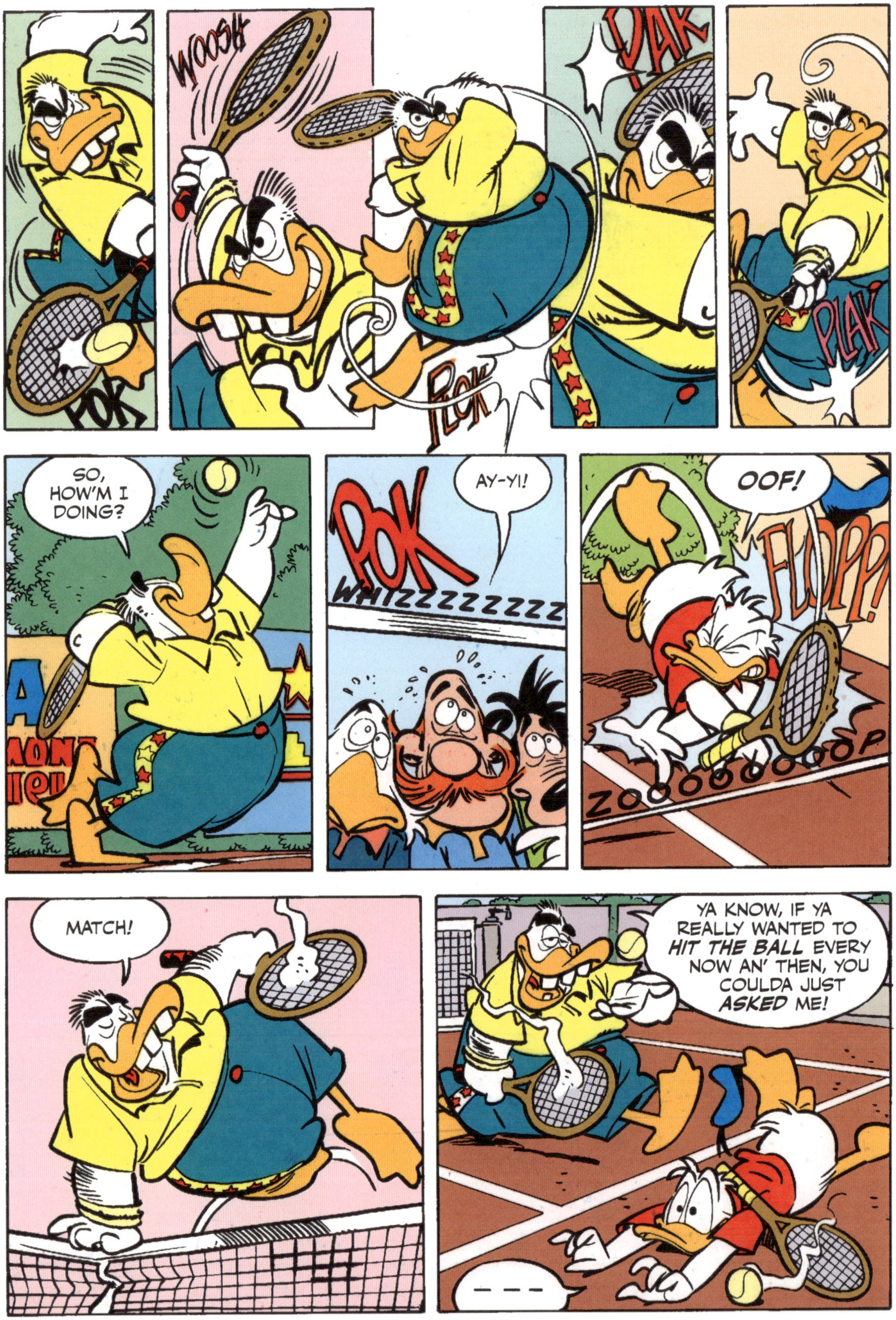

POK
WOOSH
PLOK
DAK
PLAK
SO, HOW'M I DOING?
POK
WHIZZZZZZZZZ
AY-YI!
OOF!
FLOPP!
ZOOOOOOOOOOP
MATCH!
YA KNOW, IF YA REALLY WANTED TO HIT THE BALL EVERY NOW AN' THEN, YOU COULDA JUST ASKED ME!
– – –

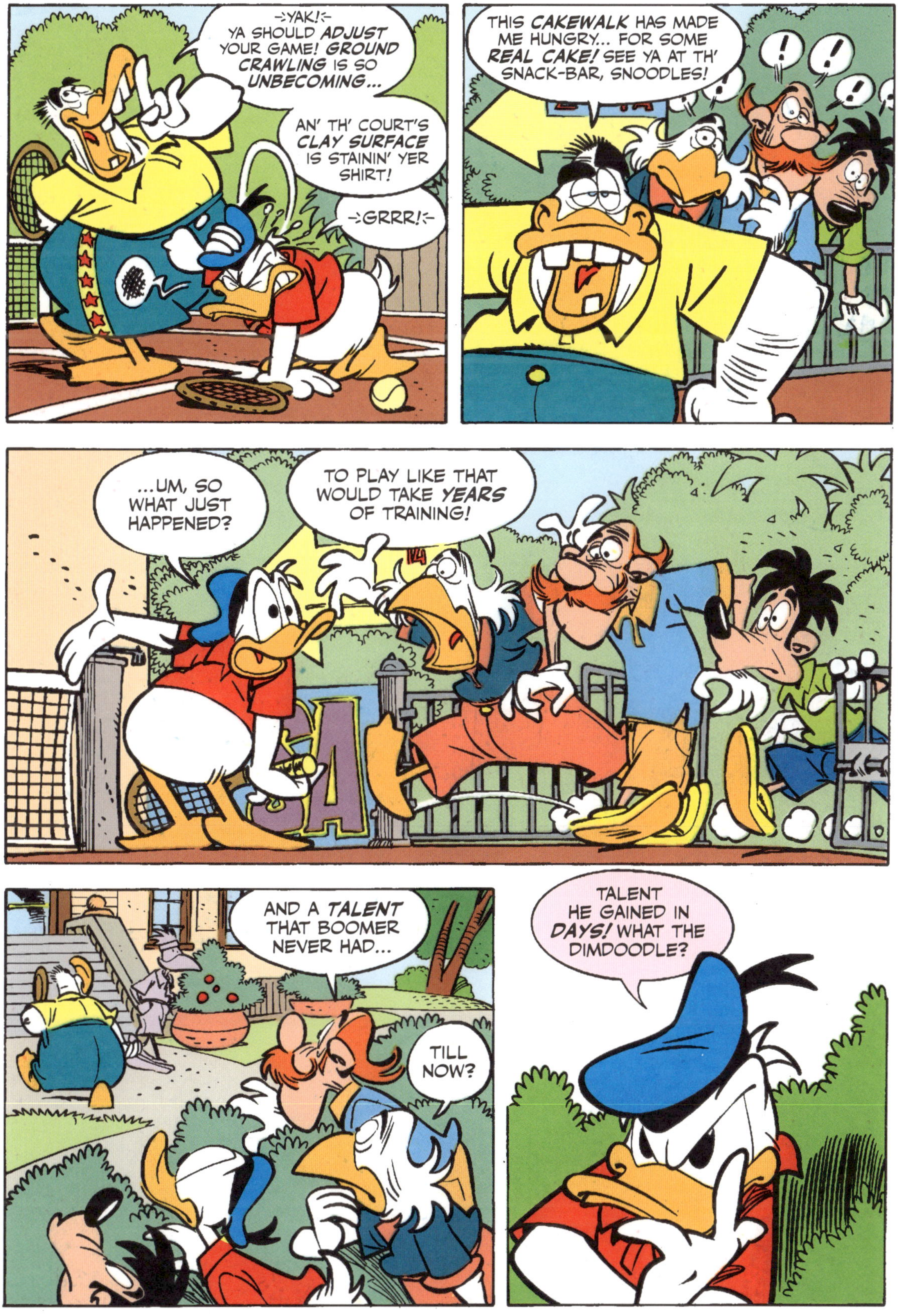
-YAK!- YA SHOULD ADJUST YOUR GAME! GROUND CRAWLING IS SO UNBECOMING...
AN' TH' COURT'S CLAY SURFACE IS STAININ' YER SHIRT!
-GRRR!-
THIS CAKEWALK HAS MADE ME HUNGRY... FOR SOME REAL CAKE! SEE YA AT TH' SNACK-BAR, SNOODLES!
...UM, SO WHAT JUST HAPPENED?
TO PLAY LIKE THAT WOULD TAKE YEARS OF TRAINING!
AND A TALENT THAT BOOMER NEVER HAD...
TILL NOW?
TALENT HE GAINED IN DAYS! WHAT THE DIMDOODLE?

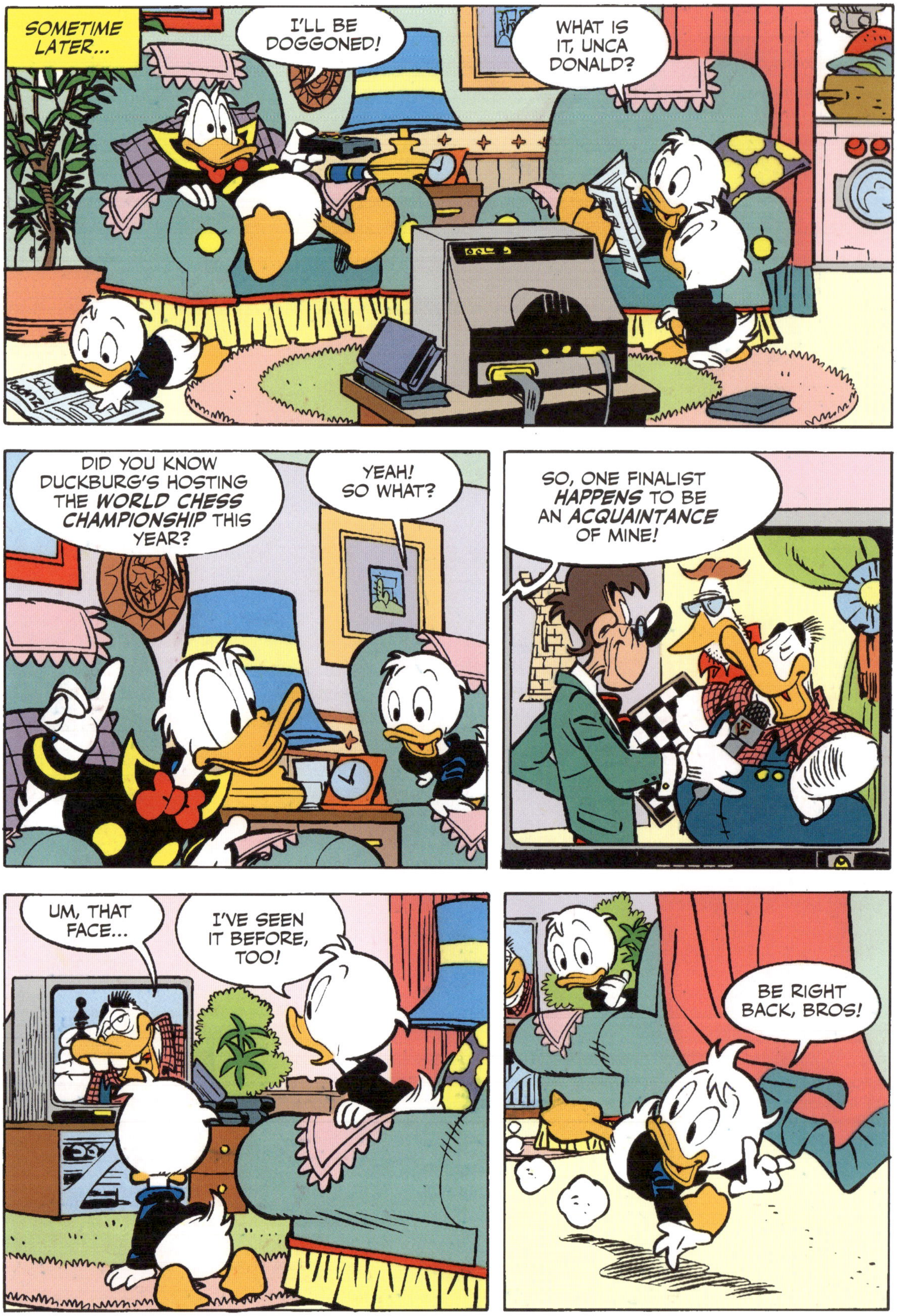
SOMETIME LATER...
I'LL BE DOGGONED!
WHAT IS IT, UNCA DONALD?
DID YOU KNOW DUCKBURG'S HOSTING THE WORLD CHESS CHAMPIONSHIP THIS YEAR?
YEAH! SO WHAT?
SO, ONE FINALIST HAPPENS TO BE AN ACQUAINTANCE OF MINE!
UM, THAT FACE...
I'VE SEEN IT BEFORE, TOO!
BE RIGHT BACK, BROS!

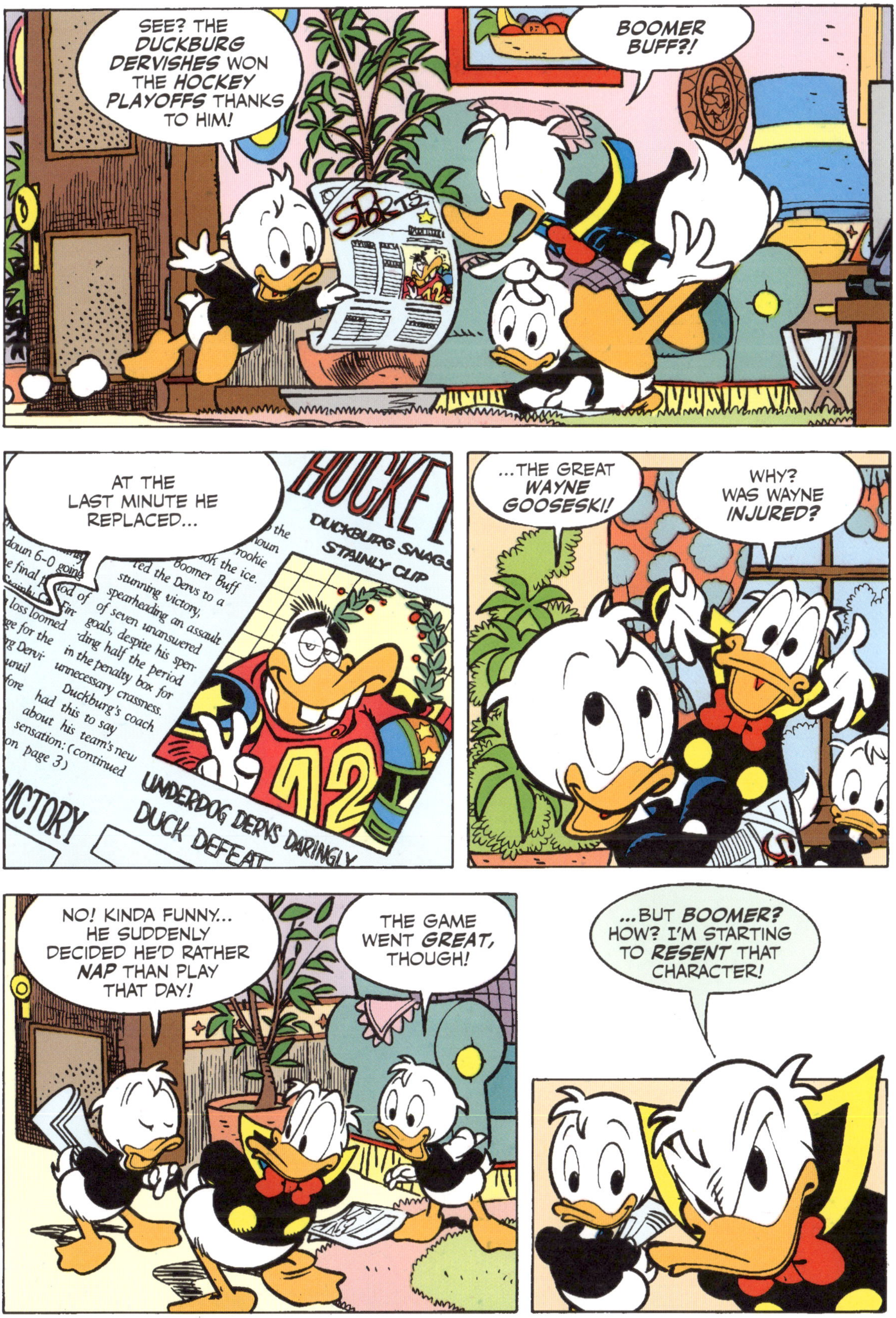

SEE? THE DUCKBURG DERVISHES WON THE HOCKEY PLAYOFFS THANKS TO HIM!
BOOMER BUFF?!
SPORTS
AT THE LAST MINUTE HE REPLACED...
HOCKEY
DUCKBURG SNAGS STAINLY CUP
UNDERDOG DERVS DARINGLY DUCK DEFEAT
VICTORY
...THE GREAT WAYNE GOOSESKI!
WHY? WAS WAYNE INJURED?
NO! KINDA FUNNY... HE SUDDENLY DECIDED HE'D RATHER NAP THAN PLAY THAT DAY!
THE GAME WENT GREAT, THOUGH!
...BUT BOOMER? HOW? I'M STARTING TO RESENT THAT CHARACTER!

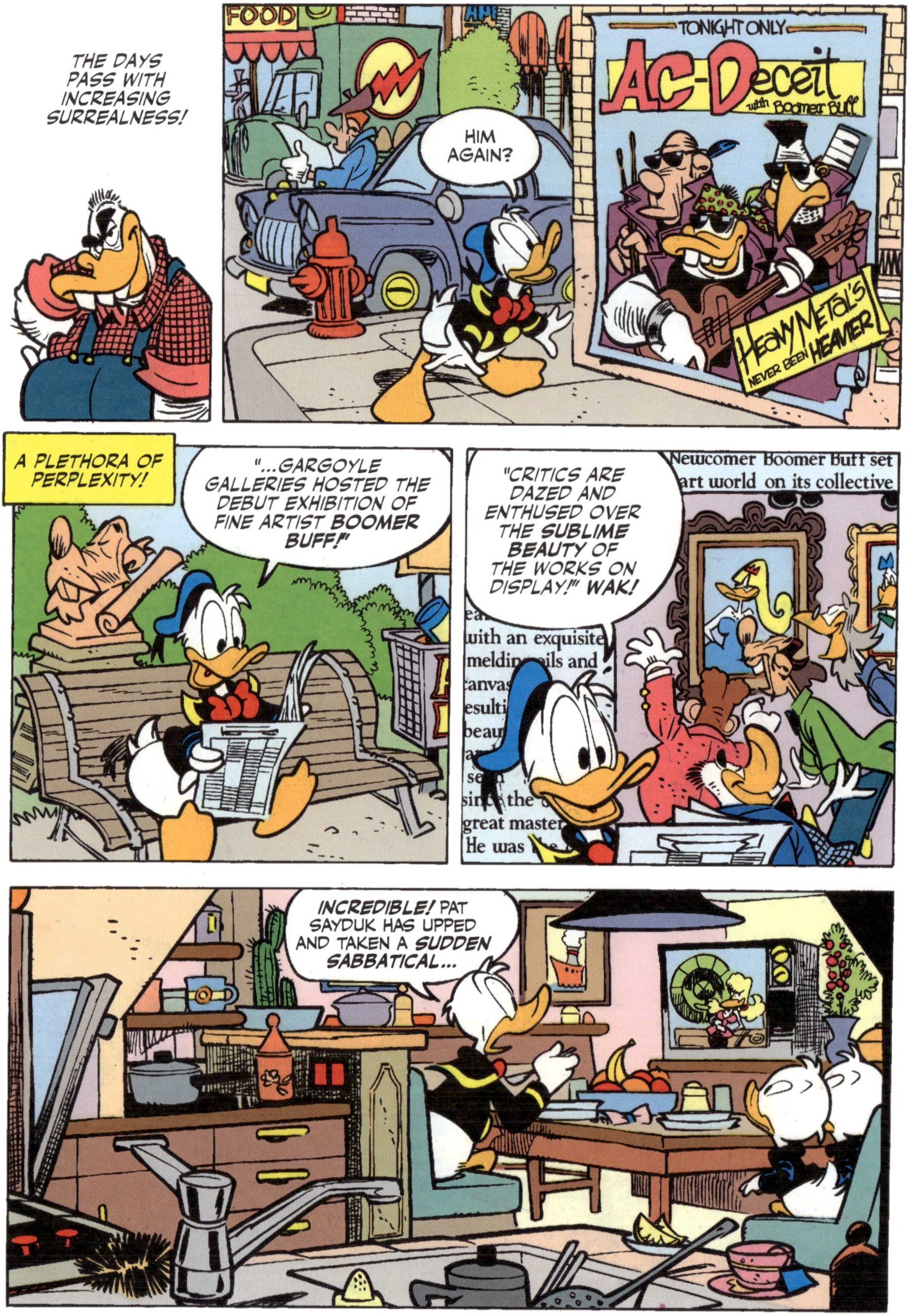
THE DAYS PASS WITH INCREASING SURREALNESS!
HIM AGAIN?
TONIGHT ONLY
Ac-Deceit
with Boomer Buff
Heavy Metal's never been Heavier
A PLETHORA OF PERPLEXITY!
"...GARGOYLE GALLERIES HOSTED THE DEBUT EXHIBITION OF FINE ARTIST BOOMER BUFF!"
"CRITICS ARE DAZED AND ENTHUSED OVER THE SUBLIME BEAUTY OF THE WORKS ON DISPLAY!" WAK!
Newcomer Boomer Buff set
art world on its collective
with an exquisite
melding oils and
great master
He was
INCREDIBLE! PAT SAYDUK HAS UPPED AND TAKEN A SUDDEN SABBATICAL...

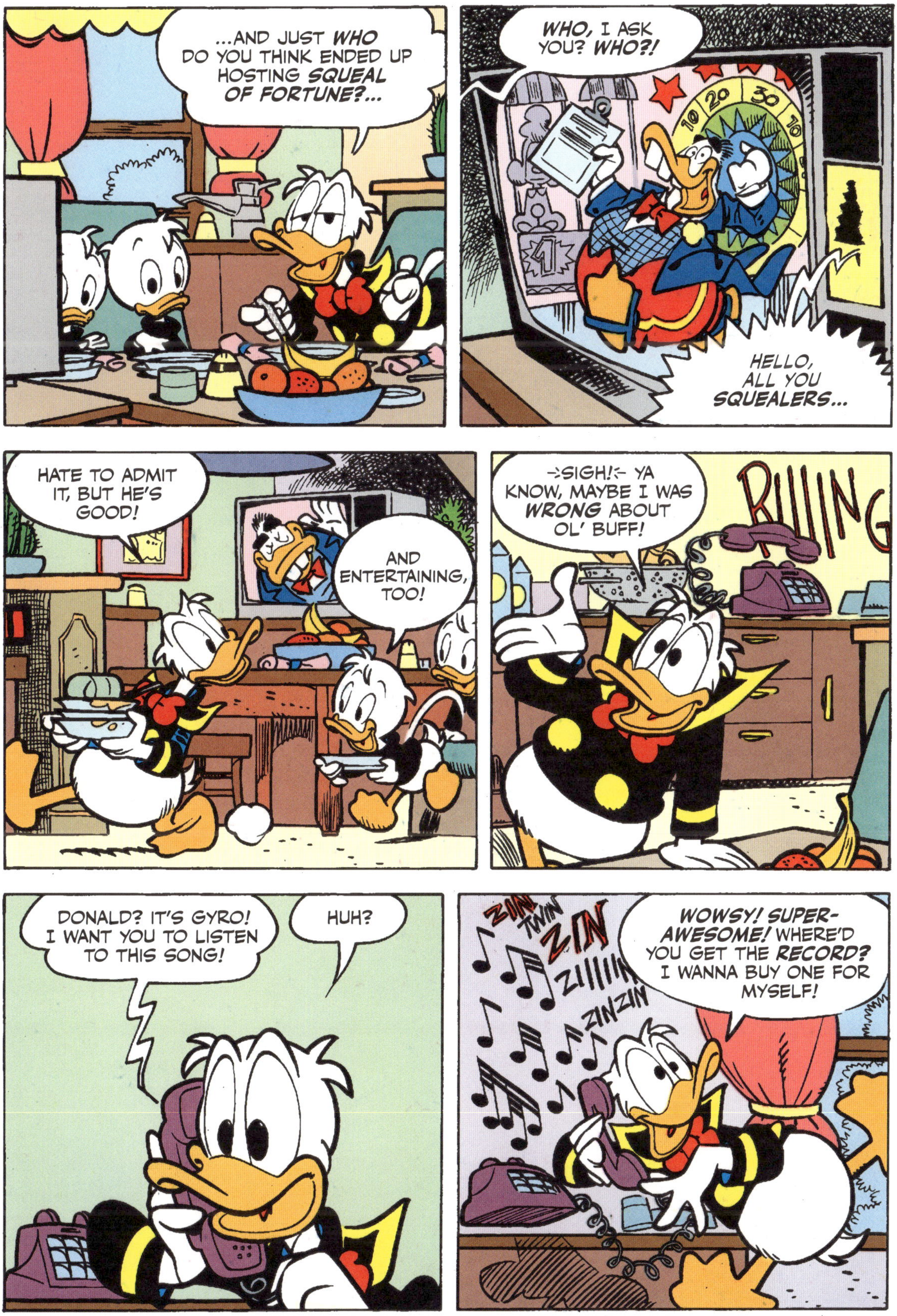

...AND JUST WHO DO YOU THINK ENDED UP HOSTING SQUEAL OF FORTUNE?...
WHO, I ASK YOU? WHO?!
HELLO, ALL YOU SQUEALERS...
HATE TO ADMIT IT, BUT HE'S GOOD!
AND ENTERTAINING, TOO!
RIIING
-SIGH!- YA KNOW, MAYBE I WAS WRONG ABOUT OL' BUFF!
DONALD? IT'S GYRO! I WANT YOU TO LISTEN TO THIS SONG!
HUH?
ZIN TWIN ZIN ZIIIIN ZINZIN
WOWSY! SUPER-AWESOME! WHERE'D YOU GET THE RECORD? I WANNA BUY ONE FOR MYSELF!

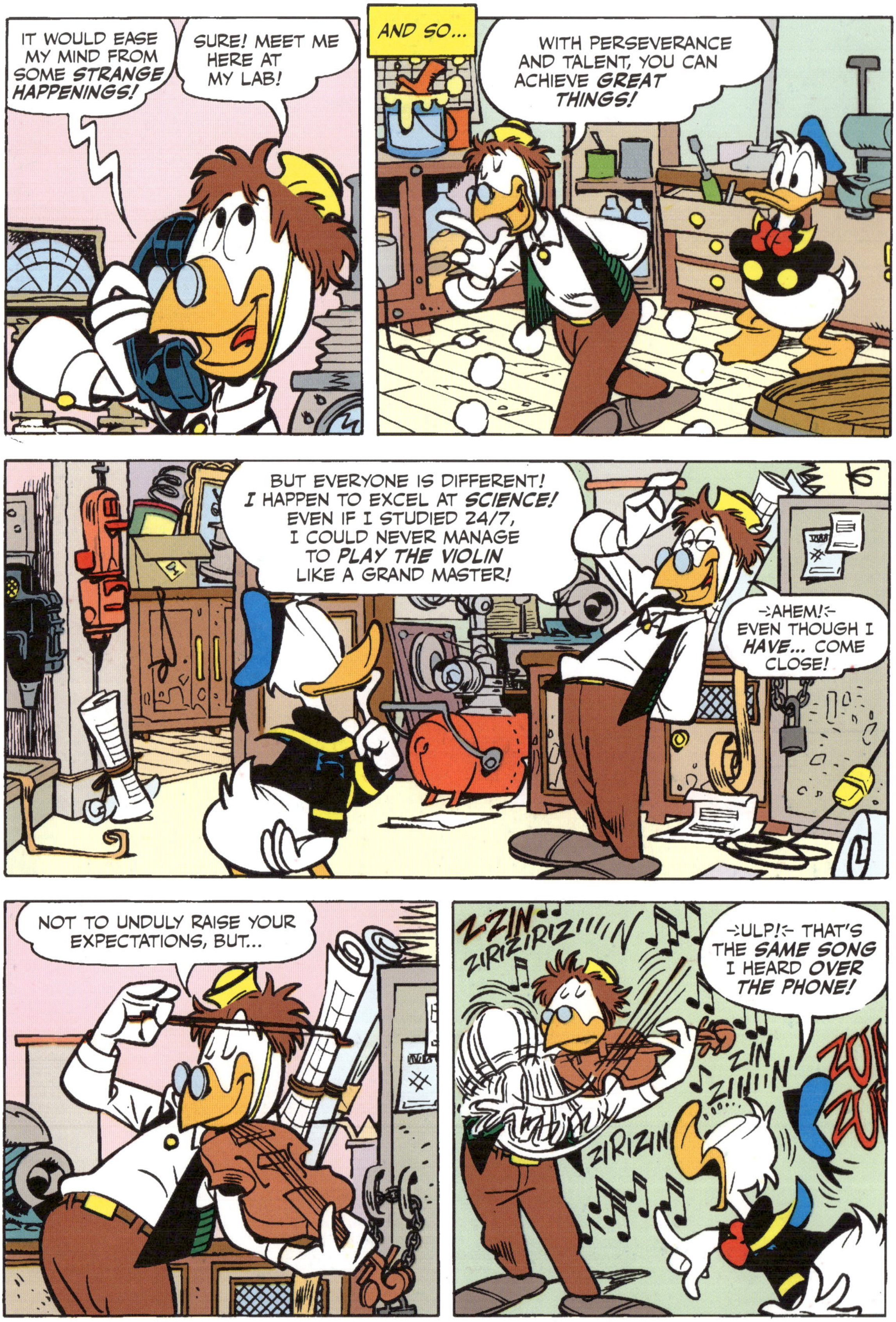

IT WOULD EASE MY MIND FROM SOME STRANGE HAPPENINGS!
SURE! MEET ME HERE AT MY LAB!
AND SO...
WITH PERSEVERANCE AND TALENT, YOU CAN ACHIEVE GREAT THINGS!
BUT EVERYONE IS DIFFERENT! I HAPPEN TO EXCEL AT SCIENCE! EVEN IF I STUDIED 24/7, I COULD NEVER MANAGE TO PLAY THE VIOLIN LIKE A GRAND MASTER!
-AHEM!- EVEN THOUGH I HAVE... COME CLOSE!
NOT TO UNDULY RAISE YOUR EXPECTATIONS, BUT...
ZZIN ZIRIZIRIZ'''N
ZIN ZIII'N
ZIRIZIN
-ULP!- THAT'S THE SAME SONG I HEARD OVER THE PHONE!

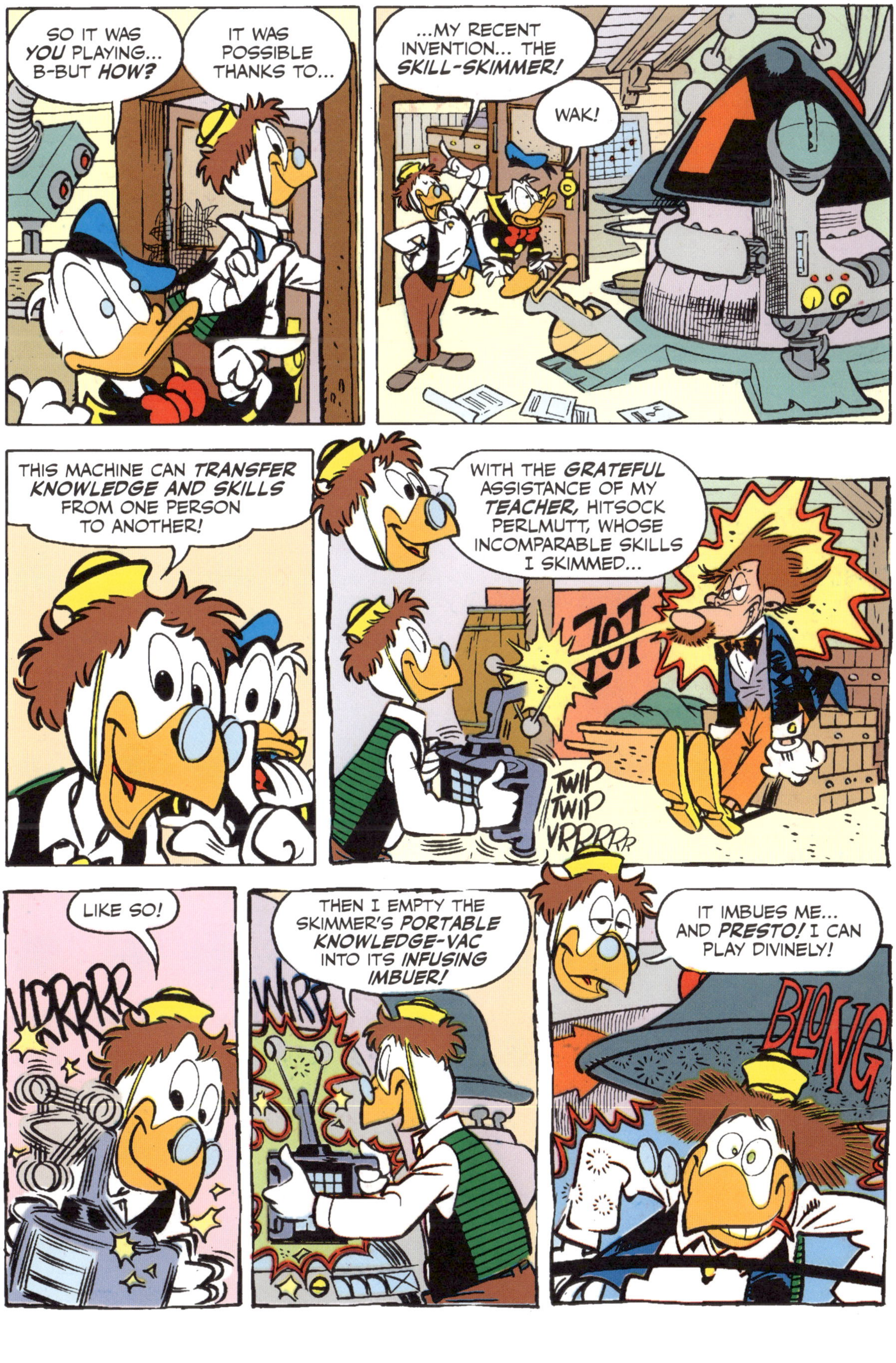
SO IT WAS YOU PLAYING... B-BUT HOW?
IT WAS POSSIBLE THANKS TO...
...MY RECENT INVENTION... THE SKILL-SKIMMER!
WAK!
THIS MACHINE CAN TRANSFER KNOWLEDGE AND SKILLS FROM ONE PERSON TO ANOTHER!
WITH THE GRATEFUL ASSISTANCE OF MY TEACHER, HITSOCK PERLMUTT, WHOSE INCOMPARABLE SKILLS I SKIMMED...
ZOT
TWIP TWIP VRRRRRR
LIKE SO!
VRRRRR
THEN I EMPTY THE SKIMMER'S PORTABLE KNOWLEDGE-VAC INTO ITS INFUSING IMBUER!
WIRR
IT IMBUES ME... AND PRESTO! I CAN PLAY DIVINELY!
BLONG

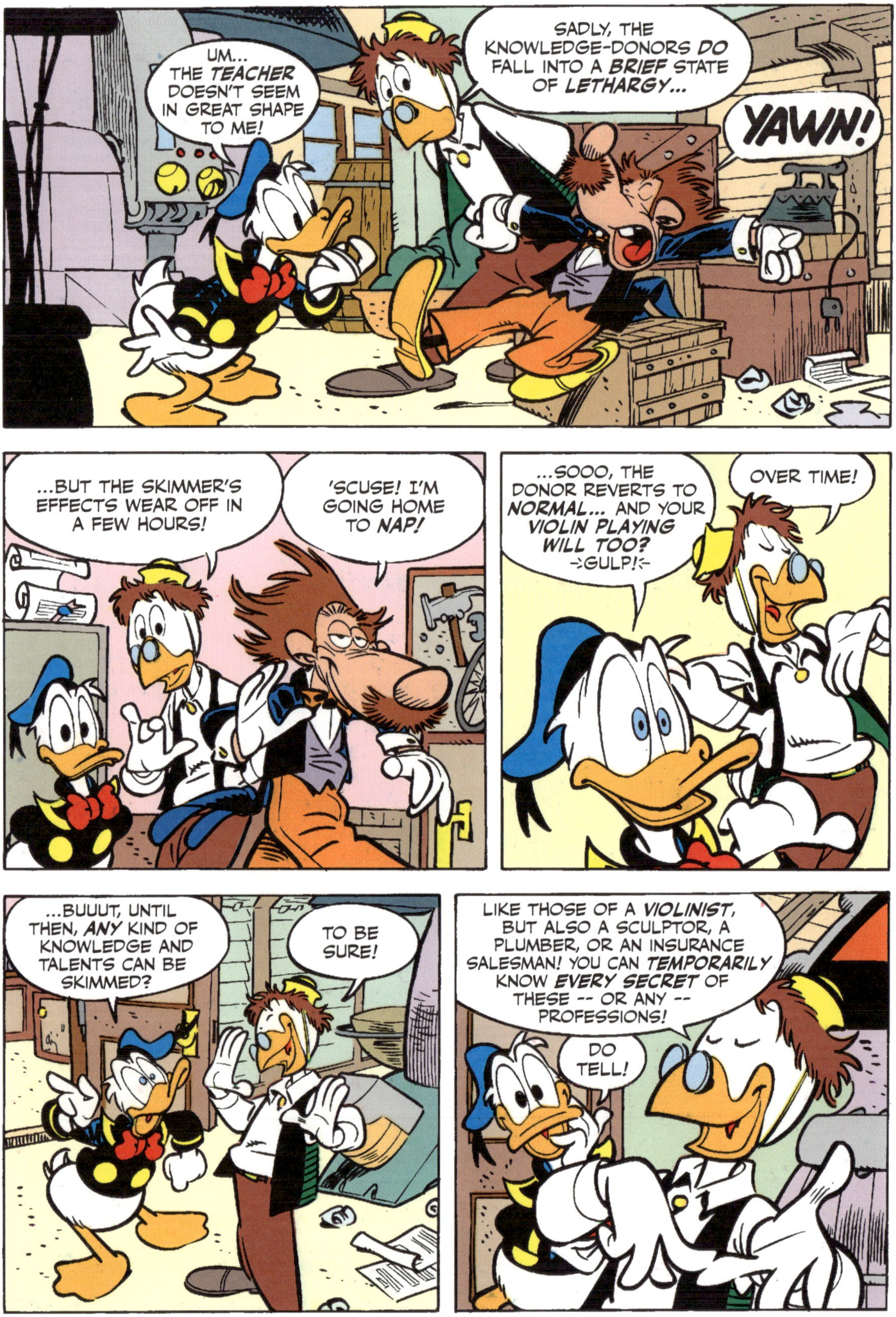
UM... THE TEACHER DOESN'T SEEM IN GREAT SHAPE TO ME!
SADLY, THE KNOWLEDGE-DONORS DO FALL INTO A BRIEF STATE OF LETHARGY...
YAWN!
...BUT THE SKIMMER'S EFFECTS WEAR OFF IN A FEW HOURS!
'SCUSE! I'M GOING HOME TO NAP!
...SOOO, THE DONOR REVERTS TO NORMAL... AND YOUR VIOLIN PLAYING WILL TOO? -GULP!-
OVER TIME!
...BUUUT, UNTIL THEN, ANY KIND OF KNOWLEDGE AND TALENTS CAN BE SKIMMED?
TO BE SURE!
LIKE THOSE OF A VIOLINIST, BUT ALSO A SCULPTOR, A PLUMBER, OR AN INSURANCE SALESMAN! YOU CAN TEMPORARILY KNOW EVERY SECRET OF THESE -- OR ANY -- PROFESSIONS!
DO TELL!

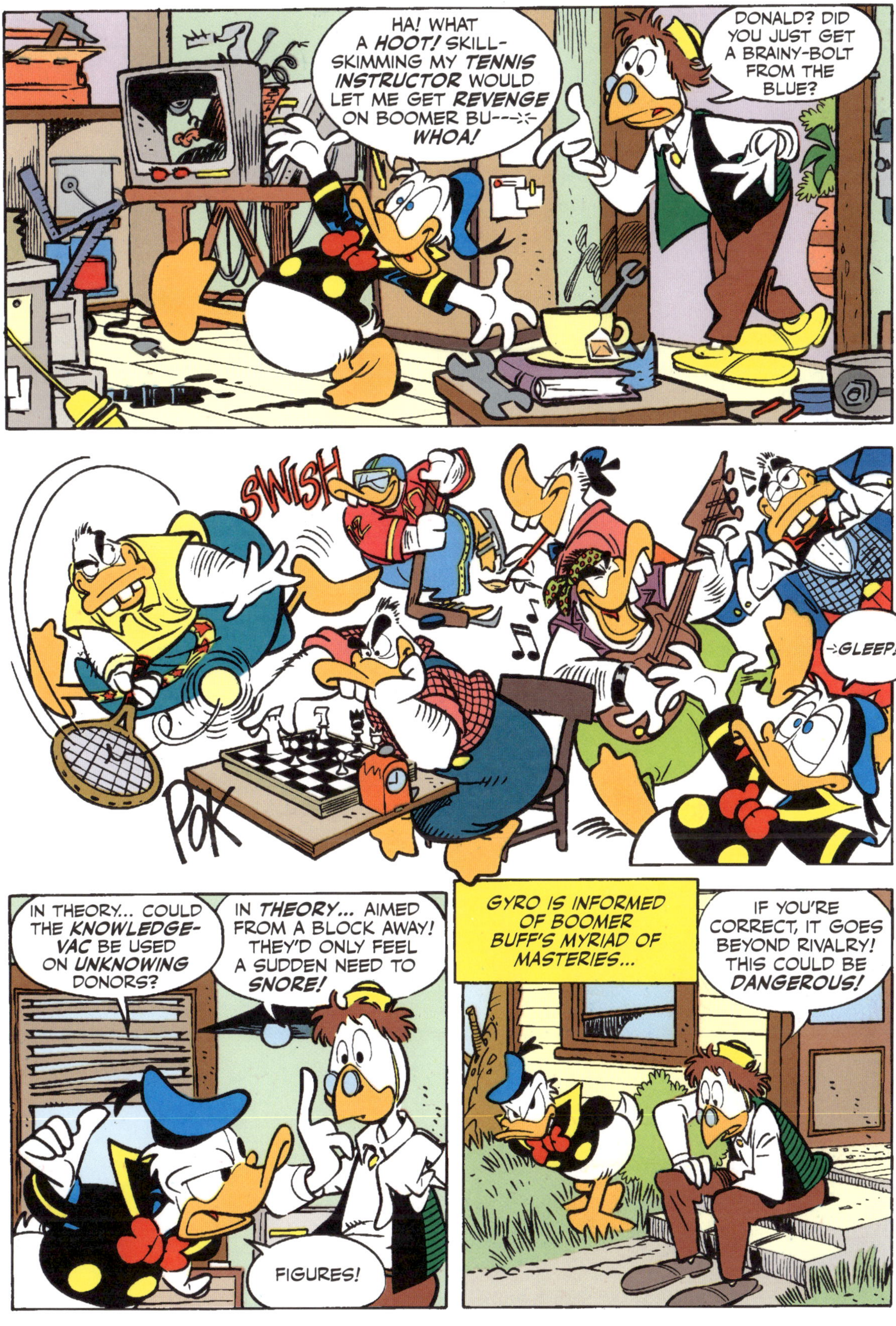
HA! WHAT A HOOT! SKILL-SKIMMING MY TENNIS INSTRUCTOR WOULD LET ME GET REVENGE ON BOOMER BU--- WHOA!
DONALD? DID YOU JUST GET A BRAINY-BOLT FROM THE BLUE?
SWISH
POK
GLEEP!
IN THEORY... COULD THE KNOWLEDGE-VAC BE USED ON UNKNOWING DONORS?
IN THEORY... AIMED FROM A BLOCK AWAY! THEY'D ONLY FEEL A SUDDEN NEED TO SNORE!
FIGURES!
GYRO IS INFORMED OF BOOMER BUFF'S MYRIAD OF MASTERIES...
IF YOU'RE CORRECT, IT GOES BEYOND RIVALRY! THIS COULD BE DANGEROUS!

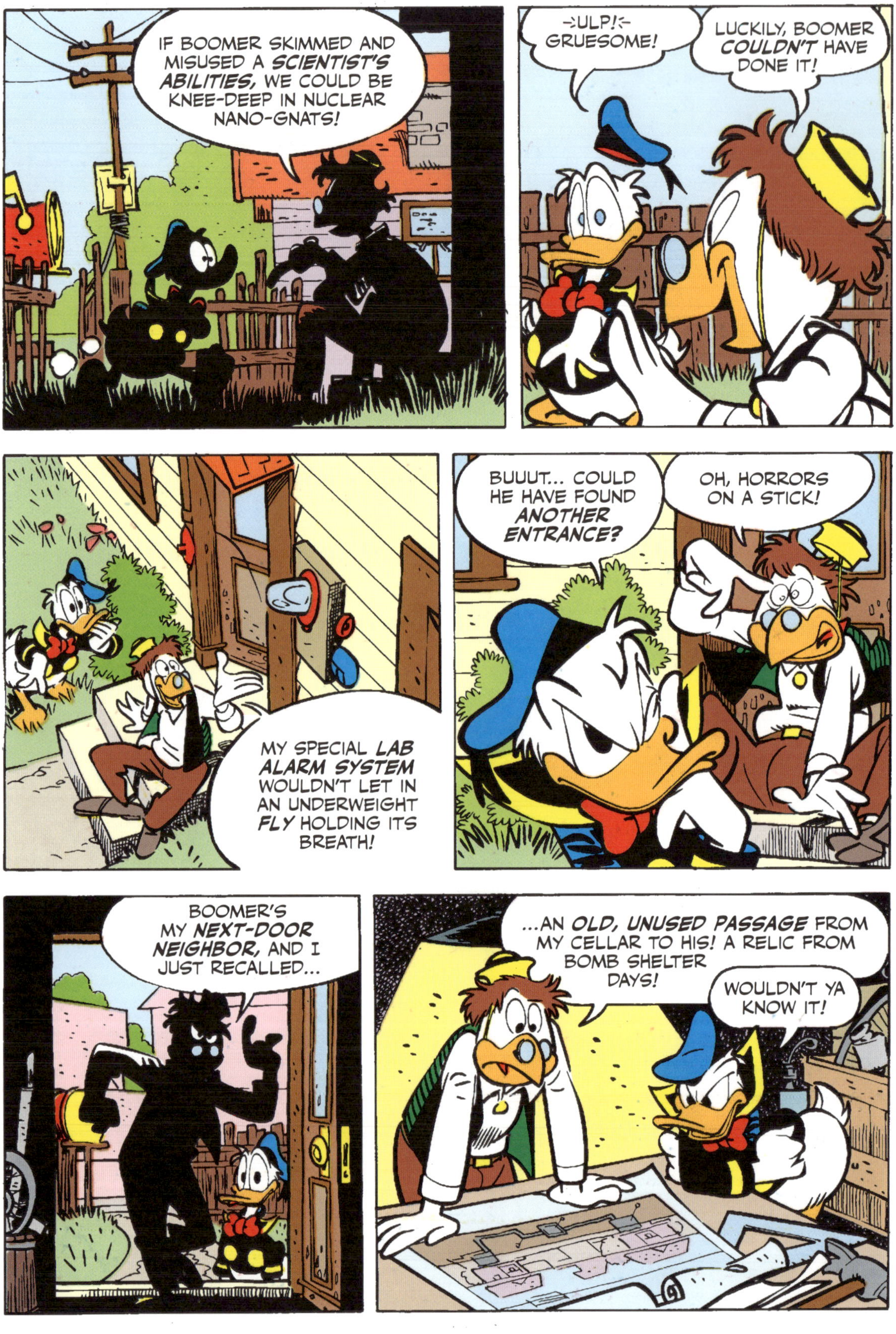
IF BOOMER SKIMMED AND MISUSED A SCIENTIST'S ABILITIES, WE COULD BE KNEE-DEEP IN NUCLEAR NANO-GNATS!
ULP! GRUESOME!
LUCKILY, BOOMER COULDN'T HAVE DONE IT!
MY SPECIAL LAB ALARM SYSTEM WOULDN'T LET IN AN UNDERWEIGHT FLY HOLDING ITS BREATH!
BUUUT... COULD HE HAVE FOUND ANOTHER ENTRANCE?
OH, HORRORS ON A STICK!
BOOMER'S MY NEXT-DOOR NEIGHBOR, AND I JUST RECALLED...
...AN OLD, UNUSED PASSAGE FROM MY CELLAR TO HIS! A RELIC FROM BOMB SHELTER DAYS!
WOULDN'T YA KNOW IT!

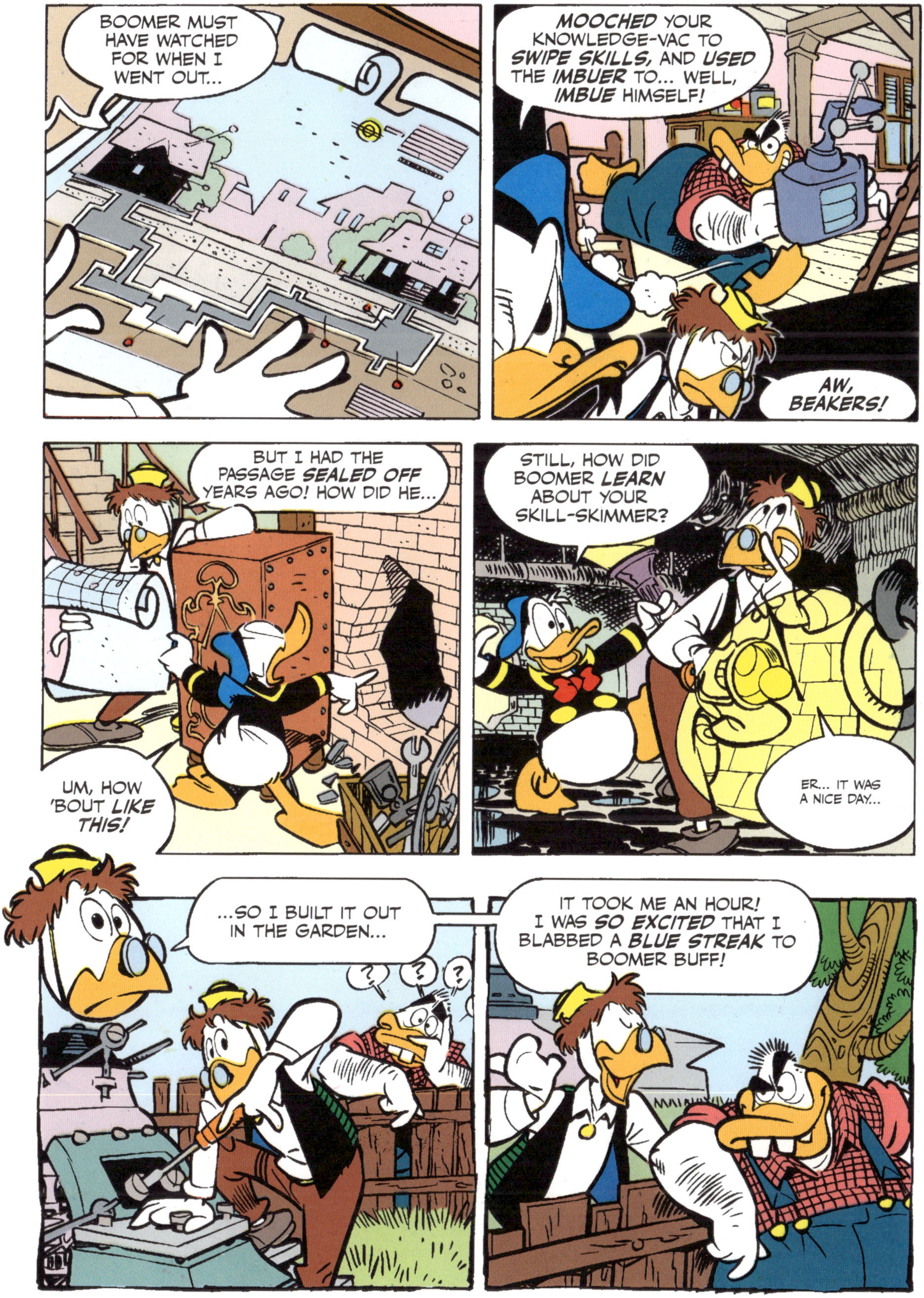
BOOMER MUST HAVE WATCHED FOR WHEN I WENT OUT...
MOOCHED YOUR KNOWLEDGE-VAC TO SWIPE SKILLS, AND USED THE IMBUER TO... WELL, IMBUE HIMSELF!
AW, BEAKERS!
BUT I HAD THE PASSAGE SEALED OFF YEARS AGO! HOW DID HE...
UM, HOW 'BOUT LIKE THIS!
STILL, HOW DID BOOMER LEARN ABOUT YOUR SKILL-SKIMMER?
ER... IT WAS A NICE DAY...
...SO I BUILT IT OUT IN THE GARDEN...
?
?
?
IT TOOK ME AN HOUR! I WAS SO EXCITED THAT I BLABBED A BLUE STREAK TO BOOMER BUFF!

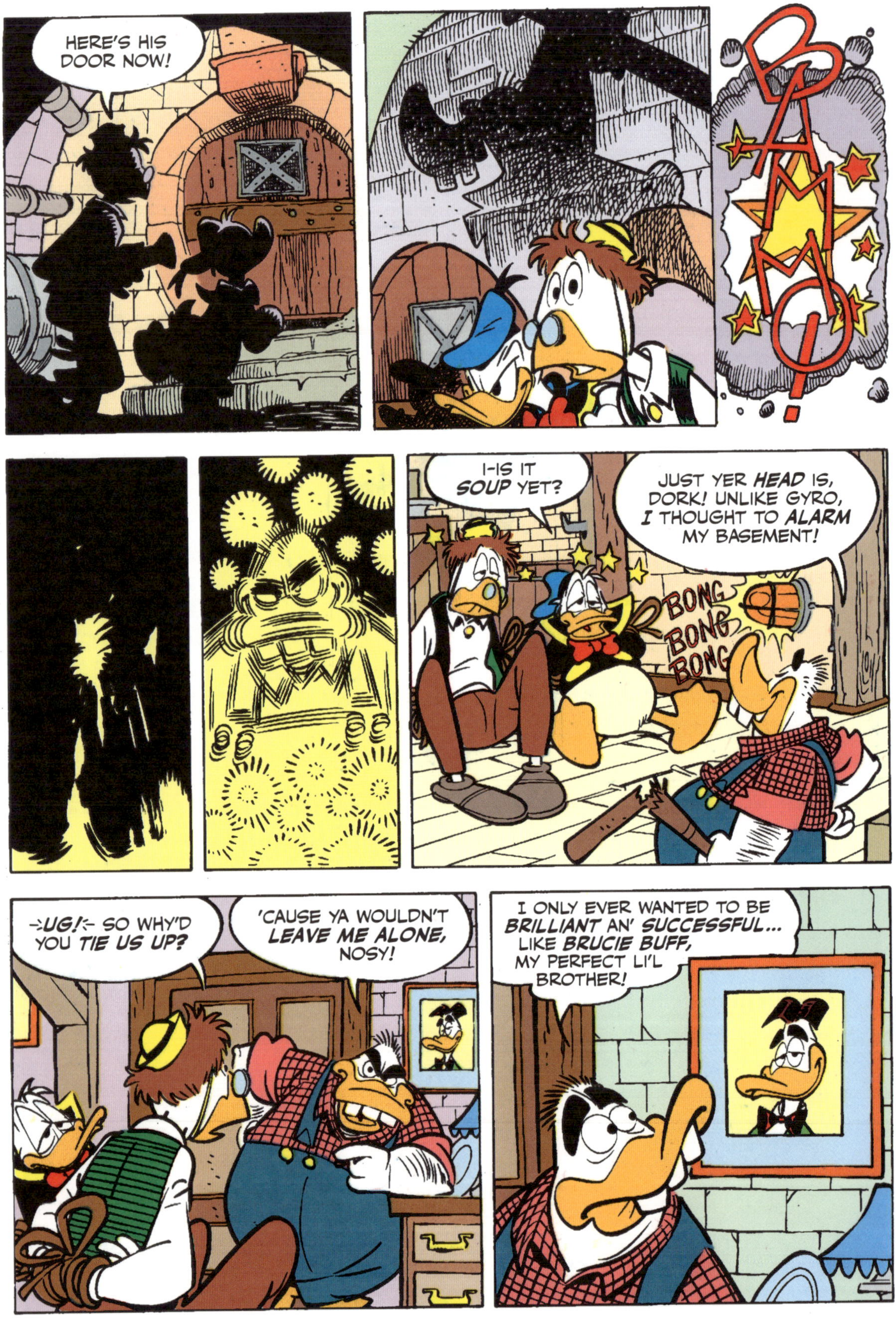
HERE'S HIS DOOR NOW!
BAMMO!
I-IS IT SOUP YET?
JUST YER HEAD IS, DORK! UNLIKE GYRO, I THOUGHT TO ALARM MY BASEMENT!
BONG BONG BONG
-UG!- SO WHY'D YOU TIE US UP?
'CAUSE YA WOULDN'T LEAVE ME ALONE, NOSY!
I ONLY EVER WANTED TO BE BRILLIANT AN' SUCCESSFUL... LIKE BRUCIE BUFF, MY PERFECT LI'L BROTHER!

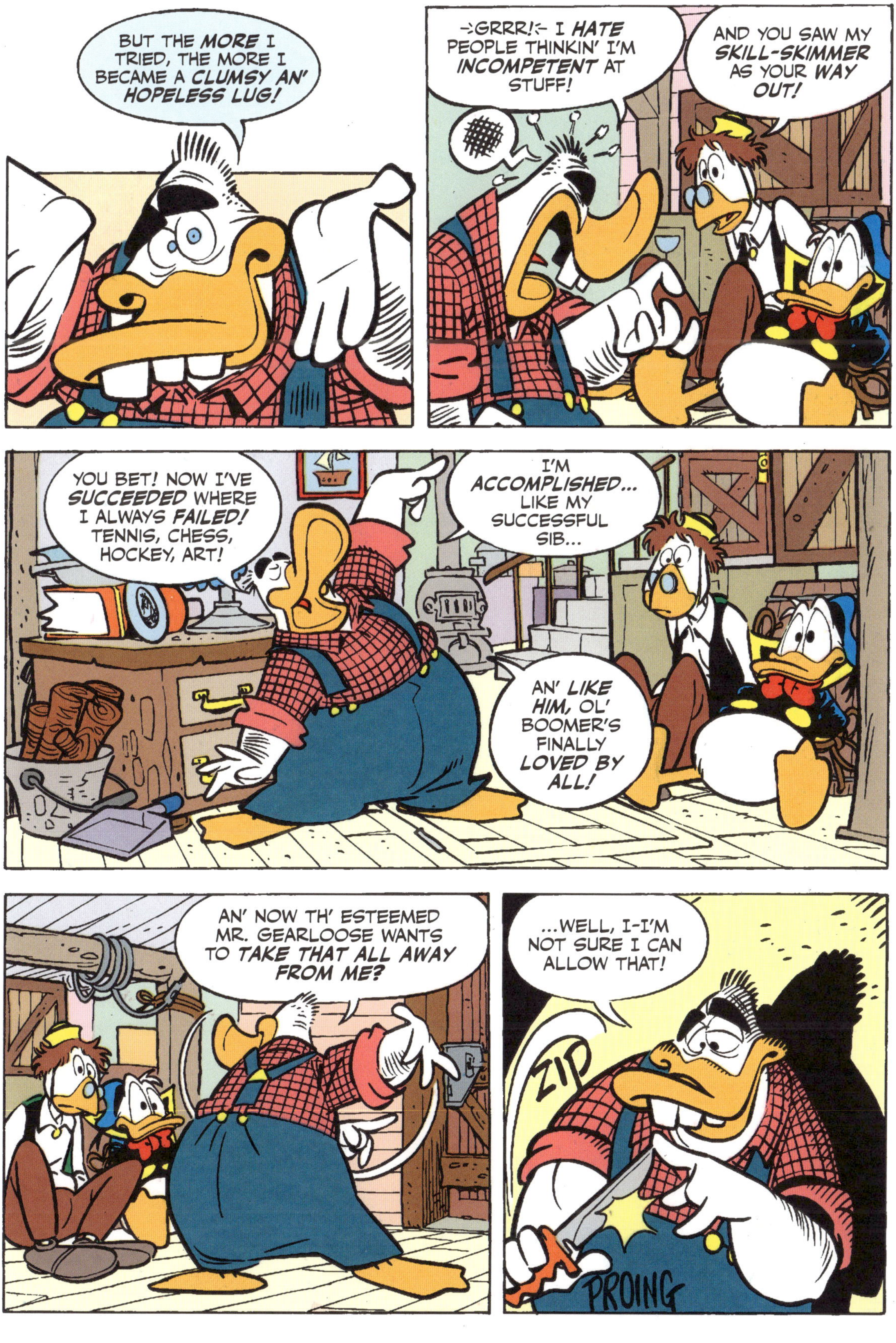
BUT THE MORE I TRIED, THE MORE I BECAME A CLUMSY AN' HOPELESS LUG!
-GRRR!- I HATE PEOPLE THINKIN' I'M INCOMPETENT AT STUFF!
AND YOU SAW MY SKILL-SKIMMER AS YOUR WAY OUT!
YOU BET! NOW I'VE SUCCEEDED WHERE I ALWAYS FAILED! TENNIS, CHESS, HOCKEY, ART!
I'M ACCOMPLISHED... LIKE MY SUCCESSFUL SIB...
AN' LIKE HIM, OL' BOOMER'S FINALLY LOVED BY ALL!
AN' NOW TH' ESTEEMED MR. GEARLOOSE WANTS TO TAKE THAT ALL AWAY FROM ME?
...WELL, I-I'M NOT SURE I CAN ALLOW THAT!
ZIP
PROING

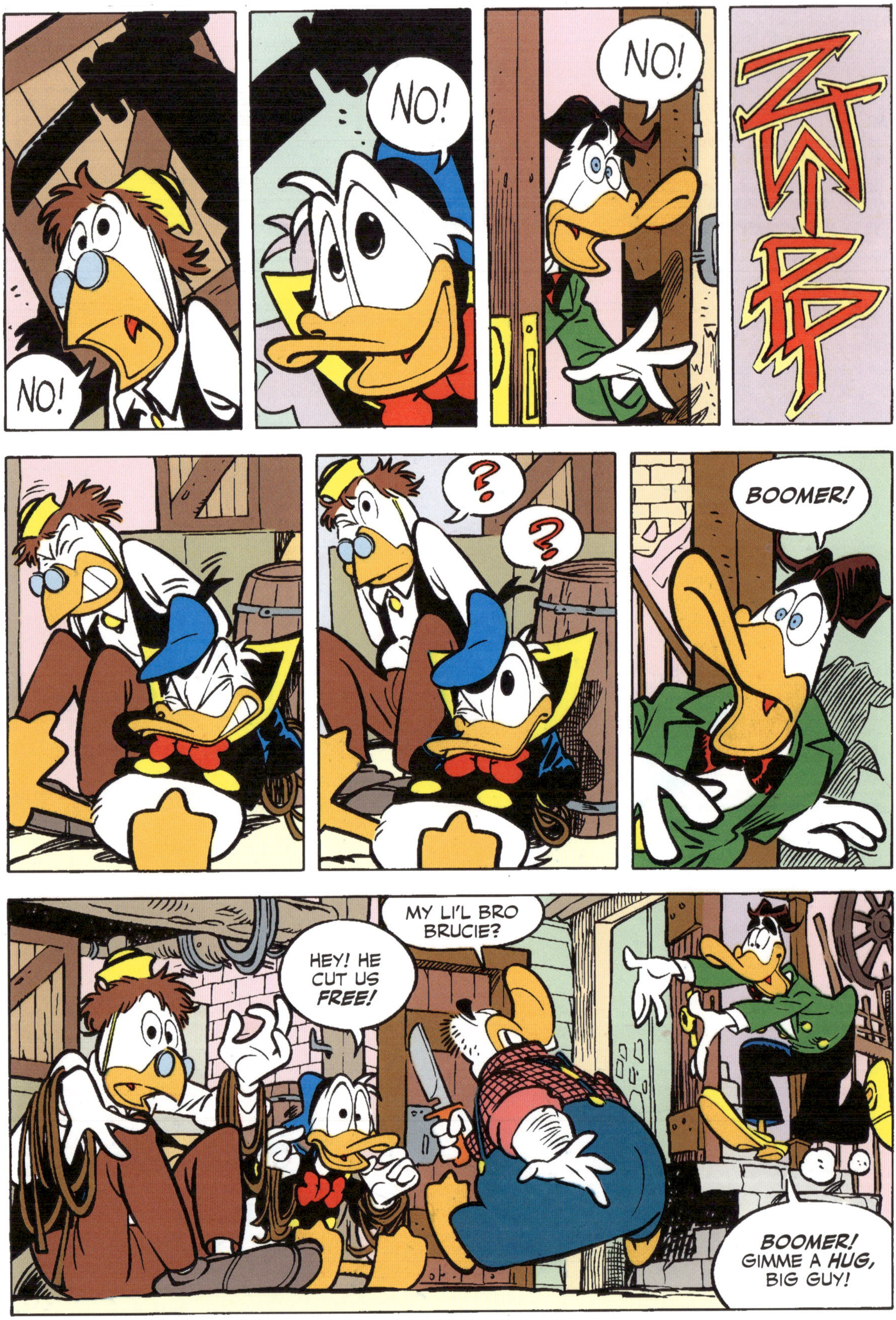
NO!
NO!
NO!
ZWPP
?
?
BOOMER!
HEY! HE CUT US FREE!
MY LI'L BRO BRUCIE?
BOOMER! GIMME A HUG, BIG GUY!

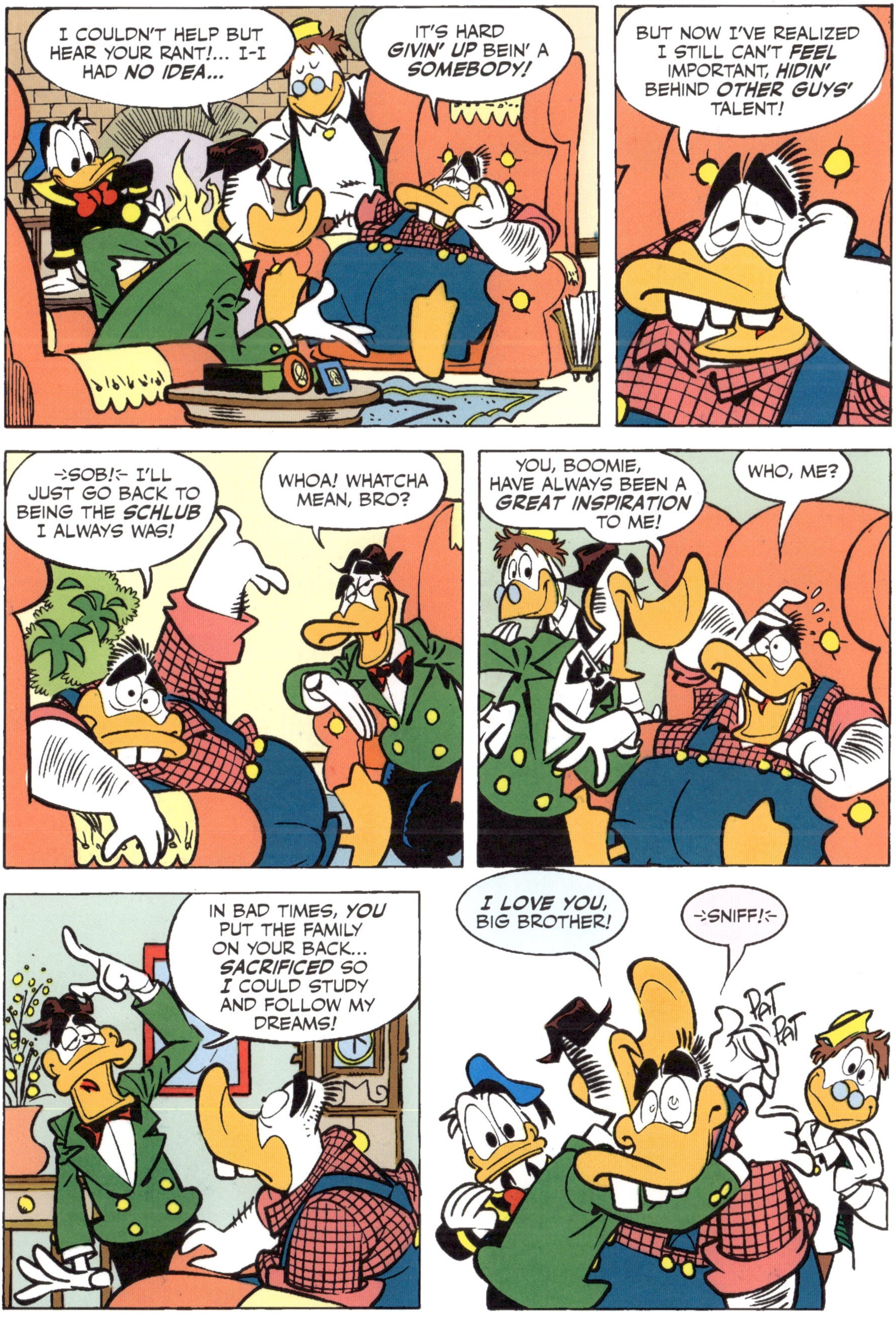
I COULDN'T HELP BUT HEAR YOUR RANT!... I-I HAD NO IDEA...
IT'S HARD GIVIN' UP BEIN' A SOMEBODY!
BUT NOW I'VE REALIZED I STILL CAN'T FEEL IMPORTANT, HIDIN' BEHIND OTHER GUYS' TALENT!
-SOB!- I'LL JUST GO BACK TO BEING THE SCHLUB I ALWAYS WAS!
WHOA! WHATCHA MEAN, BRO?
YOU, BOOMIE, HAVE ALWAYS BEEN A GREAT INSPIRATION TO ME!
WHO, ME?
IN BAD TIMES, YOU PUT THE FAMILY ON YOUR BACK... SACRIFICED SO I COULD STUDY AND FOLLOW MY DREAMS!
I LOVE YOU, BIG BROTHER!
-SNIFF!-
PAT PAT

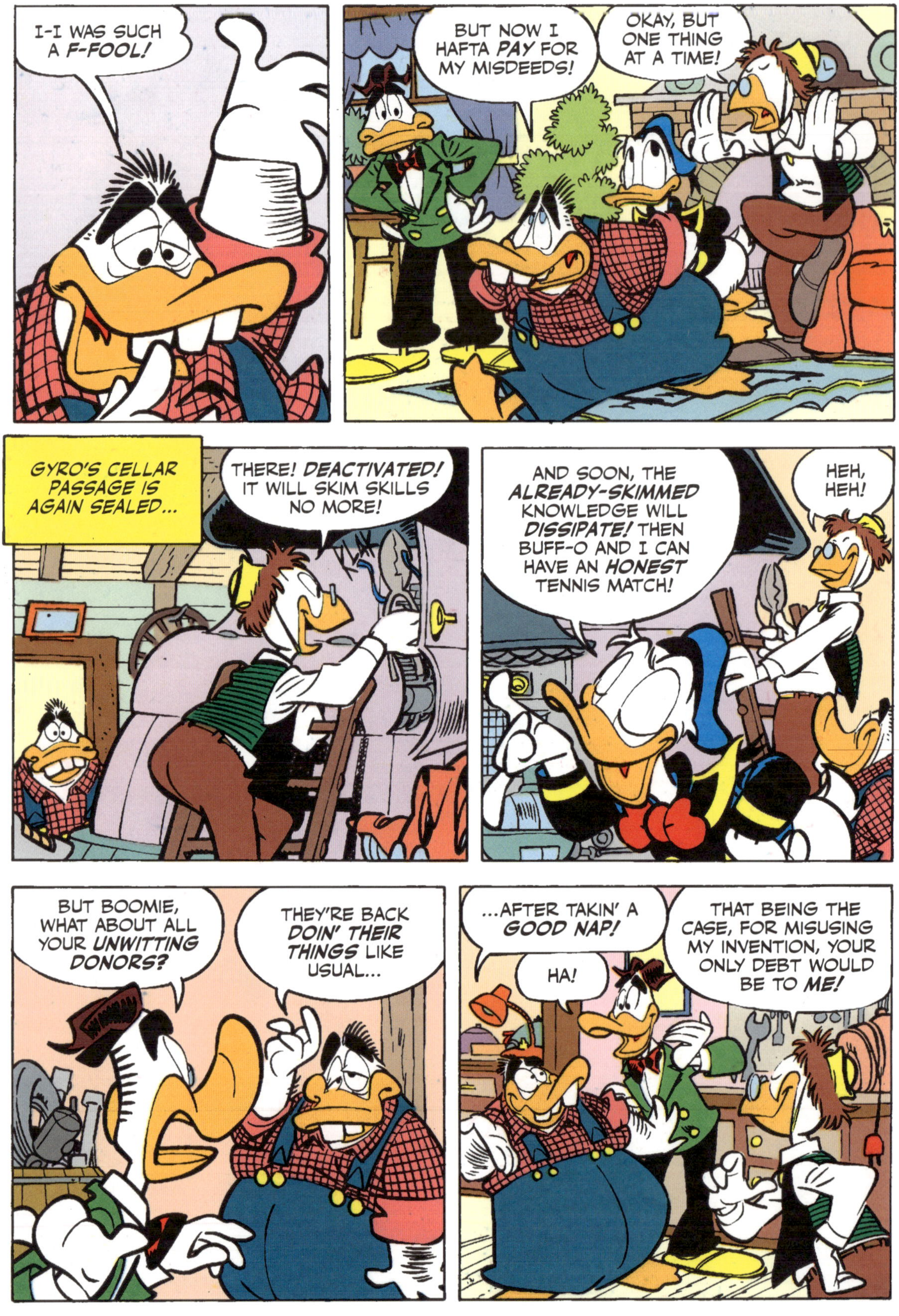
I-I WAS SUCH A F-FOOL!
BUT NOW I HAFTA PAY FOR MY MISDEEDS!
OKAY, BUT ONE THING AT A TIME!
GYRO'S CELLAR PASSAGE IS AGAIN SEALED...
THERE! DEACTIVATED! IT WILL SKIM SKILLS NO MORE!
AND SOON, THE ALREADY-SKIMMED KNOWLEDGE WILL DISSIPATE! THEN BUFF-O AND I CAN HAVE AN HONEST TENNIS MATCH!
HEH, HEH!
BUT BOOMIE, WHAT ABOUT ALL YOUR UNWITTING DONORS?
THEY'RE BACK DOIN' THEIR THINGS LIKE USUAL...
...AFTER TAKIN' A GOOD NAP!
HA!
THAT BEING THE CASE, FOR MISUSING MY INVENTION, YOUR ONLY DEBT WOULD BE TO ME!

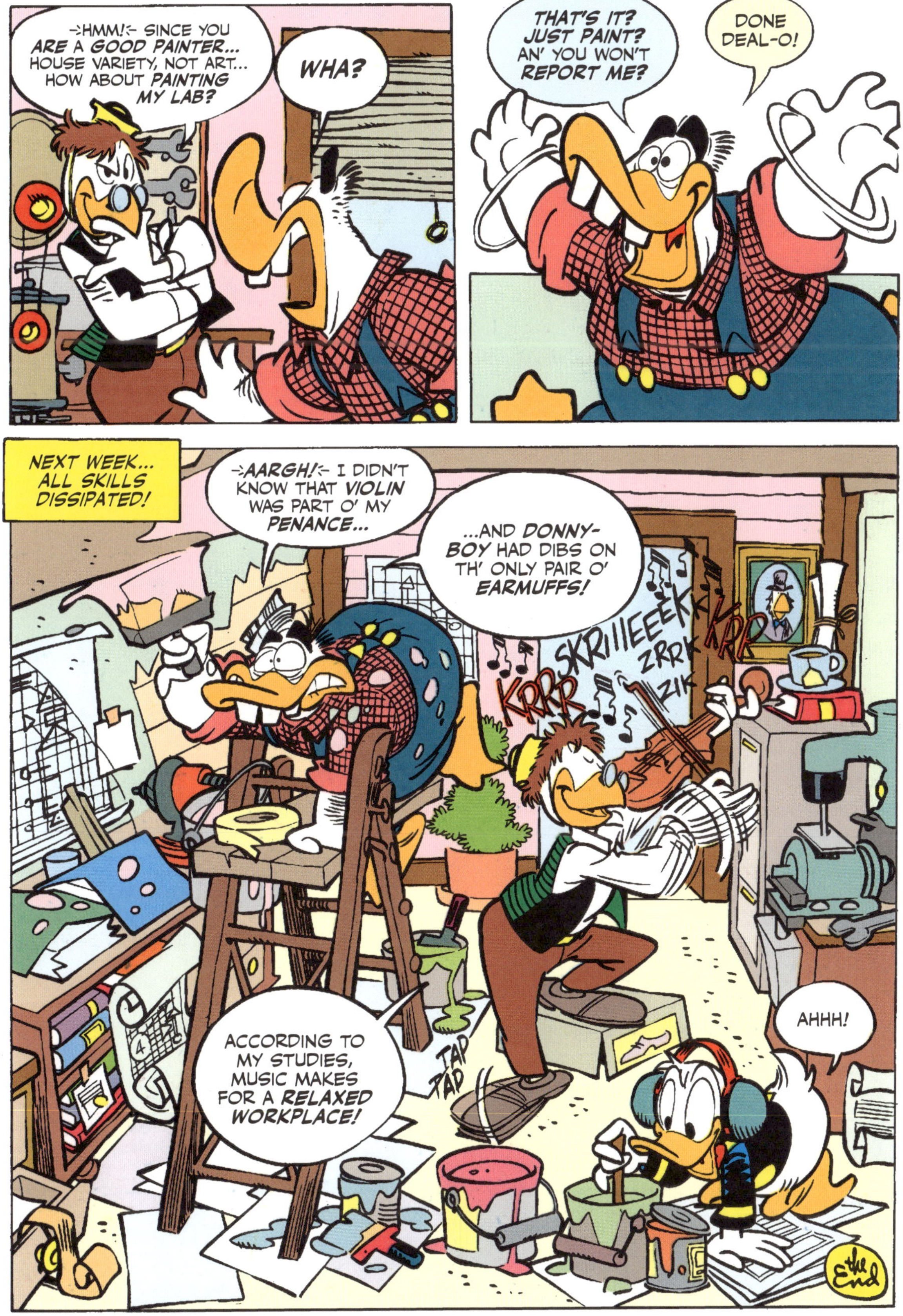

-HMM!- SINCE YOU ARE A GOOD PAINTER... HOUSE VARIETY, NOT ART... HOW ABOUT PAINTING MY LAB?
WHA?
THAT'S IT? JUST PAINT? AN' YOU WON'T REPORT ME?
DONE DEAL-O!
NEXT WEEK... ALL SKILLS DISSIPATED!
-AARGH!- I DIDN'T KNOW THAT VIOLIN WAS PART O' MY PENANCE...
...AND DONNY-BOY HAD DIBS ON TH' ONLY PAIR O' EARMUFFS!
SKRIIIEEEK
KRRR
KRR
ZRRK
ZIK
ACCORDING TO MY STUDIES, MUSIC MAKES FOR A RELAXED WORKPLACE!
TAP
TAP
AHHH!
the End

MICKEY MOUSE
YOICKS! EGAD, MEN! LOOK WHAT TH' TIME IS!
AWP!– ALMOST MIDNIGHT!
ZIP
READY ON ONE!... TWO!
I TL 3286-4A
HAPPY BIRTHDAY, MICKEY!
FOR HE'S A JOLLY GOOD FELLOW! FOR HE'S A JOLLY GOOD FELLOW! FOR HE'S A JOLLY GOOD FELLLLOW...
...THAT NOBODY CAN DENY!
UH, FELLAS... UNDER TH' CIRCUMSTANCES... SORRY, BUT I'M NOT FLATTERED!
End

TOPOLINO

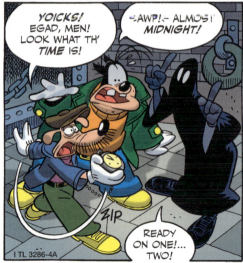

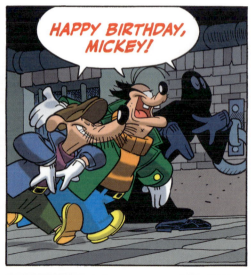

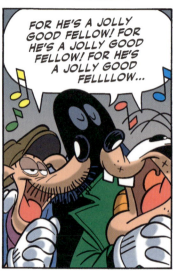

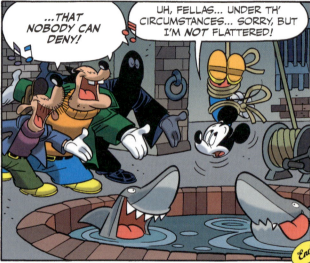

Birthday Bad Guys

Corrado Mastantuono and Disney birthday comics go together like candles and cake. In 1998, for Mickey Mouse's 70th anniversary, Mastantuono and writer Francesco Artibani produced "The River of Time," a historic conflict between Mickey and longtime arch-enemy Pete. Then two decades later, Mastantuono went back to work for Mickey's 90th—drawing a series of gag strips, like the one above, that engaged even more classic villains: the Phantom Blot and Pete's weasel sidekick Scuttle.

In between these projects, Mastantuono and Artibani created another celebrated birthday comic. December 26, 1932 had seen the first issue of the Italian Disney comic *Topolino*, published back then in an oversized mock-newspaper format. To commemorate *Topolino*'s 80th anniversary in 2012, Artibani and Mastantuono imagined what might happen if our modern Mickey were to find his name on an *actual* 1932 newspaper. How could it have gotten there? And how might a beloved bad guy—in one form or another—have been involved? •

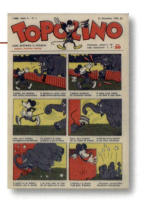

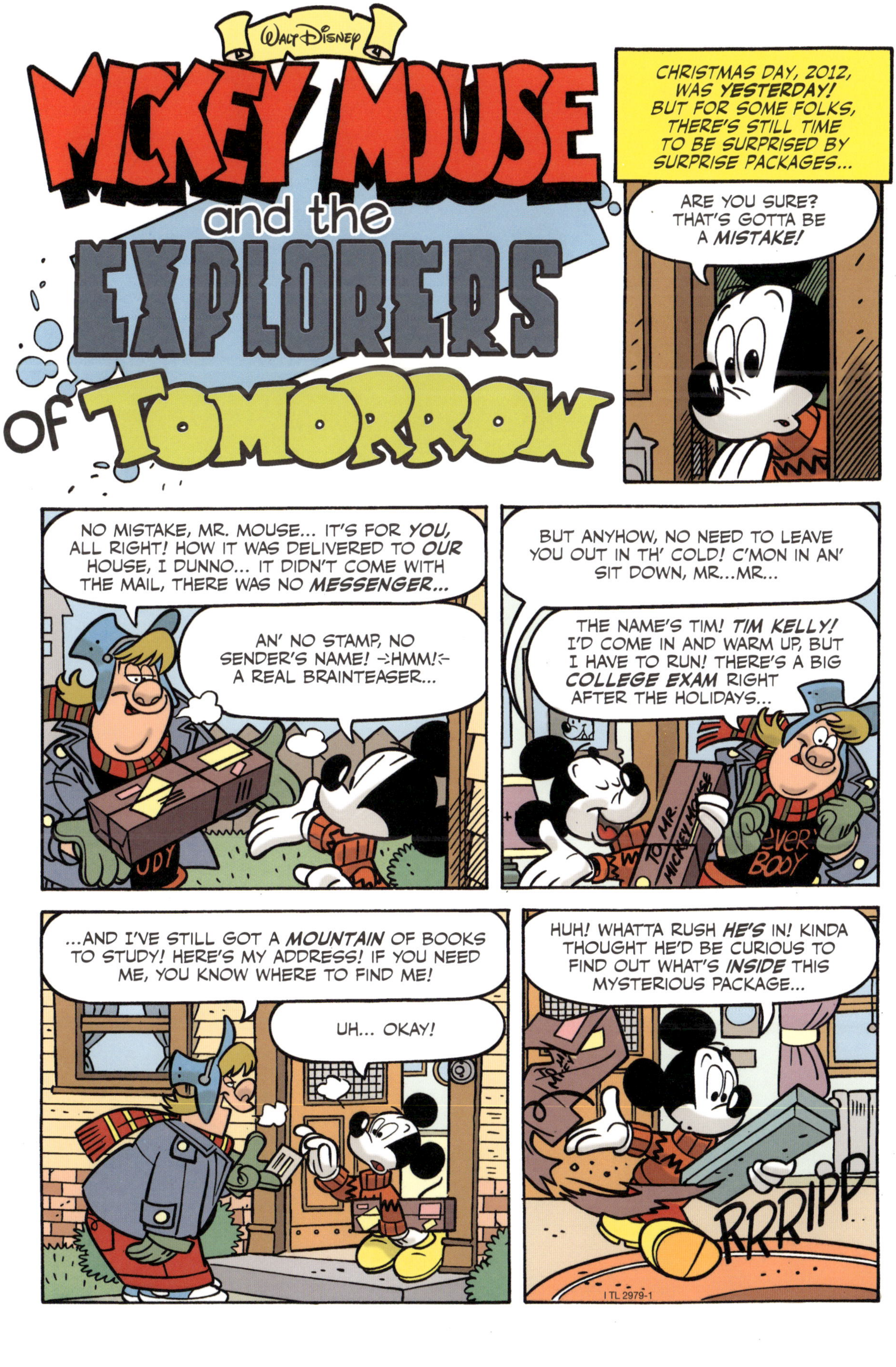
WALT DISNEY
MICKEY MOUSE and the EXPLORERS of TOMORROW
CHRISTMAS DAY, 2012, WAS YESTERDAY! BUT FOR SOME FOLKS, THERE'S STILL TIME TO BE SURPRISED BY SURPRISE PACKAGES...
ARE YOU SURE? THAT'S GOTTA BE A MISTAKE!
NO MISTAKE, MR. MOUSE... IT'S FOR YOU, ALL RIGHT! HOW IT WAS DELIVERED TO OUR HOUSE, I DUNNO... IT DIDN'T COME WITH THE MAIL, THERE WAS NO MESSENGER...
AN' NO STAMP, NO SENDER'S NAME! HMM! A REAL BRAINTEASER...
BUT ANYHOW, NO NEED TO LEAVE YOU OUT IN TH' COLD! C'MON IN AN' SIT DOWN, MR...MR...
THE NAME'S TIM! TIM KELLY! I'D COME IN AND WARM UP, BUT I HAVE TO RUN! THERE'S A BIG COLLEGE EXAM RIGHT AFTER THE HOLIDAYS...
TO MR. MICKEY MOUSE
EVERY BODY
...AND I'VE STILL GOT A MOUNTAIN OF BOOKS TO STUDY! HERE'S MY ADDRESS! IF YOU NEED ME, YOU KNOW WHERE TO FIND ME!
UH... OKAY!
HUH! WHATTA RUSH HE'S IN! KINDA THOUGHT HE'D BE CURIOUS TO FIND OUT WHAT'S INSIDE THIS MYSTERIOUS PACKAGE...
RRRIPP
I TL 2979-1

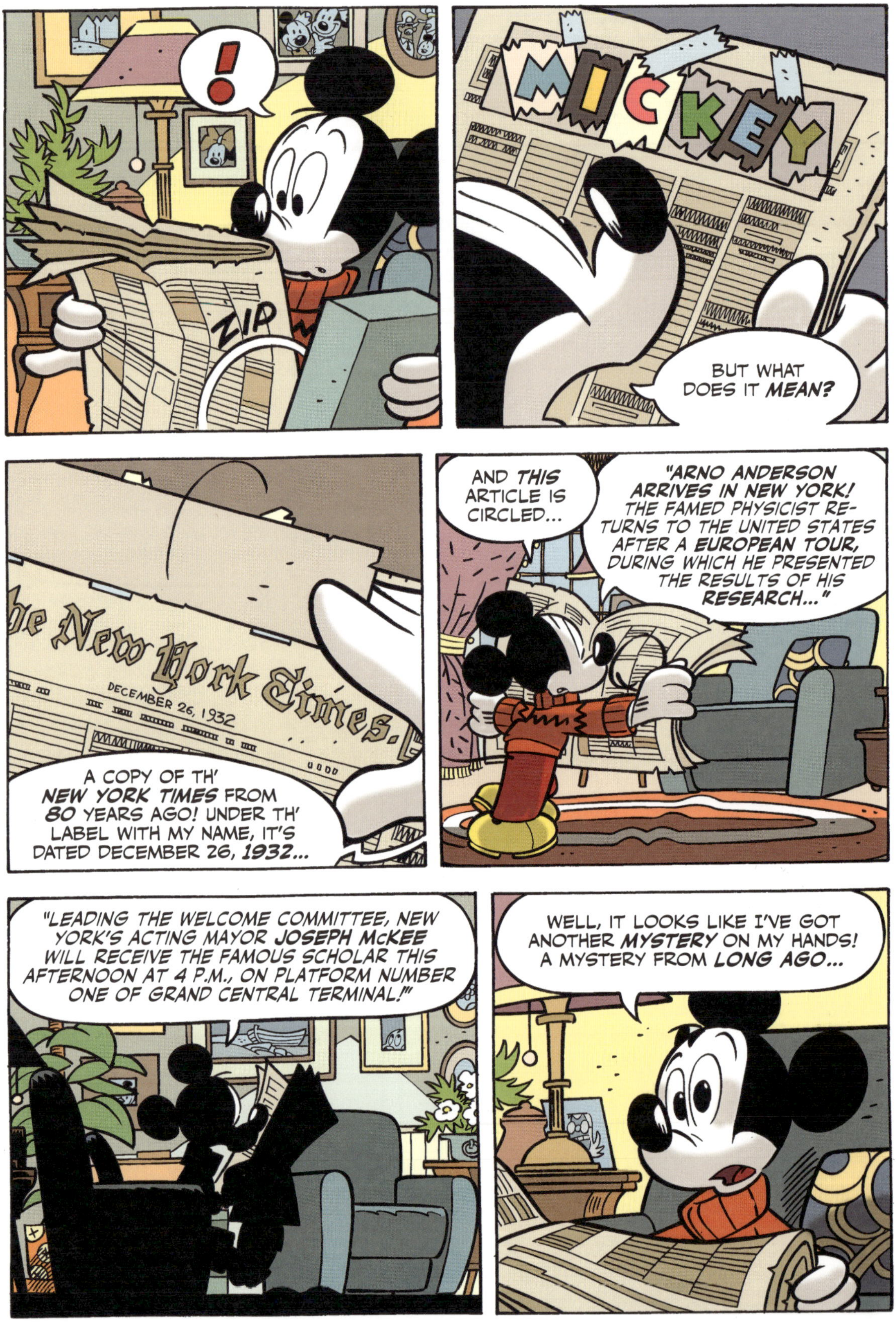
!
ZIP
MICKEY
BUT WHAT DOES IT MEAN?
The New York Times
DECEMBER 26, 1932
A COPY OF TH' NEW YORK TIMES FROM 80 YEARS AGO! UNDER TH' LABEL WITH MY NAME, IT'S DATED DECEMBER 26, 1932...
AND THIS ARTICLE IS CIRCLED...
"ARNO ANDERSON ARRIVES IN NEW YORK! THE FAMED PHYSICIST RETURNS TO THE UNITED STATES AFTER A EUROPEAN TOUR, DURING WHICH HE PRESENTED THE RESULTS OF HIS RESEARCH..."
"LEADING THE WELCOME COMMITTEE, NEW YORK'S ACTING MAYOR JOSEPH McKEE WILL RECEIVE THE FAMOUS SCHOLAR THIS AFTERNOON AT 4 P.M., ON PLATFORM NUMBER ONE OF GRAND CENTRAL TERMINAL!"
WELL, IT LOOKS LIKE I'VE GOT ANOTHER MYSTERY ON MY HANDS! A MYSTERY FROM LONG AGO...

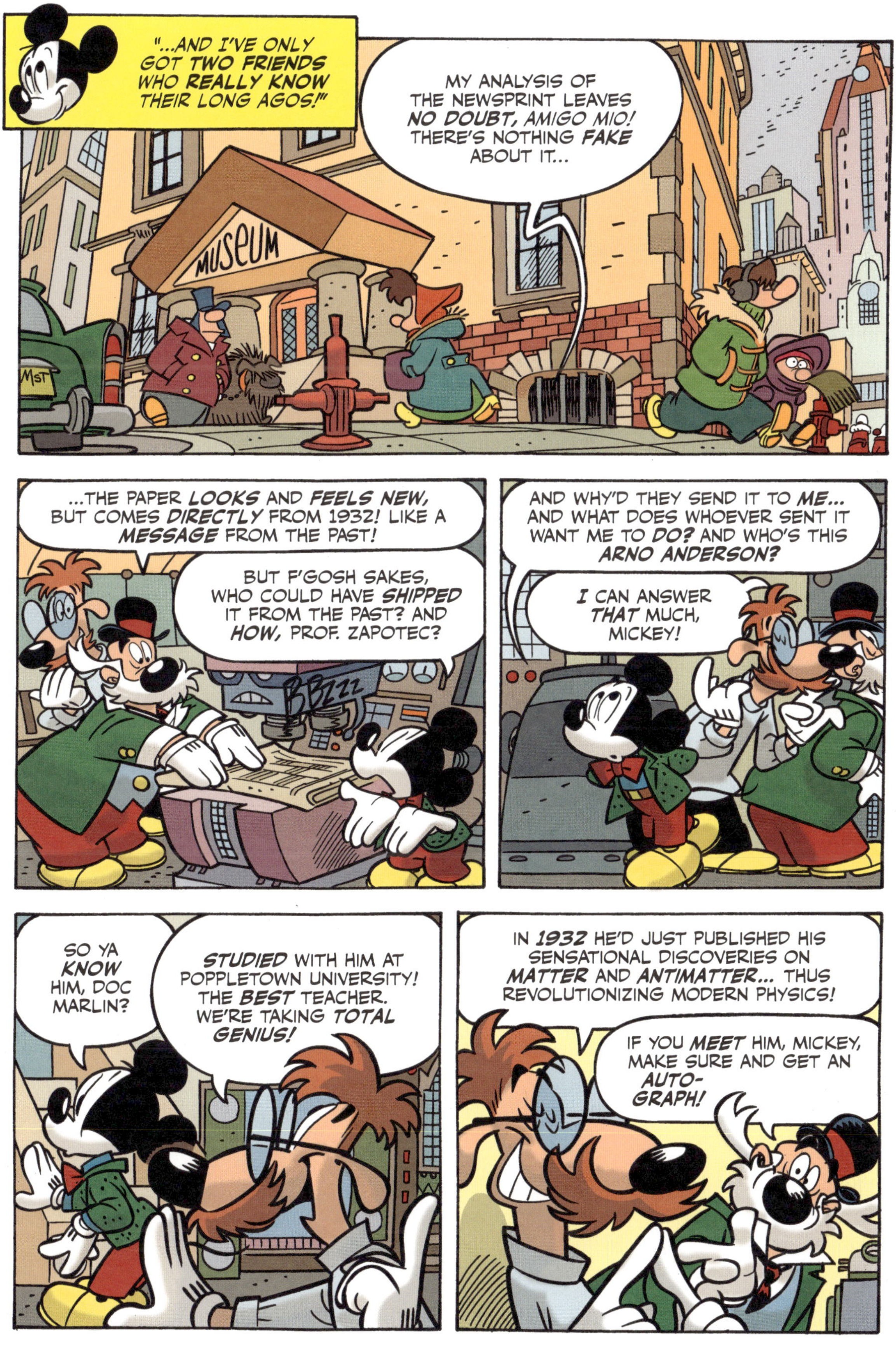
"...AND I'VE ONLY GOT TWO FRIENDS WHO REALLY KNOW THEIR LONG AGOS!"
MY ANALYSIS OF THE NEWSPRINT LEAVES NO DOUBT, AMIGO MIO! THERE'S NOTHING FAKE ABOUT IT...
MUSEUM
...THE PAPER LOOKS AND FEELS NEW, BUT COMES DIRECTLY FROM 1932! LIKE A MESSAGE FROM THE PAST!
BUT F'GOSH SAKES, WHO COULD HAVE SHIPPED IT FROM THE PAST? AND HOW, PROF. ZAPOTEC?
BZZZ
AND WHY'D THEY SEND IT TO ME... AND WHAT DOES WHOEVER SENT IT WANT ME TO DO? AND WHO'S THIS ARNO ANDERSON?
I CAN ANSWER THAT MUCH, MICKEY!
SO YA KNOW HIM, DOC MARLIN?
STUDIED WITH HIM AT POPPLETOWN UNIVERSITY! THE BEST TEACHER. WE'RE TAKING TOTAL GENIUS!
IN 1932 HE'D JUST PUBLISHED HIS SENSATIONAL DISCOVERIES ON MATTER AND ANTIMATTER... THUS REVOLUTIONIZING MODERN PHYSICS!
IF YOU MEET HIM, MICKEY, MAKE SURE AND GET AN AUTO-GRAPH!

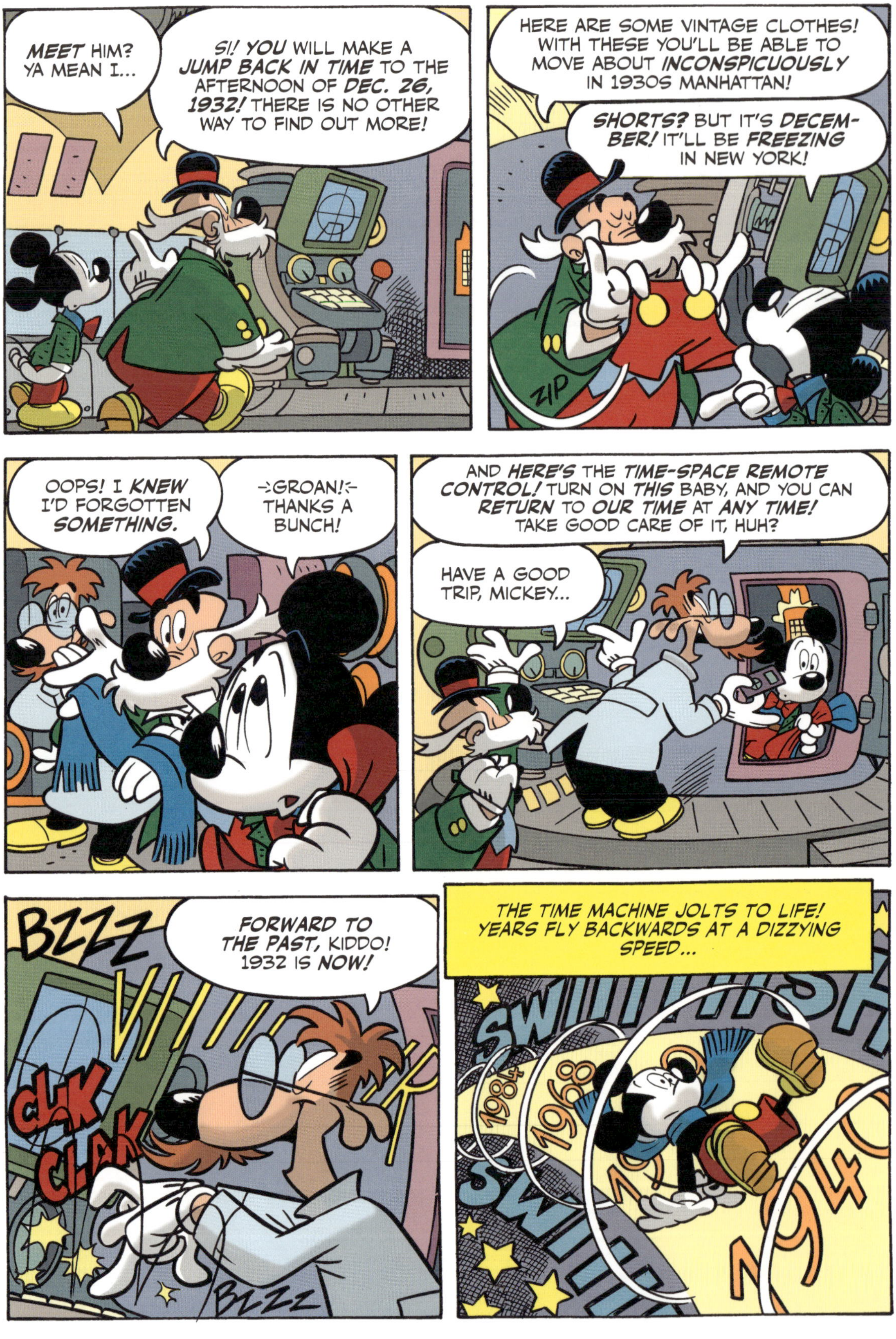
MEET HIM? YA MEAN I...
SI! YOU WILL MAKE A JUMP BACK IN TIME TO THE AFTERNOON OF DEC. 26, 1932! THERE IS NO OTHER WAY TO FIND OUT MORE!
HERE ARE SOME VINTAGE CLOTHES! WITH THESE YOU'LL BE ABLE TO MOVE ABOUT INCONSPICUOUSLY IN 1930S MANHATTAN!
SHORTS? BUT IT'S DECEMBER! IT'LL BE FREEZING IN NEW YORK!
ZIP
OOPS! I KNEW I'D FORGOTTEN SOMETHING.
-GROAN!- THANKS A BUNCH!
AND HERE'S THE TIME-SPACE REMOTE CONTROL! TURN ON THIS BABY, AND YOU CAN RETURN TO OUR TIME AT ANY TIME! TAKE GOOD CARE OF IT, HUH?
HAVE A GOOD TRIP, MICKEY...
BZZZ
FORWARD TO THE PAST, KIDDO! 1932 IS NOW!
CLIK CLAK
BZZZ
THE TIME MACHINE JOLTS TO LIFE! YEARS FLY BACKWARDS AT A DIZZYING SPEED...
SWIIIISH
1984
1968
1940
SWIIII

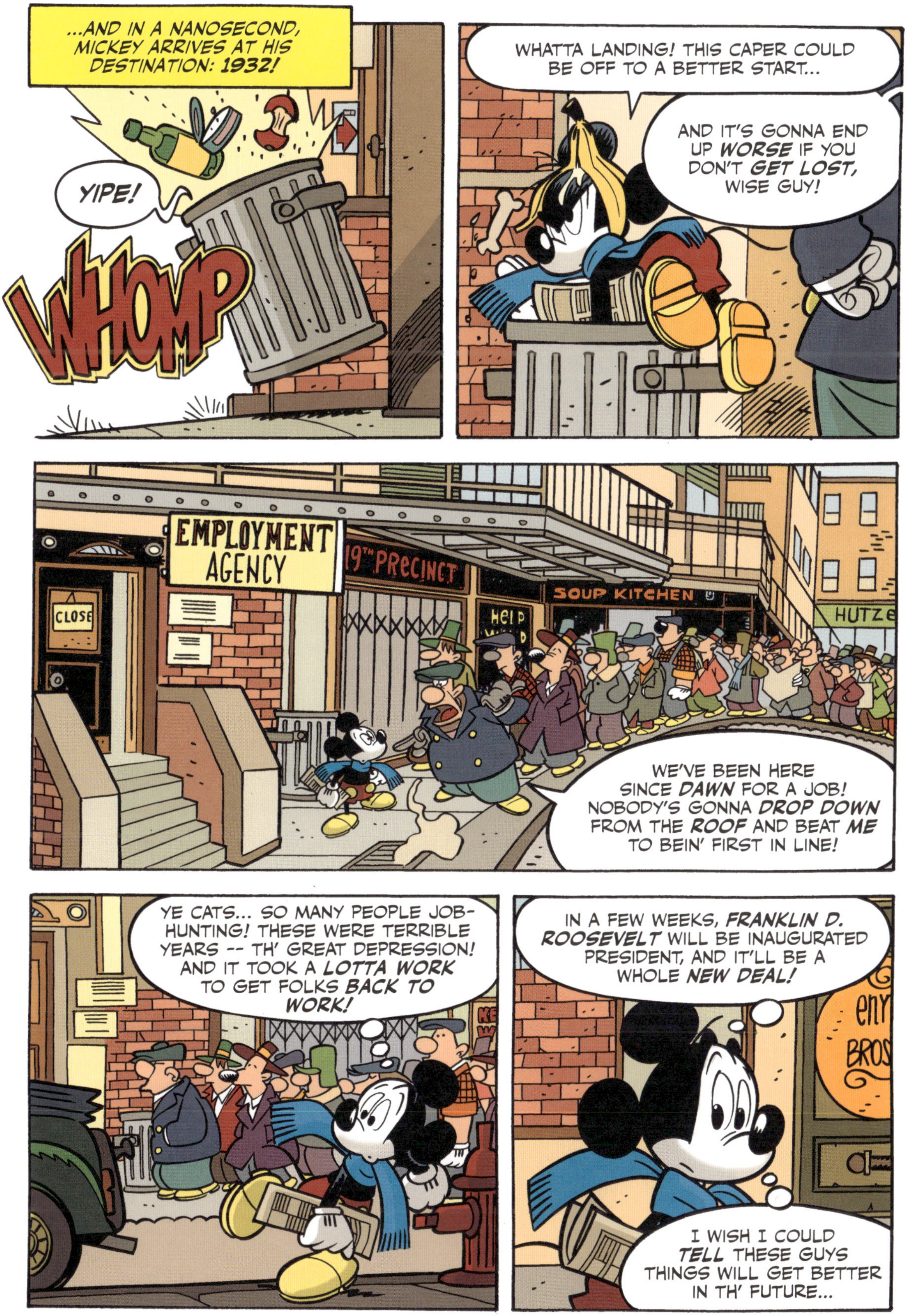
...AND IN A NANOSECOND, MICKEY ARRIVES AT HIS DESTINATION: 1932!
YIPE!
WHOMP
WHATTA LANDING! THIS CAPER COULD BE OFF TO A BETTER START...
AND IT'S GONNA END UP WORSE IF YOU DON'T GET LOST, WISE GUY!
EMPLOYMENT AGENCY
CLOSE
19TH PRECINCT
SOUP KITCHEN
HUTZE
WE'VE BEEN HERE SINCE DAWN FOR A JOB! NOBODY'S GONNA DROP DOWN FROM THE ROOF AND BEAT ME TO BEIN' FIRST IN LINE!
YE CATS... SO MANY PEOPLE JOB-HUNTING! THESE WERE TERRIBLE YEARS -- TH' GREAT DEPRESSION! AND IT TOOK A LOTTA WORK TO GET FOLKS BACK TO WORK!
IN A FEW WEEKS, FRANKLIN D. ROOSEVELT WILL BE INAUGURATED PRESIDENT, AND IT'LL BE A WHOLE NEW DEAL!
I WISH I COULD TELL THESE GUYS THINGS WILL GET BETTER IN TH' FUTURE...

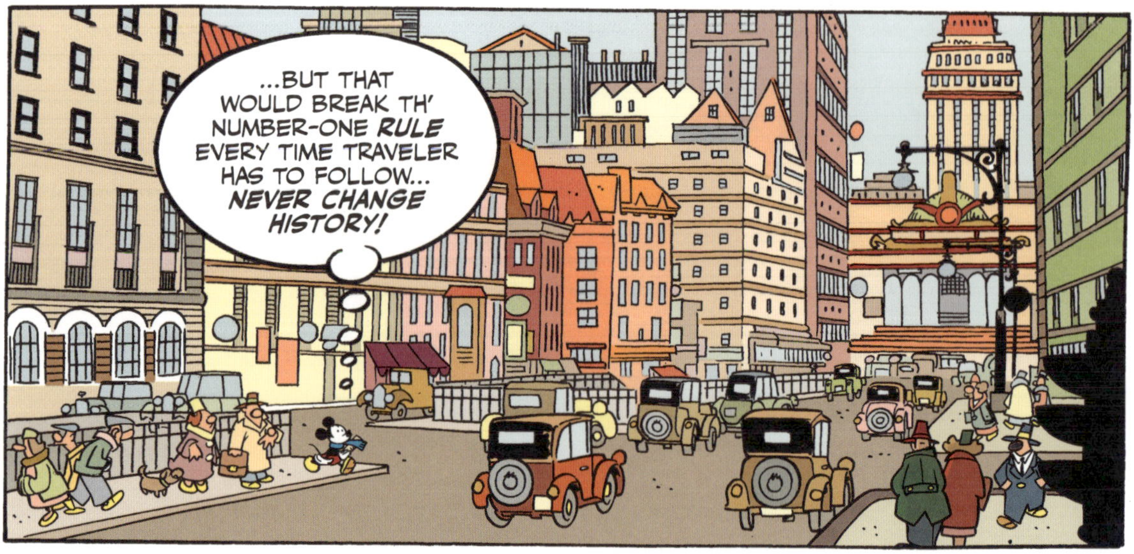
...BUT THAT WOULD BREAK TH' NUMBER-ONE RULE EVERY TIME TRAVELER HAS TO FOLLOW... NEVER CHANGE HISTORY!

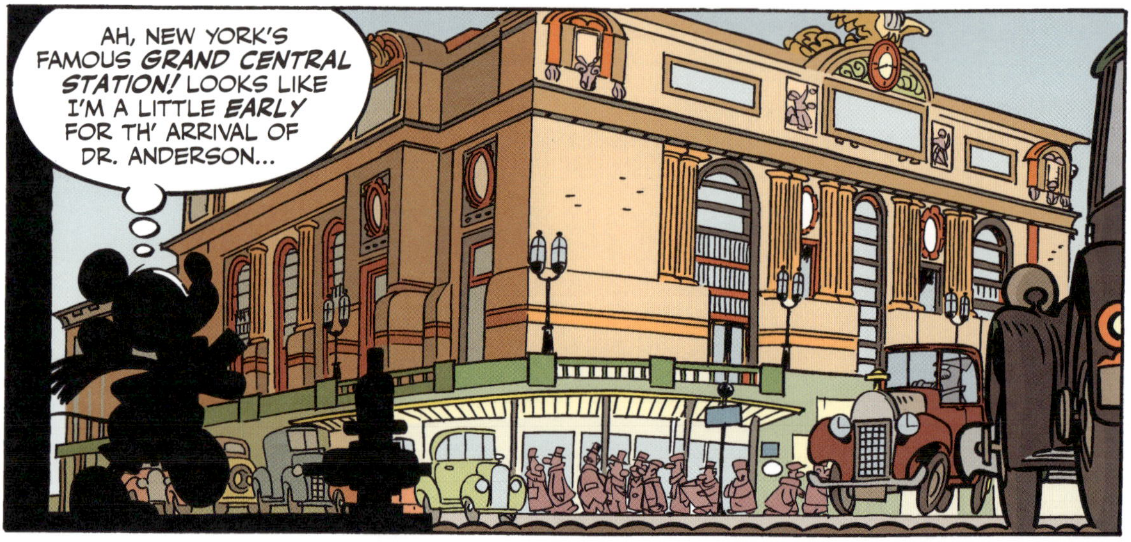
AH, NEW YORK'S FAMOUS GRAND CENTRAL STATION! LOOKS LIKE I'M A LITTLE EARLY FOR TH' ARRIVAL OF DR. ANDERSON...

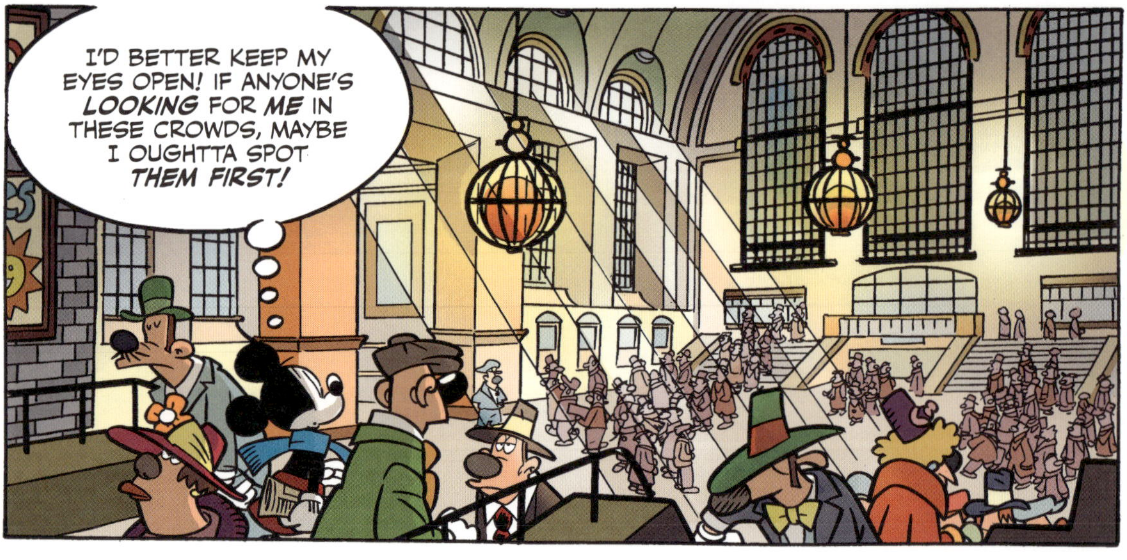
I'D BETTER KEEP MY EYES OPEN! IF ANYONE'S LOOKING FOR ME IN THESE CROWDS, MAYBE I OUGHTTA SPOT THEM FIRST!

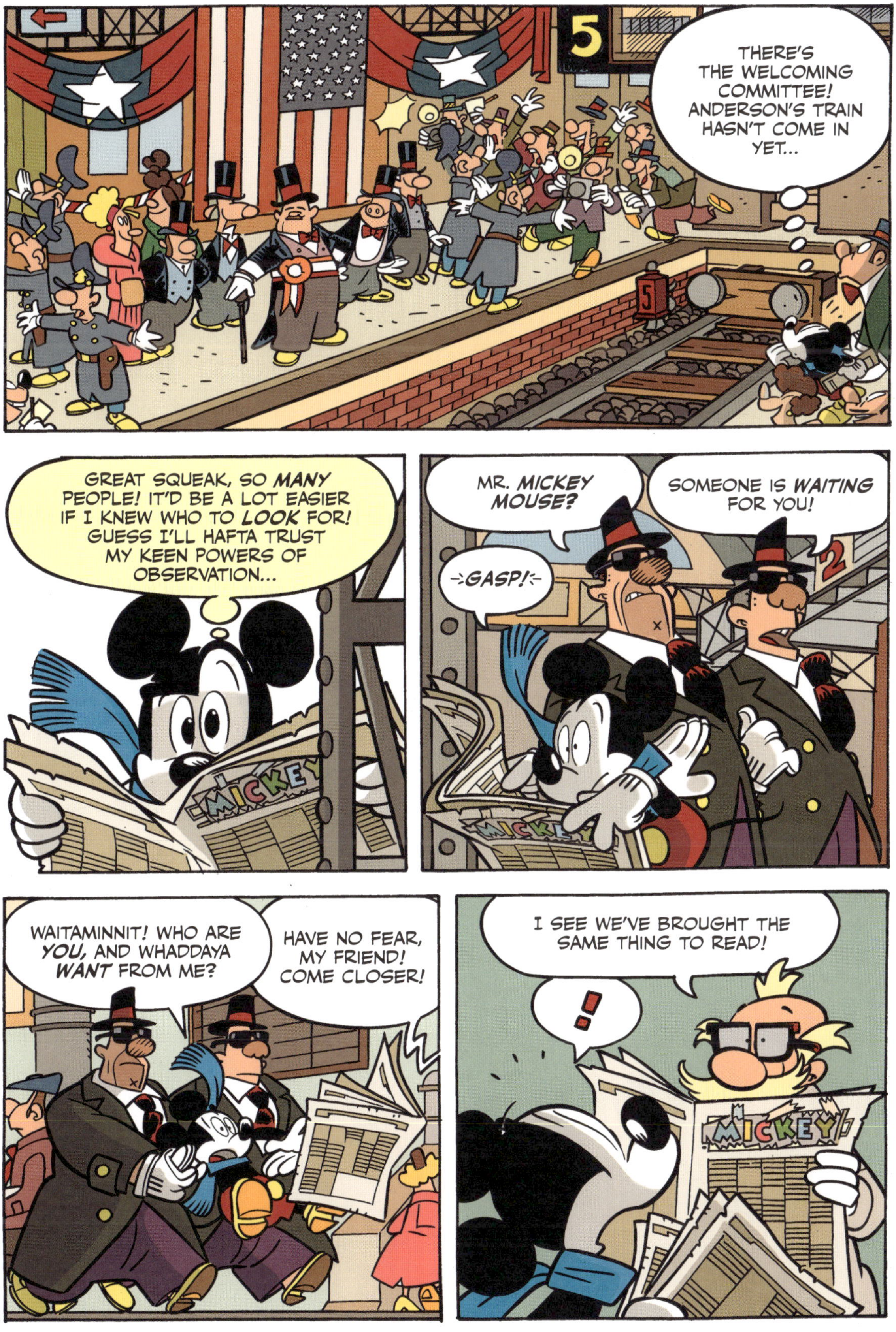
5
THERE'S THE WELCOMING COMMITTEE! ANDERSON'S TRAIN HASN'T COME IN YET...
GREAT SQUEAK, SO MANY PEOPLE! IT'D BE A LOT EASIER IF I KNEW WHO TO LOOK FOR! GUESS I'LL HAFTA TRUST MY KEEN POWERS OF OBSERVATION...
MICKEY
MR. MICKEY MOUSE?
SOMEONE IS WAITING FOR YOU!
-GASP!-
MICKEY
WAITAMINNIT! WHO ARE YOU, AND WHADDAYA WANT FROM ME?
HAVE NO FEAR, MY FRIEND! COME CLOSER!
I SEE WE'VE BROUGHT THE SAME THING TO READ!
!
MICKEY

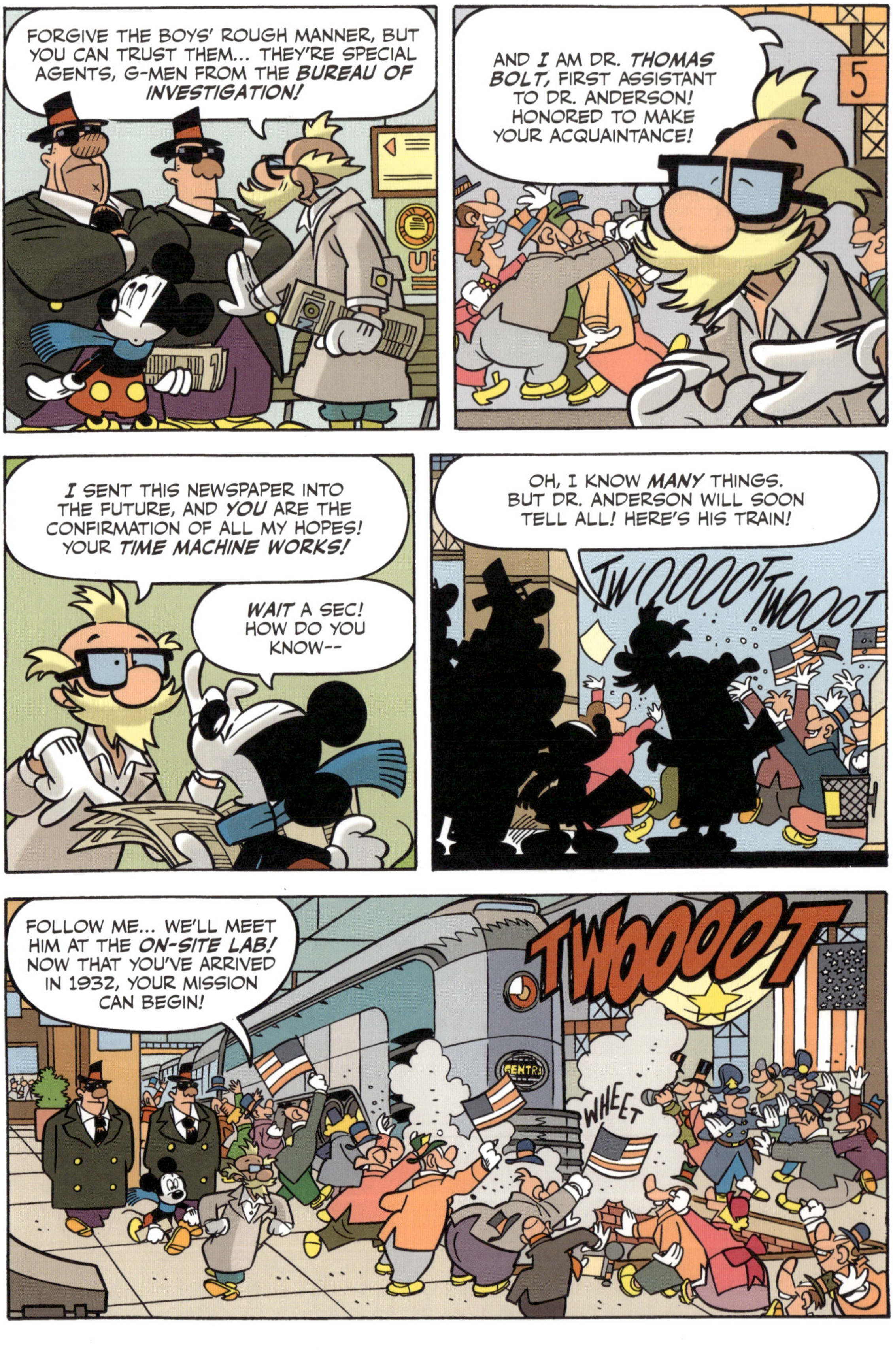
FORGIVE THE BOYS' ROUGH MANNER, BUT YOU CAN TRUST THEM... THEY'RE SPECIAL AGENTS, G-MEN FROM THE BUREAU OF INVESTIGATION!
AND I AM DR. THOMAS BOLT, FIRST ASSISTANT TO DR. ANDERSON! HONORED TO MAKE YOUR ACQUAINTANCE!
5
I SENT THIS NEWSPAPER INTO THE FUTURE, AND YOU ARE THE CONFIRMATION OF ALL MY HOPES! YOUR TIME MACHINE WORKS!
WAIT A SEC! HOW DO YOU KNOW--
OH, I KNOW MANY THINGS. BUT DR. ANDERSON WILL SOON TELL ALL! HERE'S HIS TRAIN!
TWOOOOT TWOOOT
FOLLOW ME... WE'LL MEET HIM AT THE ON-SITE LAB! NOW THAT YOU'VE ARRIVED IN 1932, YOUR MISSION CAN BEGIN!
TWOOOOT
WHEET

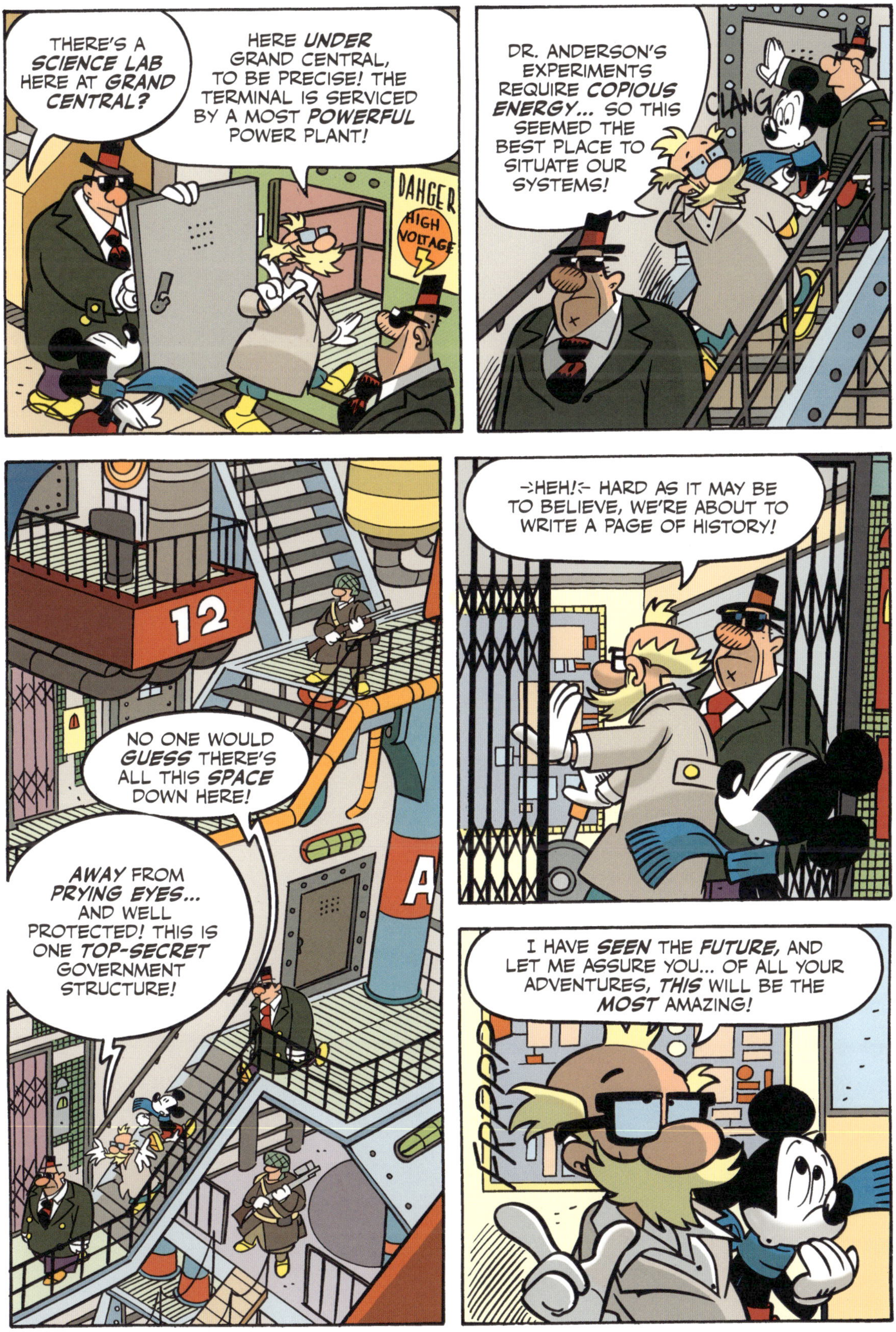
THERE'S A SCIENCE LAB HERE AT GRAND CENTRAL?
HERE UNDER GRAND CENTRAL, TO BE PRECISE! THE TERMINAL IS SERVICED BY A MOST POWERFUL POWER PLANT!
DANGER
HIGH VOLTAGE
DR. ANDERSON'S EXPERIMENTS REQUIRE COPIOUS ENERGY... SO THIS SEEMED THE BEST PLACE TO SITUATE OUR SYSTEMS!
CLANG
12
NO ONE WOULD GUESS THERE'S ALL THIS SPACE DOWN HERE!
AWAY FROM PRYING EYES... AND WELL PROTECTED! THIS IS ONE TOP-SECRET GOVERNMENT STRUCTURE!
A
–HEH!– HARD AS IT MAY BE TO BELIEVE, WE'RE ABOUT TO WRITE A PAGE OF HISTORY!
I HAVE SEEN THE FUTURE, AND LET ME ASSURE YOU... OF ALL YOUR ADVENTURES, THIS WILL BE THE MOST AMAZING!
FRRRR

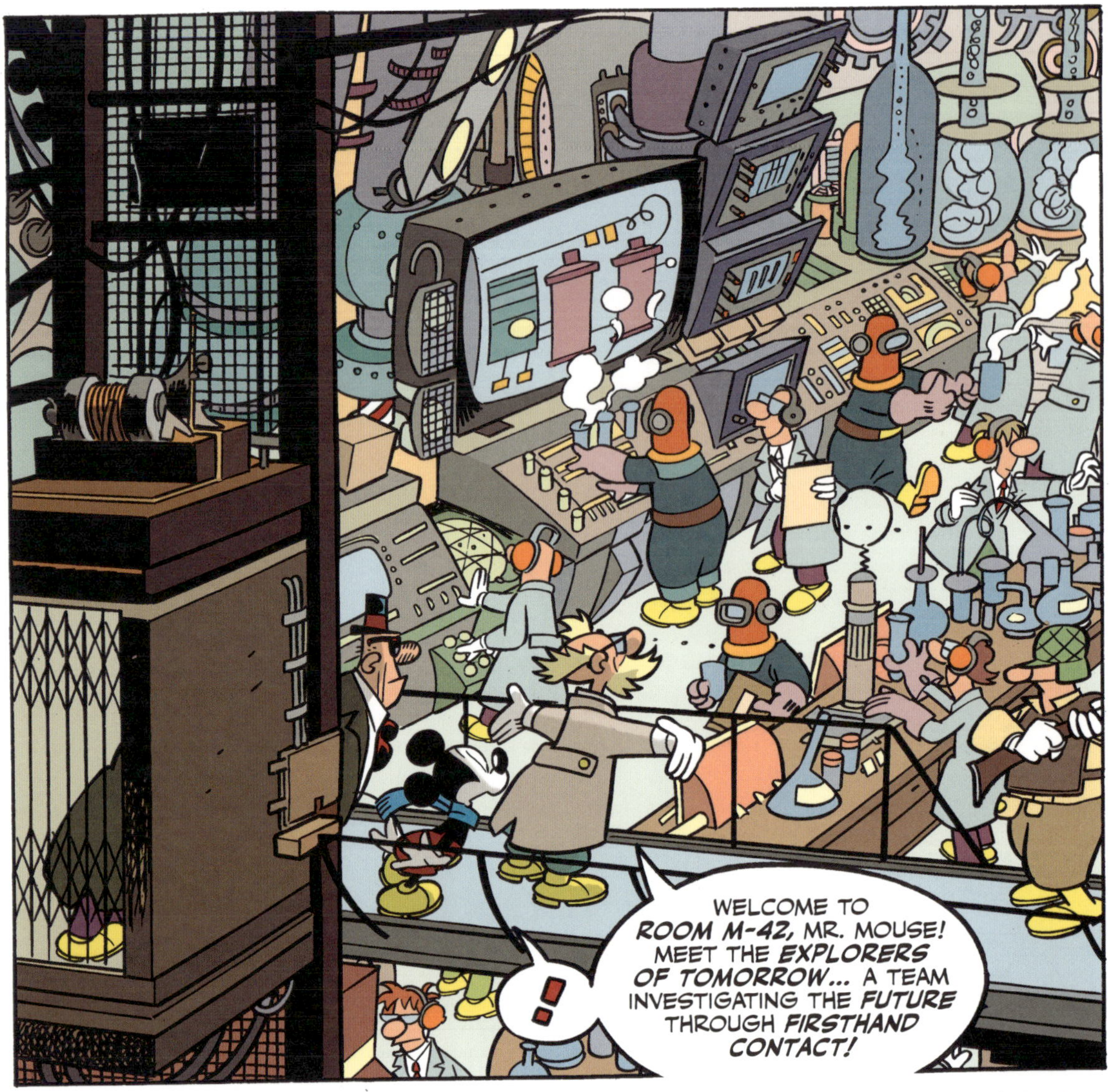
!
WELCOME TO ROOM M-42, MR. MOUSE! MEET THE EXPLORERS OF TOMORROW... A TEAM INVESTIGATING THE FUTURE THROUGH FIRSTHAND CONTACT!

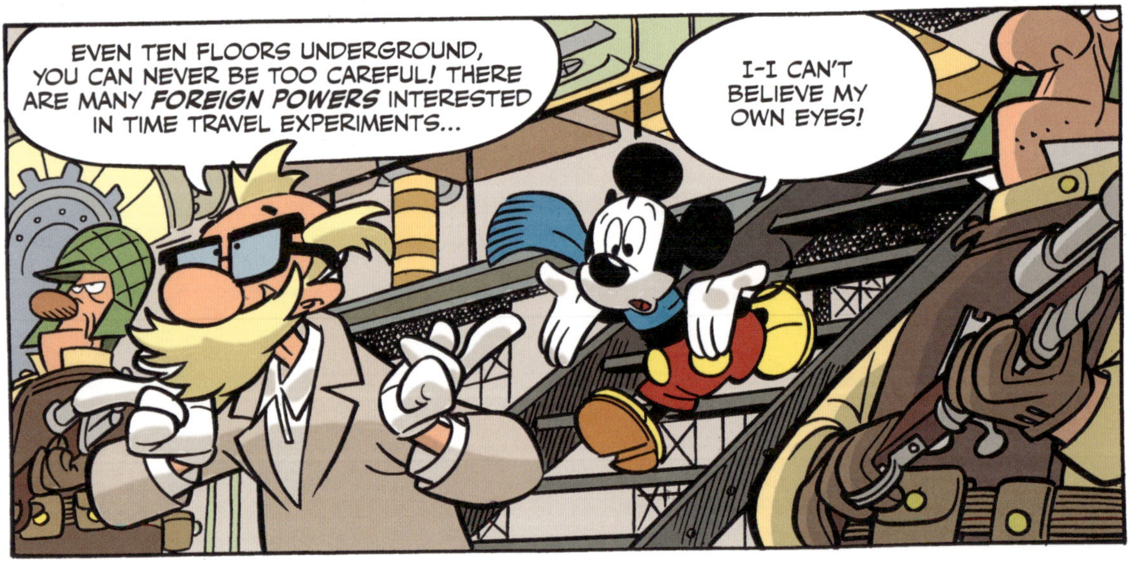
EVEN TEN FLOORS UNDERGROUND, YOU CAN NEVER BE TOO CAREFUL! THERE ARE MANY FOREIGN POWERS INTERESTED IN TIME TRAVEL EXPERIMENTS...
I-I CAN'T BELIEVE MY OWN EYES!

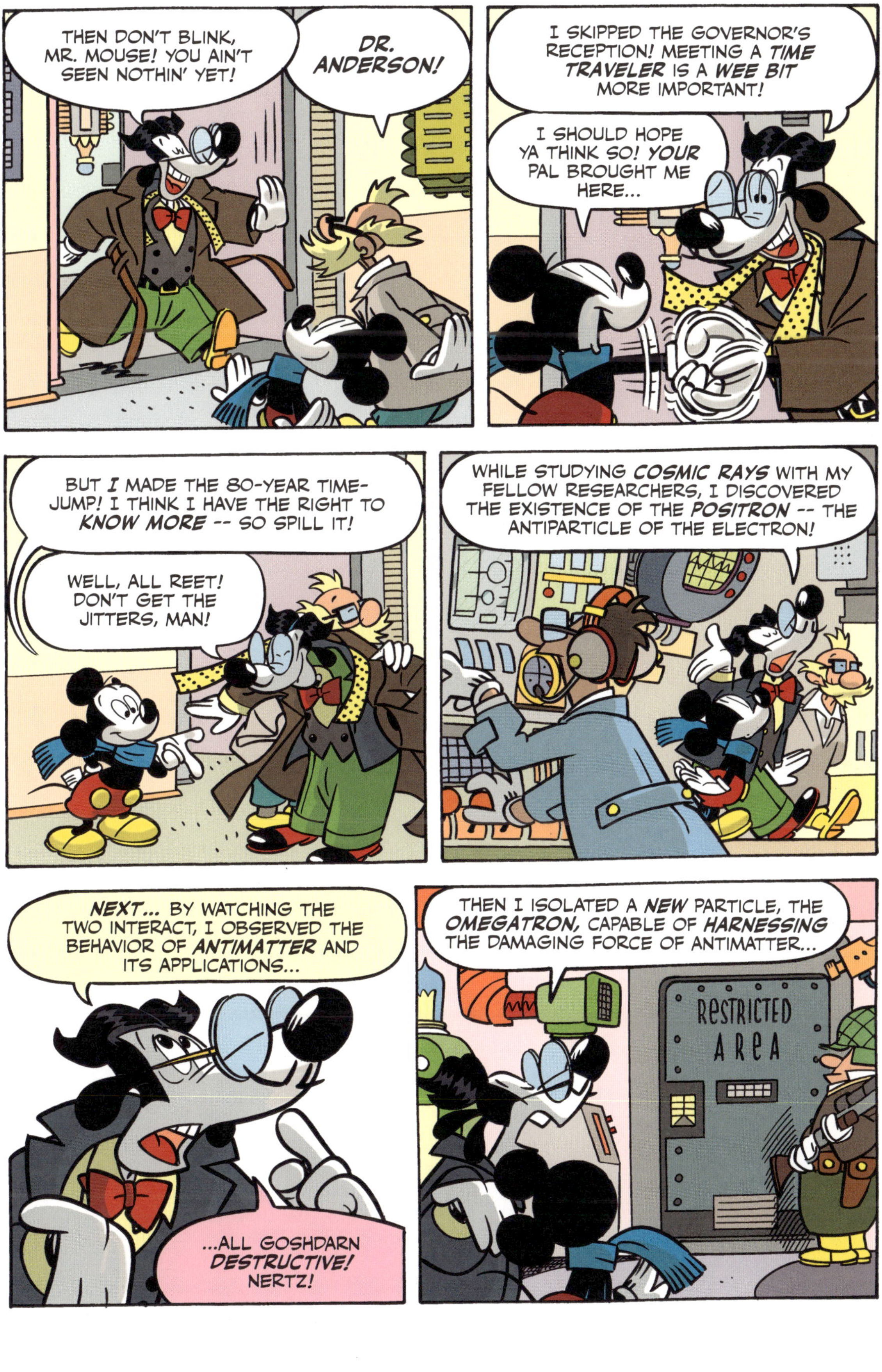
THEN DON'T BLINK, MR. MOUSE! YOU AIN'T SEEN NOTHIN' YET!
DR. ANDERSON!
I SKIPPED THE GOVERNOR'S RECEPTION! MEETING A TIME TRAVELER IS A WEE BIT MORE IMPORTANT!
I SHOULD HOPE YA THINK SO! YOUR PAL BROUGHT ME HERE...
BUT I MADE THE 80-YEAR TIME-JUMP! I THINK I HAVE THE RIGHT TO KNOW MORE -- SO SPILL IT!
WELL, ALL REET! DON'T GET THE JITTERS, MAN!
WHILE STUDYING COSMIC RAYS WITH MY FELLOW RESEARCHERS, I DISCOVERED THE EXISTENCE OF THE POSITRON -- THE ANTIPARTICLE OF THE ELECTRON!
NEXT... BY WATCHING THE TWO INTERACT, I OBSERVED THE BEHAVIOR OF ANTIMATTER AND ITS APPLICATIONS...
...ALL GOSHDARN DESTRUCTIVE! NERTZ!
THEN I ISOLATED A NEW PARTICLE, THE OMEGATRON, CAPABLE OF HARNESSING THE DAMAGING FORCE OF ANTIMATTER...
RESTRICTED AREA

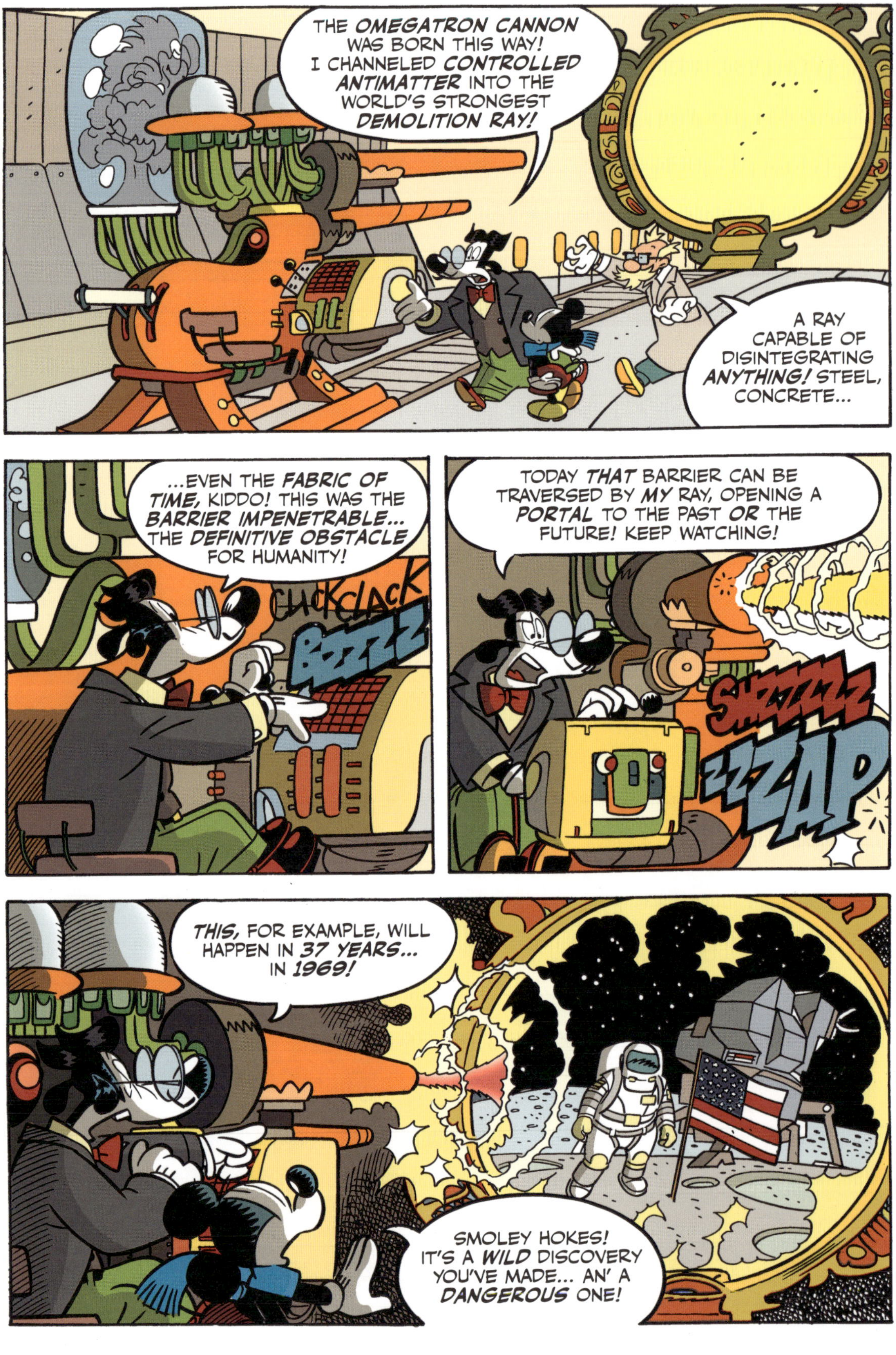
THE OMEGATRON CANNON WAS BORN THIS WAY! I CHANNELED CONTROLLED ANTIMATTER INTO THE WORLD'S STRONGEST DEMOLITION RAY!
A RAY CAPABLE OF DISINTEGRATING ANYTHING! STEEL, CONCRETE...
...EVEN THE FABRIC OF TIME, KIDDO! THIS WAS THE BARRIER IMPENETRABLE... THE DEFINITIVE OBSTACLE FOR HUMANITY!
CLICKCLACK
BZZZZ
TODAY THAT BARRIER CAN BE TRAVERSED BY MY RAY, OPENING A PORTAL TO THE PAST OR THE FUTURE! KEEP WATCHING!
SHZZZZZ
ZZZAP
THIS, FOR EXAMPLE, WILL HAPPEN IN 37 YEARS... IN 1969!
SMOLEY HOKES! IT'S A WILD DISCOVERY YOU'VE MADE... AN' A DANGEROUS ONE!

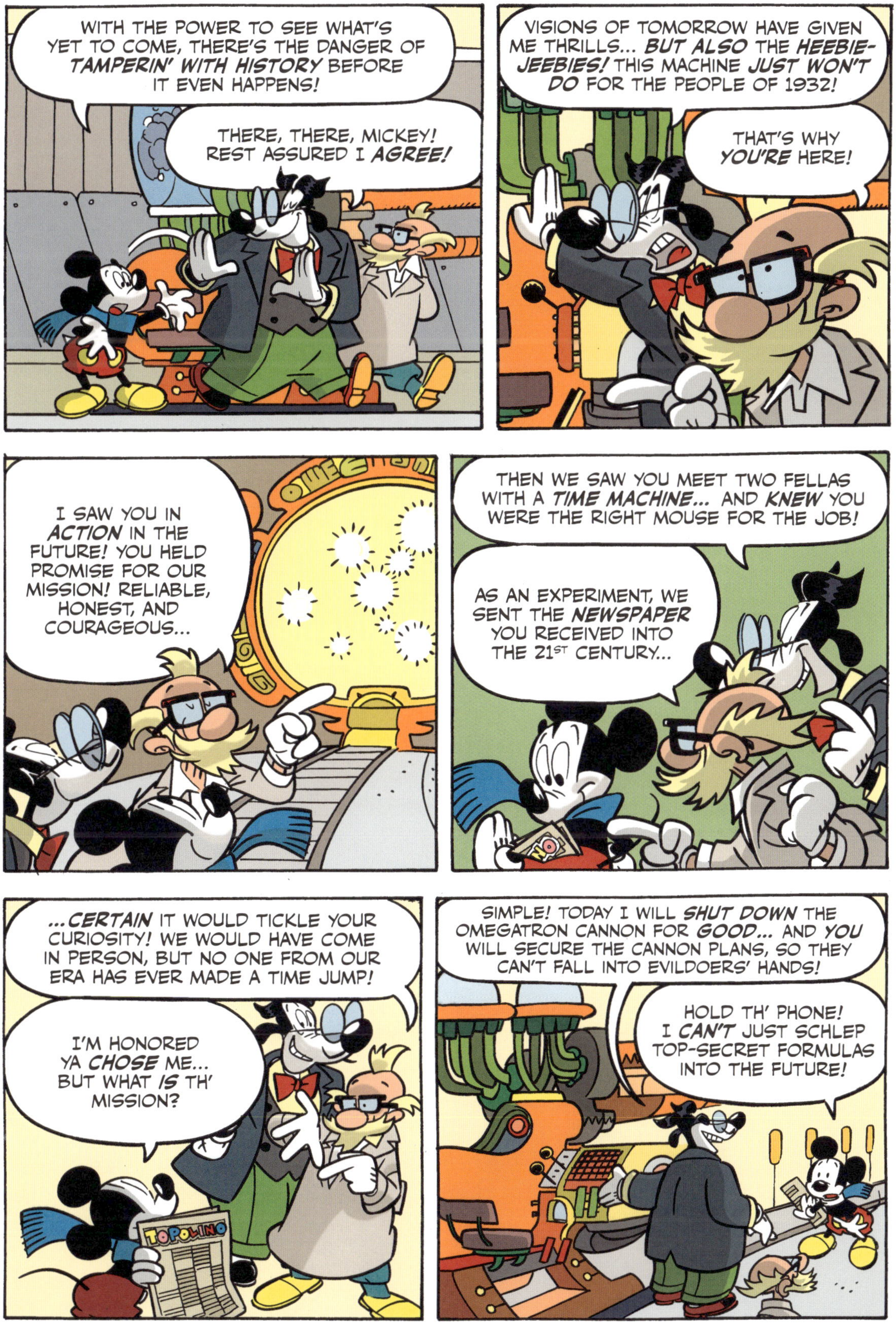
WITH THE POWER TO SEE WHAT'S YET TO COME, THERE'S THE DANGER OF TAMPERIN' WITH HISTORY BEFORE IT EVEN HAPPENS!
THERE, THERE, MICKEY! REST ASSURED I AGREE!
VISIONS OF TOMORROW HAVE GIVEN ME THRILLS... BUT ALSO THE HEEBIE-JEEBIES! THIS MACHINE JUST WON'T DO FOR THE PEOPLE OF 1932!
THAT'S WHY YOU'RE HERE!
I SAW YOU IN ACTION IN THE FUTURE! YOU HELD PROMISE FOR OUR MISSION! RELIABLE, HONEST, AND COURAGEOUS...
THEN WE SAW YOU MEET TWO FELLAS WITH A TIME MACHINE... AND KNEW YOU WERE THE RIGHT MOUSE FOR THE JOB!
AS AN EXPERIMENT, WE SENT THE NEWSPAPER YOU RECEIVED INTO THE 21ST CENTURY...
...CERTAIN IT WOULD TICKLE YOUR CURIOSITY! WE WOULD HAVE COME IN PERSON, BUT NO ONE FROM OUR ERA HAS EVER MADE A TIME JUMP!
I'M HONORED YA CHOSE ME... BUT WHAT IS TH' MISSION?
TOPOLINO
SIMPLE! TODAY I WILL SHUT DOWN THE OMEGATRON CANNON FOR GOOD... AND YOU WILL SECURE THE CANNON PLANS, SO THEY CAN'T FALL INTO EVILDOERS' HANDS!
HOLD TH' PHONE! I CAN'T JUST SCHLEP TOP-SECRET FORMULAS INTO THE FUTURE!

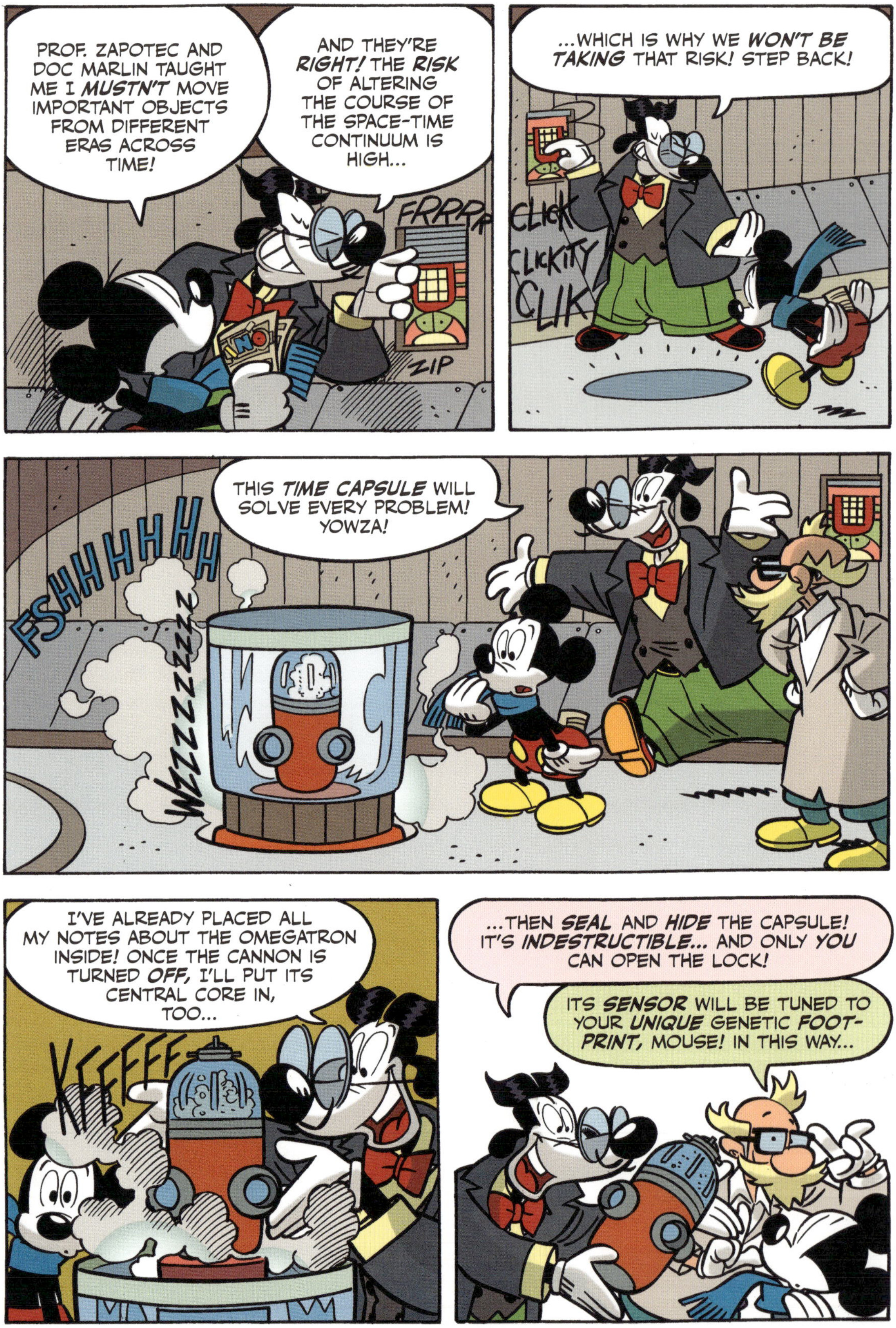
PROF. ZAPOTEC AND DOC MARLIN TAUGHT ME I MUSTN'T MOVE IMPORTANT OBJECTS FROM DIFFERENT ERAS ACROSS TIME!
AND THEY'RE RIGHT! THE RISK OF ALTERING THE COURSE OF THE SPACE-TIME CONTINUUM IS HIGH...
FRRRR
ZIP
...WHICH IS WHY WE WON'T BE TAKING THAT RISK! STEP BACK!
CLICK
CLICKITY
CLIK
THIS TIME CAPSULE WILL SOLVE EVERY PROBLEM! YOWZA!
FSHHHHHHH
WZZZZZZZZZ
I'VE ALREADY PLACED ALL MY NOTES ABOUT THE OMEGATRON INSIDE! ONCE THE CANNON IS TURNED OFF, I'LL PUT ITS CENTRAL CORE IN, TOO...
KFFFFF
...THEN SEAL AND HIDE THE CAPSULE! IT'S INDESTRUCTIBLE... AND ONLY YOU CAN OPEN THE LOCK!
ITS SENSOR WILL BE TUNED TO YOUR UNIQUE GENETIC FOOT-PRINT, MOUSE! IN THIS WAY...

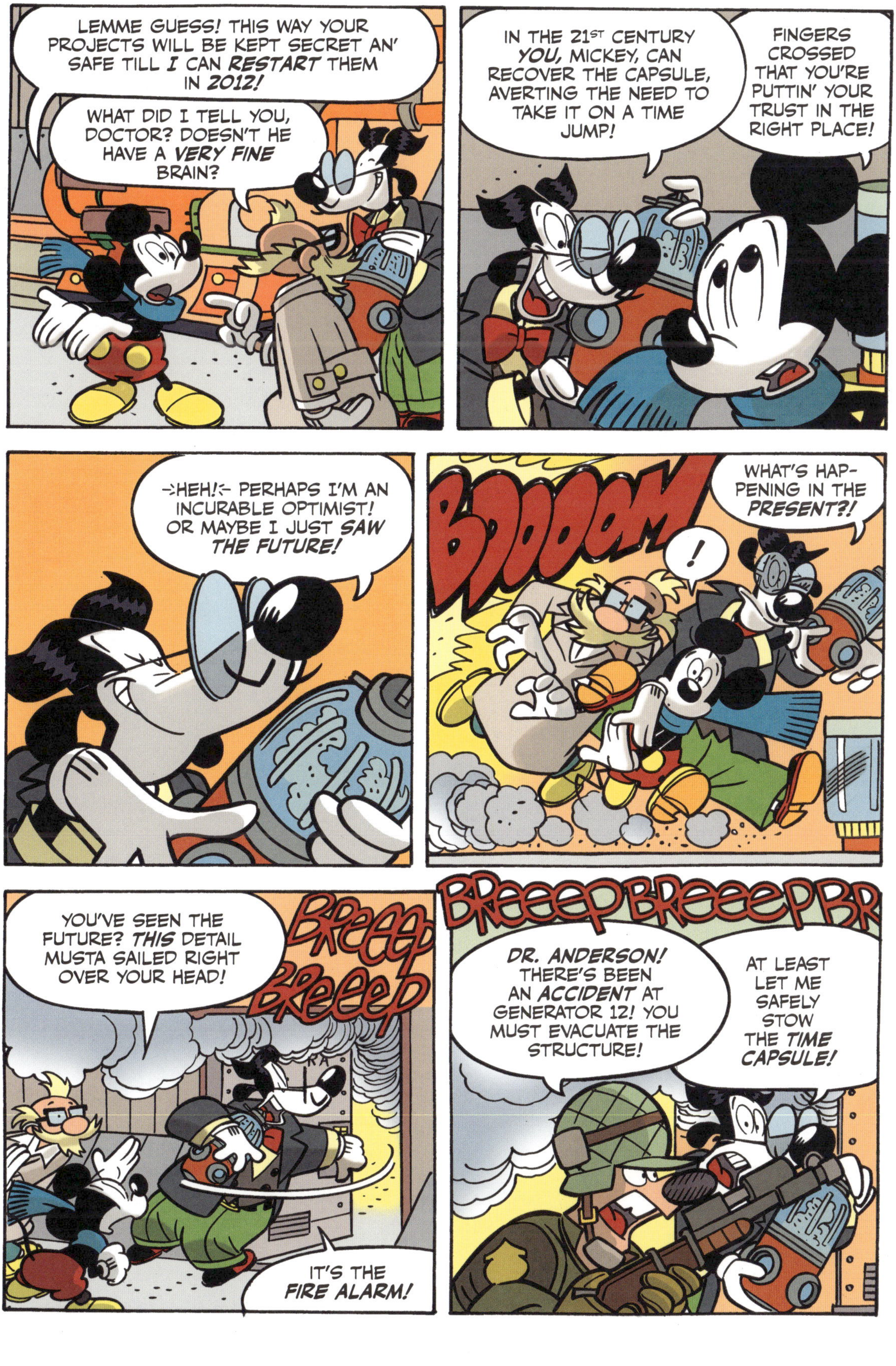
LEMME GUESS! THIS WAY YOUR PROJECTS WILL BE KEPT SECRET AN' SAFE TILL I CAN RESTART THEM IN 2012!
WHAT DID I TELL YOU, DOCTOR? DOESN'T HE HAVE A VERY FINE BRAIN?
IN THE 21ST CENTURY YOU, MICKEY, CAN RECOVER THE CAPSULE, AVERTING THE NEED TO TAKE IT ON A TIME JUMP!
FINGERS CROSSED THAT YOU'RE PUTTIN' YOUR TRUST IN THE RIGHT PLACE!
-HEH!- PERHAPS I'M AN INCURABLE OPTIMIST! OR MAYBE I JUST SAW THE FUTURE!
BOOOOM
!
WHAT'S HAP-PENING IN THE PRESENT?!
YOU'VE SEEN THE FUTURE? THIS DETAIL MUSTA SAILED RIGHT OVER YOUR HEAD!
BREEEP BREEEP
IT'S THE FIRE ALARM!
BREEEP BREEEEP BR
DR. ANDERSON! THERE'S BEEN AN ACCIDENT AT GENERATOR 12! YOU MUST EVACUATE THE STRUCTURE!
AT LEAST LET ME SAFELY STOW THE TIME CAPSULE!

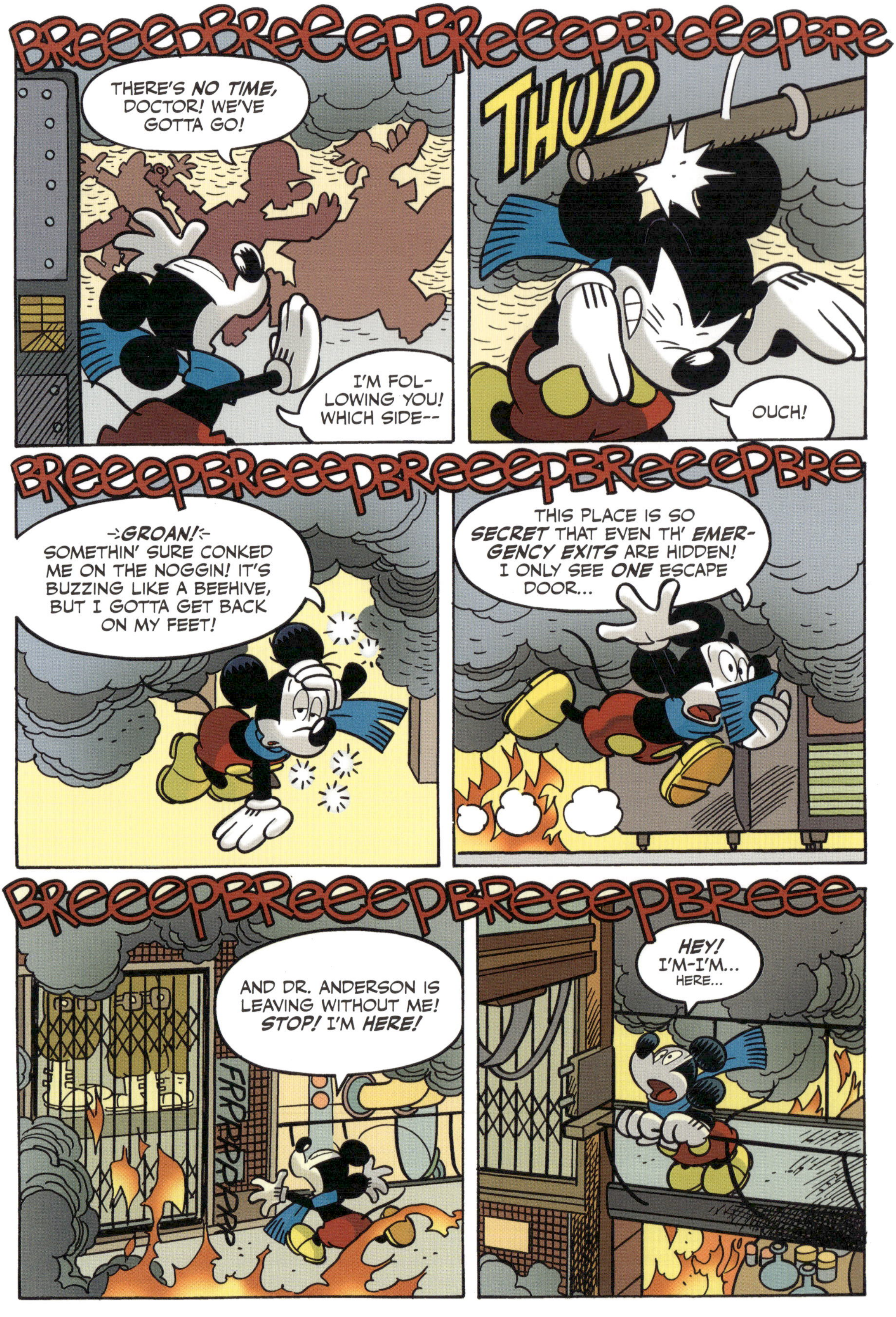

BREEEPBREEEPBREEEPBREEEPBRE
THERE'S *NO TIME,* DOCTOR! WE'VE GOTTA GO!
I'M FOL-LOWING YOU! WHICH SIDE--
THUD
OUCH!
BREEEPBREEEPBREEEPBREEEPBRE
-GROAN!- SOMETHIN' SURE CONKED ME ON THE NOGGIN! IT'S BUZZING LIKE A BEEHIVE, BUT I GOTTA GET BACK ON MY FEET!
THIS PLACE IS SO *SECRET* THAT EVEN TH' *EMER-GENCY EXITS* ARE HIDDEN! I ONLY SEE *ONE* ESCAPE DOOR...
BREEEPBREEEPBREEEPBREEE
AND DR. ANDERSON IS LEAVING WITHOUT ME! *STOP!* I'M *HERE!*
HEY! I'M-I'M... HERE...

WE MUST GO BACK IMMEDIATELY! MICKEY MOUSE IS STILL DOWN THERE!
A RECOVERY TEAM WILL BE DISPATCHED ONCE WE REACH THE UPPER LEVEL!
THAT MAY BE TOO LATE! WHY, OH, WHY DIDN'T THE FIREFIGHTING SYSTEM TURN ON?
COULDN'T TELL YOU, DR. BOLT! I JUST FOLLOW ORDERS!
-ULP!- WHAT'S HAPPENING?
IT'S COMING FROM THE SHAFT BELOW! STAND BACK, DOCTOR!
THUMP THUMP THUMP
YOU! OPEN THE HATCH SLOWLY... AND BE READY TO DISARM!
HEY! GO EASY WITH YOUR OWN WEAPONS...
MICKEY!
MY LUCKY SCARF JUST SAVED MY LIFE! YOU DON'T WANT TO RUIN IT WITH A FEW TOO MANY HOLES!

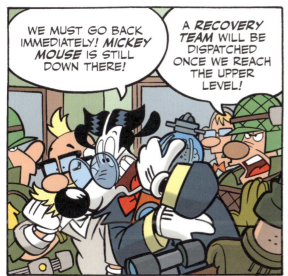

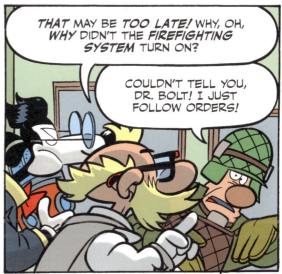

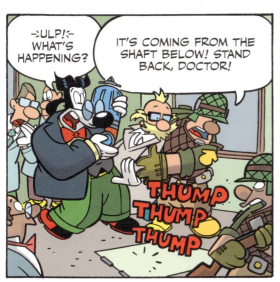

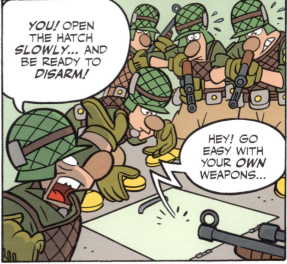

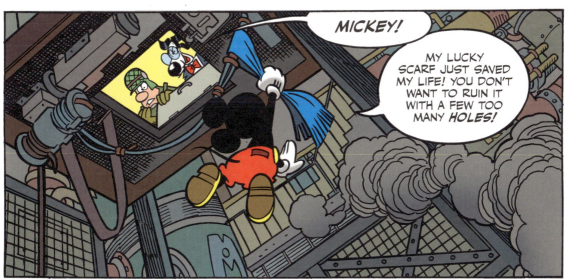

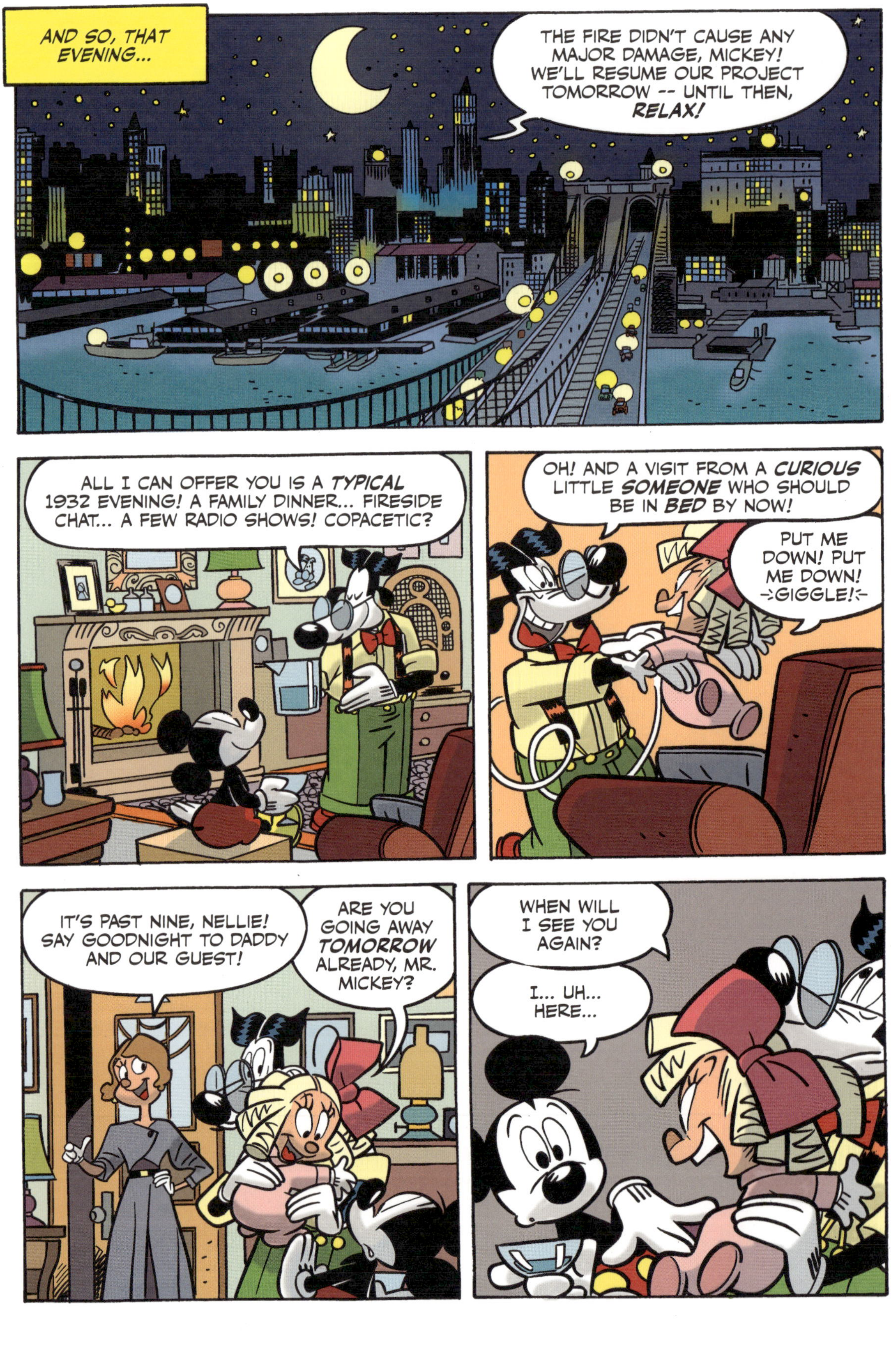
AND SO, THAT EVENING...
THE FIRE DIDN'T CAUSE ANY MAJOR DAMAGE, MICKEY! WE'LL RESUME OUR PROJECT TOMORROW -- UNTIL THEN, RELAX!
ALL I CAN OFFER YOU IS A TYPICAL 1932 EVENING! A FAMILY DINNER... FIRESIDE CHAT... A FEW RADIO SHOWS! COPACETIC?
OH! AND A VISIT FROM A CURIOUS LITTLE SOMEONE WHO SHOULD BE IN BED BY NOW!
PUT ME DOWN! PUT ME DOWN! GIGGLE!
IT'S PAST NINE, NELLIE! SAY GOODNIGHT TO DADDY AND OUR GUEST!
ARE YOU GOING AWAY TOMORROW ALREADY, MR. MICKEY?
WHEN WILL I SEE YOU AGAIN?
I... UH... HERE...

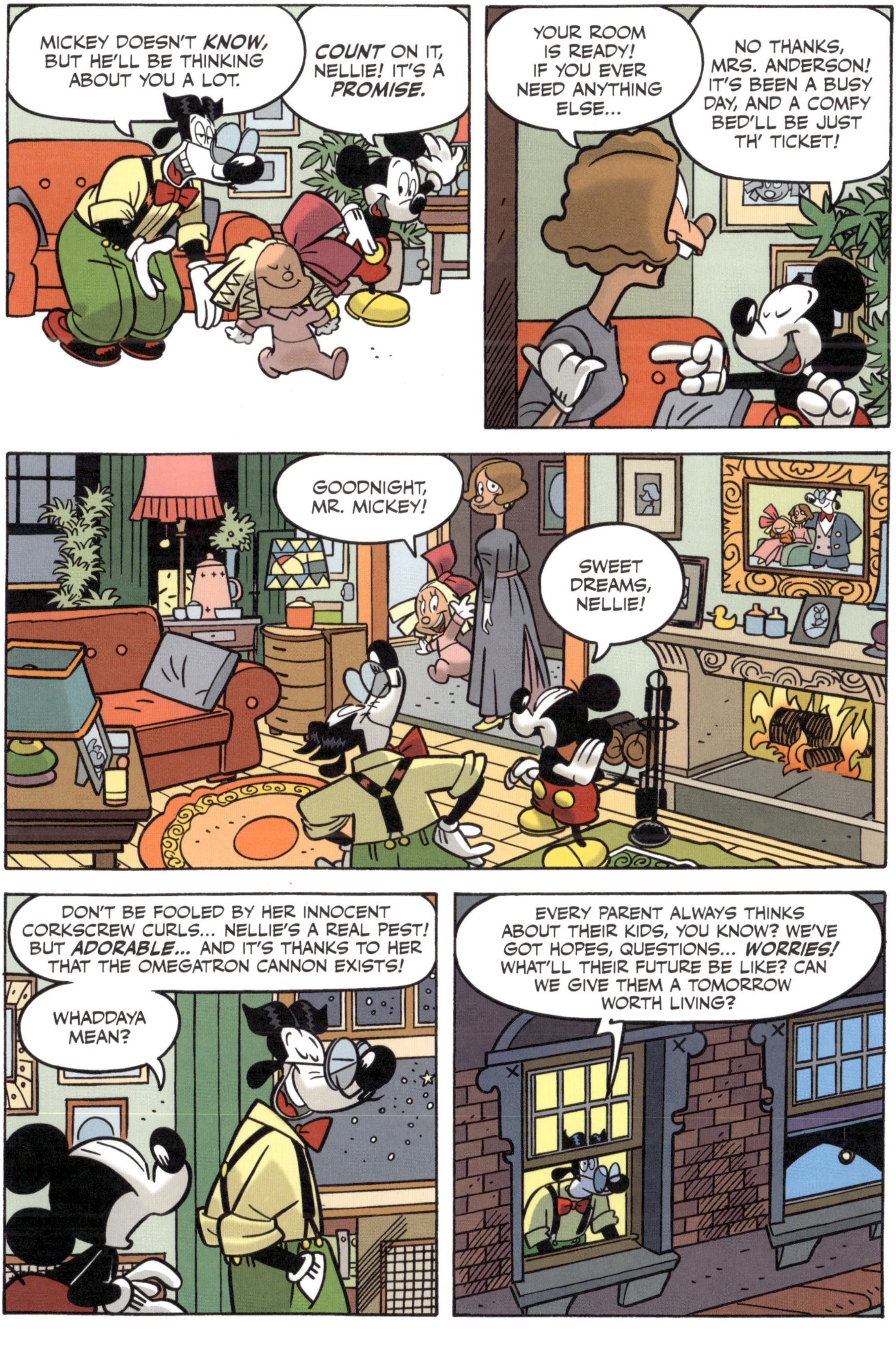
MICKEY DOESN'T KNOW, BUT HE'LL BE THINKING ABOUT YOU A LOT.
COUNT ON IT, NELLIE! IT'S A PROMISE.
YOUR ROOM IS READY! IF YOU EVER NEED ANYTHING ELSE...
NO THANKS, MRS. ANDERSON! IT'S BEEN A BUSY DAY, AND A COMFY BED'LL BE JUST TH' TICKET!
GOODNIGHT, MR. MICKEY!
SWEET DREAMS, NELLIE!
DON'T BE FOOLED BY HER INNOCENT CORKSCREW CURLS... NELLIE'S A REAL PEST! BUT ADORABLE... AND IT'S THANKS TO HER THAT THE OMEGATRON CANNON EXISTS!
WHADDAYA MEAN?
EVERY PARENT ALWAYS THINKS ABOUT THEIR KIDS, YOU KNOW? WE'VE GOT HOPES, QUESTIONS... WORRIES! WHAT'LL THEIR FUTURE BE LIKE? CAN WE GIVE THEM A TOMORROW WORTH LIVING?

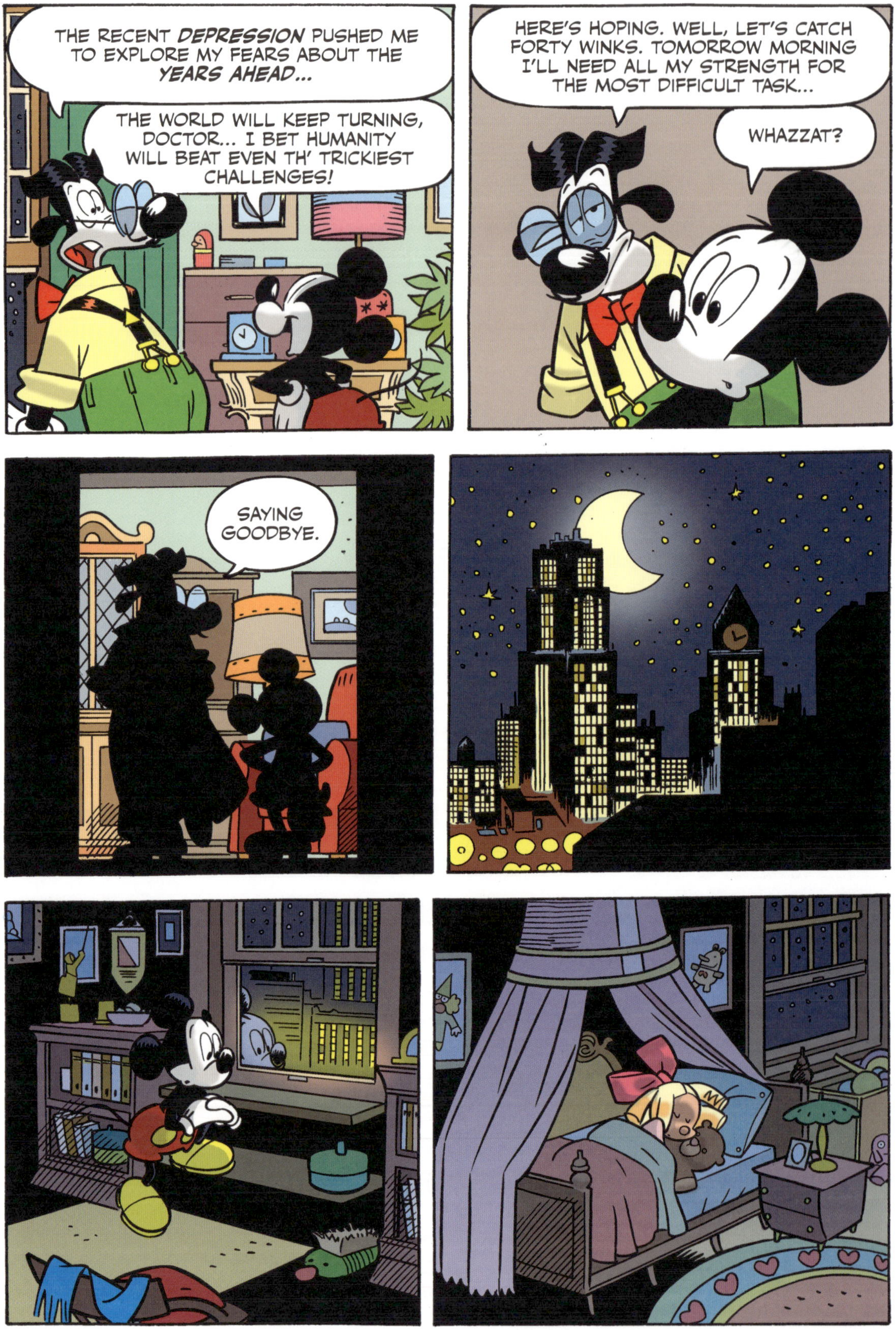
THE RECENT ***DEPRESSION*** PUSHED ME TO EXPLORE MY FEARS ABOUT THE ***YEARS AHEAD...***
THE WORLD WILL KEEP TURNING, DOCTOR... I BET HUMANITY WILL BEAT EVEN TH' TRICKIEST CHALLENGES!
HERE'S HOPING. WELL, LET'S CATCH FORTY WINKS. TOMORROW MORNING I'LL NEED ALL MY STRENGTH FOR THE MOST DIFFICULT TASK...
WHAZZAT?
SAYING GOODBYE.

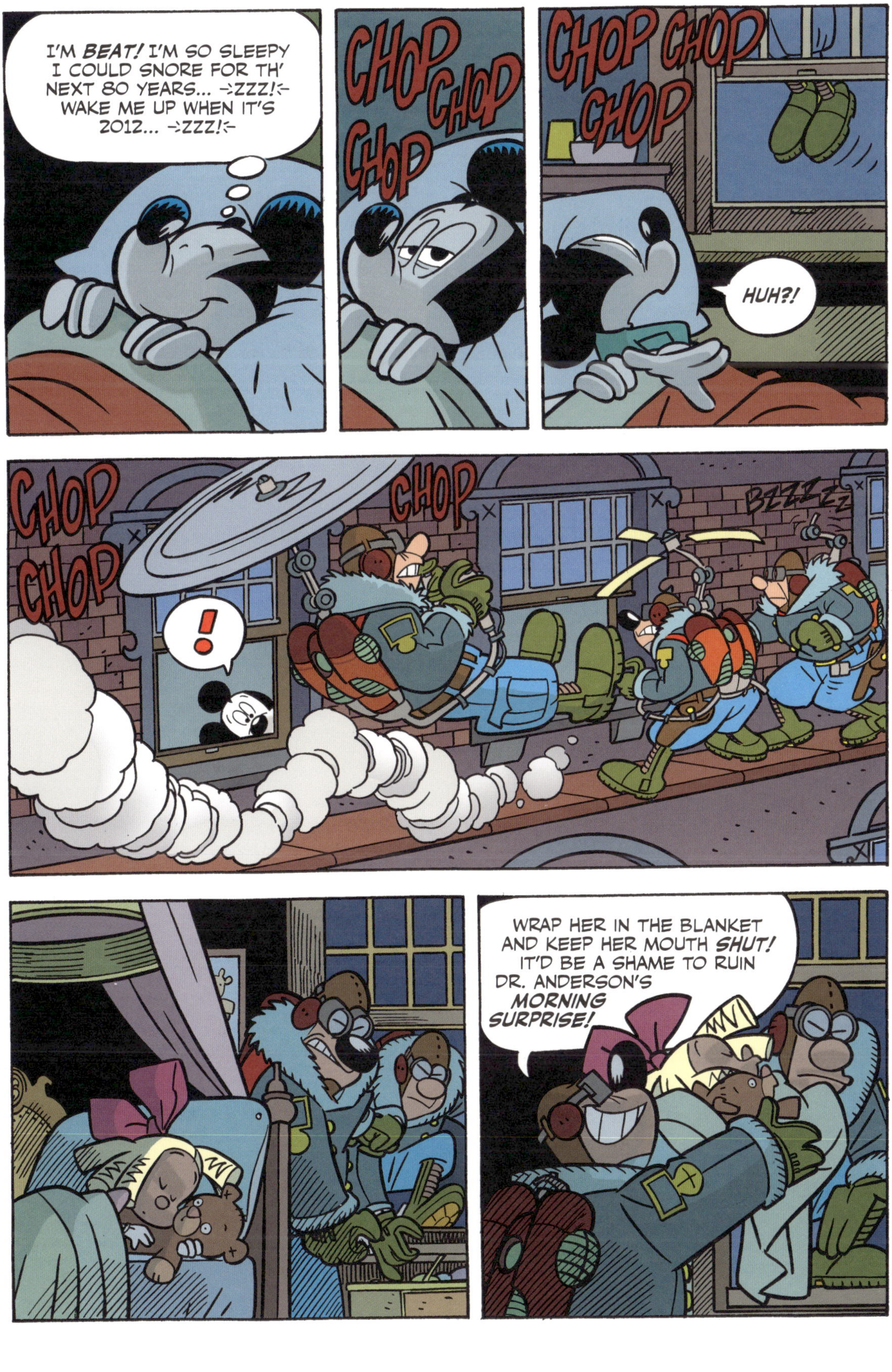
I'M BEAT! I'M SO SLEEPY I COULD SNORE FOR TH' NEXT 80 YEARS... ➛ZZZ!➛ WAKE ME UP WHEN IT'S 2012... ➛ZZZ!➛
CHOP CHOP CHOP
CHOP CHOP CHOP
HUH?!
CHOP CHOP
CHOP
BZZZZZ
!
WRAP HER IN THE BLANKET AND KEEP HER MOUTH SHUT! IT'D BE A SHAME TO RUIN DR. ANDERSON'S MORNING SURPRISE!

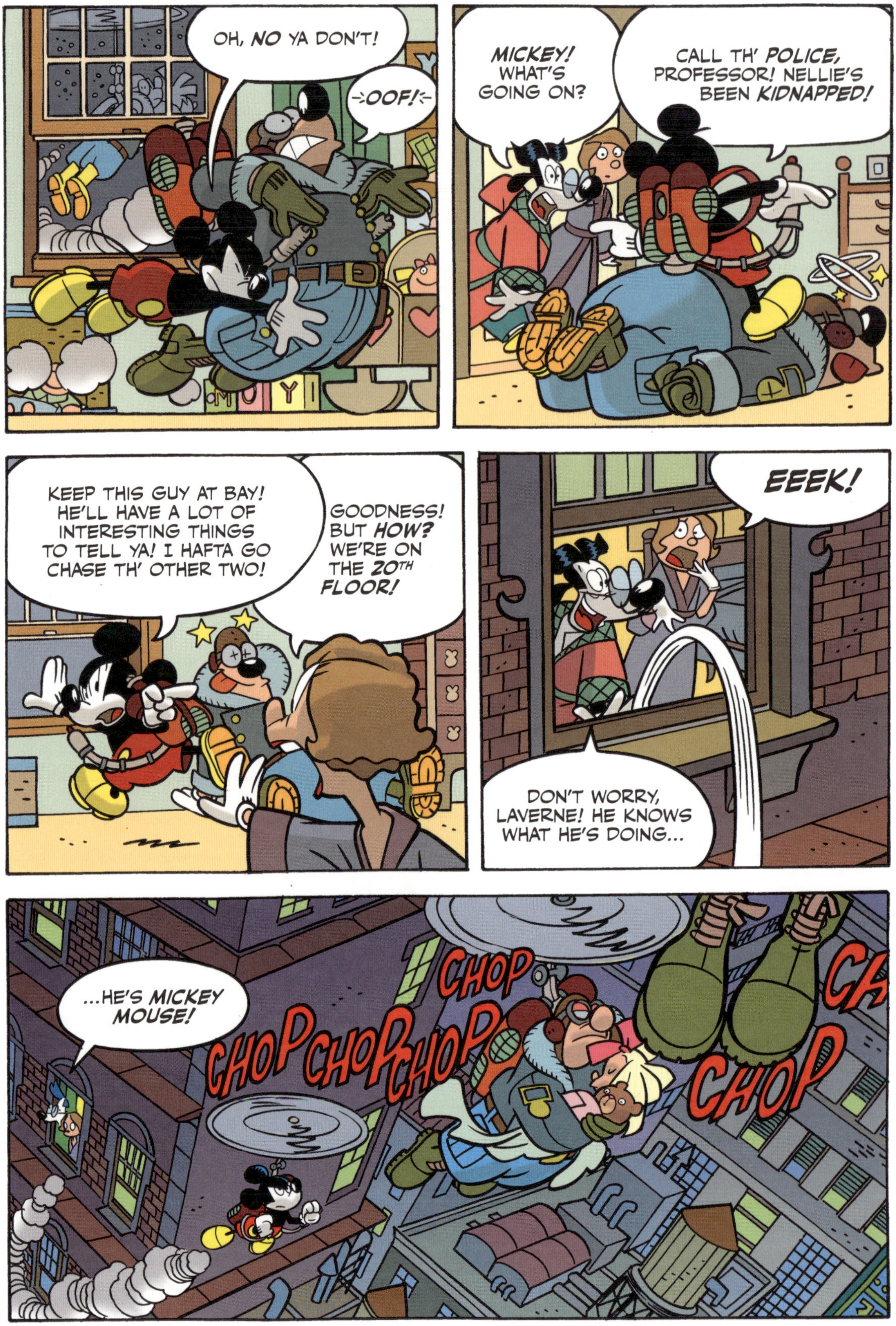
OH, NO YA DON'T!
OOF!
MICKEY! WHAT'S GOING ON?
CALL TH' POLICE, PROFESSOR! NELLIE'S BEEN KIDNAPPED!
KEEP THIS GUY AT BAY! HE'LL HAVE A LOT OF INTERESTING THINGS TO TELL YA! I HAFTA GO CHASE TH' OTHER TWO!
GOODNESS! BUT HOW? WE'RE ON THE 20TH FLOOR!
EEEK!
DON'T WORRY, LAVERNE! HE KNOWS WHAT HE'S DOING...
...HE'S MICKEY MOUSE!
CHOP CHOP CHOP
CHOP
CHOP
CHOP
CH

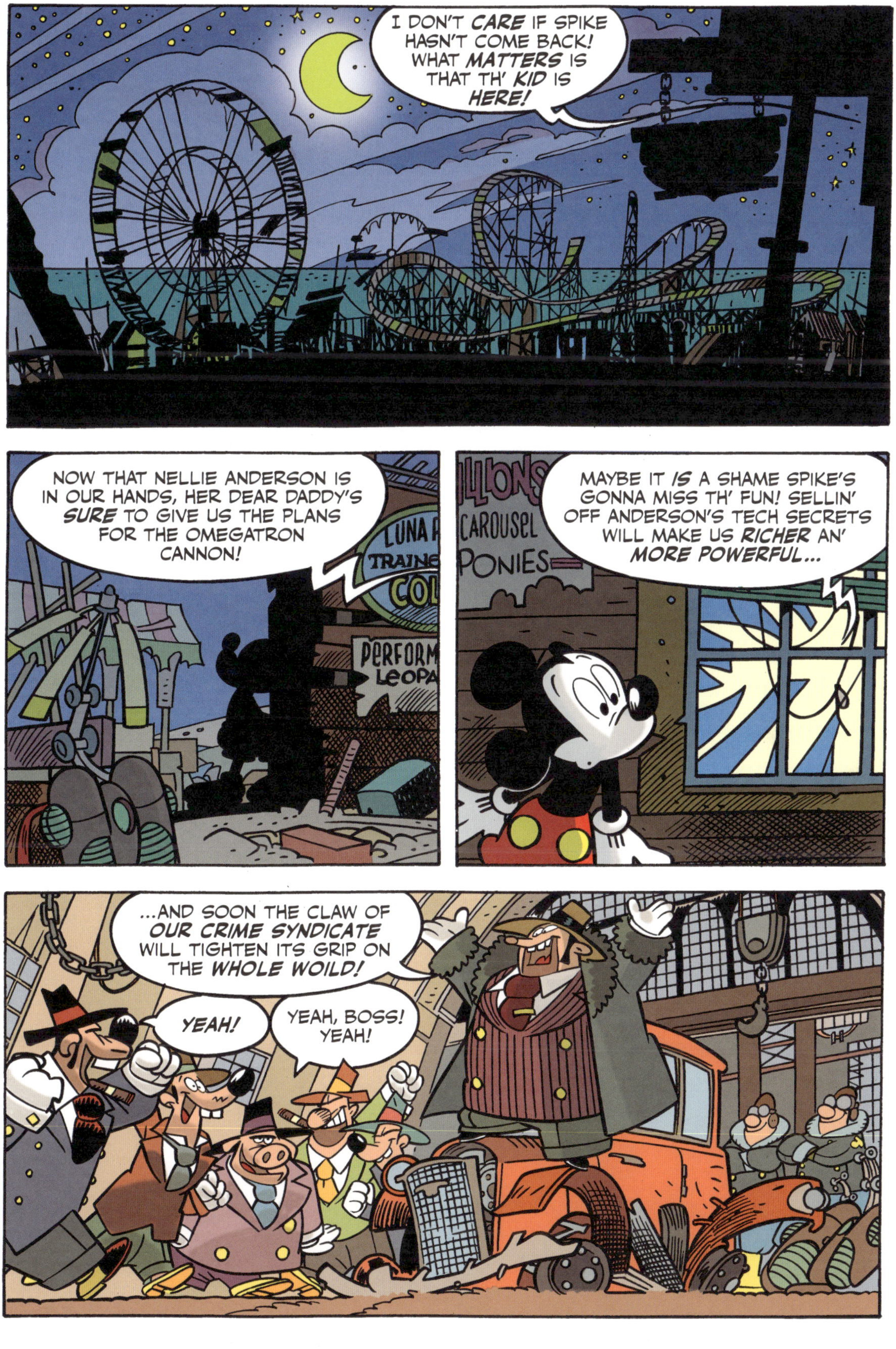
I DON'T *CARE* IF SPIKE HASN'T COME BACK! WHAT *MATTERS* IS THAT TH' *KID* IS *HERE!*
NOW THAT NELLIE ANDERSON IS IN OUR HANDS, HER DEAR DADDY'S *SURE* TO GIVE US THE PLANS FOR THE OMEGATRON CANNON!
CAROUSEL
PONIES
MAYBE IT *IS* A SHAME SPIKE'S GONNA MISS TH' FUN! SELLIN' OFF ANDERSON'S TECH SECRETS WILL MAKE US *RICHER* AN' *MORE POWERFUL...*
...AND SOON THE CLAW OF *OUR CRIME SYNDICATE* WILL TIGHTEN ITS GRIP ON THE *WHOLE WOILD!*
YEAH!
YEAH, BOSS! YEAH!

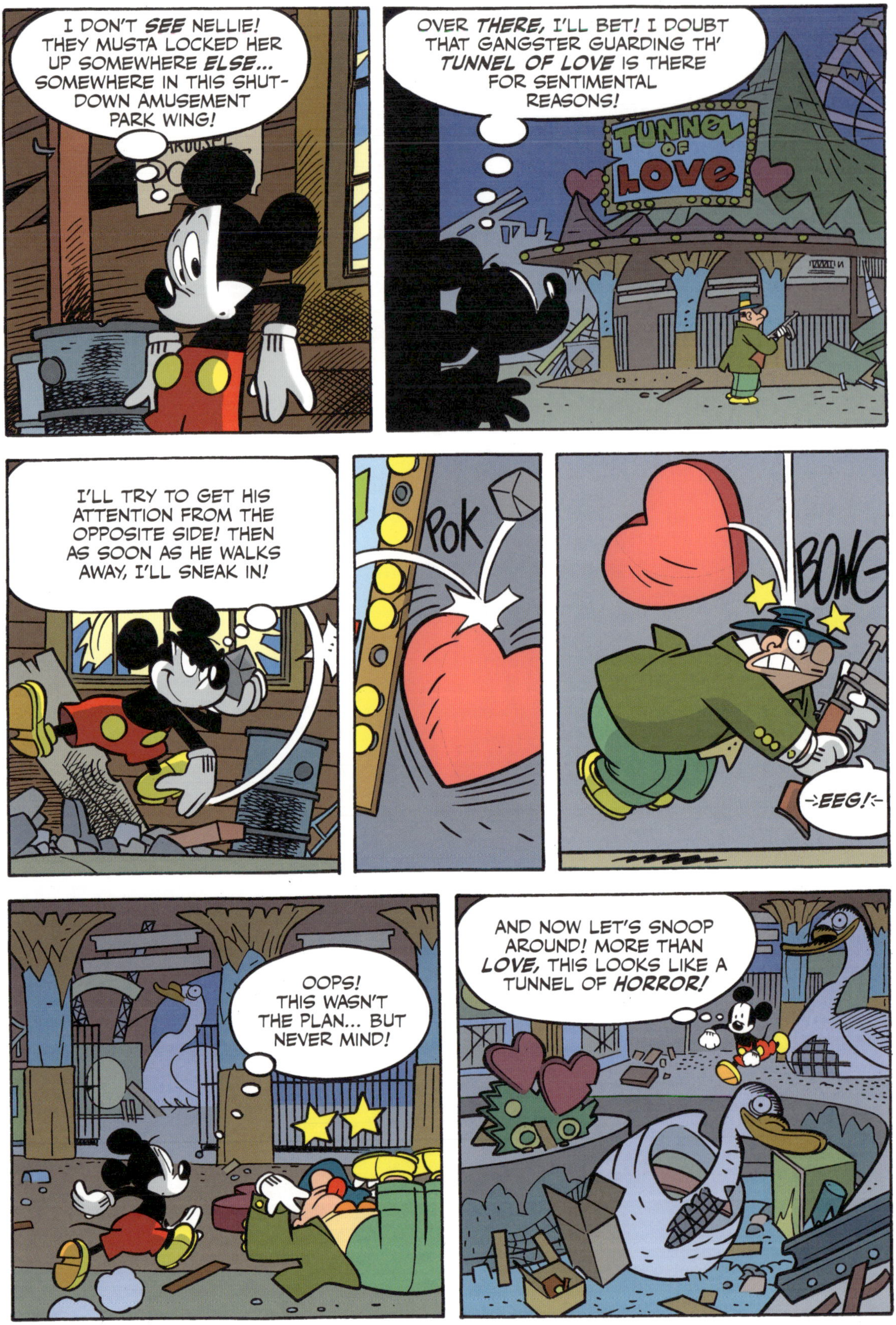
I DON'T SEE NELLIE! THEY MUSTA LOCKED HER UP SOMEWHERE ELSE... SOMEWHERE IN THIS SHUT-DOWN AMUSEMENT PARK WING!
OVER THERE, I'LL BET! I DOUBT THAT GANGSTER GUARDING TH' TUNNEL OF LOVE IS THERE FOR SENTIMENTAL REASONS!
TUNNEL OF LOVE
I'LL TRY TO GET HIS ATTENTION FROM THE OPPOSITE SIDE! THEN AS SOON AS HE WALKS AWAY, I'LL SNEAK IN!
POK
BONG
EEG!
OOPS! THIS WASN'T THE PLAN... BUT NEVER MIND!
AND NOW LET'S SNOOP AROUND! MORE THAN LOVE, THIS LOOKS LIKE A TUNNEL OF HORROR!

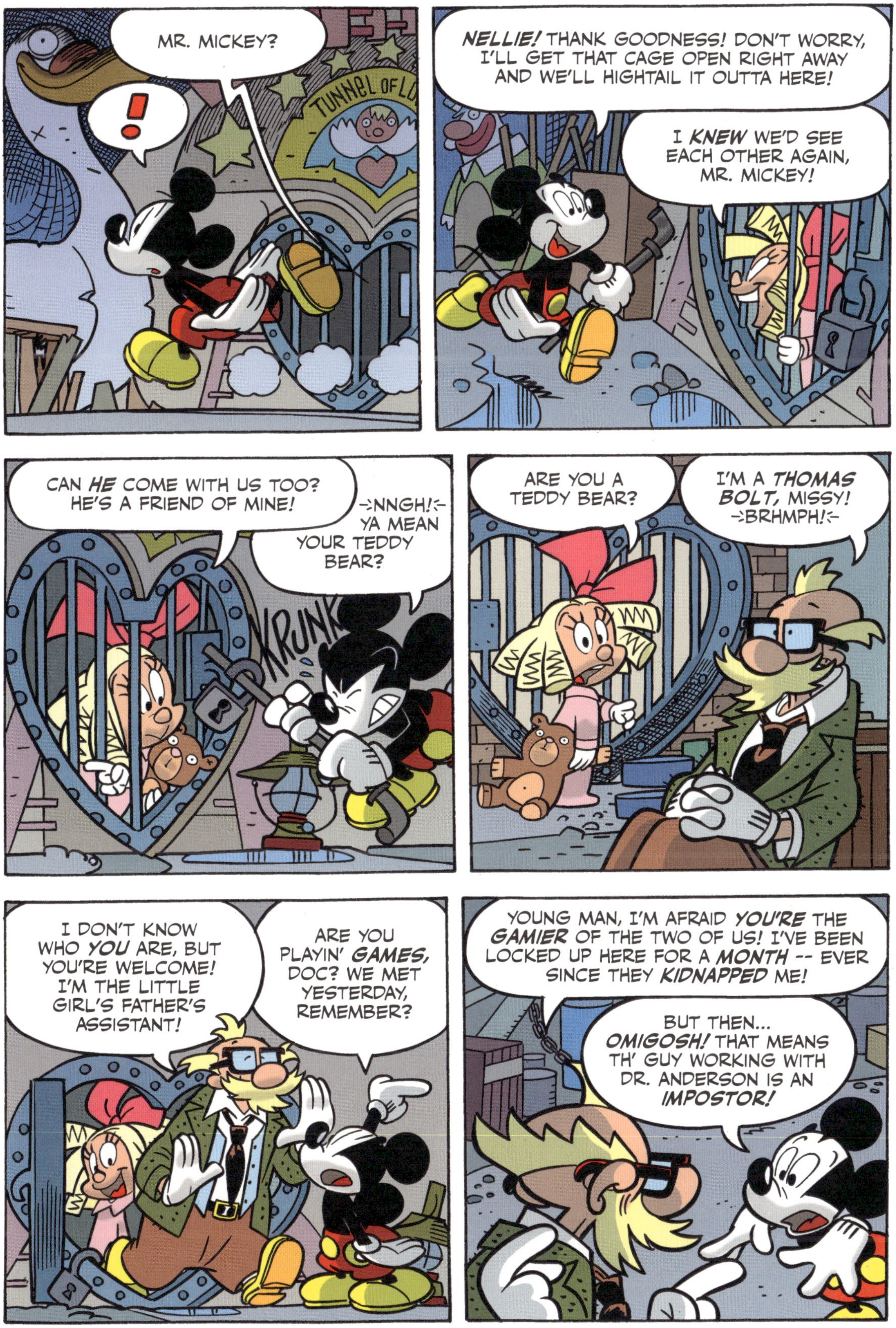

MR. MICKEY?
!
NELLIE! THANK GOODNESS! DON'T WORRY, I'LL GET THAT CAGE OPEN RIGHT AWAY AND WE'LL HIGHTAIL IT OUTTA HERE!
I KNEW WE'D SEE EACH OTHER AGAIN, MR. MICKEY!
CAN HE COME WITH US TOO? HE'S A FRIEND OF MINE!
-NNGH!- YA MEAN YOUR TEDDY BEAR?
KRUNK
ARE YOU A TEDDY BEAR?
I'M A THOMAS BOLT, MISSY! -BRHMPH!-
I DON'T KNOW WHO YOU ARE, BUT YOU'RE WELCOME! I'M THE LITTLE GIRL'S FATHER'S ASSISTANT!
ARE YOU PLAYIN' GAMES, DOC? WE MET YESTERDAY, REMEMBER?
YOUNG MAN, I'M AFRAID YOU'RE THE GAMIER OF THE TWO OF US! I'VE BEEN LOCKED UP HERE FOR A MONTH -- EVER SINCE THEY KIDNAPPED ME!
BUT THEN... OMIGOSH! THAT MEANS TH' GUY WORKING WITH DR. ANDERSON IS AN IMPOSTOR!

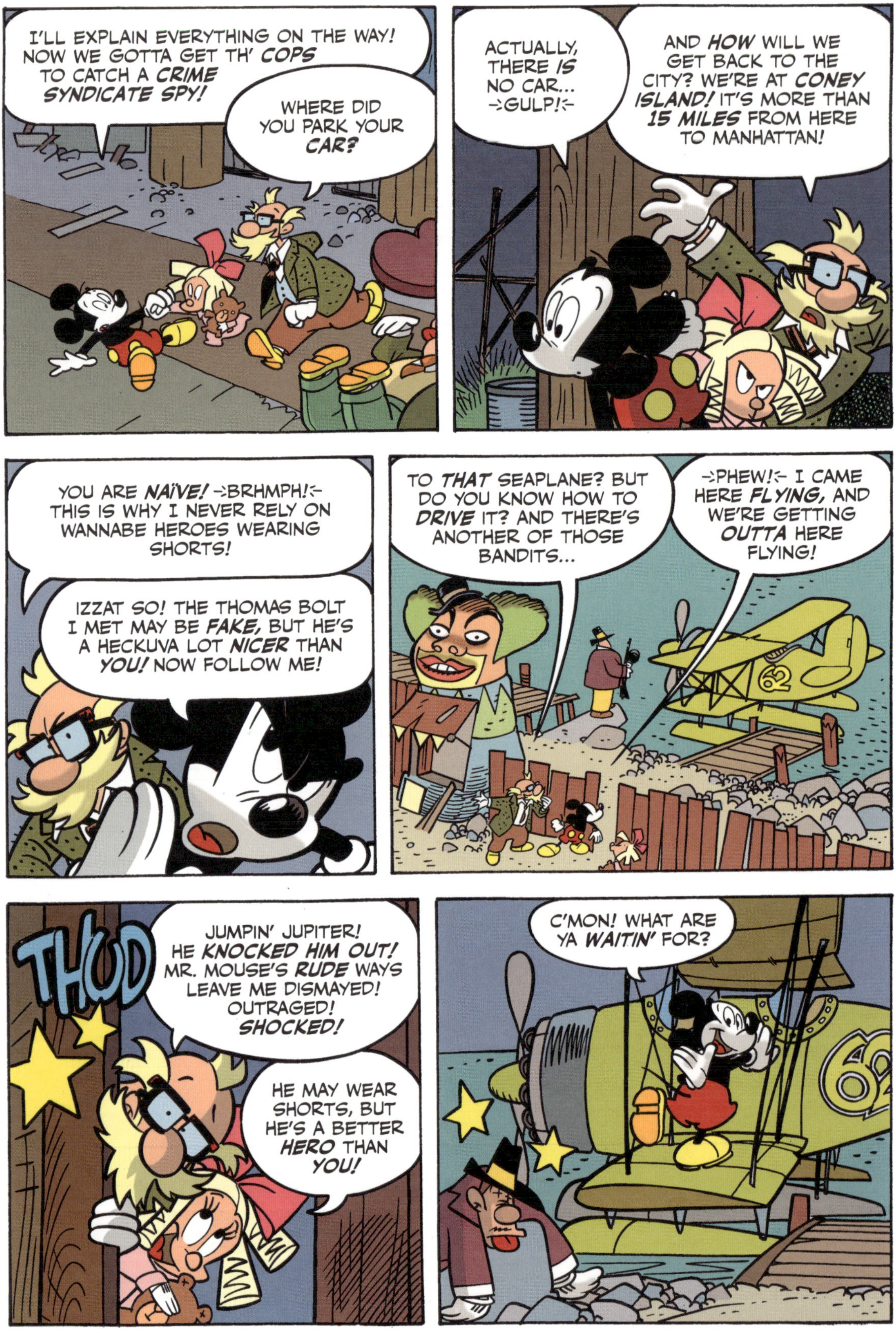
I'LL EXPLAIN EVERYTHING ON THE WAY! NOW WE GOTTA GET TH' COPS TO CATCH A CRIME SYNDICATE SPY!
WHERE DID YOU PARK YOUR CAR?
ACTUALLY, THERE IS NO CAR... GULP!
AND HOW WILL WE GET BACK TO THE CITY? WE'RE AT CONEY ISLAND! IT'S MORE THAN 15 MILES FROM HERE TO MANHATTAN!
YOU ARE NAÏVE! BRHMPH! THIS IS WHY I NEVER RELY ON WANNABE HEROES WEARING SHORTS!
IZZAT SO! THE THOMAS BOLT I MET MAY BE FAKE, BUT HE'S A HECKUVA LOT NICER THAN YOU! NOW FOLLOW ME!
TO THAT SEAPLANE? BUT DO YOU KNOW HOW TO DRIVE IT? AND THERE'S ANOTHER OF THOSE BANDITS...
PHEW! I CAME HERE FLYING, AND WE'RE GETTING OUTTA HERE FLYING!
THUD
JUMPIN' JUPITER! HE KNOCKED HIM OUT! MR. MOUSE'S RUDE WAYS LEAVE ME DISMAYED! OUTRAGED! SHOCKED!
HE MAY WEAR SHORTS, BUT HE'S A BETTER HERO THAN YOU!
C'MON! WHAT ARE YA WAITIN' FOR?

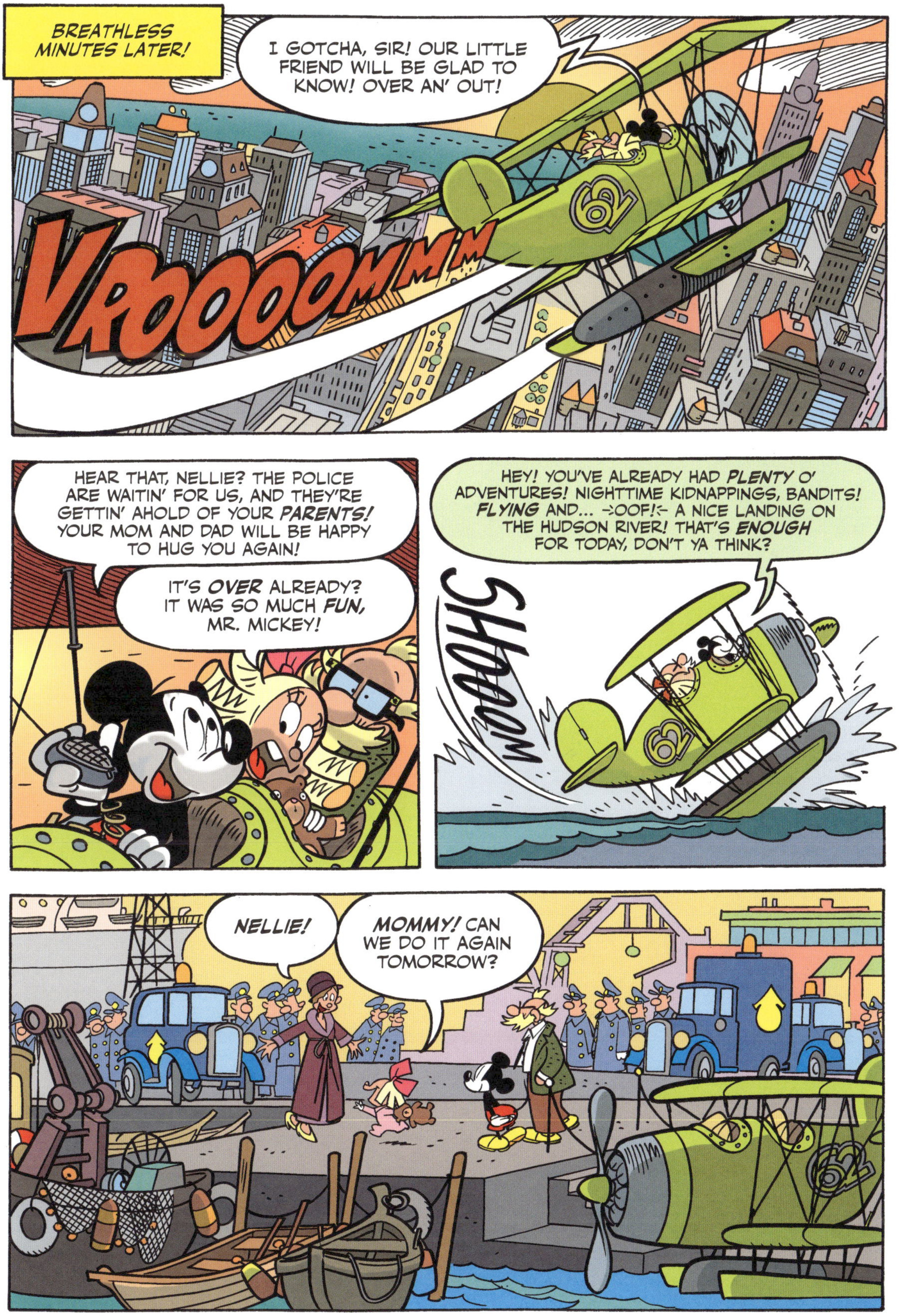

BREATHLESS MINUTES LATER!
I GOTCHA, SIR! OUR LITTLE FRIEND WILL BE GLAD TO KNOW! OVER AN' OUT!
VROOOOOMMM
HEAR THAT, NELLIE? THE POLICE ARE WAITIN' FOR US, AND THEY'RE GETTIN' AHOLD OF YOUR PARENTS! YOUR MOM AND DAD WILL BE HAPPY TO HUG YOU AGAIN!
IT'S OVER ALREADY? IT WAS SO MUCH FUN, MR. MICKEY!
HEY! YOU'VE ALREADY HAD PLENTY O' ADVENTURES! NIGHTTIME KIDNAPPINGS, BANDITS! FLYING AND... ->OOF!<- A NICE LANDING ON THE HUDSON RIVER! THAT'S ENOUGH FOR TODAY, DON'T YA THINK?
SHOOOOM
NELLIE!
MOMMY! CAN WE DO IT AGAIN TOMORROW?

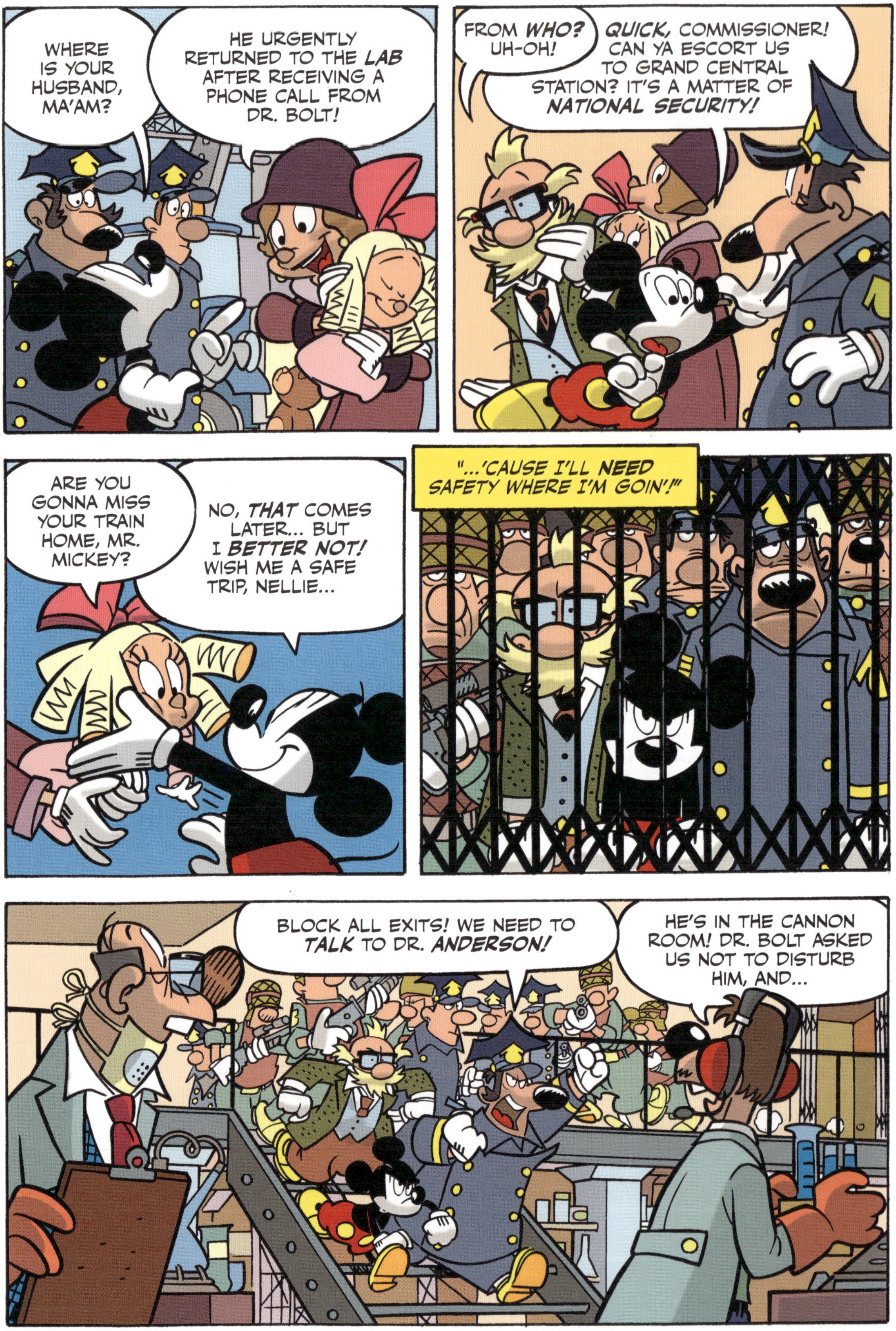
WHERE IS YOUR HUSBAND, MA'AM?
HE URGENTLY RETURNED TO THE LAB AFTER RECEIVING A PHONE CALL FROM DR. BOLT!
FROM WHO? UH-OH!
QUICK, COMMISSIONER! CAN YA ESCORT US TO GRAND CENTRAL STATION? IT'S A MATTER OF NATIONAL SECURITY!
ARE YOU GONNA MISS YOUR TRAIN HOME, MR. MICKEY?
NO, THAT COMES LATER... BUT I BETTER NOT! WISH ME A SAFE TRIP, NELLIE...
"...'CAUSE I'LL NEED SAFETY WHERE I'M GOIN'!"
BLOCK ALL EXITS! WE NEED TO TALK TO DR. ANDERSON!
HE'S IN THE CANNON ROOM! DR. BOLT ASKED US NOT TO DISTURB HIM, AND...

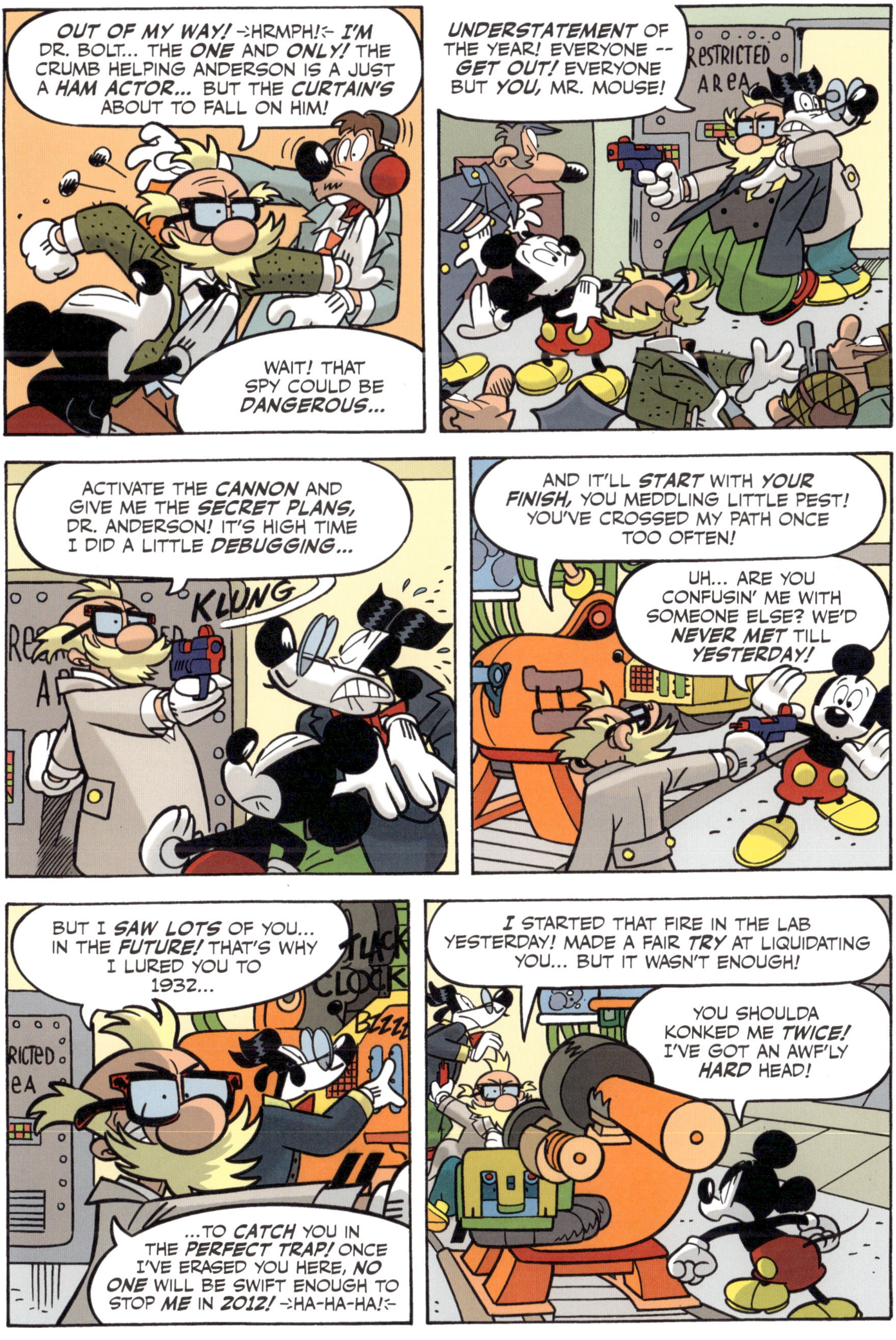
OUT OF MY WAY! -HRMPH!- I'M DR. BOLT... THE ONE AND ONLY! THE CRUMB HELPING ANDERSON IS A JUST A HAM ACTOR... BUT THE CURTAIN'S ABOUT TO FALL ON HIM!
WAIT! THAT SPY COULD BE DANGEROUS...
UNDERSTATEMENT OF THE YEAR! EVERYONE -- GET OUT! EVERYONE BUT YOU, MR. MOUSE!
RESTRICTED AREA
ACTIVATE THE CANNON AND GIVE ME THE SECRET PLANS, DR. ANDERSON! IT'S HIGH TIME I DID A LITTLE DEBUGGING...
KLUNG
AND IT'LL START WITH YOUR FINISH, YOU MEDDLING LITTLE PEST! YOU'VE CROSSED MY PATH ONCE TOO OFTEN!
UH... ARE YOU CONFUSIN' ME WITH SOMEONE ELSE? WE'D NEVER MET TILL YESTERDAY!
BUT I SAW LOTS OF YOU... IN THE FUTURE! THAT'S WHY I LURED YOU TO 1932...
TLACK
CLOCK
BZZZZ
...TO CATCH YOU IN THE PERFECT TRAP! ONCE I'VE ERASED YOU HERE, NO ONE WILL BE SWIFT ENOUGH TO STOP ME IN 2012! -HA-HA-HA!-
I STARTED THAT FIRE IN THE LAB YESTERDAY! MADE A FAIR TRY AT LIQUIDATING YOU... BUT IT WASN'T ENOUGH!
YOU SHOULDA KONKED ME TWICE! I'VE GOT AN AWF'LY HARD HEAD!

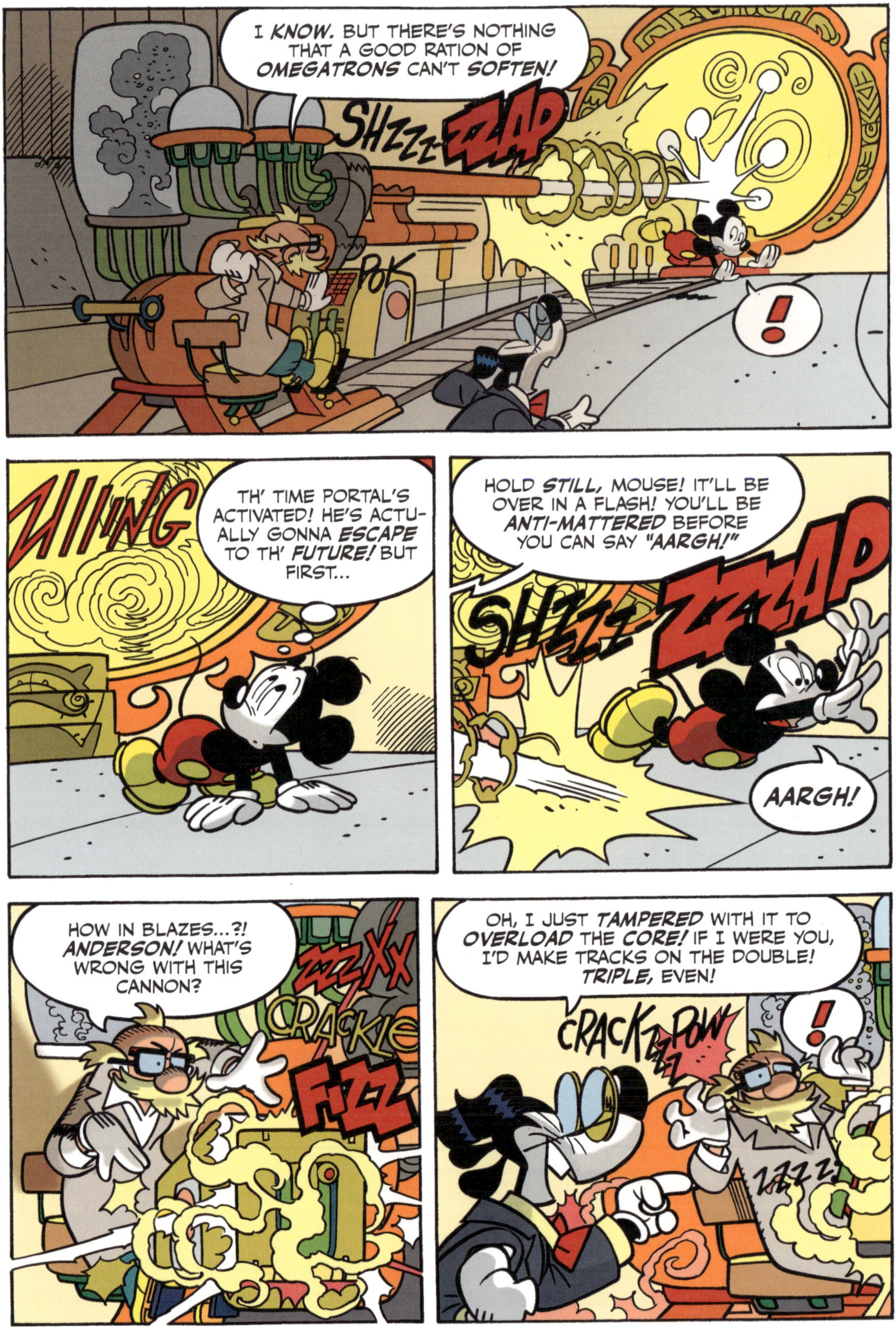
I KNOW. BUT THERE'S NOTHING THAT A GOOD RATION OF OMEGATRONS CAN'T SOFTEN!
SHZZZ-ZZAP
POK
!
ZIIING
TH' TIME PORTAL'S ACTIVATED! HE'S ACTUALLY GONNA ESCAPE TO TH' FUTURE! BUT FIRST...
HOLD STILL, MOUSE! IT'LL BE OVER IN A FLASH! YOU'LL BE ANTI-MATTERED BEFORE YOU CAN SAY "AARGH!"
SHZZZ-ZZZAP
AARGH!
HOW IN BLAZES...?! ANDERSON! WHAT'S WRONG WITH THIS CANNON?
ZZZZXX
CRACKLE
FIZZ
OH, I JUST TAMPERED WITH IT TO OVERLOAD THE CORE! IF I WERE YOU, I'D MAKE TRACKS ON THE DOUBLE! TRIPLE, EVEN!
CRACK
POW
!

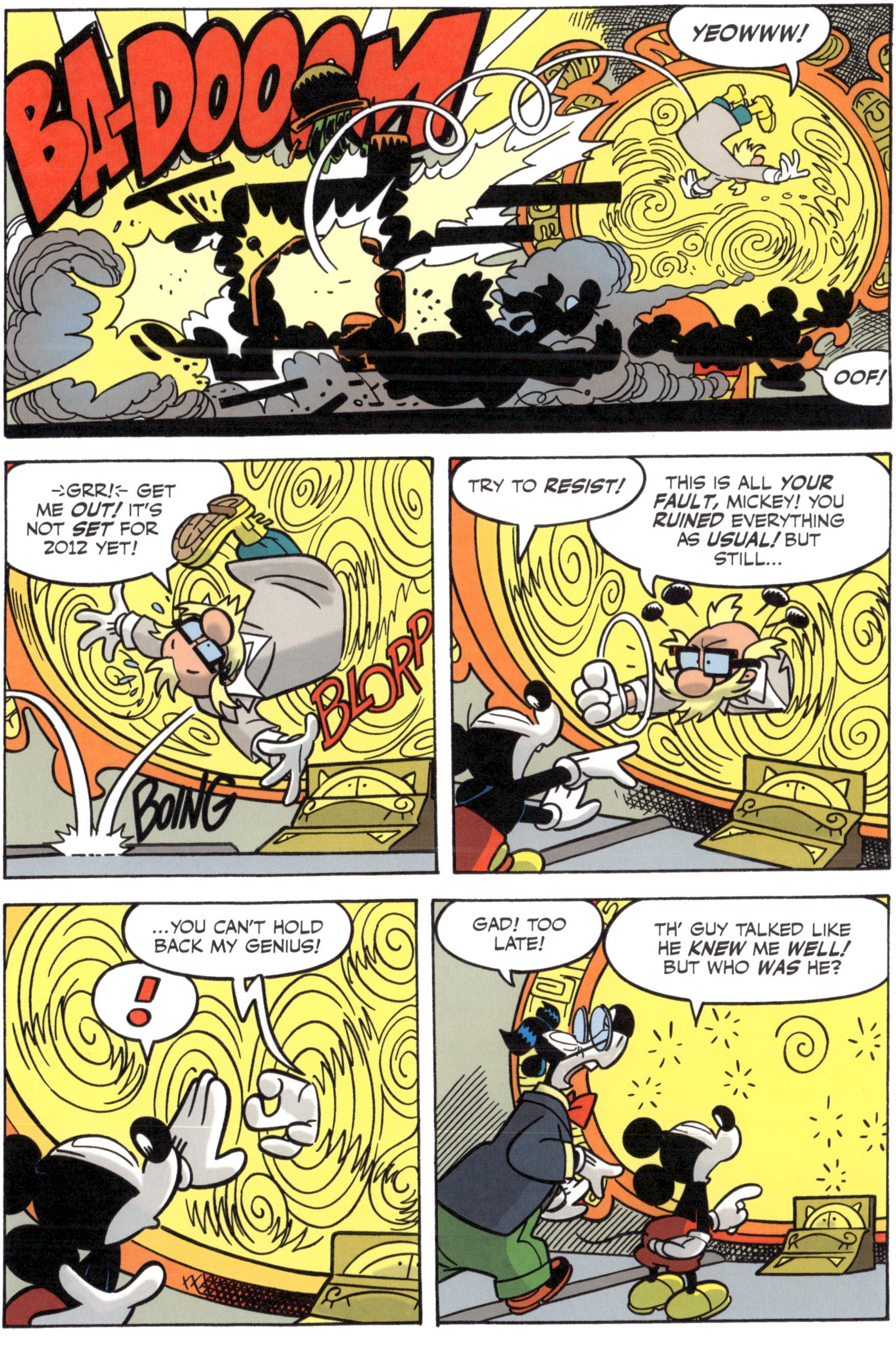
BA-DOOOM
YEOWWW!
OOF!
-GRR!- GET ME OUT! IT'S NOT SET FOR 2012 YET!
BLORP
BOING
TRY TO RESIST!
THIS IS ALL YOUR FAULT, MICKEY! YOU RUINED EVERYTHING AS USUAL! BUT STILL...
...YOU CAN'T HOLD BACK MY GENIUS!
!
GAD! TOO LATE!
TH' GUY TALKED LIKE HE KNEW ME WELL! BUT WHO WAS HE?

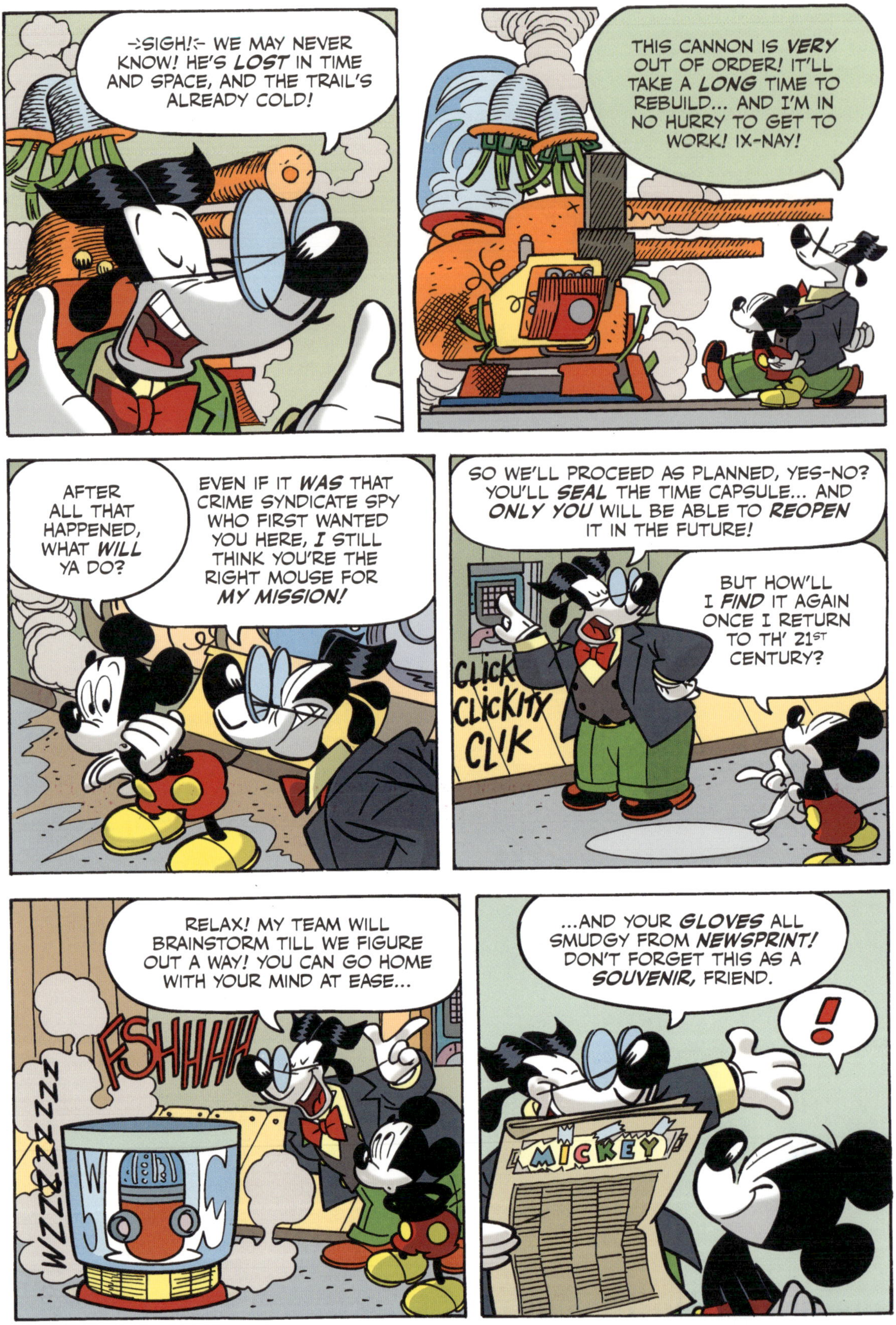
-SIGH!- WE MAY NEVER KNOW! HE'S LOST IN TIME AND SPACE, AND THE TRAIL'S ALREADY COLD!
THIS CANNON IS VERY OUT OF ORDER! IT'LL TAKE A LONG TIME TO REBUILD... AND I'M IN NO HURRY TO GET TO WORK! IX-NAY!
AFTER ALL THAT HAPPENED, WHAT WILL YA DO?
EVEN IF IT WAS THAT CRIME SYNDICATE SPY WHO FIRST WANTED YOU HERE, I STILL THINK YOU'RE THE RIGHT MOUSE FOR MY MISSION!
SO WE'LL PROCEED AS PLANNED, YES-NO? YOU'LL SEAL THE TIME CAPSULE... AND ONLY YOU WILL BE ABLE TO REOPEN IT IN THE FUTURE!
CLICK CLICKITY CLIK
BUT HOW'LL I FIND IT AGAIN ONCE I RETURN TO TH' 21ST CENTURY?
RELAX! MY TEAM WILL BRAINSTORM TILL WE FIGURE OUT A WAY! YOU CAN GO HOME WITH YOUR MIND AT EASE...
FSHHHH
WZZZZZZZ
...AND YOUR GLOVES ALL SMUDGY FROM NEWSPRINT! DON'T FORGET THIS AS A SOUVENIR, FRIEND.
!
MICKEY

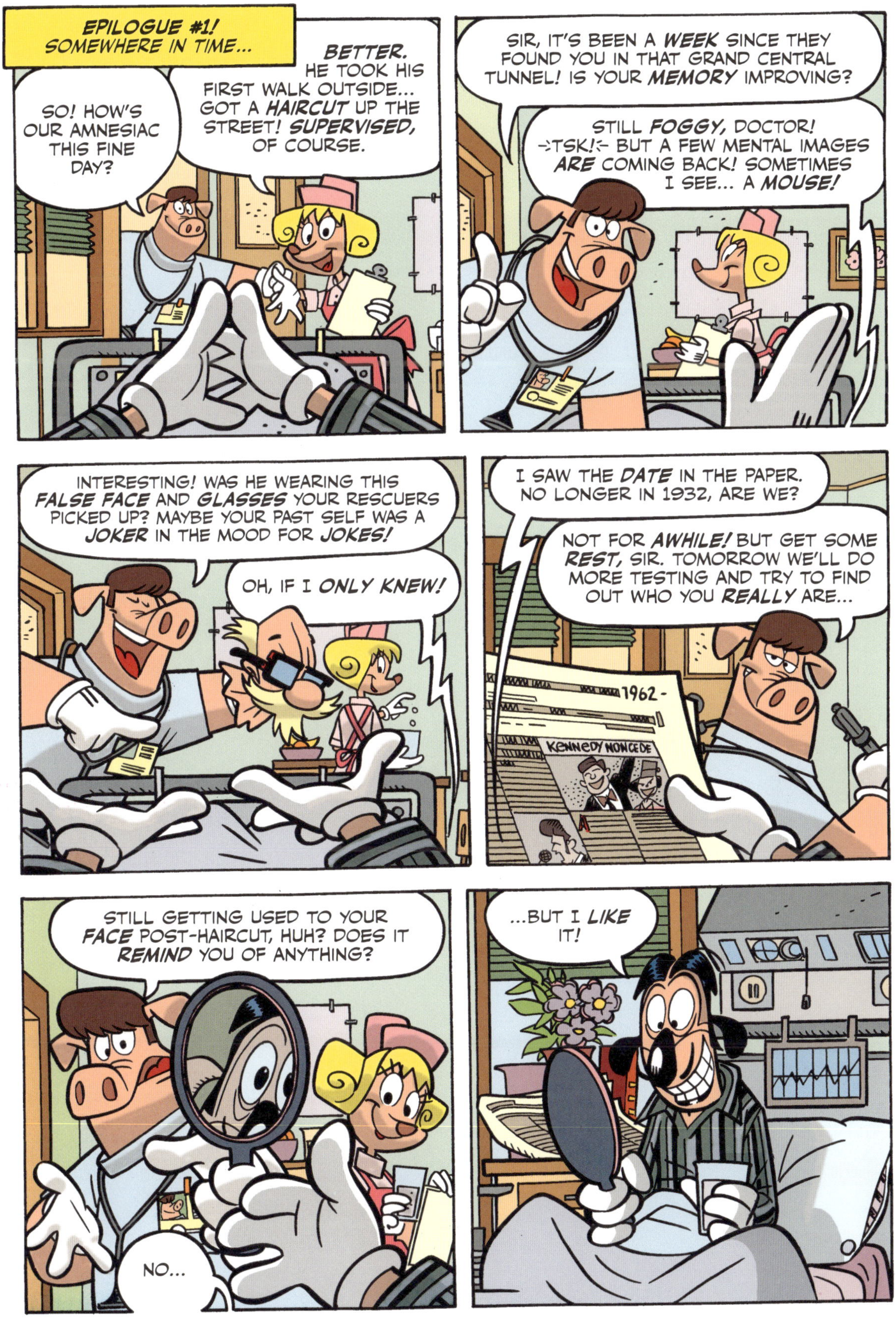
EPILOGUE #1! SOMEWHERE IN TIME...
SO! HOW'S OUR AMNESIAC THIS FINE DAY?
BETTER. HE TOOK HIS FIRST WALK OUTSIDE... GOT A HAIRCUT UP THE STREET! SUPERVISED, OF COURSE.
SIR, IT'S BEEN A WEEK SINCE THEY FOUND YOU IN THAT GRAND CENTRAL TUNNEL! IS YOUR MEMORY IMPROVING?
STILL FOGGY, DOCTOR! →TSK!← BUT A FEW MENTAL IMAGES ARE COMING BACK! SOMETIMES I SEE... A MOUSE!
INTERESTING! WAS HE WEARING THIS FALSE FACE AND GLASSES YOUR RESCUERS PICKED UP? MAYBE YOUR PAST SELF WAS A JOKER IN THE MOOD FOR JOKES!
OH, IF I ONLY KNEW!
I SAW THE DATE IN THE PAPER. NO LONGER IN 1932, ARE WE?
NOT FOR AWHILE! BUT GET SOME REST, SIR. TOMORROW WE'LL DO MORE TESTING AND TRY TO FIND OUT WHO YOU REALLY ARE...
1962
KENNEDY NONCEDE
STILL GETTING USED TO YOUR FACE POST-HAIRCUT, HUH? DOES IT REMIND YOU OF ANYTHING?
NO...
...BUT I LIKE IT!

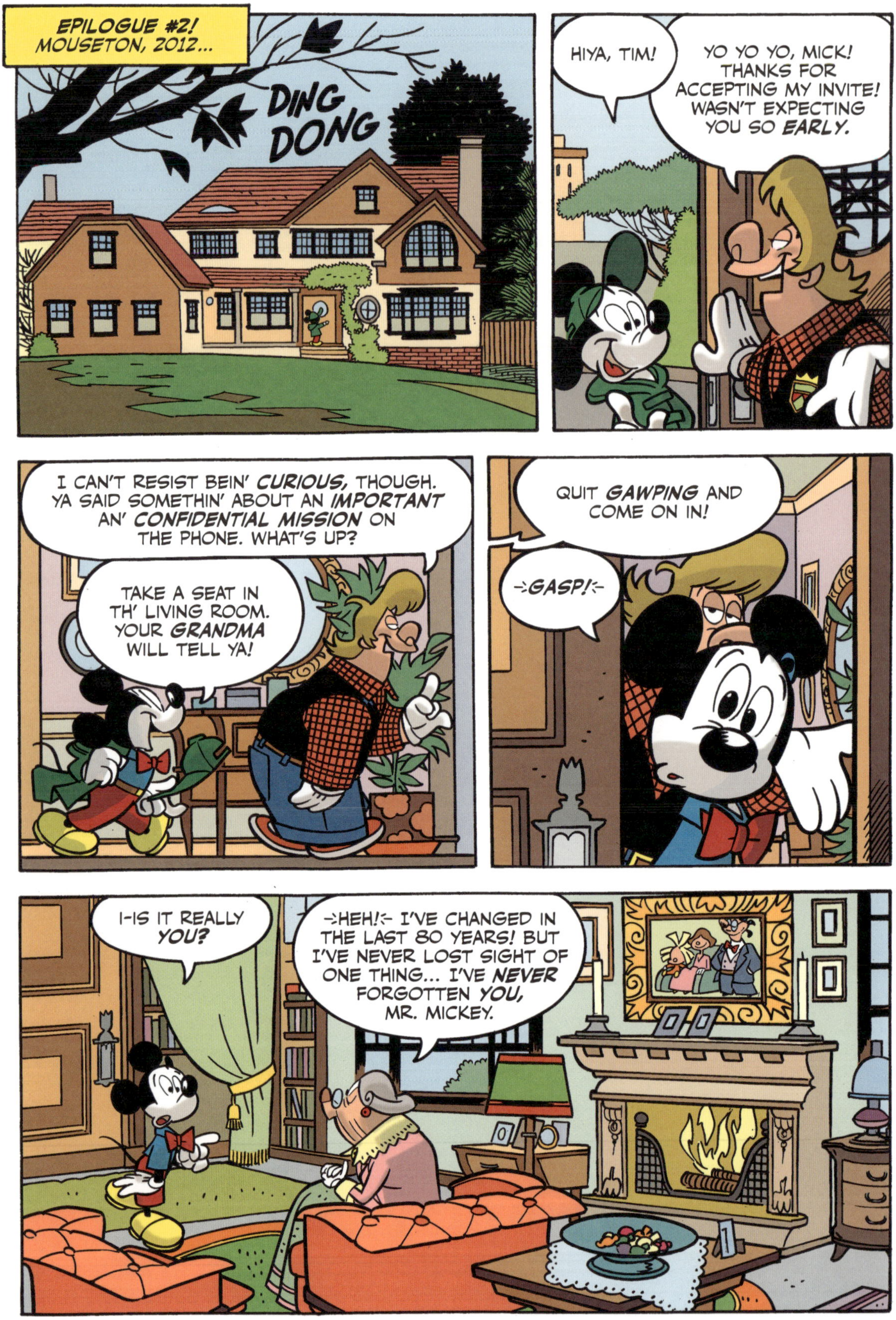
EPILOGUE #2! MOUSETON, 2012...
DING DONG
HIYA, TIM!
YO YO YO, MICK! THANKS FOR ACCEPTING MY INVITE! WASN'T EXPECTING YOU SO EARLY.
I CAN'T RESIST BEIN' CURIOUS, THOUGH. YA SAID SOMETHIN' ABOUT AN IMPORTANT AN' CONFIDENTIAL MISSION ON THE PHONE. WHAT'S UP?
TAKE A SEAT IN TH' LIVING ROOM. YOUR GRANDMA WILL TELL YA!
QUIT GAWPING AND COME ON IN!
GASP!
I-IS IT REALLY YOU?
HEH! I'VE CHANGED IN THE LAST 80 YEARS! BUT I'VE NEVER LOST SIGHT OF ONE THING... I'VE NEVER FORGOTTEN YOU, MR. MICKEY.

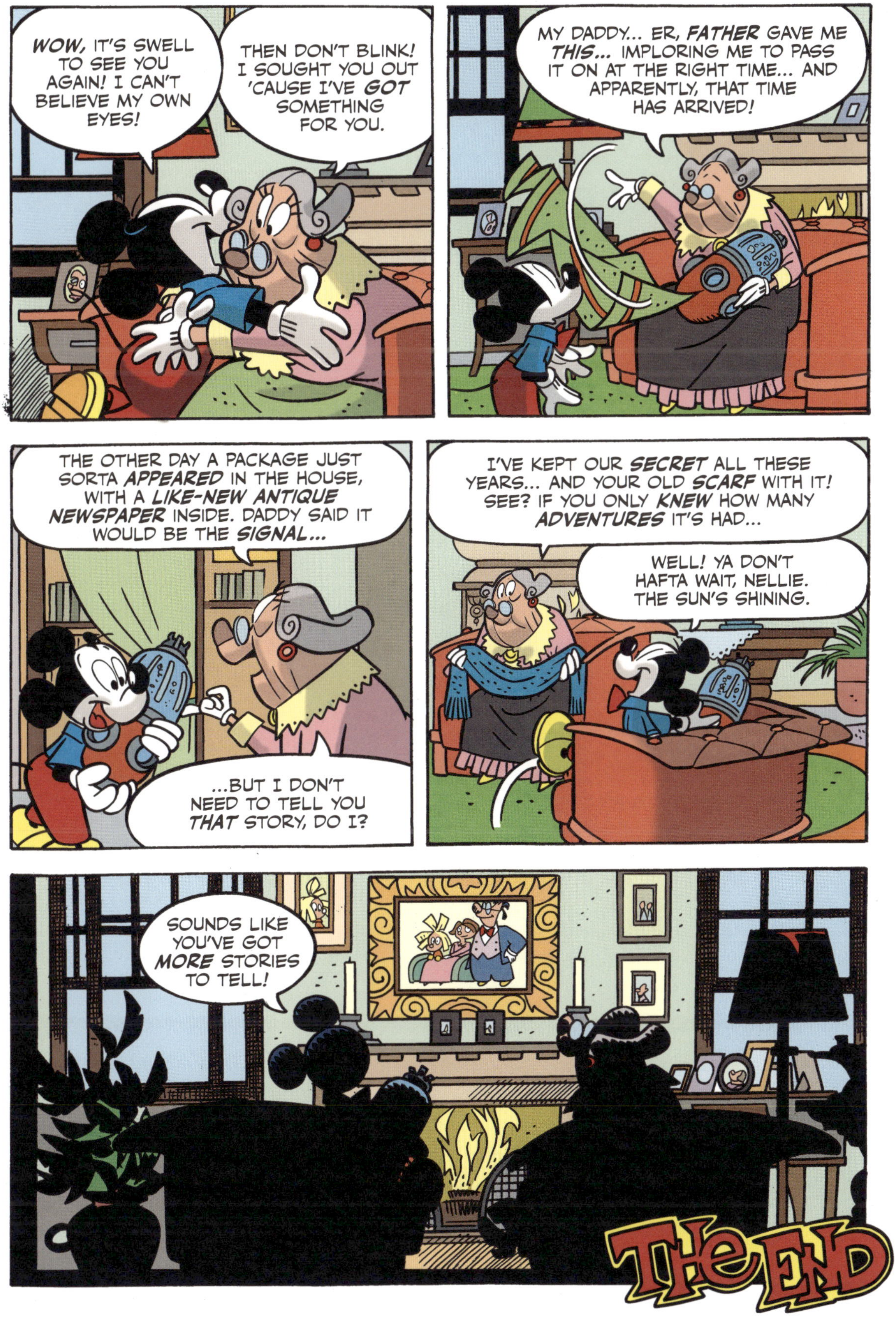
WOW, IT'S SWELL TO SEE YOU AGAIN! I CAN'T BELIEVE MY OWN EYES!
THEN DON'T BLINK! I SOUGHT YOU OUT 'CAUSE I'VE GOT SOMETHING FOR YOU.
MY DADDY... ER, FATHER GAVE ME THIS... IMPLORING ME TO PASS IT ON AT THE RIGHT TIME... AND APPARENTLY, THAT TIME HAS ARRIVED!
THE OTHER DAY A PACKAGE JUST SORTA APPEARED IN THE HOUSE, WITH A LIKE-NEW ANTIQUE NEWSPAPER INSIDE. DADDY SAID IT WOULD BE THE SIGNAL...
...BUT I DON'T NEED TO TELL YOU THAT STORY, DO I?
I'VE KEPT OUR SECRET ALL THESE YEARS... AND YOUR OLD SCARF WITH IT! SEE? IF YOU ONLY KNEW HOW MANY ADVENTURES IT'S HAD...
WELL! YA DON'T HAFTA WAIT, NELLIE. THE SUN'S SHINING.
SOUNDS LIKE YOU'VE GOT MORE STORIES TO TELL!
THE END

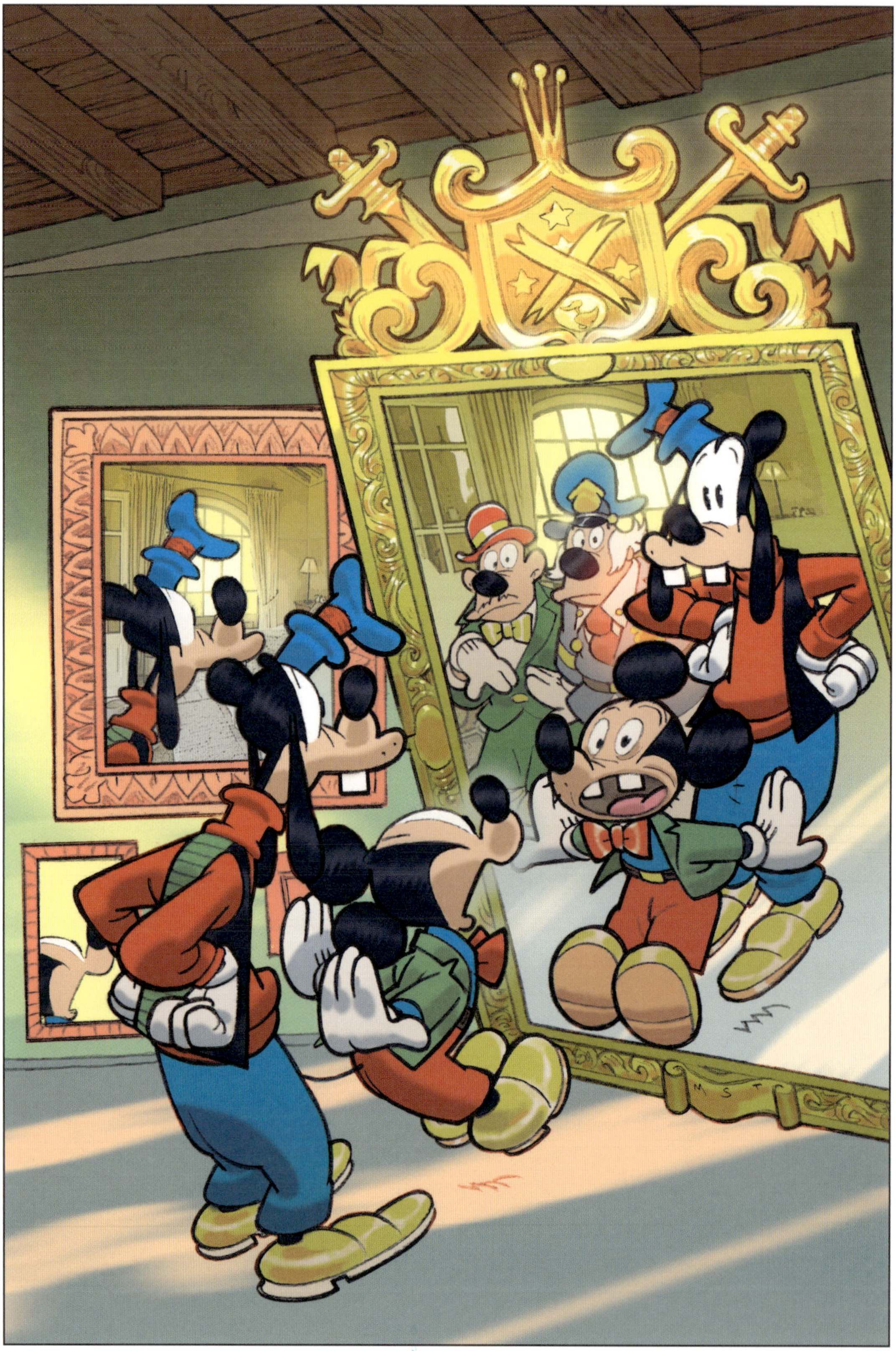

Cover art illustrating "Mouse in the Mirror," first published on Italian *Disney BIG* 117 (January 2018). Art and color by Corrado Mastantuono.

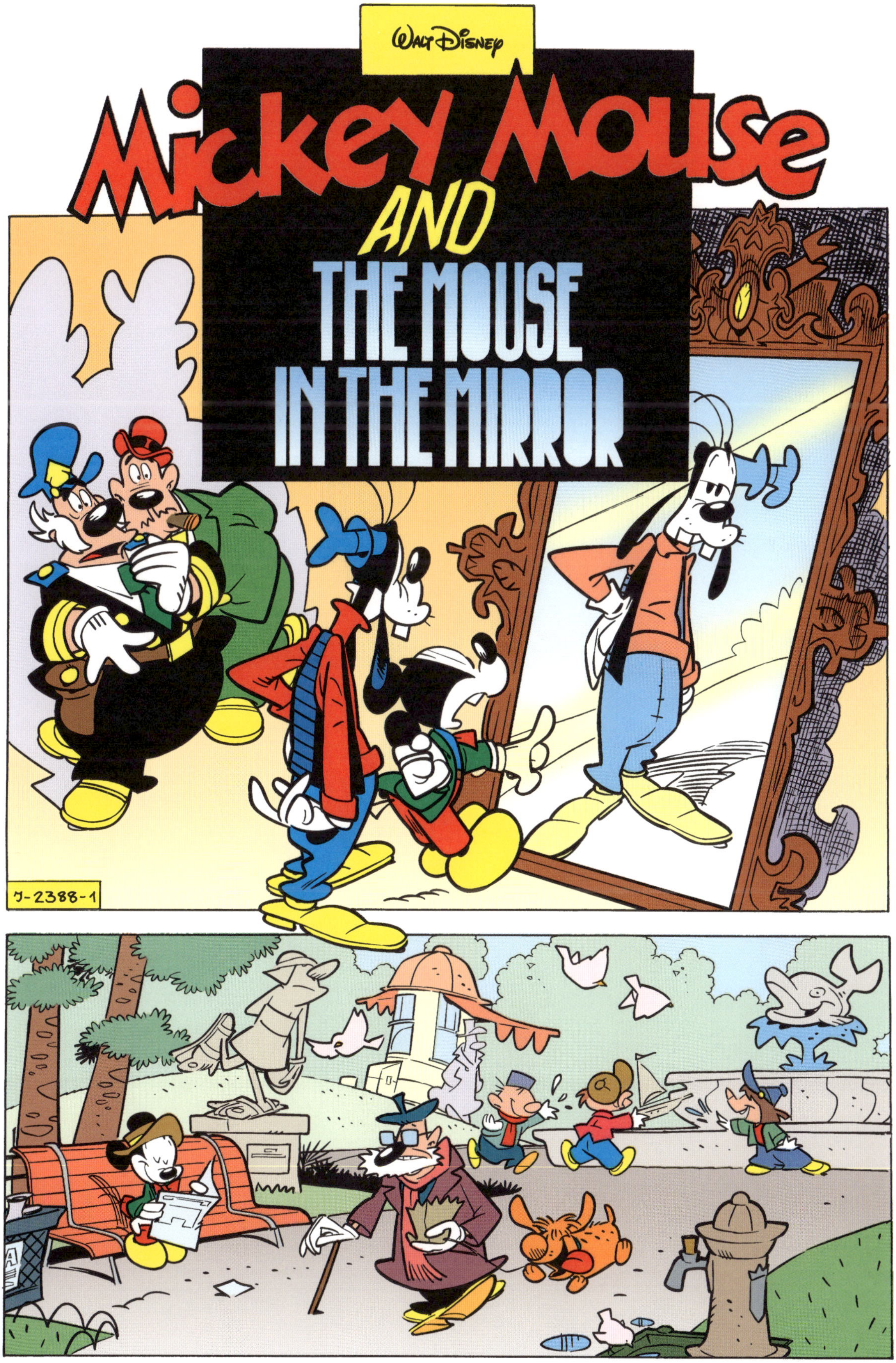
Walt Disney
Mickey Mouse
AND
THE MOUSE IN THE MIRROR
J-2388-1

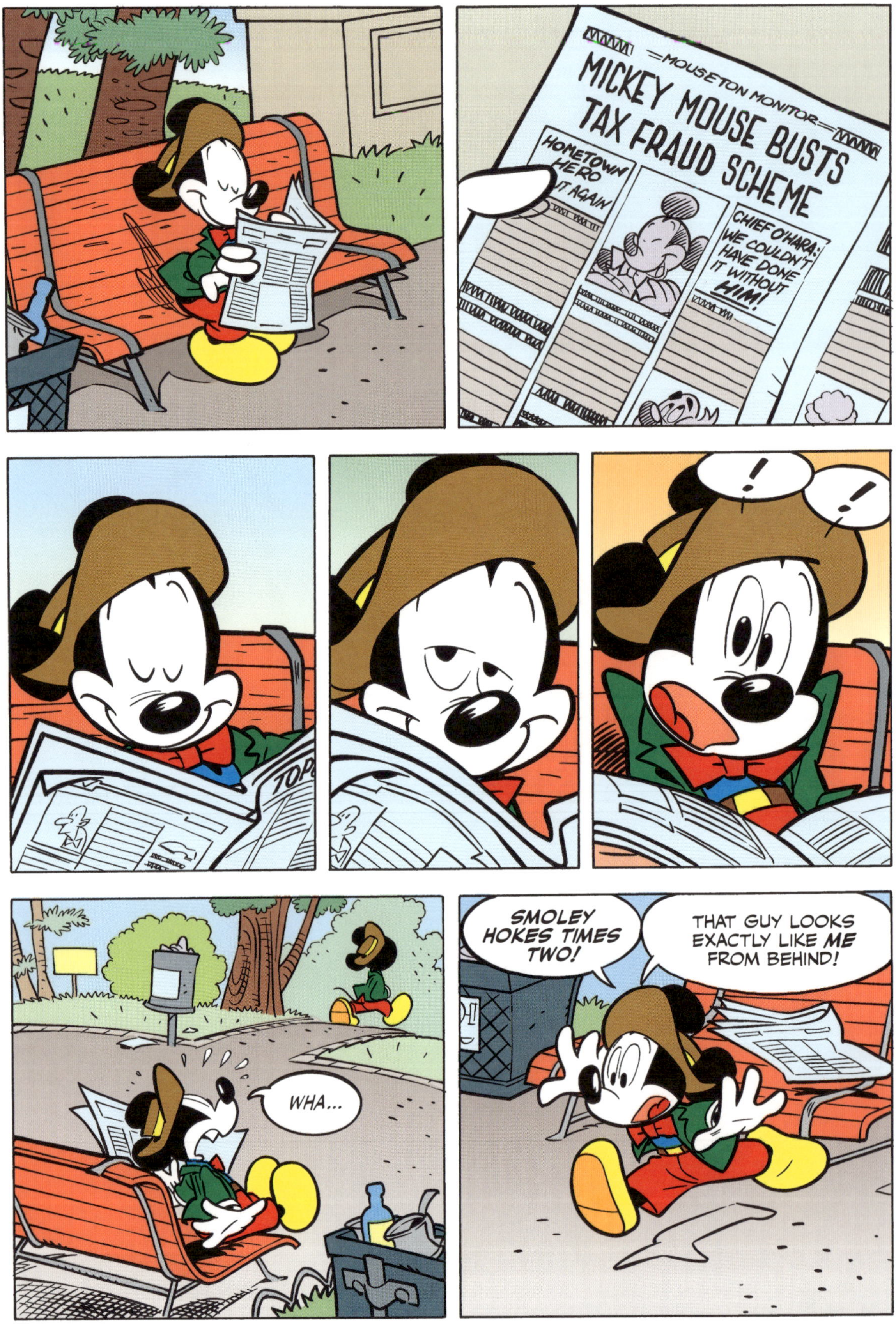

MOUSETON MONITOR
MICKEY MOUSE BUSTS TAX FRAUD SCHEME
HOMETOWN HERO
IT AGAIN
CHIEF O'HARA: WE COULDN'T HAVE DONE IT WITHOUT *HIM*!
WHA...
SMOLEY HOKES TIMES TWO!
THAT GUY LOOKS EXACTLY LIKE *ME* FROM BEHIND!

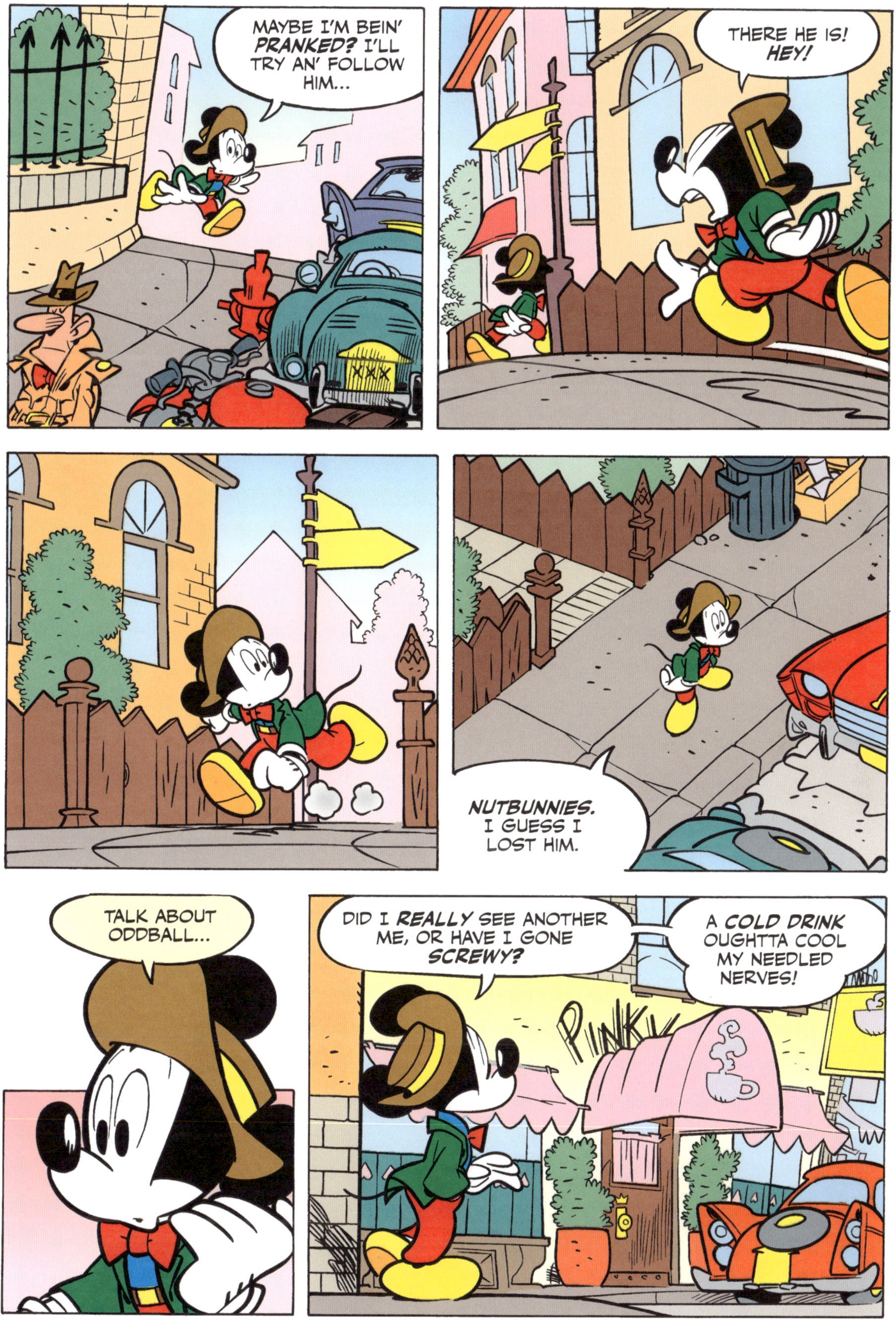
MAYBE I'M BEIN' *PRANKED?* I'LL TRY AN' FOLLOW HIM...
THERE HE IS! *HEY!*
NUTBUNNIES. I GUESS I LOST HIM.
TALK ABOUT ODDBALL...
DID I *REALLY* SEE ANOTHER ME, OR HAVE I GONE *SCREWY?*
A *COLD DRINK* OUGHTTA COOL MY NEEDLED NERVES!

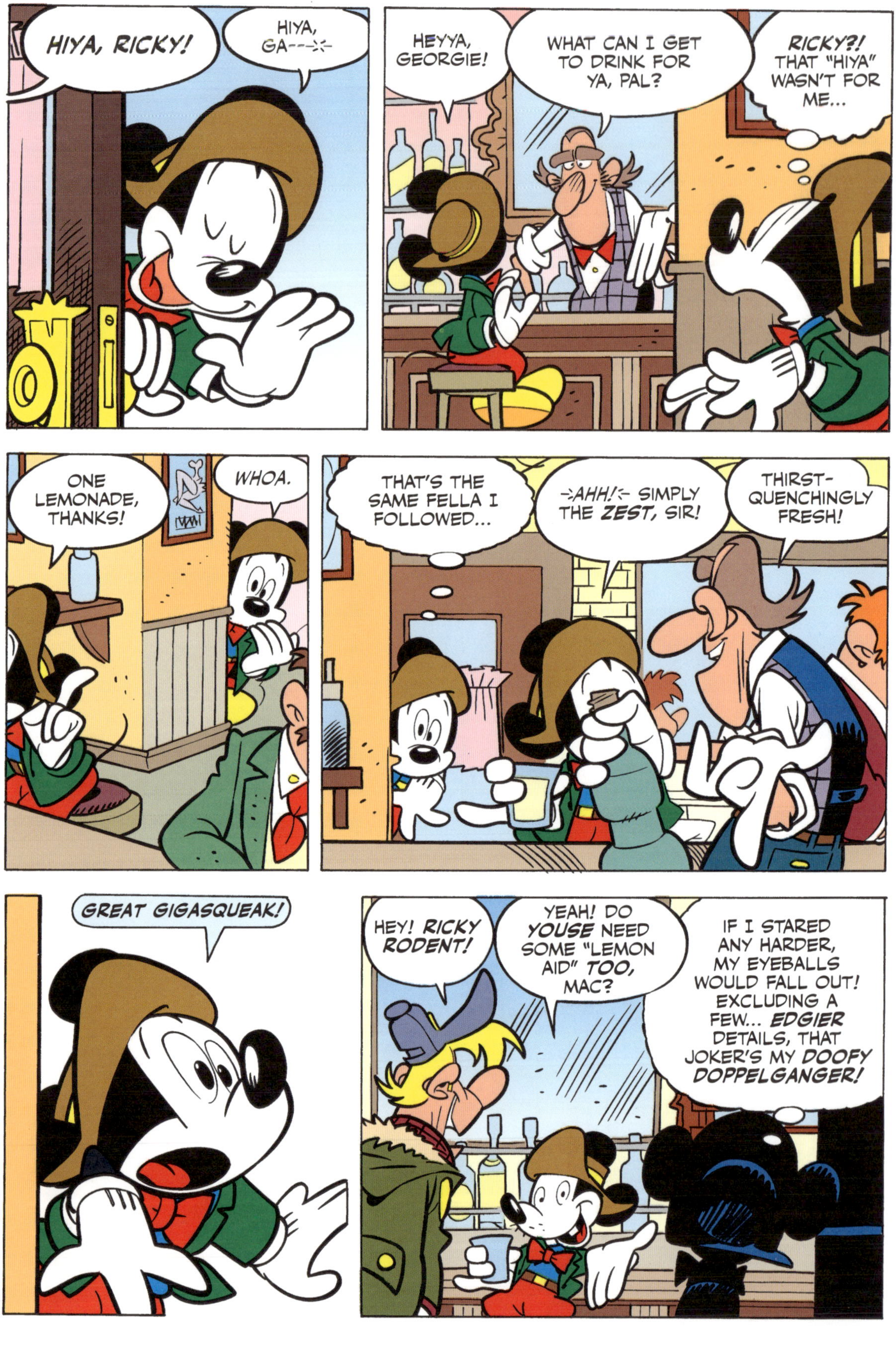
HIYA, RICKY!
HIYA, GA--
HEYYA, GEORGIE!
WHAT CAN I GET TO DRINK FOR YA, PAL?
RICKY?! THAT "HIYA" WASN'T FOR ME...
ONE LEMONADE, THANKS!
WHOA.
THAT'S THE SAME FELLA I FOLLOWED...
AHH! SIMPLY THE ZEST, SIR!
THIRST-QUENCHINGLY FRESH!
GREAT GIGASQUEAK!
HEY! RICKY RODENT!
YEAH! DO YOUSE NEED SOME "LEMON AID" TOO, MAC?
IF I STARED ANY HARDER, MY EYEBALLS WOULD FALL OUT! EXCLUDING A FEW... EDGIER DETAILS, THAT JOKER'S MY DOOFY DOPPELGANGER!

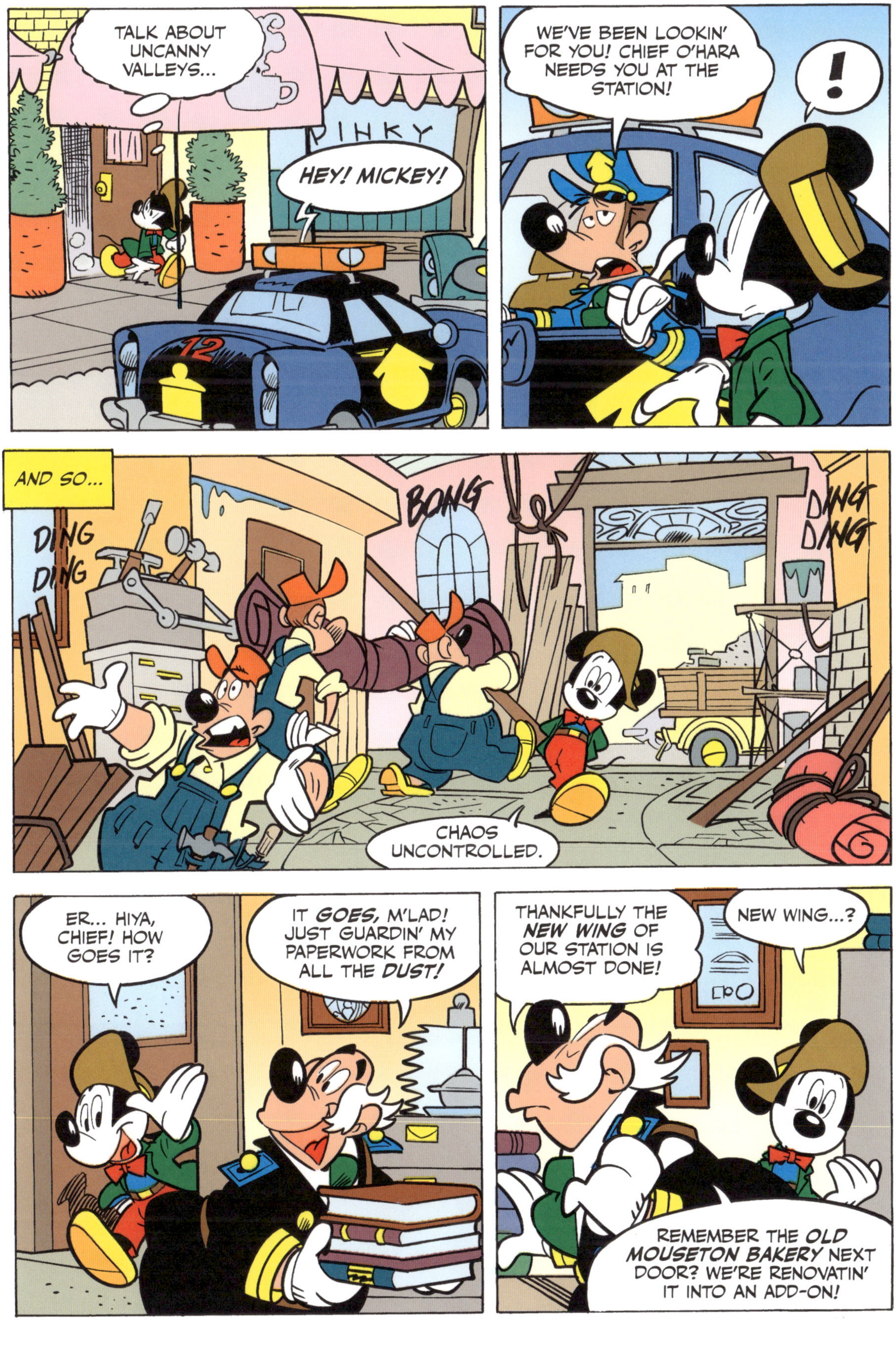
TALK ABOUT UNCANNY VALLEYS...
HEY! MICKEY!
WE'VE BEEN LOOKIN' FOR YOU! CHIEF O'HARA NEEDS YOU AT THE STATION!
!
AND SO...
DING DING
BONG
DING DING
CHAOS UNCONTROLLED.
ER... HIYA, CHIEF! HOW GOES IT?
IT *GOES,* M'LAD! JUST GUARDIN' MY PAPERWORK FROM ALL THE *DUST!*
THANKFULLY THE *NEW WING* OF OUR STATION IS ALMOST DONE!
NEW WING...?
REMEMBER THE *OLD MOUSETON BAKERY* NEXT DOOR? WE'RE RENOVATIN' IT INTO AN ADD-ON!

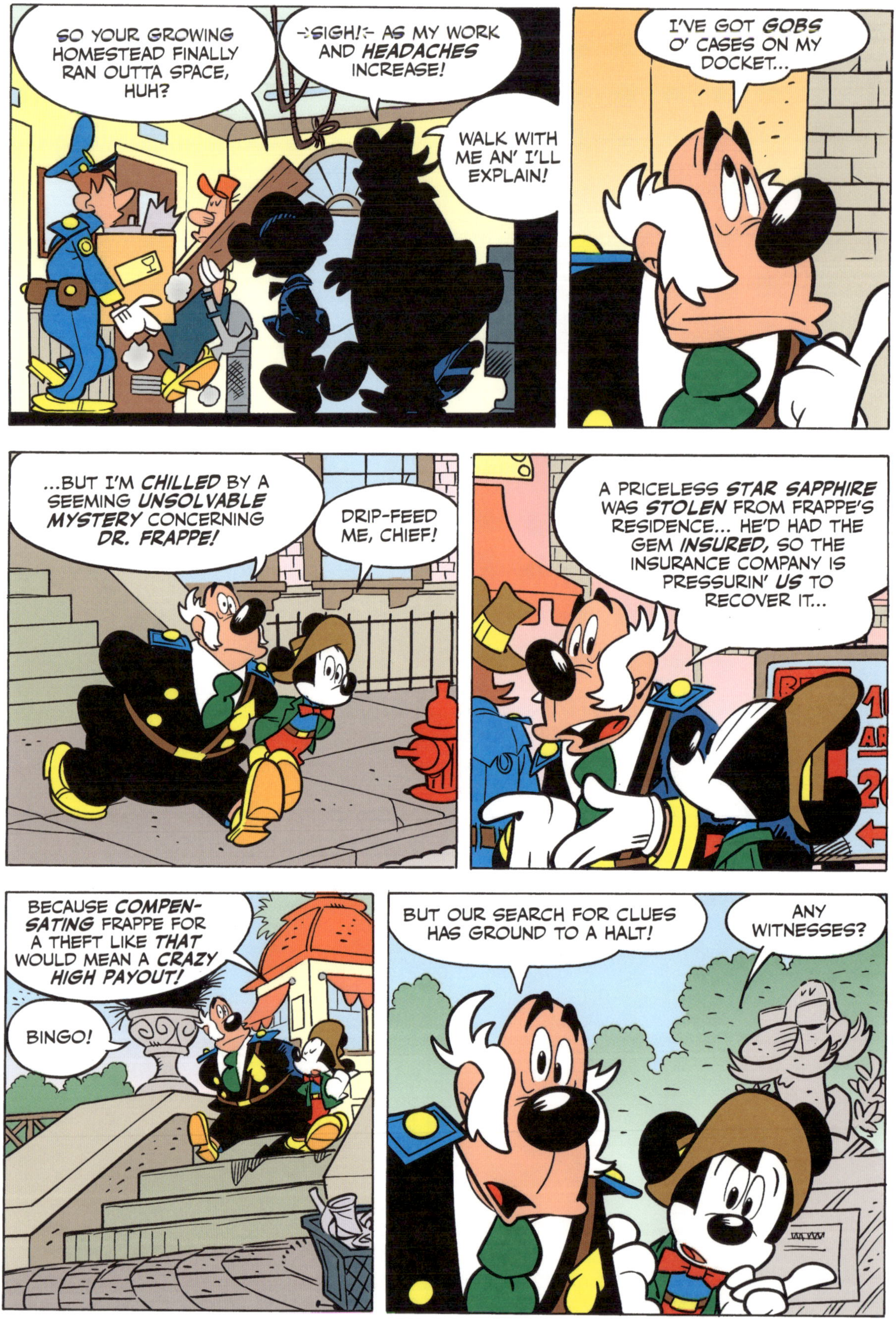
SO YOUR GROWING HOMESTEAD FINALLY RAN OUTTA SPACE, HUH?
-SIGH!- AS MY WORK AND HEADACHES INCREASE!
WALK WITH ME AN' I'LL EXPLAIN!
I'VE GOT GOBS O' CASES ON MY DOCKET...
...BUT I'M CHILLED BY A SEEMING UNSOLVABLE MYSTERY CONCERNING DR. FRAPPE!
DRIP-FEED ME, CHIEF!
A PRICELESS STAR SAPPHIRE WAS STOLEN FROM FRAPPE'S RESIDENCE... HE'D HAD THE GEM INSURED, SO THE INSURANCE COMPANY IS PRESSURIN' US TO RECOVER IT...
BECAUSE COMPEN-SATING FRAPPE FOR A THEFT LIKE THAT WOULD MEAN A CRAZY HIGH PAYOUT!
BINGO!
BUT OUR SEARCH FOR CLUES HAS GROUND TO A HALT!
ANY WITNESSES?

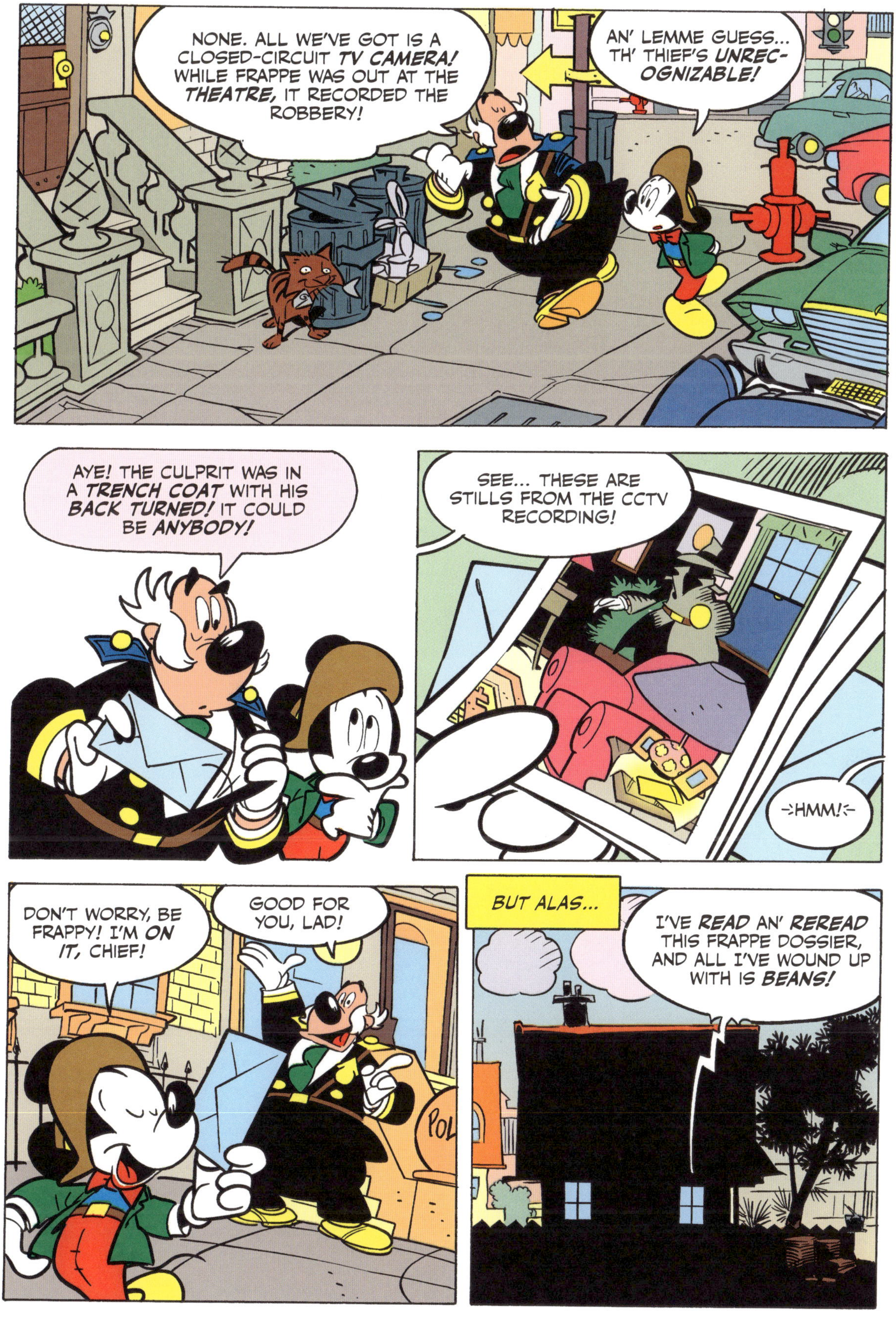
NONE. ALL WE'VE GOT IS A CLOSED-CIRCUIT TV CAMERA! WHILE FRAPPE WAS OUT AT THE THEATRE, IT RECORDED THE ROBBERY!
AN' LEMME GUESS... TH' THIEF'S UNRECOGNIZABLE!
AYE! THE CULPRIT WAS IN A TRENCH COAT WITH HIS BACK TURNED! IT COULD BE ANYBODY!
SEE... THESE ARE STILLS FROM THE CCTV RECORDING!
HMM!
DON'T WORRY, BE FRAPPY! I'M ON IT, CHIEF!
GOOD FOR YOU, LAD!
BUT ALAS...
I'VE READ AN' REREAD THIS FRAPPE DOSSIER, AND ALL I'VE WOUND UP WITH IS BEANS!

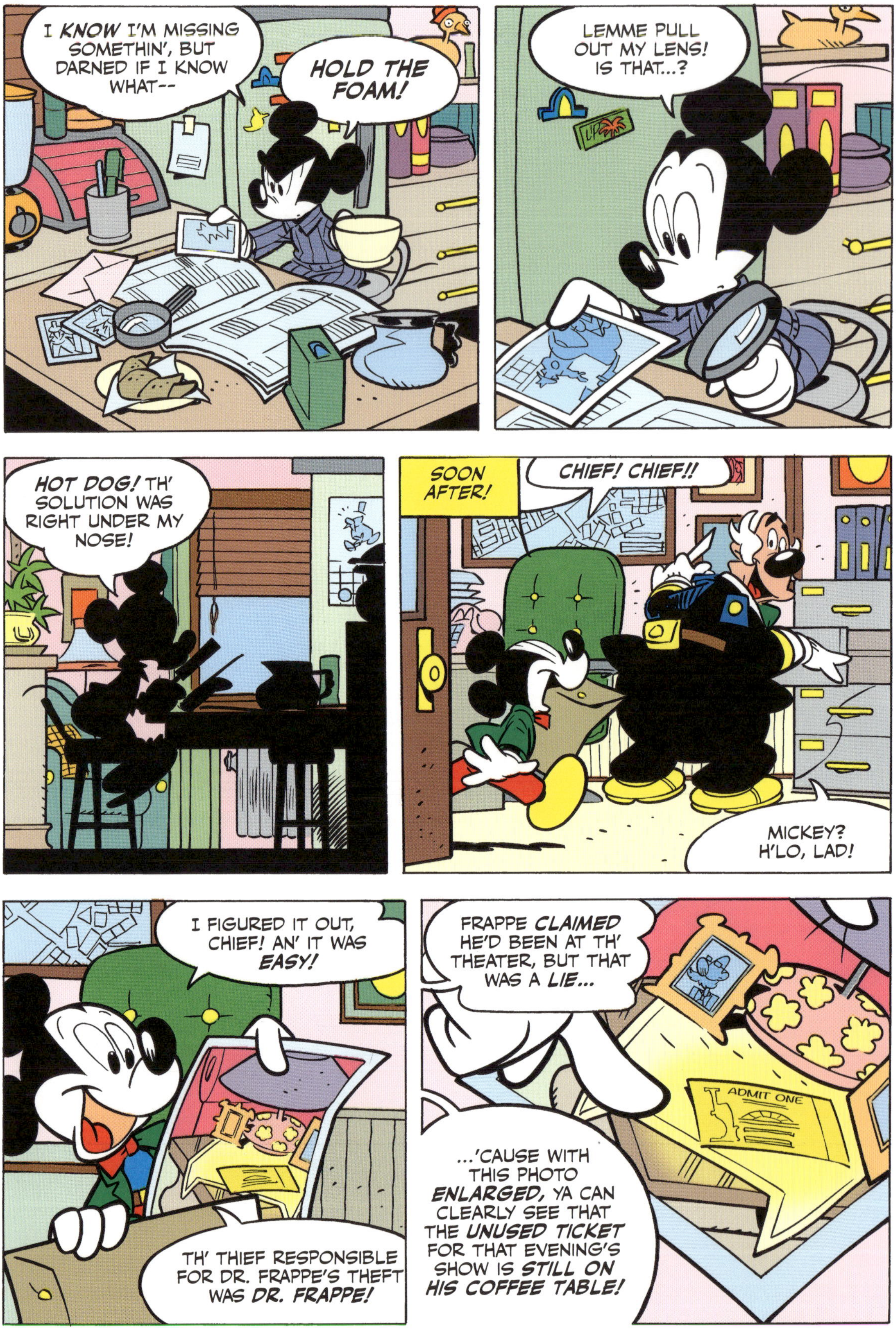

I KNOW I'M MISSING SOMETHIN', BUT DARNED IF I KNOW WHAT--
HOLD THE FOAM!
LEMME PULL OUT MY LENS! IS THAT...?
UP
HOT DOG! TH' SOLUTION WAS RIGHT UNDER MY NOSE!
SOON AFTER!
CHIEF! CHIEF!!
MICKEY? H'LO, LAD!
I FIGURED IT OUT, CHIEF! AN' IT WAS EASY!
TH' THIEF RESPONSIBLE FOR DR. FRAPPE'S THEFT WAS DR. FRAPPE!
FRAPPE CLAIMED HE'D BEEN AT TH' THEATER, BUT THAT WAS A LIE...
ADMIT ONE
...'CAUSE WITH THIS PHOTO ENLARGED, YA CAN CLEARLY SEE THAT THE UNUSED TICKET FOR THAT EVENING'S SHOW IS STILL ON HIS COFFEE TABLE!

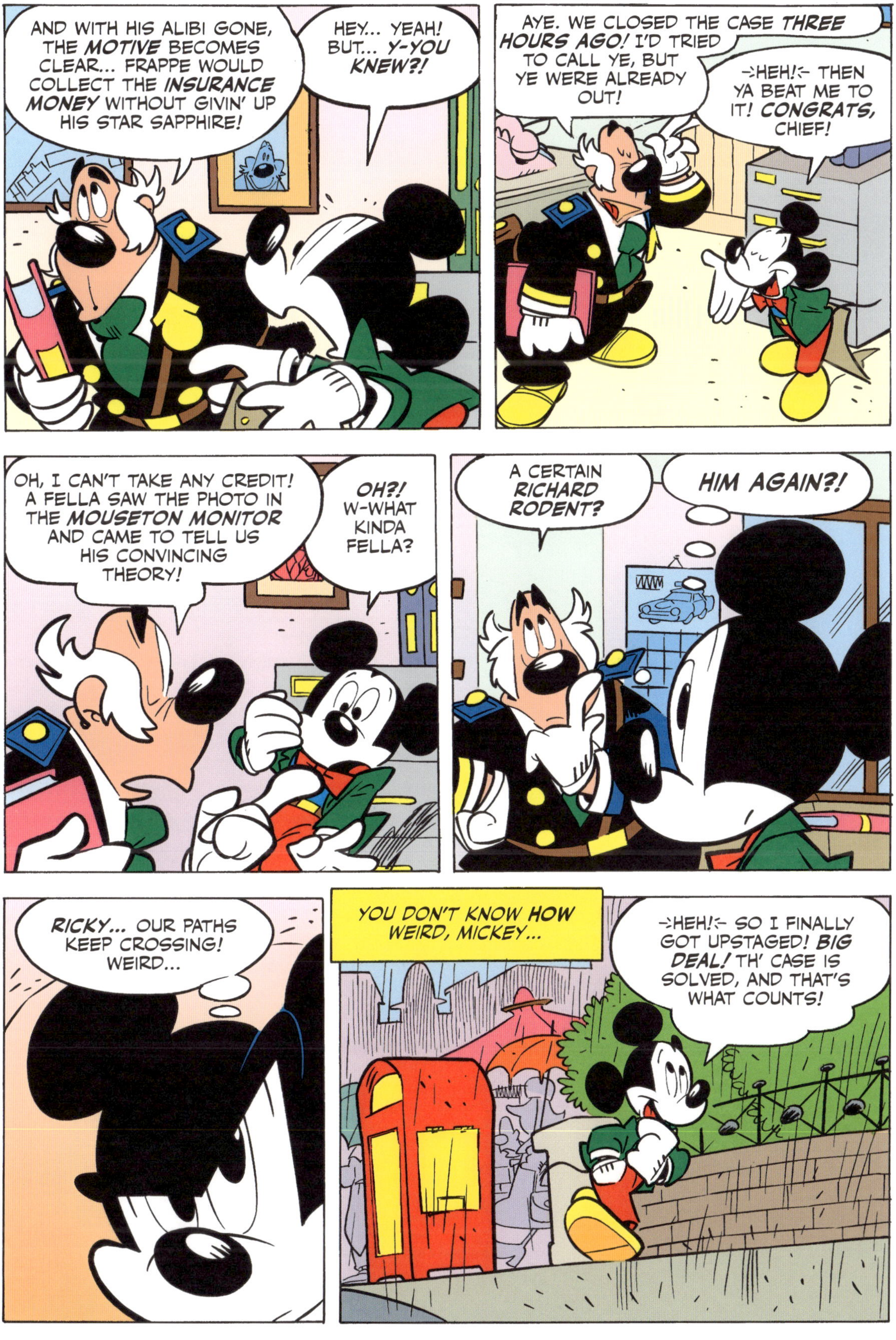
AND WITH HIS ALIBI GONE, THE MOTIVE BECOMES CLEAR... FRAPPE WOULD COLLECT THE INSURANCE MONEY WITHOUT GIVIN' UP HIS STAR SAPPHIRE!
HEY... YEAH! BUT... Y-YOU KNEW?!
AYE. WE CLOSED THE CASE THREE HOURS AGO! I'D TRIED TO CALL YE, BUT YE WERE ALREADY OUT!
HEH! THEN YA BEAT ME TO IT! CONGRATS, CHIEF!
OH, I CAN'T TAKE ANY CREDIT! A FELLA SAW THE PHOTO IN THE MOUSETON MONITOR AND CAME TO TELL US HIS CONVINCING THEORY!
OH?! W-WHAT KINDA FELLA?
A CERTAIN RICHARD RODENT?
HIM AGAIN?!
RICKY... OUR PATHS KEEP CROSSING! WEIRD...
YOU DON'T KNOW HOW WEIRD, MICKEY...
HEH! SO I FINALLY GOT UPSTAGED! BIG DEAL! TH' CASE IS SOLVED, AND THAT'S WHAT COUNTS!

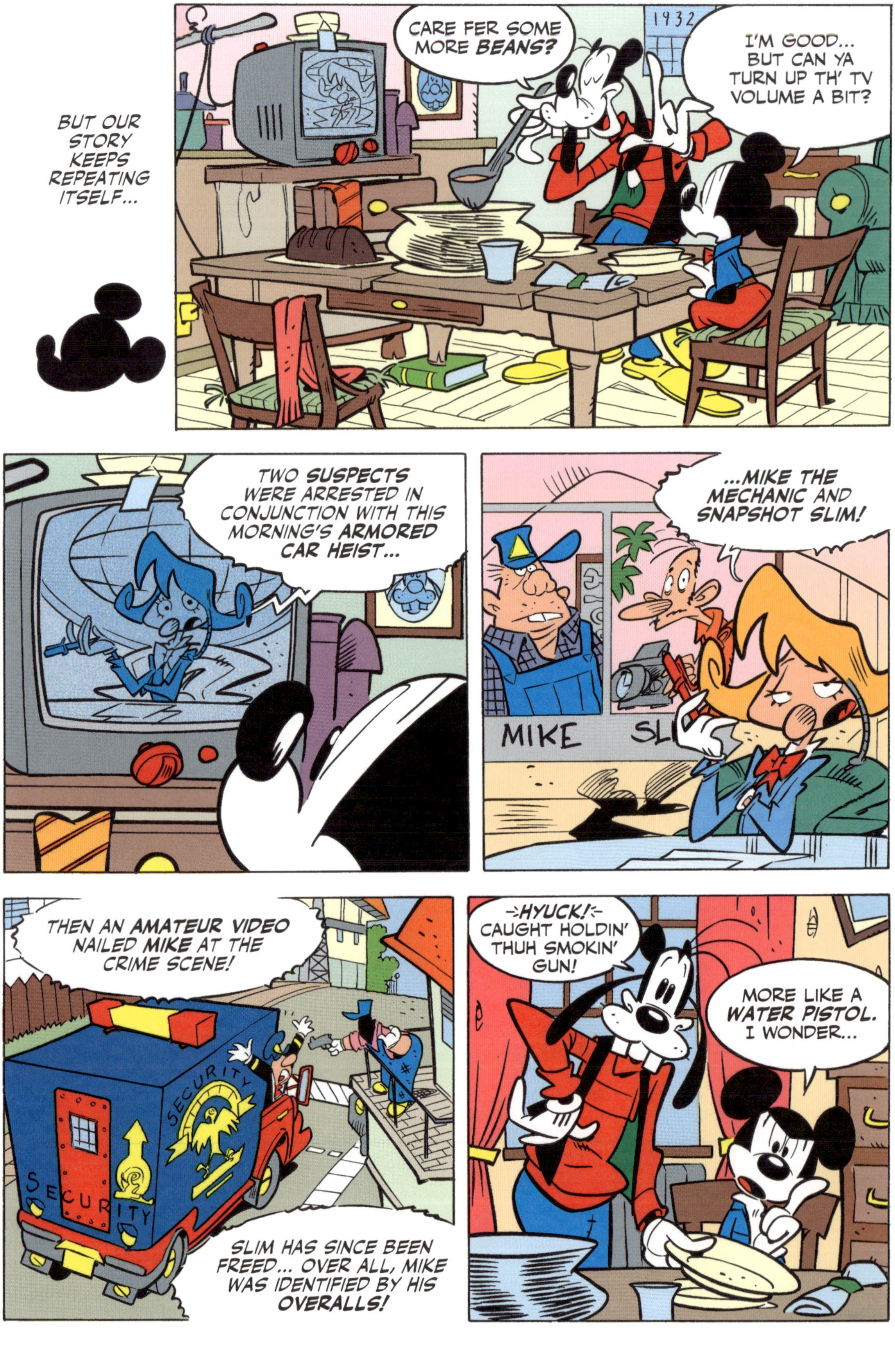
BUT OUR STORY KEEPS REPEATING ITSELF...
1932
CARE FER SOME MORE BEANS?
I'M GOOD... BUT CAN YA TURN UP TH' TV VOLUME A BIT?
TWO SUSPECTS WERE ARRESTED IN CONJUNCTION WITH THIS MORNING'S ARMORED CAR HEIST...
...MIKE THE MECHANIC AND SNAPSHOT SLIM!
MIKE
THEN AN AMATEUR VIDEO NAILED MIKE AT THE CRIME SCENE!
SECURITY
SECURITY
SLIM HAS SINCE BEEN FREED... OVER ALL, MIKE WAS IDENTIFIED BY HIS OVERALLS!
HYUCK! CAUGHT HOLDIN' THUH SMOKIN' GUN!
MORE LIKE A WATER PISTOL. I WONDER...

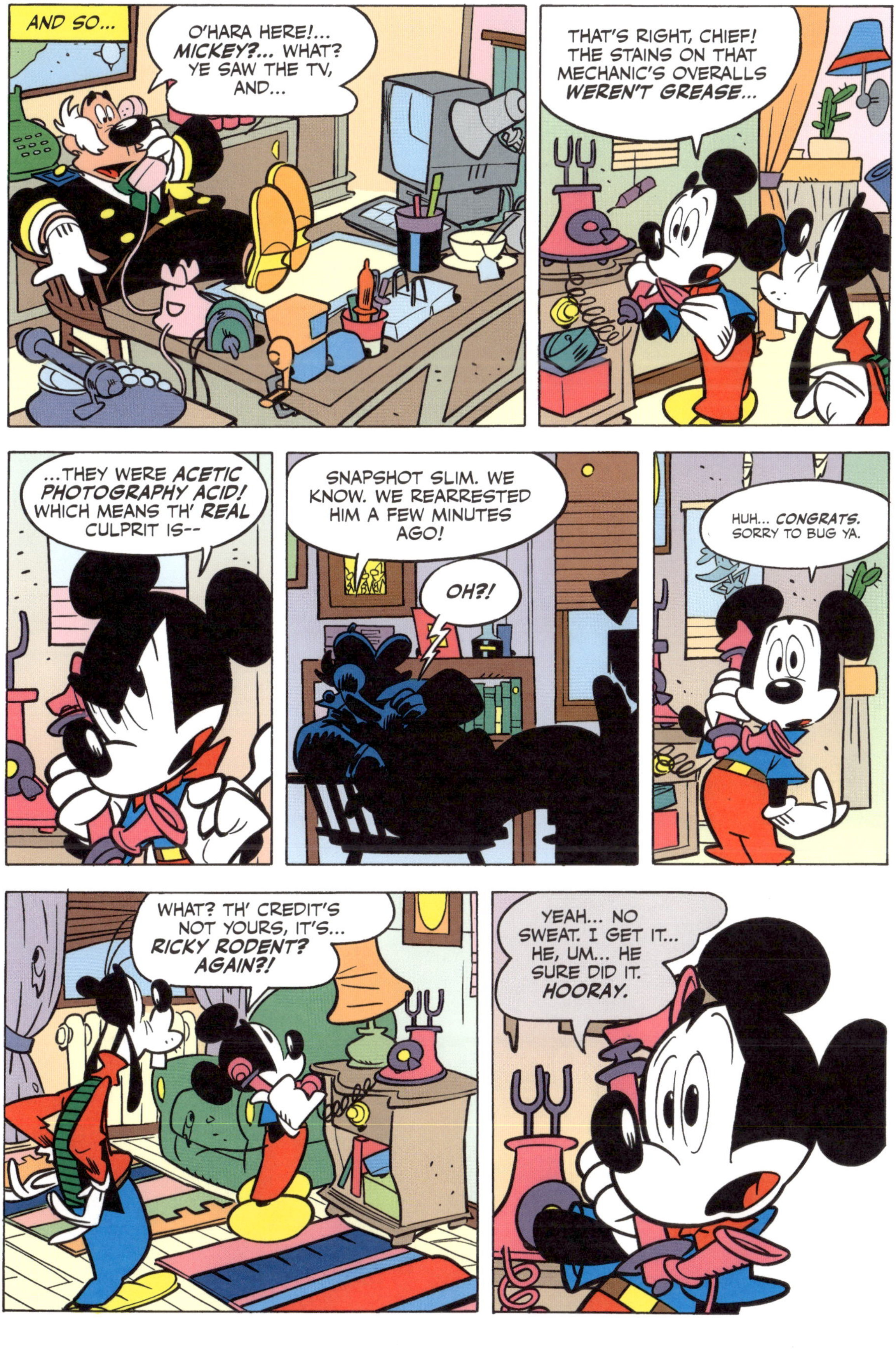

AND SO...
O'HARA HERE!... MICKEY?... WHAT? YE SAW THE TV, AND...
THAT'S RIGHT, CHIEF! THE STAINS ON THAT MECHANIC'S OVERALLS WEREN'T GREASE...
...THEY WERE ACETIC PHOTOGRAPHY ACID! WHICH MEANS TH' REAL CULPRIT IS--
SNAPSHOT SLIM. WE KNOW. WE REARRESTED HIM A FEW MINUTES AGO!
OH?!
HUH... CONGRATS. SORRY TO BUG YA.
WHAT? TH' CREDIT'S NOT YOURS, IT'S... RICKY RODENT? AGAIN?!
YEAH... NO SWEAT. I GET IT... HE, UM... HE SURE DID IT. HOORAY.

AND SO IT GOES...
HIYA, CHIEF! YEAH, I FOUND THE SOLUTION TO--
ALREADY SOLVED?!... ->SIGH!<- HIM AGAIN... NO, IT'S... I'M GOOD.
->SIGH!<- I'VE STOPPED BEING THE MAIN CHARACTER IN MY OWN LIFE! MAKING MYSELF USEFUL MADE ME FEEL USEFUL... IMPORTANT...
NOWADAYS I'M LATE TO ANYTHING AN' EVERYTHING!
THUS...
OOH! GOT CHANGE FOR SOME ICE CREAM?
YEAH, BUT I WAS GONNA USE IT TO BUY A PAPER...
ICE CREAM
EXTRY! EXTRY! RICKY RODENT FOILS BANK ROBBERY!
READ TH' EXPLOITS OF MOUSETON'S NEWEST HERO!
!
!

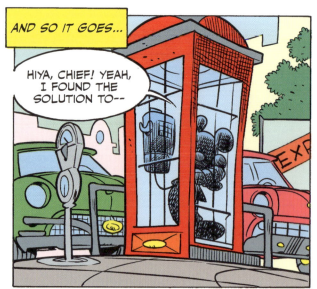

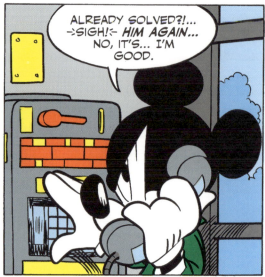

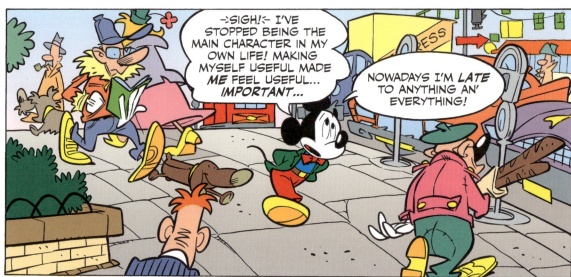

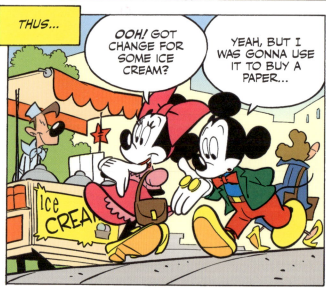

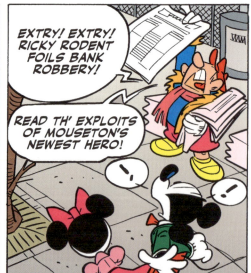

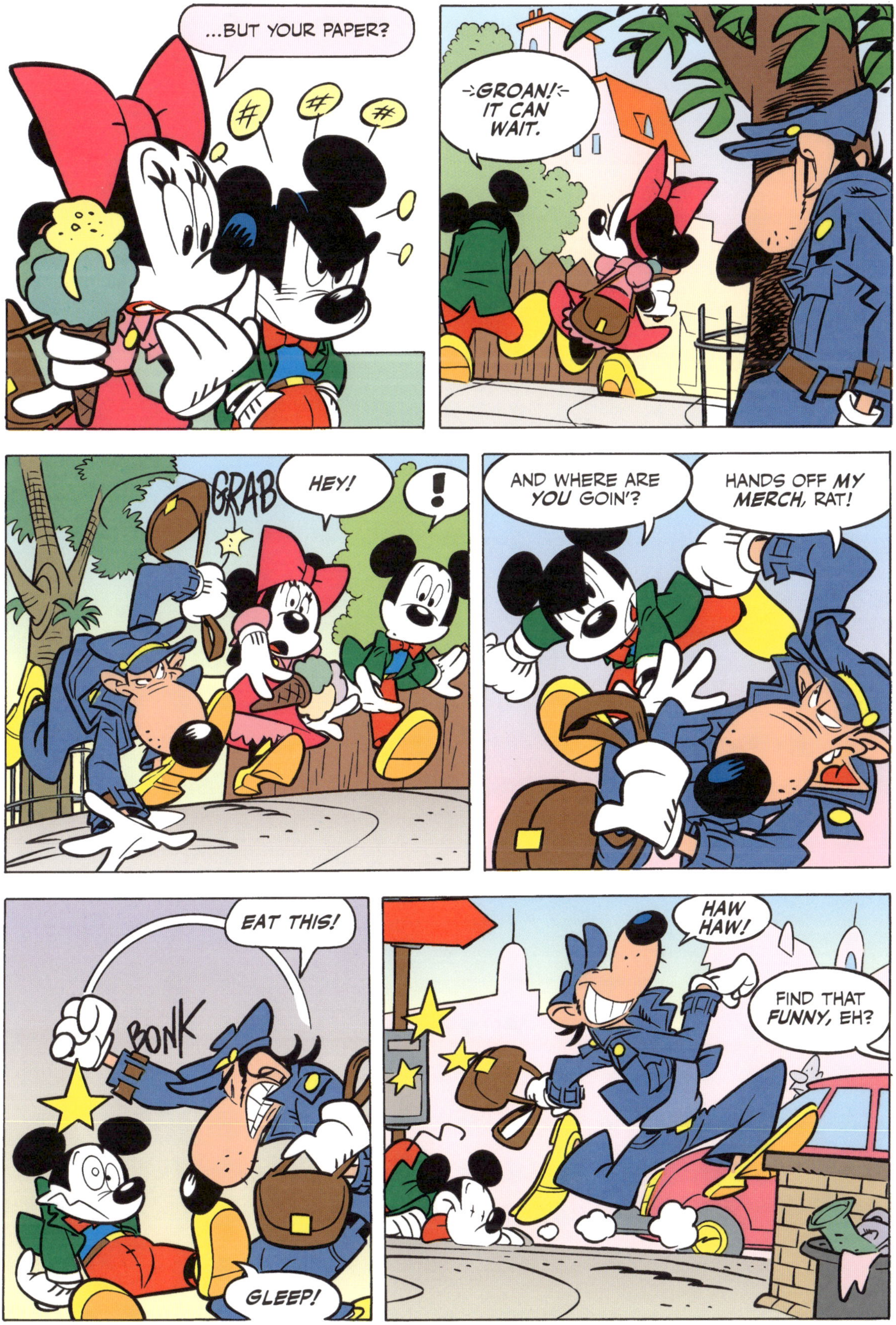
...BUT YOUR PAPER?
#
#
#
GROAN! IT CAN WAIT.
GRAB
HEY!
!
AND WHERE ARE YOU GOIN'?
HANDS OFF MY MERCH, RAT!
EAT THIS!
BONK
GLEEP!
HAW HAW!
FIND THAT FUNNY, EH?

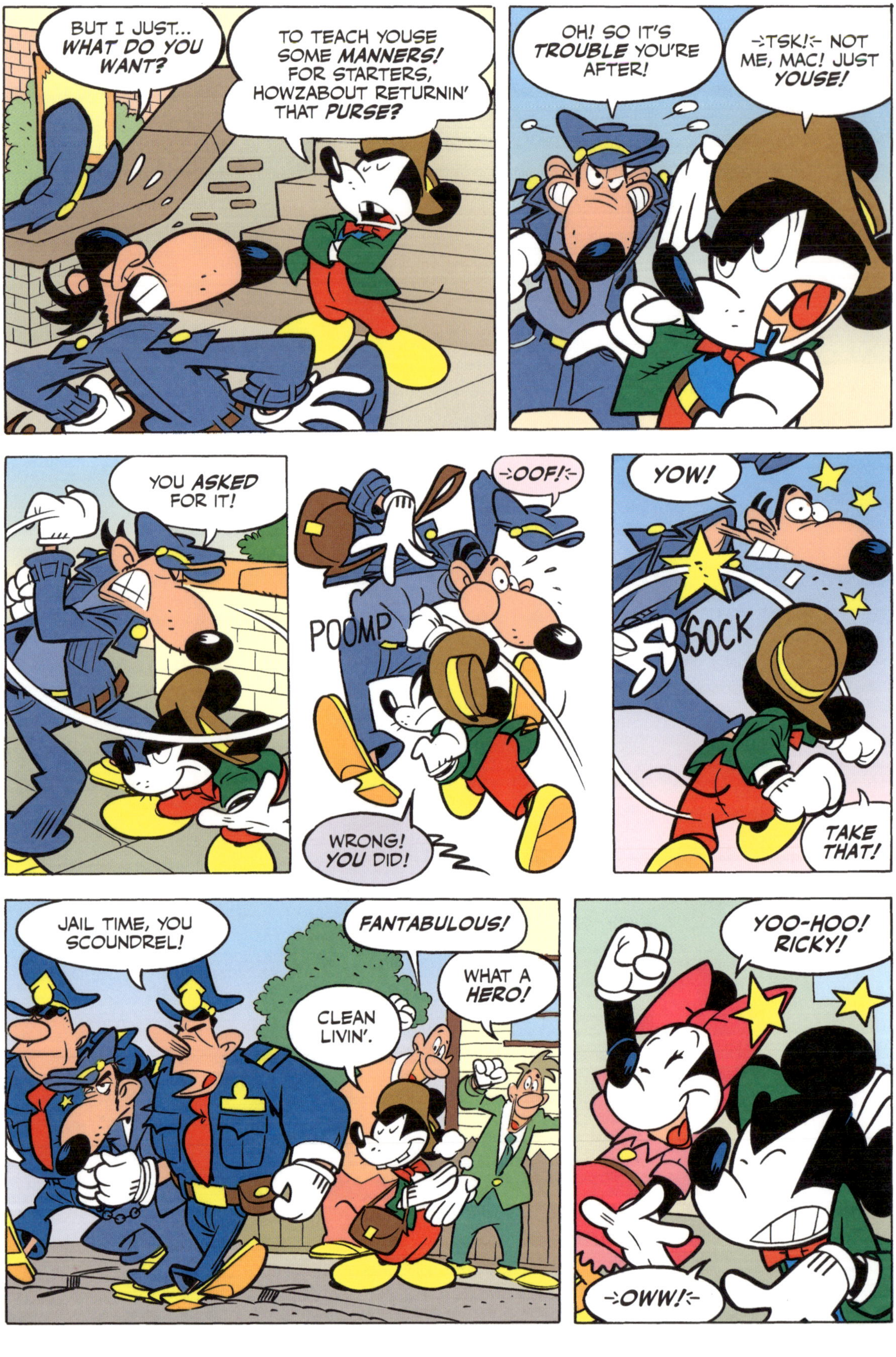

BUT I JUST... WHAT DO YOU WANT?
TO TEACH YOUSE SOME MANNERS! FOR STARTERS, HOWZABOUT RETURNIN' THAT PURSE?
OH! SO IT'S TROUBLE YOU'RE AFTER!
TSK! NOT ME, MAC! JUST YOUSE!
YOU ASKED FOR IT!
OOF!
POOMP
WRONG! YOU DID!
YOW!
SOCK
TAKE THAT!
JAIL TIME, YOU SCOUNDREL!
FANTABULOUS!
CLEAN LIVIN'.
WHAT A HERO!
YOO-HOO! RICKY!
OWW!

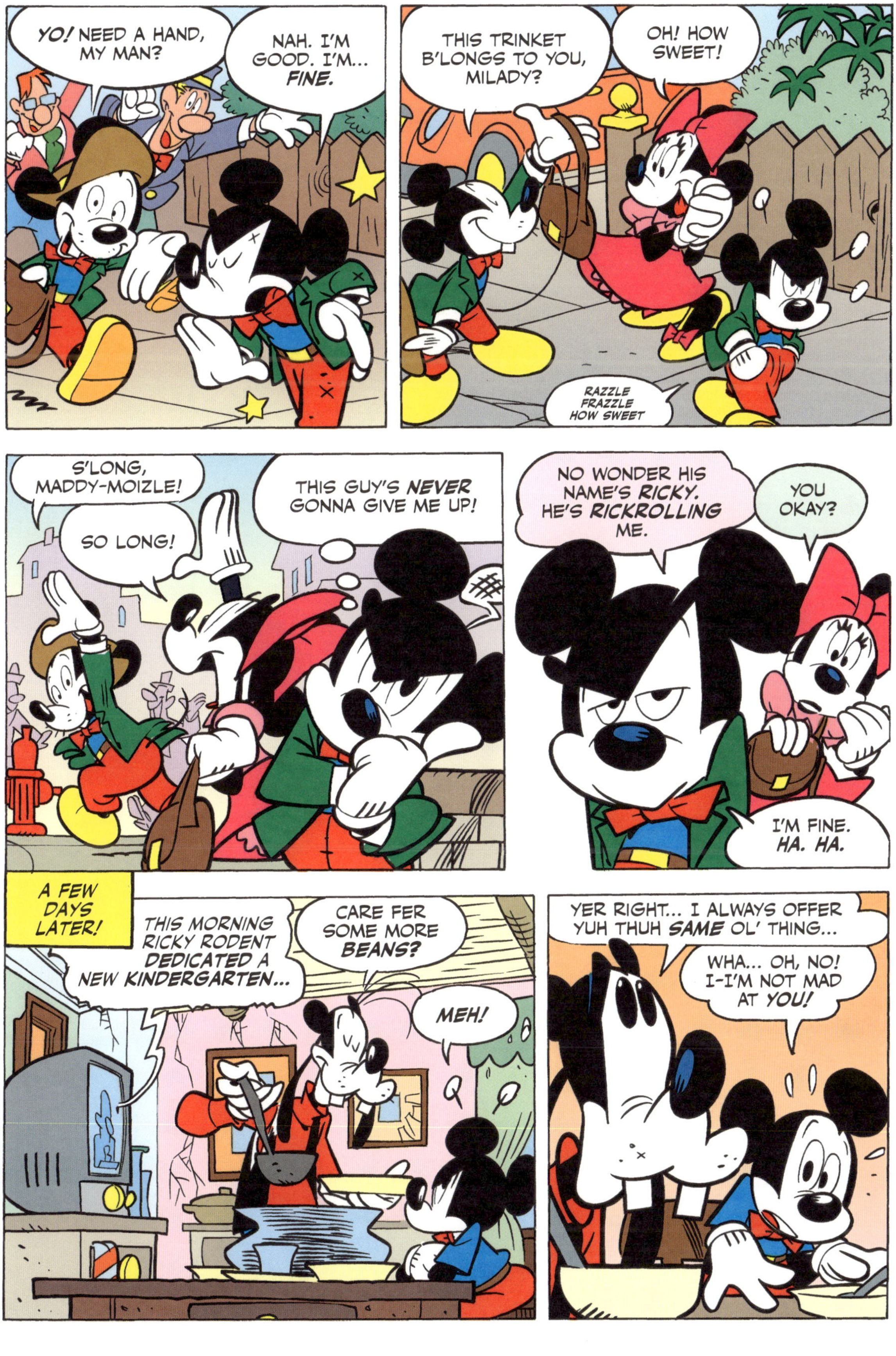
YO! NEED A HAND, MY MAN?
NAH. I'M GOOD. I'M... FINE.
THIS TRINKET B'LONGS TO YOU, MILADY?
OH! HOW SWEET!
RAZZLE FRAZZLE HOW SWEET
S'LONG, MADDY-MOIZLE!
SO LONG!
THIS GUY'S NEVER GONNA GIVE ME UP!
NO WONDER HIS NAME'S RICKY. HE'S RICKROLLING ME.
YOU OKAY?
I'M FINE. HA. HA.
A FEW DAYS LATER!
THIS MORNING RICKY RODENT DEDICATED A NEW KINDERGARTEN...
CARE FER SOME MORE BEANS?
MEH!
YER RIGHT... I ALWAYS OFFER YUH THUH SAME OL' THING...
WHA... OH, NO! I-I'M NOT MAD AT YOU!

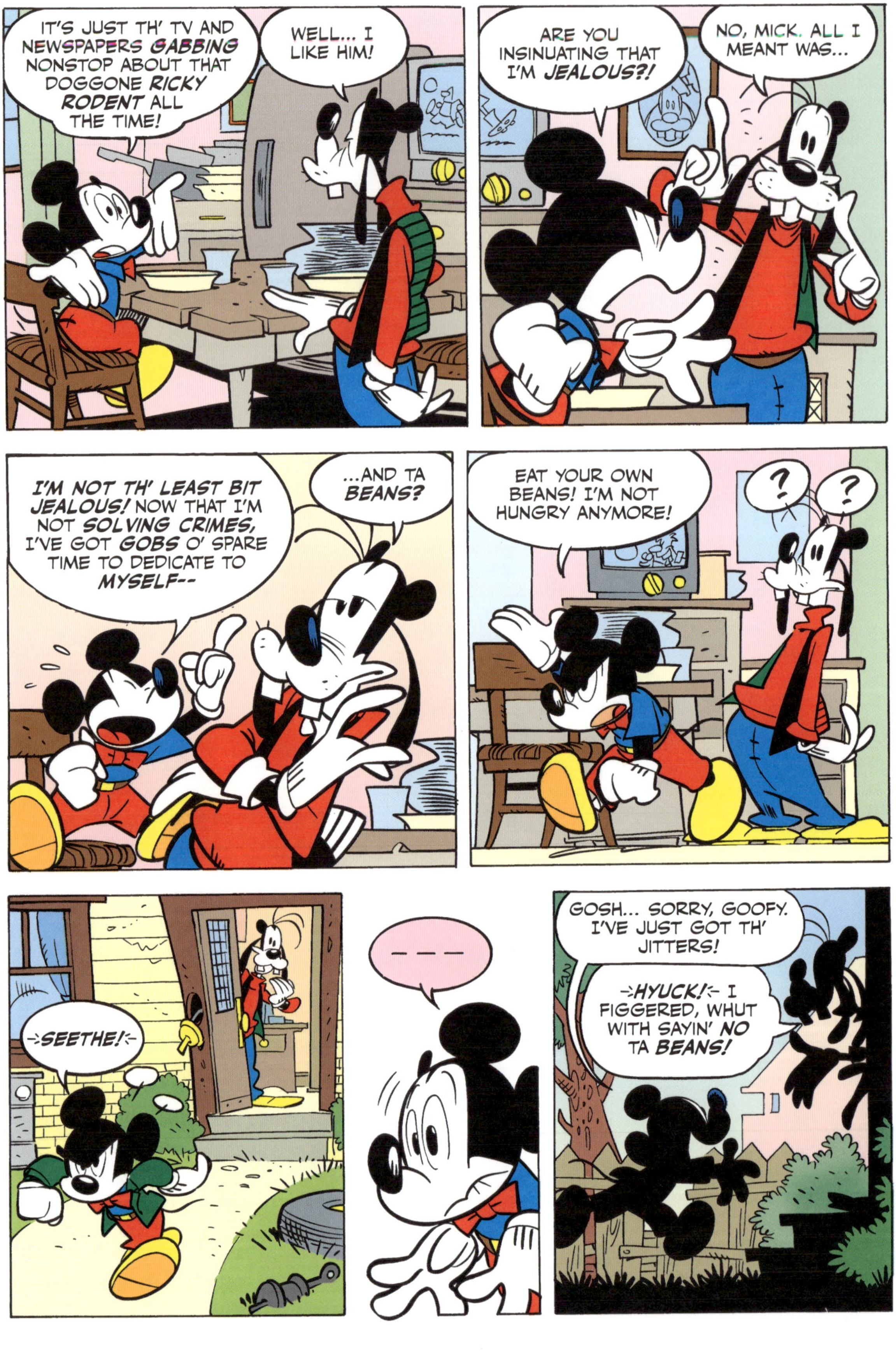
IT'S JUST TH' TV AND NEWSPAPERS GABBING NONSTOP ABOUT THAT DOGGONE RICKY RODENT ALL THE TIME!
WELL... I LIKE HIM!
ARE YOU INSINUATING THAT I'M JEALOUS?!
NO, MICK. ALL I MEANT WAS...
I'M NOT TH' LEAST BIT JEALOUS! NOW THAT I'M NOT SOLVING CRIMES, I'VE GOT GOBS O' SPARE TIME TO DEDICATE TO MYSELF--
...AND TA BEANS?
EAT YOUR OWN BEANS! I'M NOT HUNGRY ANYMORE!
? ?
SEETHE!
– – –
GOSH... SORRY, GOOFY. I'VE JUST GOT TH' JITTERS!
HYUCK! I FIGGERED, WHUT WITH SAYIN' NO TA BEANS!

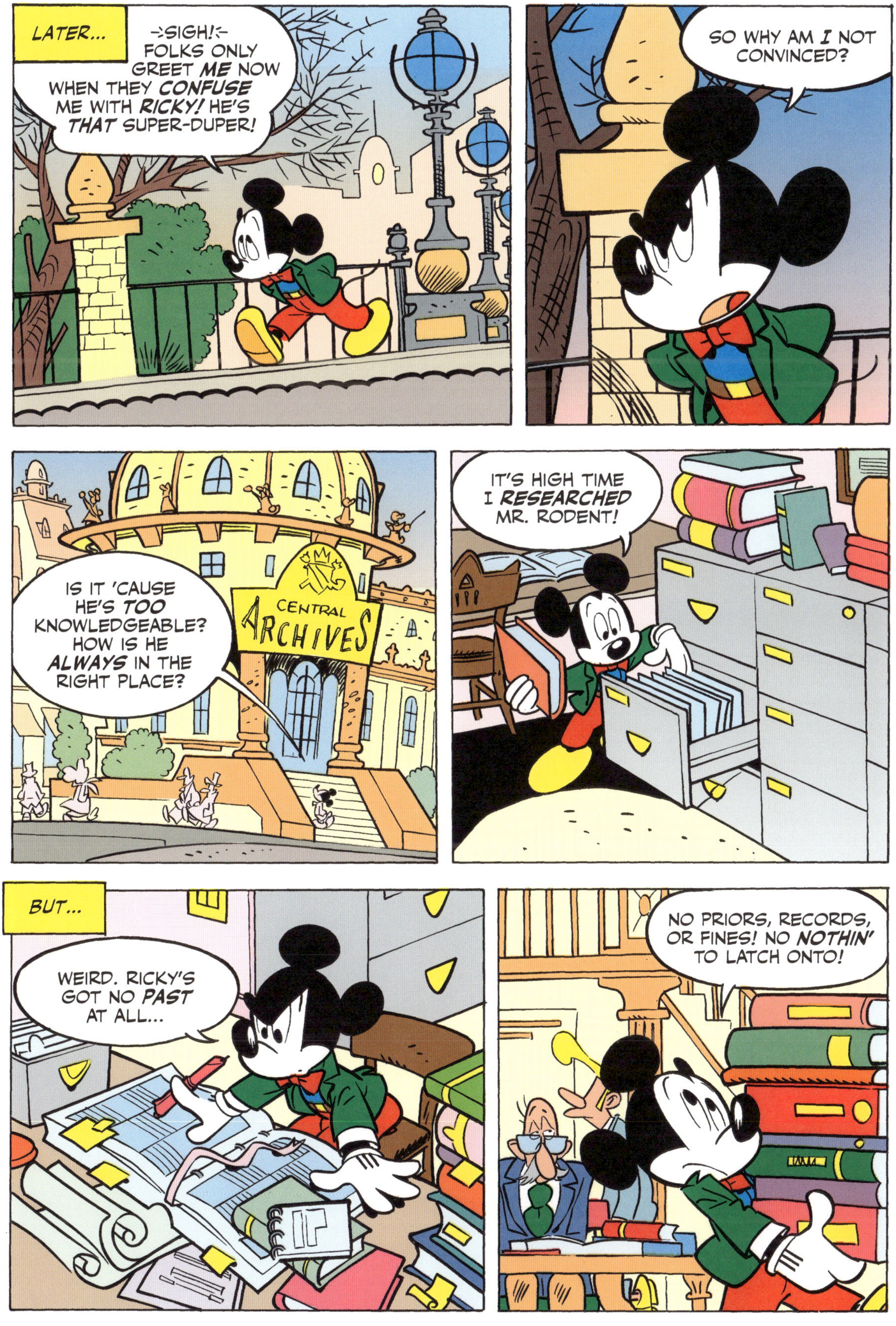

LATER...
-SIGH!- FOLKS ONLY GREET ME NOW WHEN THEY CONFUSE ME WITH RICKY! HE'S THAT SUPER-DUPER!
SO WHY AM I NOT CONVINCED?
IS IT 'CAUSE HE'S TOO KNOWLEDGEABLE? HOW IS HE ALWAYS IN THE RIGHT PLACE?
CENTRAL ARCHIVES
IT'S HIGH TIME I RESEARCHED MR. RODENT!
BUT...
WEIRD. RICKY'S GOT NO PAST AT ALL...
NO PRIORS, RECORDS, OR FINES! NO NOTHIN' TO LATCH ONTO!

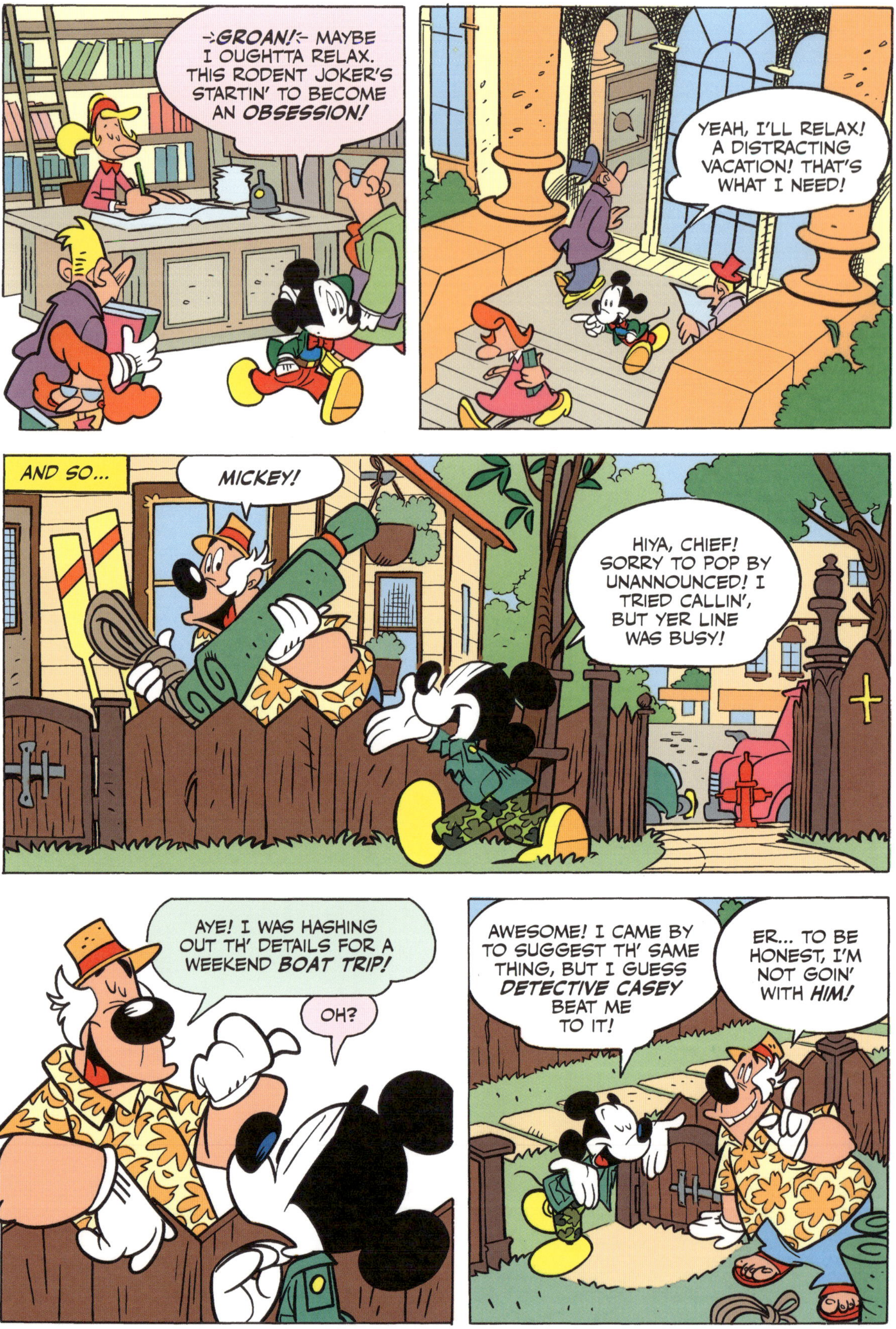

-GROAN!- MAYBE I OUGHTTA RELAX. THIS RODENT JOKER'S STARTIN' TO BECOME AN OBSESSION!
YEAH, I'LL RELAX! A DISTRACTING VACATION! THAT'S WHAT I NEED!
AND SO...
MICKEY!
HIYA, CHIEF! SORRY TO POP BY UNANNOUNCED! I TRIED CALLIN', BUT YER LINE WAS BUSY!
AYE! I WAS HASHING OUT TH' DETAILS FOR A WEEKEND BOAT TRIP!
OH?
AWESOME! I CAME BY TO SUGGEST TH' SAME THING, BUT I GUESS DETECTIVE CASEY BEAT ME TO IT!
ER... TO BE HONEST, I'M NOT GOIN' WITH HIM!

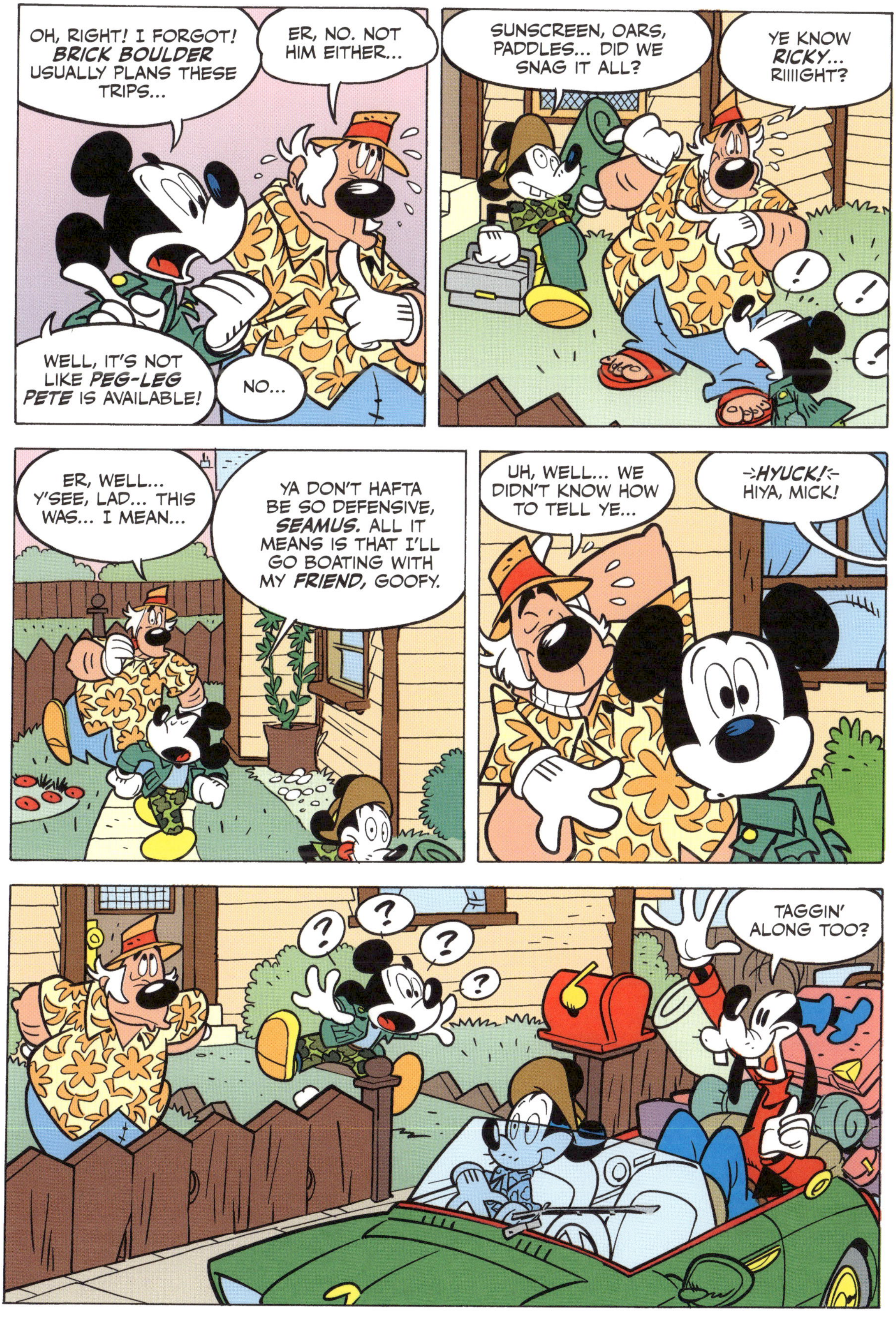
OH, RIGHT! I FORGOT! BRICK BOULDER USUALLY PLANS THESE TRIPS...
ER, NO. NOT HIM EITHER...
WELL, IT'S NOT LIKE PEG-LEG PETE IS AVAILABLE!
NO...
SUNSCREEN, OARS, PADDLES... DID WE SNAG IT ALL?
YE KNOW RICKY... RIIIIGHT?
!
!
!
ER, WELL... Y'SEE, LAD... THIS WAS... I MEAN...
YA DON'T HAFTA BE SO DEFENSIVE, SEAMUS. ALL IT MEANS IS THAT I'LL GO BOATING WITH MY FRIEND, GOOFY.
UH, WELL... WE DIDN'T KNOW HOW TO TELL YE...
HYUCK! HIYA, MICK!
?
?
?
?
TAGGIN' ALONG TOO?

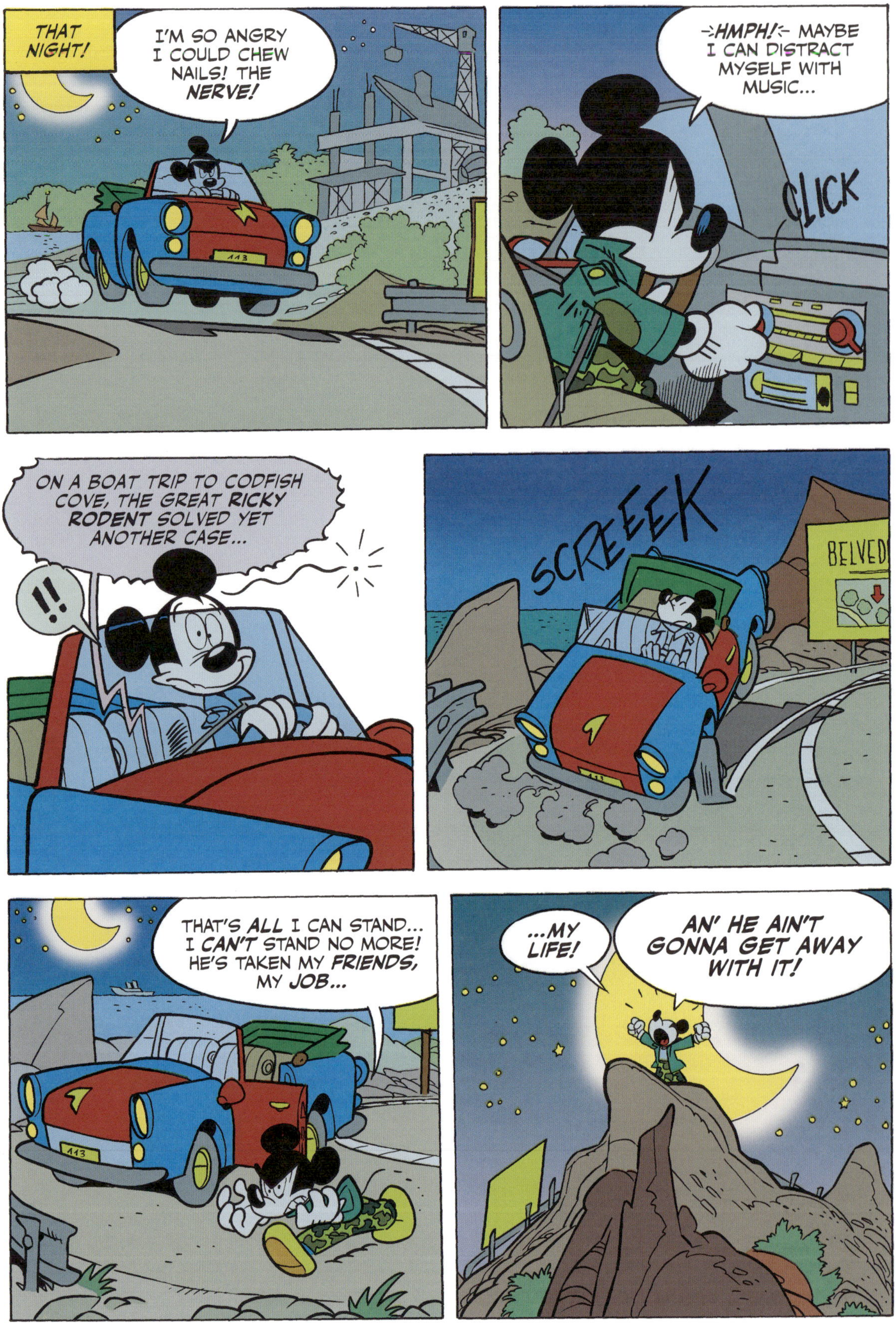
THAT NIGHT!
I'M SO ANGRY I COULD CHEW NAILS! THE NERVE!
HMPH! MAYBE I CAN DISTRACT MYSELF WITH MUSIC...
CLICK
ON A BOAT TRIP TO CODFISH COVE, THE GREAT RICKY RODENT SOLVED YET ANOTHER CASE...
!!
SCREEEK
BELVED
THAT'S ALL I CAN STAND... I CAN'T STAND NO MORE! HE'S TAKEN MY FRIENDS, MY JOB...
...MY LIFE!
AN' HE AIN'T GONNA GET AWAY WITH IT!

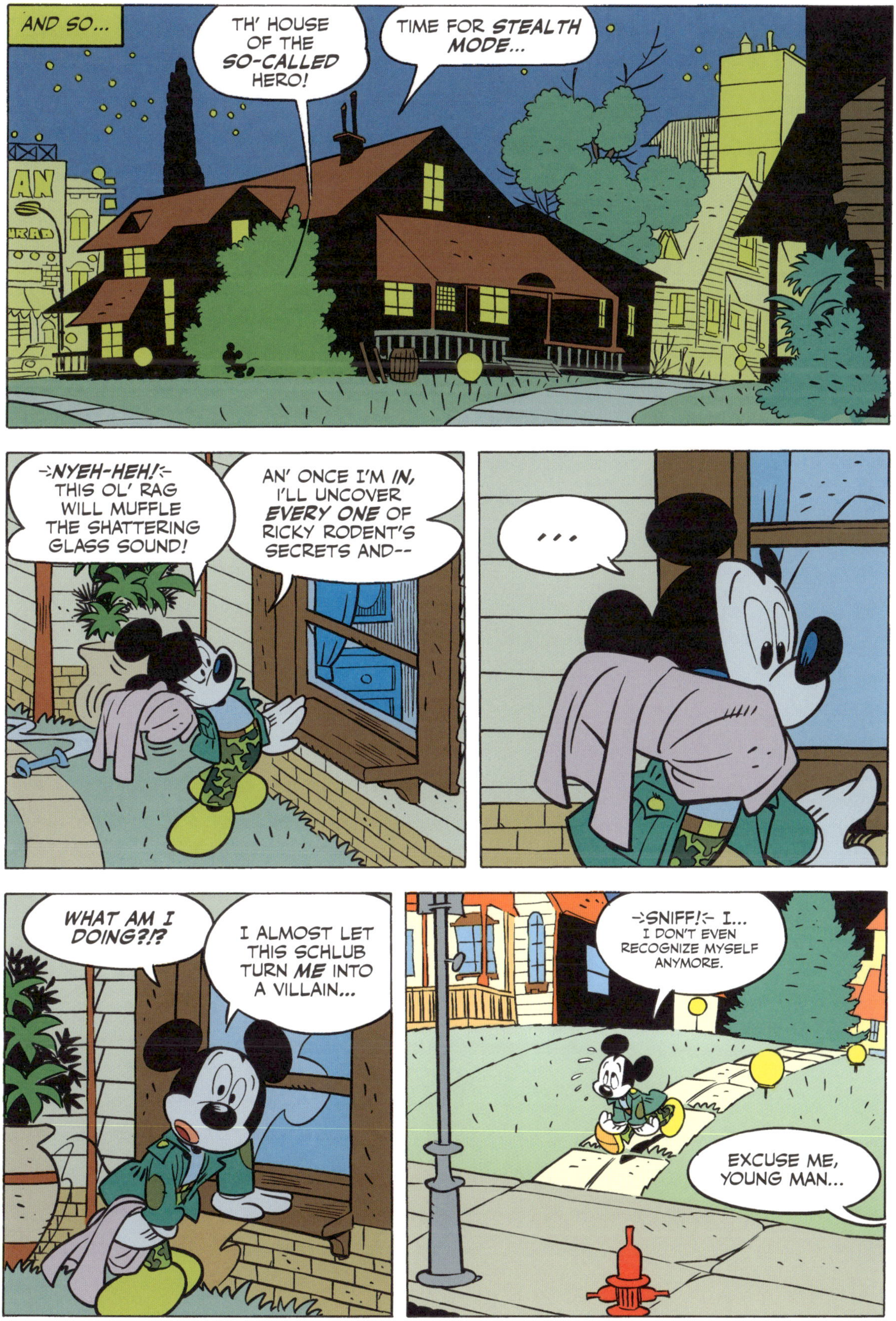
AND SO...
TH' HOUSE OF THE SO-CALLED HERO!
TIME FOR STEALTH MODE...
NYEH-HEH! THIS OL' RAG WILL MUFFLE THE SHATTERING GLASS SOUND!
AN' ONCE I'M IN, I'LL UNCOVER EVERY ONE OF RICKY RODENT'S SECRETS AND--
...
WHAT AM I DOING?!?
I ALMOST LET THIS SCHLUB TURN ME INTO A VILLAIN...
SNIFF! I... I DON'T EVEN RECOGNIZE MYSELF ANYMORE.
EXCUSE ME, YOUNG MAN...

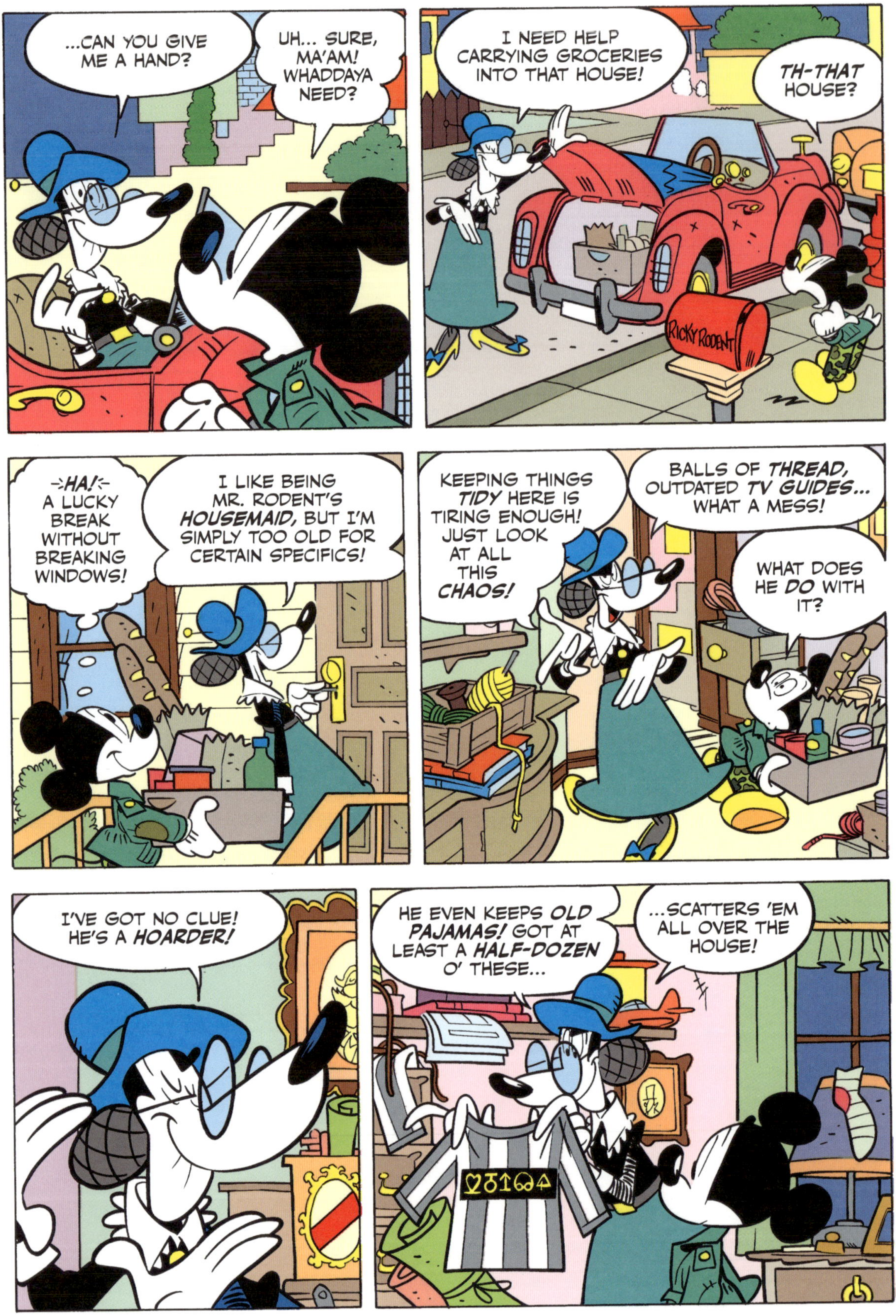
...CAN YOU GIVE ME A HAND?
UH... SURE, MA'AM! WHADDAYA NEED?
I NEED HELP CARRYING GROCERIES INTO THAT HOUSE!
TH-THAT HOUSE?
RICKY RODENT
HA! A LUCKY BREAK WITHOUT BREAKING WINDOWS!
I LIKE BEING MR. RODENT'S HOUSEMAID, BUT I'M SIMPLY TOO OLD FOR CERTAIN SPECIFICS!
KEEPING THINGS TIDY HERE IS TIRING ENOUGH! JUST LOOK AT ALL THIS CHAOS!
BALLS OF THREAD, OUTDATED TV GUIDES... WHAT A MESS!
WHAT DOES HE DO WITH IT?
I'VE GOT NO CLUE! HE'S A HOARDER!
HE EVEN KEEPS OLD PAJAMAS! GOT AT LEAST A HALF-DOZEN O' THESE...
...SCATTERS 'EM ALL OVER THE HOUSE!

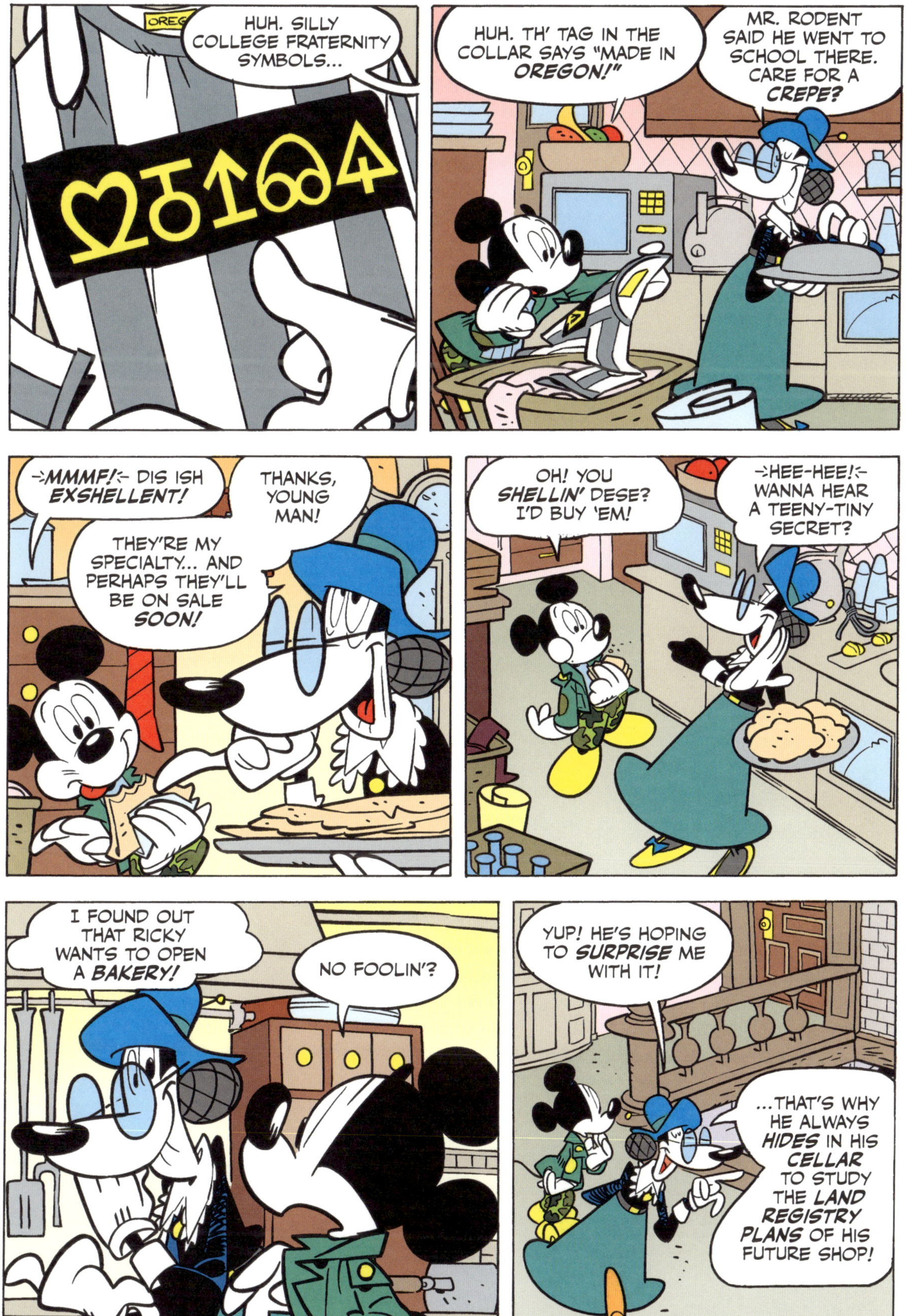
OREG
HUH. SILLY COLLEGE FRATERNITY SYMBOLS...
HUH. TH' TAG IN THE COLLAR SAYS "MADE IN OREGON!"
MR. RODENT SAID HE WENT TO SCHOOL THERE. CARE FOR A CREPE?
MMMF! DIS ISH EXSHELLENT!
THANKS, YOUNG MAN!
THEY'RE MY SPECIALTY... AND PERHAPS THEY'LL BE ON SALE SOON!
OH! YOU SHELLIN' DESE? I'D BUY 'EM!
HEE-HEE! WANNA HEAR A TEENY-TINY SECRET?
I FOUND OUT THAT RICKY WANTS TO OPEN A BAKERY!
NO FOOLIN'?
YUP! HE'S HOPING TO SURPRISE ME WITH IT!
...THAT'S WHY HE ALWAYS HIDES IN HIS CELLAR TO STUDY THE LAND REGISTRY PLANS OF HIS FUTURE SHOP!

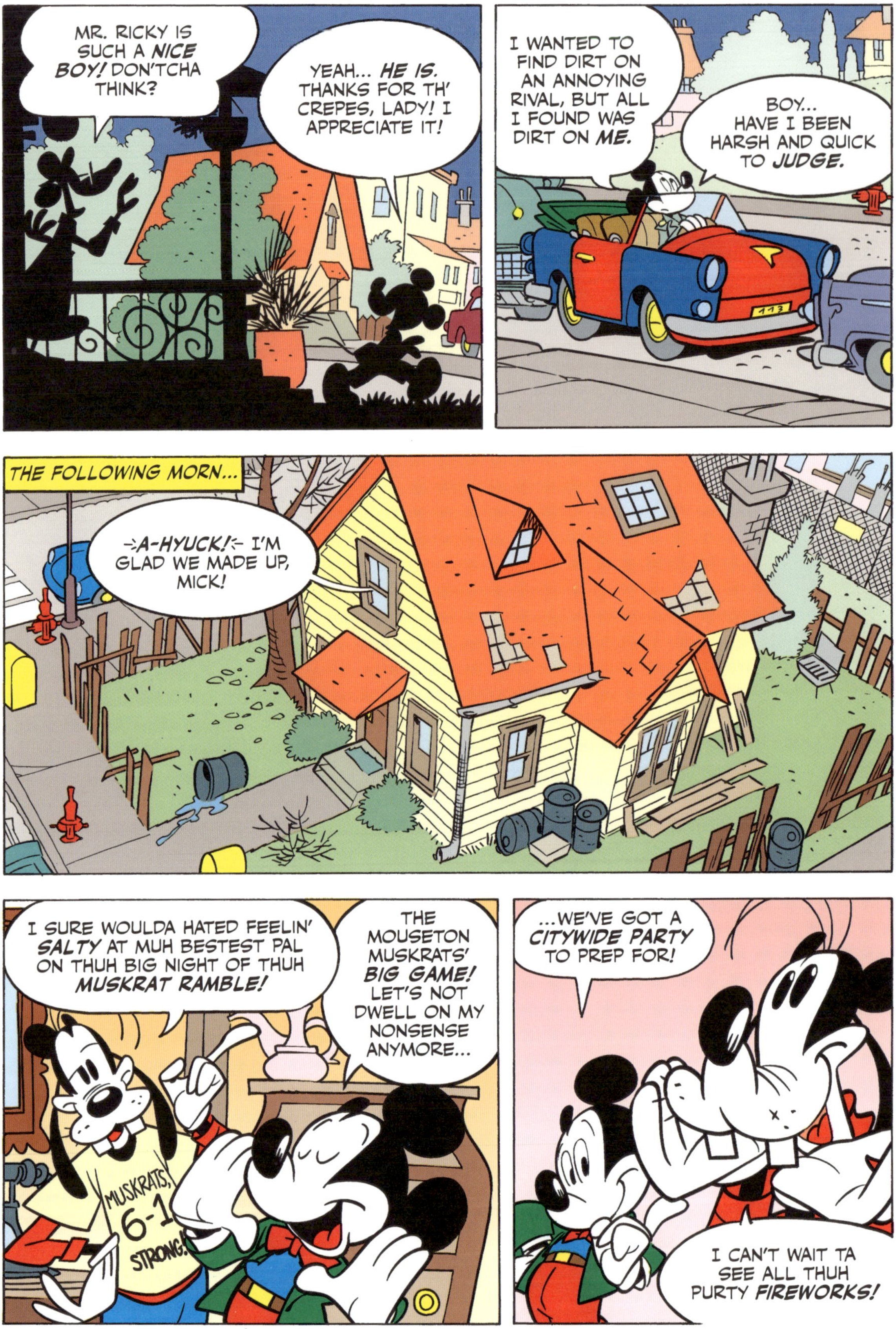
MR. RICKY IS SUCH A NICE BOY! DON'TCHA THINK?
YEAH... HE IS. THANKS FOR TH' CREPES, LADY! I APPRECIATE IT!
I WANTED TO FIND DIRT ON AN ANNOYING RIVAL, BUT ALL I FOUND WAS DIRT ON ME.
BOY... HAVE I BEEN HARSH AND QUICK TO JUDGE.
THE FOLLOWING MORN...
A-HYUCK! I'M GLAD WE MADE UP, MICK!
I SURE WOULDA HATED FEELIN' SALTY AT MUH BESTEST PAL ON THUH BIG NIGHT OF THUH MUSKRAT RAMBLE!
MUSKRATS, 6-1 STRONG!
THE MOUSETON MUSKRATS' BIG GAME! LET'S NOT DWELL ON MY NONSENSE ANYMORE...
...WE'VE GOT A CITYWIDE PARTY TO PREP FOR!
I CAN'T WAIT TA SEE ALL THUH PURTY FIREWORKS!

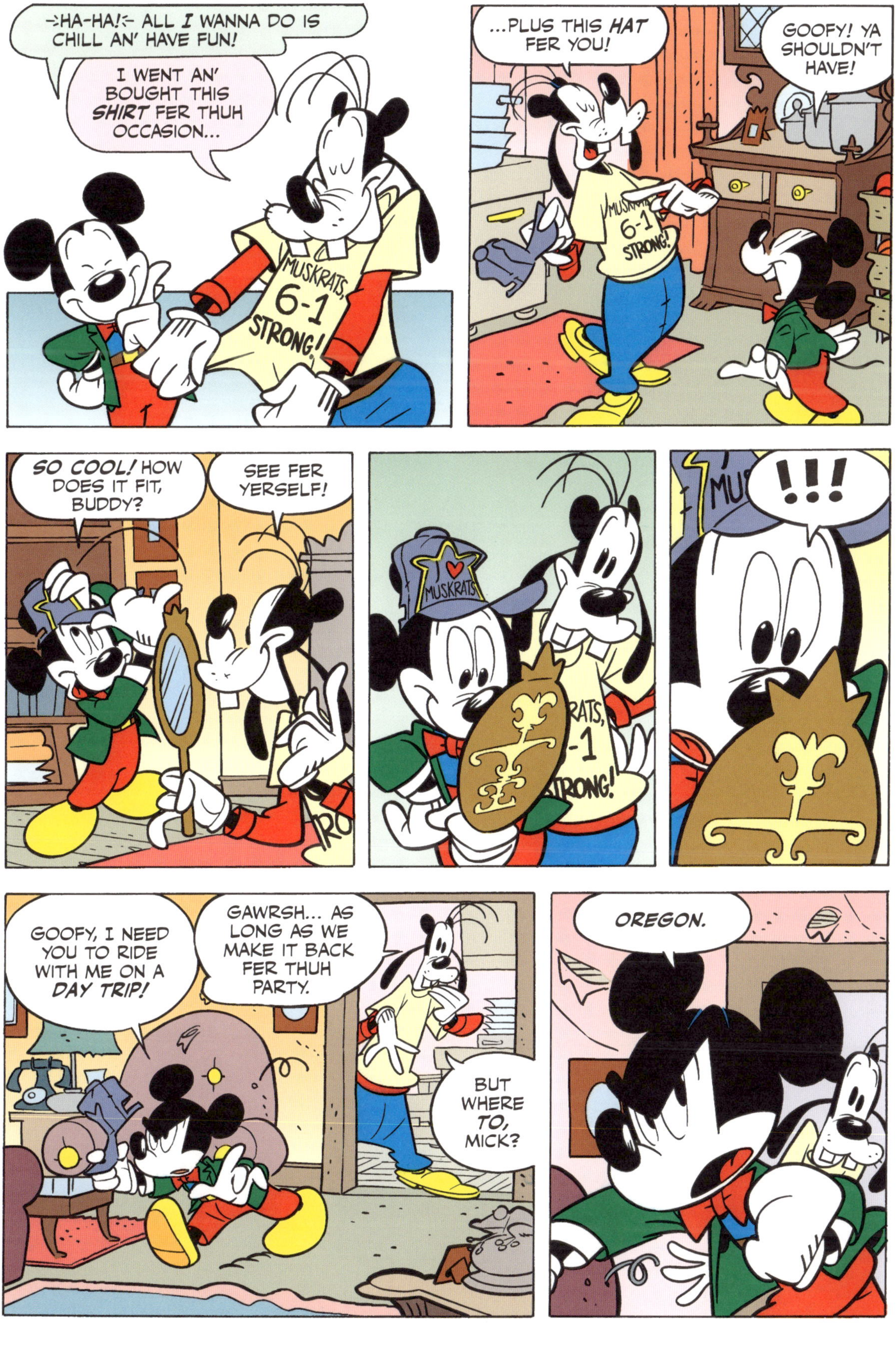

HA-HA! ALL I WANNA DO IS CHILL AN' HAVE FUN!
I WENT AN' BOUGHT THIS SHIRT FER THUH OCCASION...
MUSKRATS, 6-1 STRONG!
...PLUS THIS HAT FER YOU!
GOOFY! YA SHOULDN'T HAVE!
SO COOL! HOW DOES IT FIT, BUDDY?
SEE FER YERSELF!
I ♥ MUSKRATS
!!!
GOOFY, I NEED YOU TO RIDE WITH ME ON A DAY TRIP!
GAWRSH... AS LONG AS WE MAKE IT BACK FER THUH PARTY.
BUT WHERE TO, MICK?
OREGON.

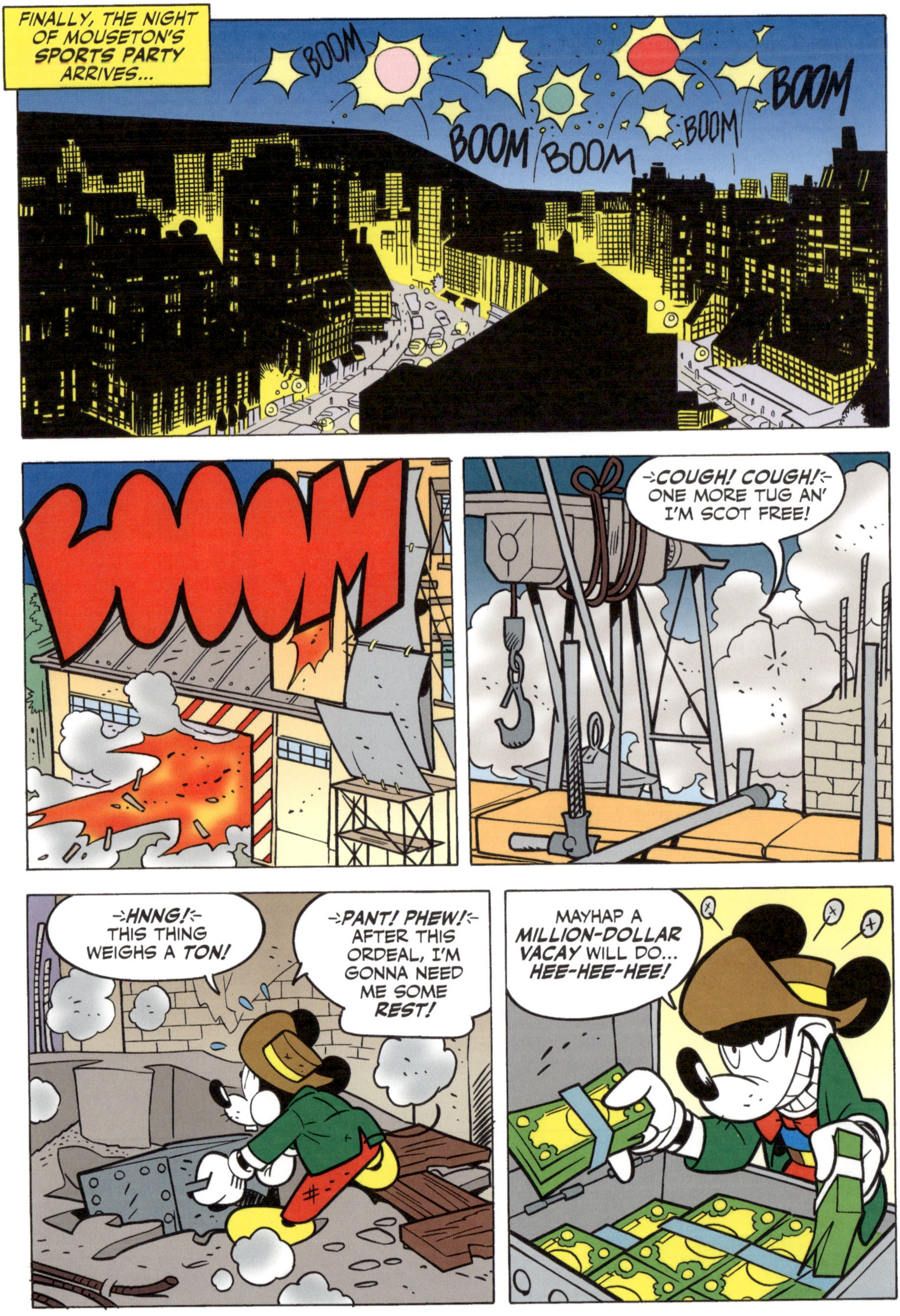
FINALLY, THE NIGHT OF MOUSETON'S SPORTS PARTY ARRIVES...
BOOM
BOOM
BOOM
BOOM
BOOM
BOOOM
-COUGH! COUGH!- ONE MORE TUG AN' I'M SCOT FREE!
-HNNG!- THIS THING WEIGHS A TON!
-PANT! PHEW!- AFTER THIS ORDEAL, I'M GONNA NEED ME SOME REST!
MAYHAP A MILLION-DOLLAR VACAY WILL DO... HEE-HEE-HEE!

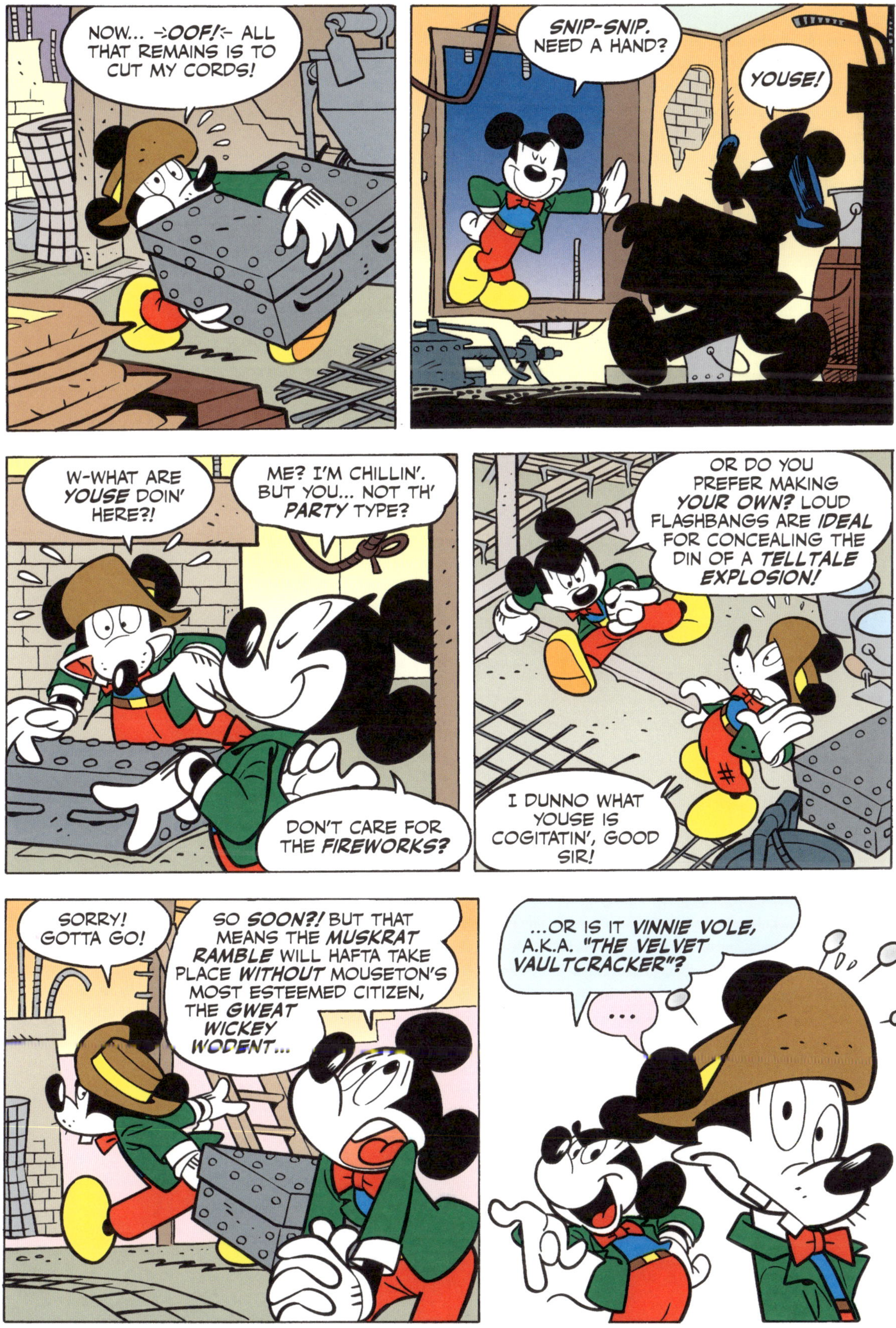

NOW... OOF! ALL THAT REMAINS IS TO CUT MY CORDS!
SNIP-SNIP. NEED A HAND?
YOUSE!
W-WHAT ARE YOUSE DOIN' HERE?!
ME? I'M CHILLIN'. BUT YOU... NOT TH' PARTY TYPE?
DON'T CARE FOR THE FIREWORKS?
OR DO YOU PREFER MAKING YOUR OWN? LOUD FLASHBANGS ARE IDEAL FOR CONCEALING THE DIN OF A TELLTALE EXPLOSION!
I DUNNO WHAT YOUSE IS COGITATIN', GOOD SIR!
SORRY! GOTTA GO!
SO SOON?! BUT THAT MEANS THE MUSKRAT RAMBLE WILL HAFTA TAKE PLACE WITHOUT MOUSETON'S MOST ESTEEMED CITIZEN, THE GWEAT WICKEY WODENT...
...OR IS IT VINNIE VOLE, A.K.A. "THE VELVET VAULTCRACKER"?
...

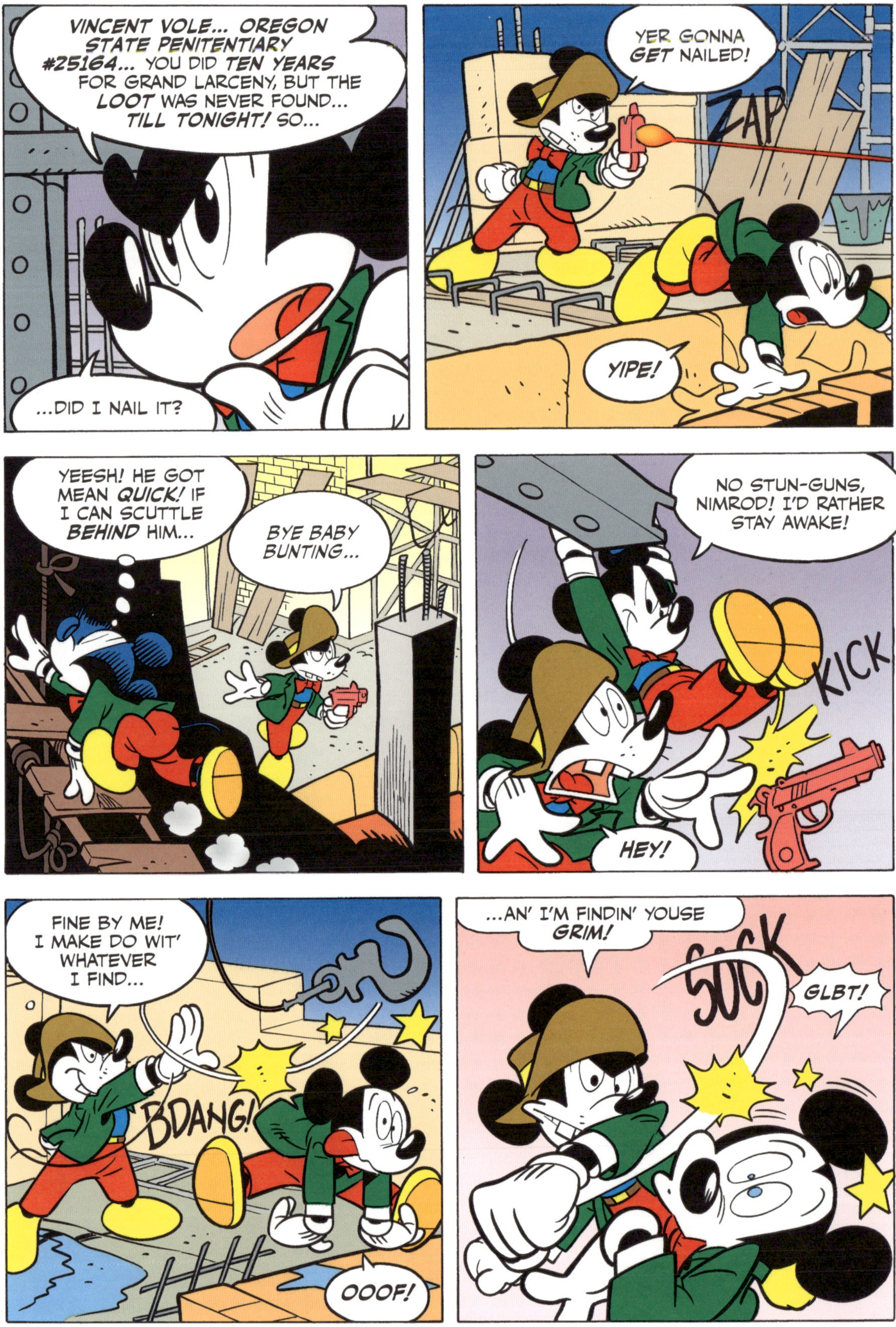
VINCENT VOLE... OREGON STATE PENITENTIARY #25164... YOU DID TEN YEARS FOR GRAND LARCENY, BUT THE LOOT WAS NEVER FOUND... TILL TONIGHT! SO...
...DID I NAIL IT?
YER GONNA GET NAILED!
ZAP
YIPE!
YEESH! HE GOT MEAN QUICK! IF I CAN SCUTTLE BEHIND HIM...
BYE BABY BUNTING...
NO STUN-GUNS, NIMROD! I'D RATHER STAY AWAKE!
KICK
HEY!
FINE BY ME! I MAKE DO WIT' WHATEVER I FIND...
BDANG!
OOOF!
...AN' I'M FINDIN' YOUSE GRIM!
SOCK
GLBT!

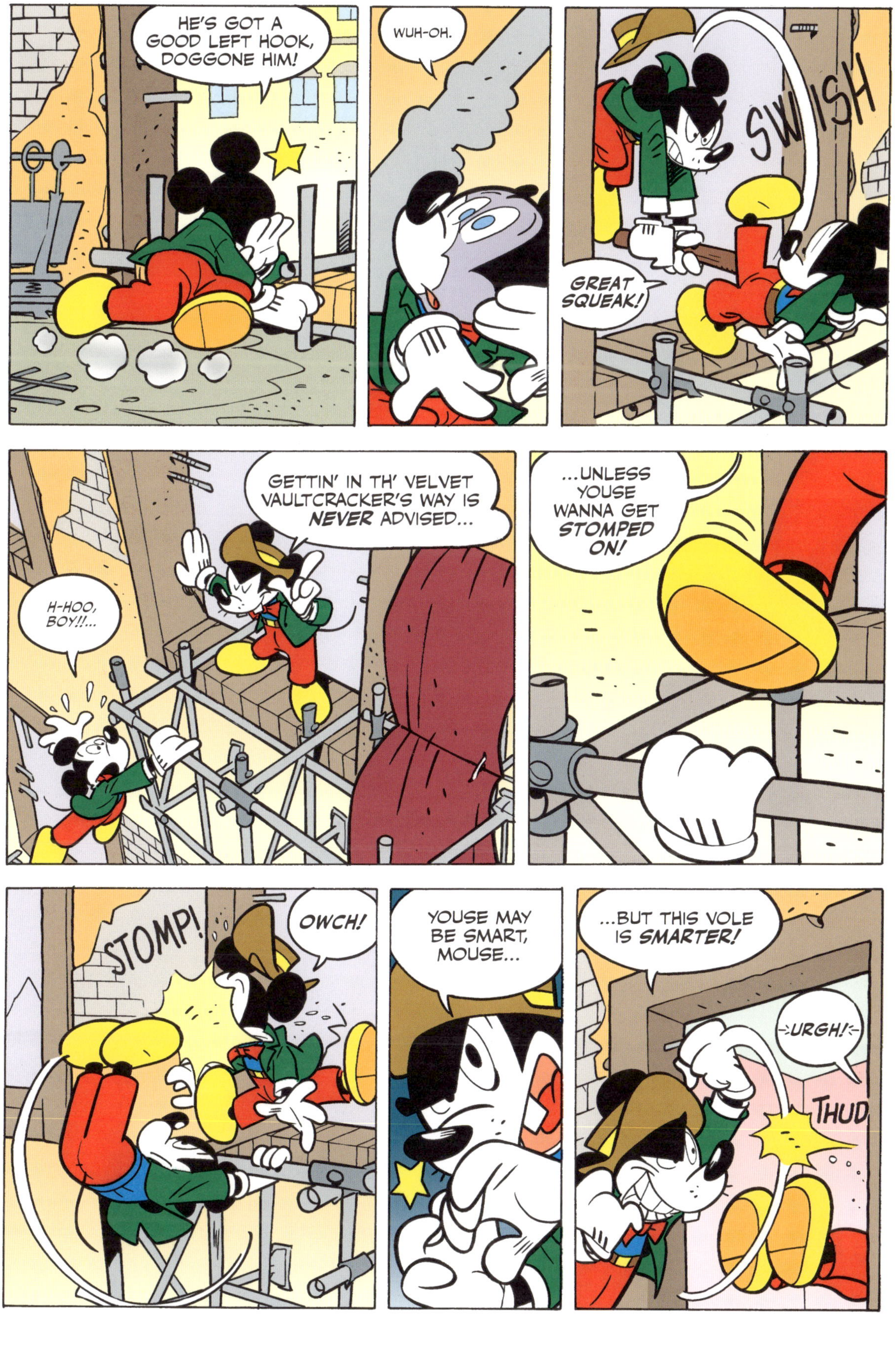
HE'S GOT A GOOD LEFT HOOK, DOGGONE HIM!
WUH-OH.
SWISH
GREAT SQUEAK!
GETTIN' IN TH' VELVET VAULTCRACKER'S WAY IS NEVER ADVISED...
H-HOO, BOY!!...
...UNLESS YOUSE WANNA GET STOMPED ON!
STOMP!
OWCH!
YOUSE MAY BE SMART, MOUSE...
...BUT THIS VOLE IS SMARTER!
URGH!
THUD

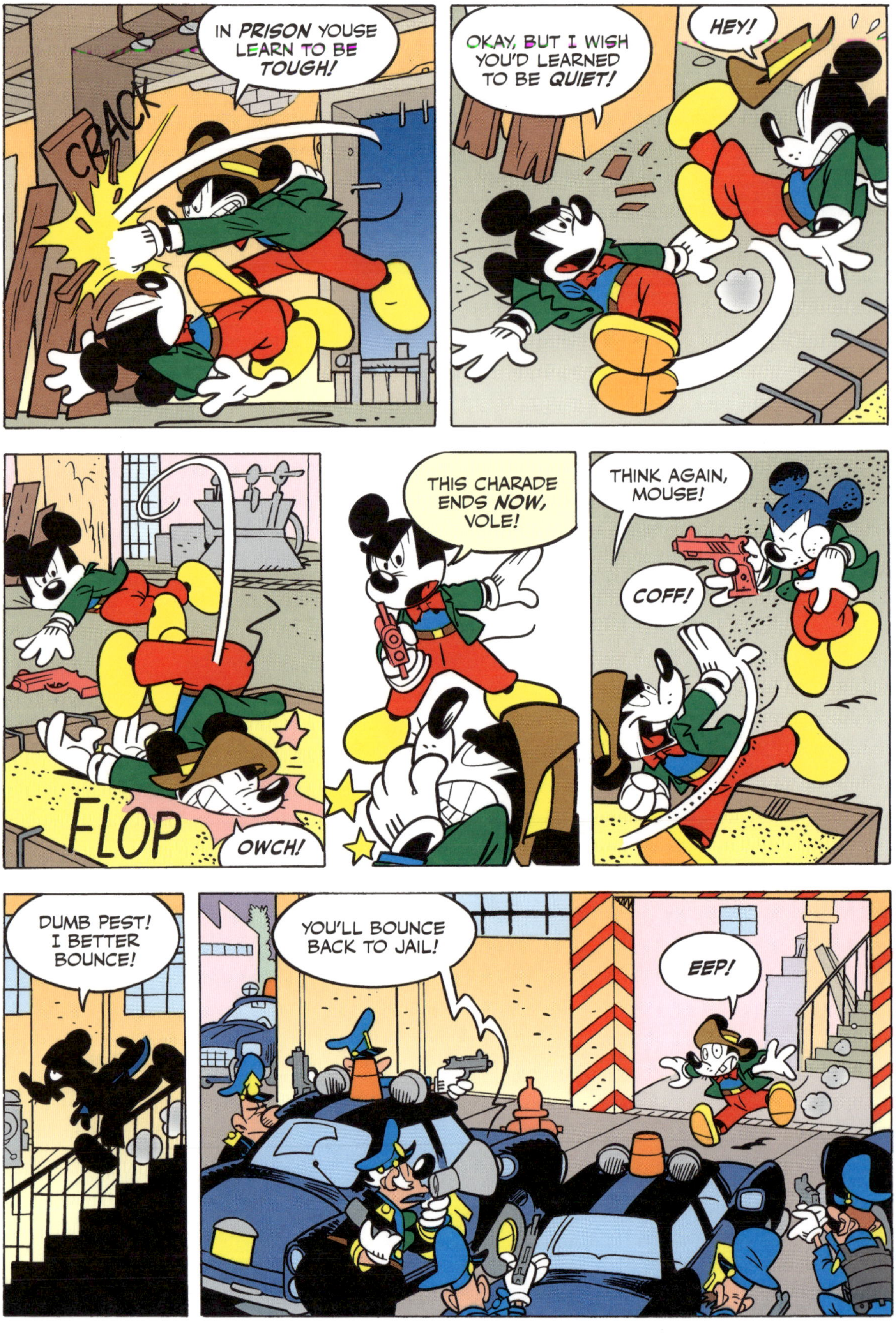
CRACK
IN PRISON YOUSE LEARN TO BE TOUGH!
OKAY, BUT I WISH YOU'D LEARNED TO BE QUIET!
HEY!
FLOP
OWCH!
THIS CHARADE ENDS NOW, VOLE!
THINK AGAIN, MOUSE!
COFF!
DUMB PEST! I BETTER BOUNCE!
YOU'LL BOUNCE BACK TO JAIL!
EEP!

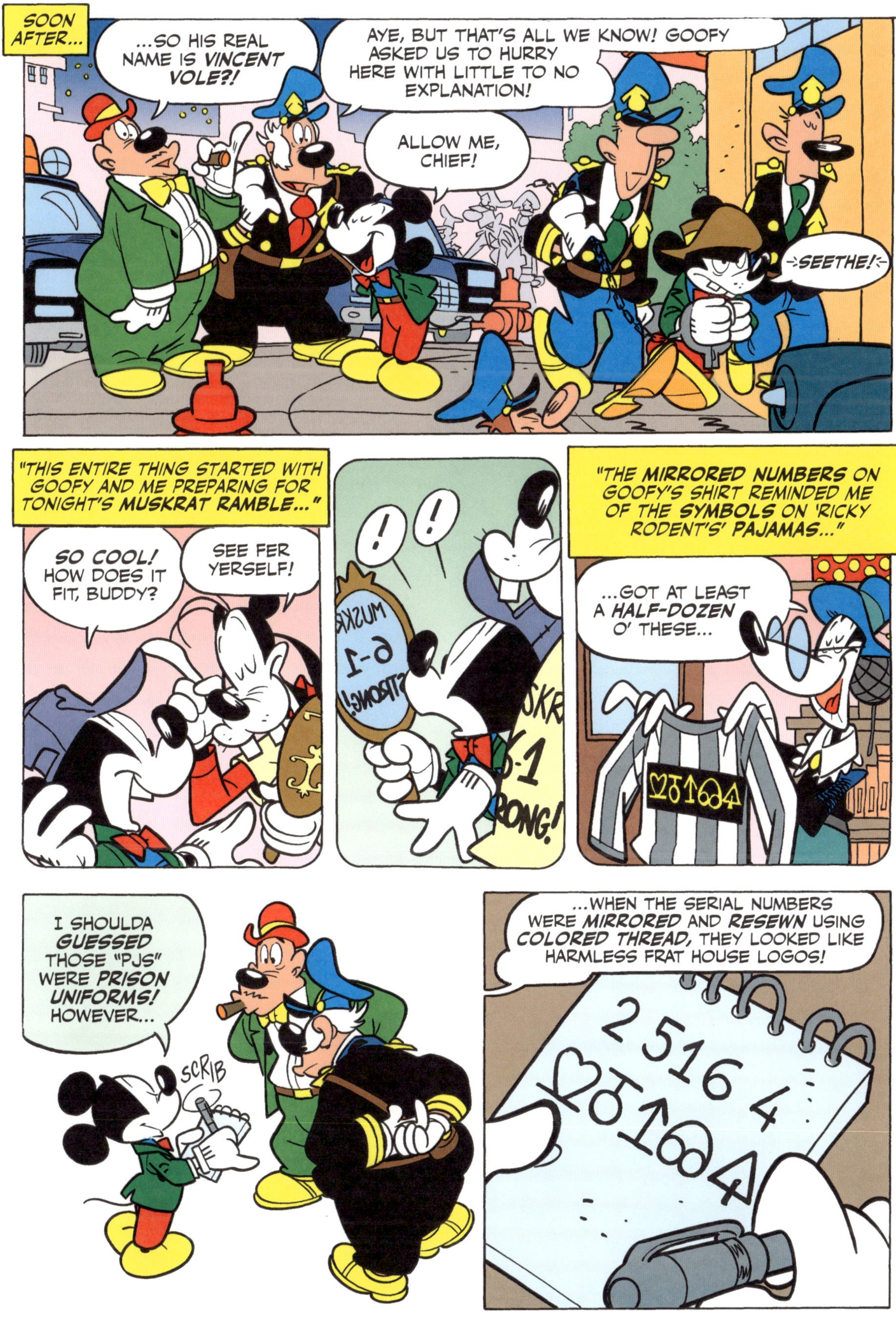
SOON AFTER...
...SO HIS REAL NAME IS VINCENT VOLE?!
AYE, BUT THAT'S ALL WE KNOW! GOOFY ASKED US TO HURRY HERE WITH LITTLE TO NO EXPLANATION!
ALLOW ME, CHIEF!
-SEETHE!-
"THIS ENTIRE THING STARTED WITH GOOFY AND ME PREPARING FOR TONIGHT'S MUSKRAT RAMBLE..."
SO COOL! HOW DOES IT FIT, BUDDY?
SEE FER YERSELF!
! !
"THE MIRRORED NUMBERS ON GOOFY'S SHIRT REMINDED ME OF THE SYMBOLS ON 'RICKY RODENT'S' PAJAMAS..."
...GOT AT LEAST A HALF-DOZEN O' THESE...
I SHOULDA GUESSED THOSE "PJS" WERE PRISON UNIFORMS! HOWEVER...
SCRIB
...WHEN THE SERIAL NUMBERS WERE MIRRORED AND RESEWN USING COLORED THREAD, THEY LOOKED LIKE HARMLESS FRAT HOUSE LOGOS!
2 5 16 4

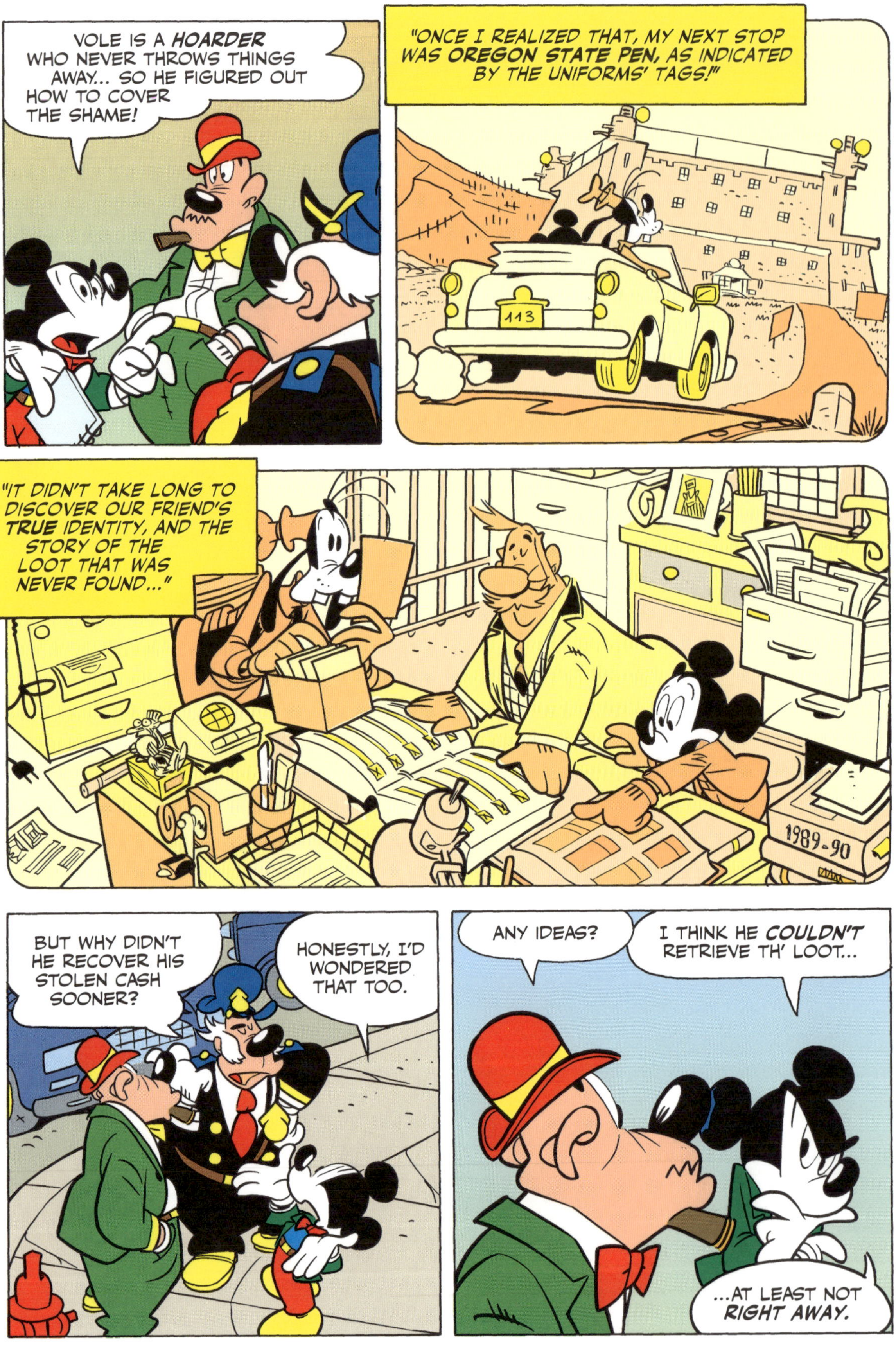
VOLE IS A *HOARDER* WHO NEVER THROWS THINGS AWAY... SO HE FIGURED OUT HOW TO COVER THE SHAME!
"ONCE I REALIZED THAT, MY NEXT STOP WAS **OREGON STATE PEN,** AS INDICATED BY THE UNIFORMS' TAGS!"
113
"IT DIDN'T TAKE LONG TO DISCOVER OUR FRIEND'S **TRUE** IDENTITY, AND THE STORY OF THE LOOT THAT WAS NEVER FOUND..."
1989-90
BUT WHY DIDN'T HE RECOVER HIS STOLEN CASH SOONER?
HONESTLY, I'D WONDERED THAT TOO.
ANY IDEAS?
I THINK HE *COULDN'T* RETRIEVE TH' LOOT...
...AT LEAST NOT *RIGHT AWAY.*

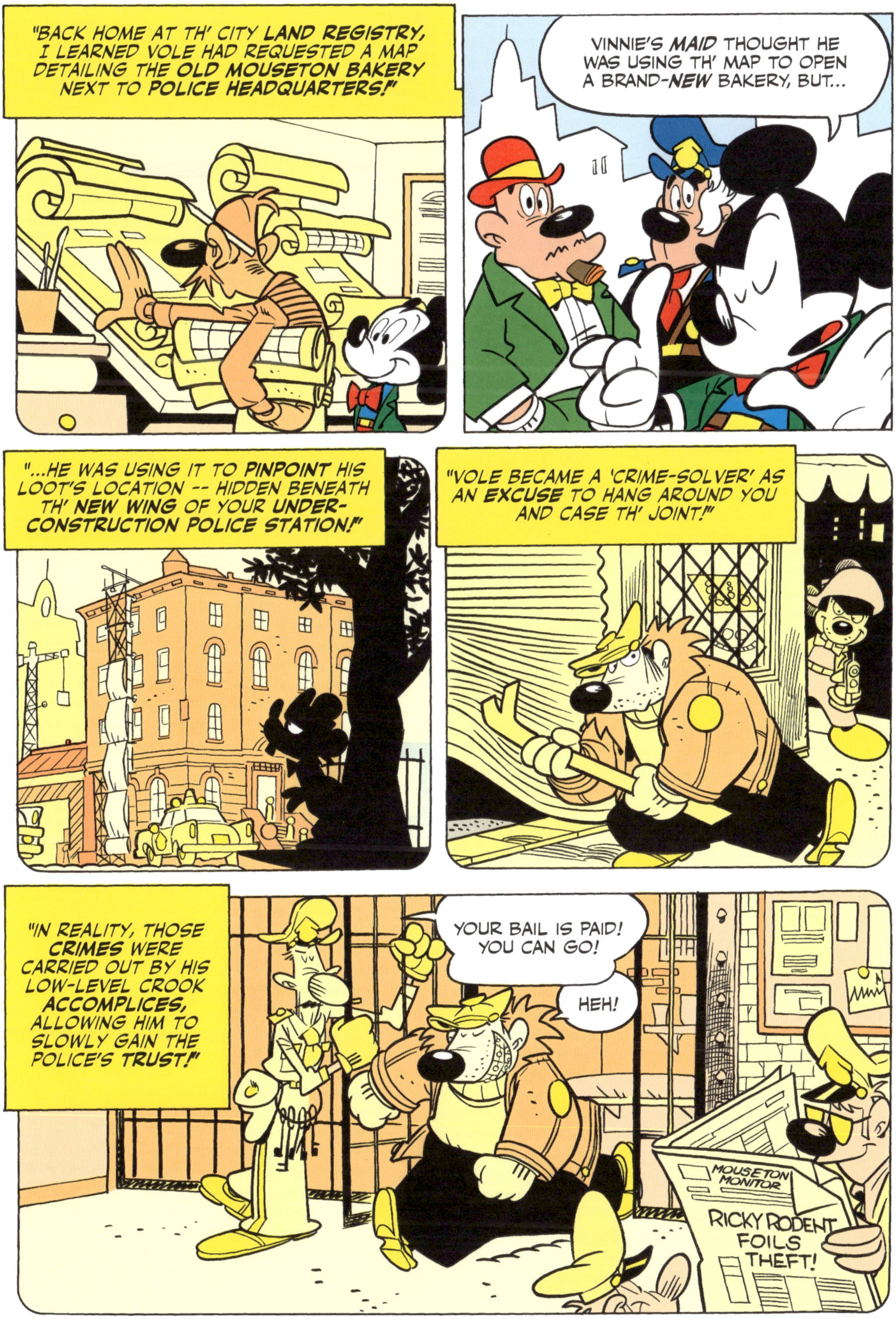

"BACK HOME AT TH' CITY LAND REGISTRY, I LEARNED VOLE HAD REQUESTED A MAP DETAILING THE OLD MOUSETON BAKERY NEXT TO POLICE HEADQUARTERS!"
VINNIE'S MAID THOUGHT HE WAS USING TH' MAP TO OPEN A BRAND-NEW BAKERY, BUT...
"...HE WAS USING IT TO PINPOINT HIS LOOT'S LOCATION -- HIDDEN BENEATH TH' NEW WING OF YOUR UNDER-CONSTRUCTION POLICE STATION!"
"VOLE BECAME A 'CRIME-SOLVER' AS AN EXCUSE TO HANG AROUND YOU AND CASE TH' JOINT!"
"IN REALITY, THOSE CRIMES WERE CARRIED OUT BY HIS LOW-LEVEL CROOK ACCOMPLICES, ALLOWING HIM TO SLOWLY GAIN THE POLICE'S TRUST!"
YOUR BAIL IS PAID! YOU CAN GO!
HEH!
MOUSETON MONITOR
RICKY RODENT FOILS THEFT!

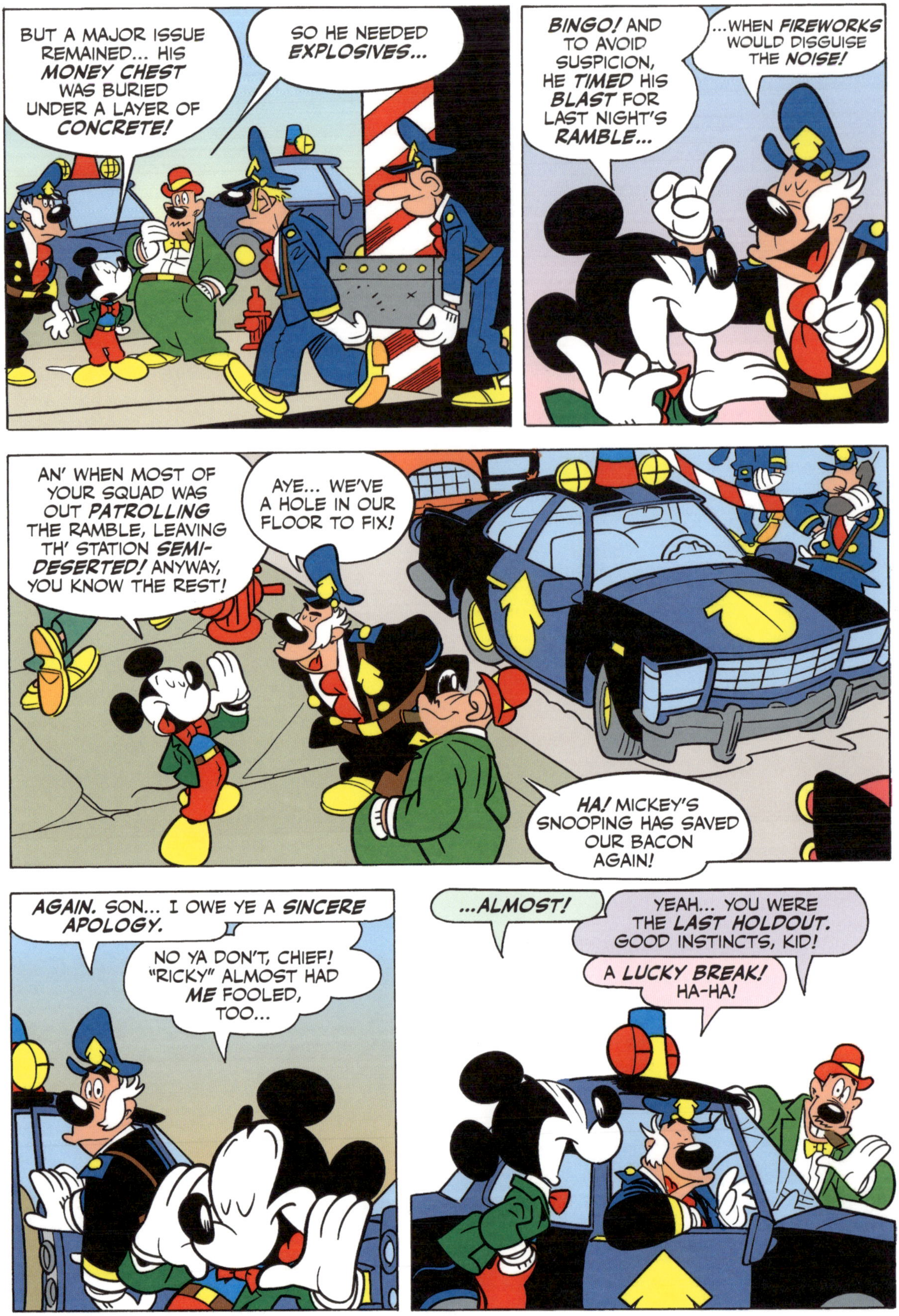
BUT A MAJOR ISSUE REMAINED... HIS MONEY CHEST WAS BURIED UNDER A LAYER OF CONCRETE!
SO HE NEEDED EXPLOSIVES...
BINGO! AND TO AVOID SUSPICION, HE TIMED HIS BLAST FOR LAST NIGHT'S RAMBLE...
...WHEN FIREWORKS WOULD DISGUISE THE NOISE!
AN' WHEN MOST OF YOUR SQUAD WAS OUT PATROLLING THE RAMBLE, LEAVING TH' STATION SEMI-DESERTED! ANYWAY, YOU KNOW THE REST!
AYE... WE'VE A HOLE IN OUR FLOOR TO FIX!
HA! MICKEY'S SNOOPING HAS SAVED OUR BACON AGAIN!
AGAIN. SON... I OWE YE A SINCERE APOLOGY.
NO YA DON'T, CHIEF! "RICKY" ALMOST HAD ME FOOLED, TOO...
...ALMOST!
YEAH... YOU WERE THE LAST HOLDOUT. GOOD INSTINCTS, KID!
A LUCKY BREAK! HA-HA!

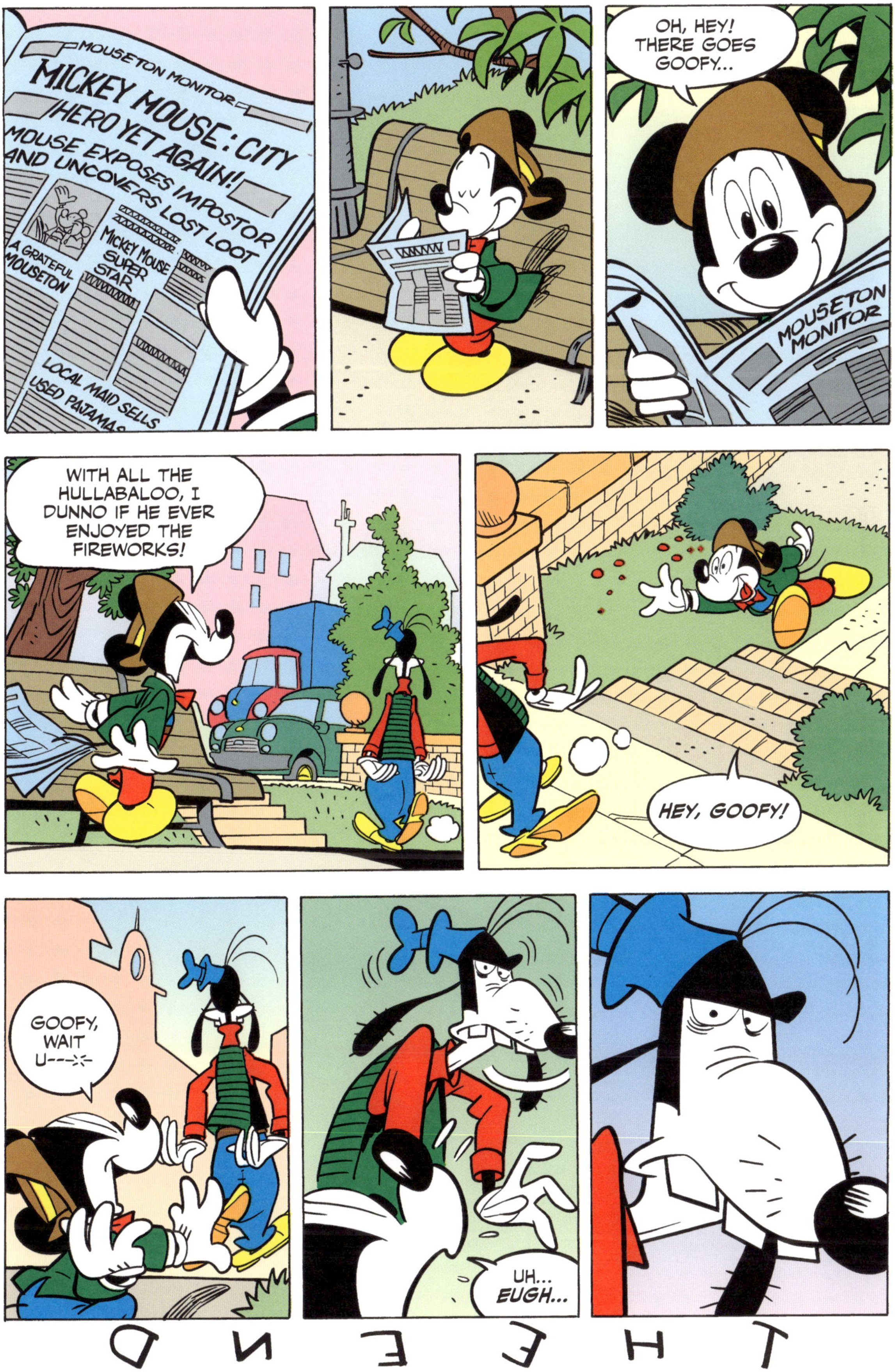
MOUSETON MONITOR
MICKEY MOUSE: CITY HERO YET AGAIN!
MOUSE EXPOSES IMPOSTOR AND UNCOVERS LOST LOOT
A GRATEFUL MOUSETON
MICKEY MOUSE SUPER STAR
LOCAL MAID SELLS USED PAJAMAS
OH, HEY! THERE GOES GOOFY...
MOUSETON MONITOR
WITH ALL THE HULLABALOO, I DUNNO IF HE EVER ENJOYED THE FIREWORKS!
HEY, GOOFY!
GOOFY, WAIT U---
UH... EUGH...
THE END

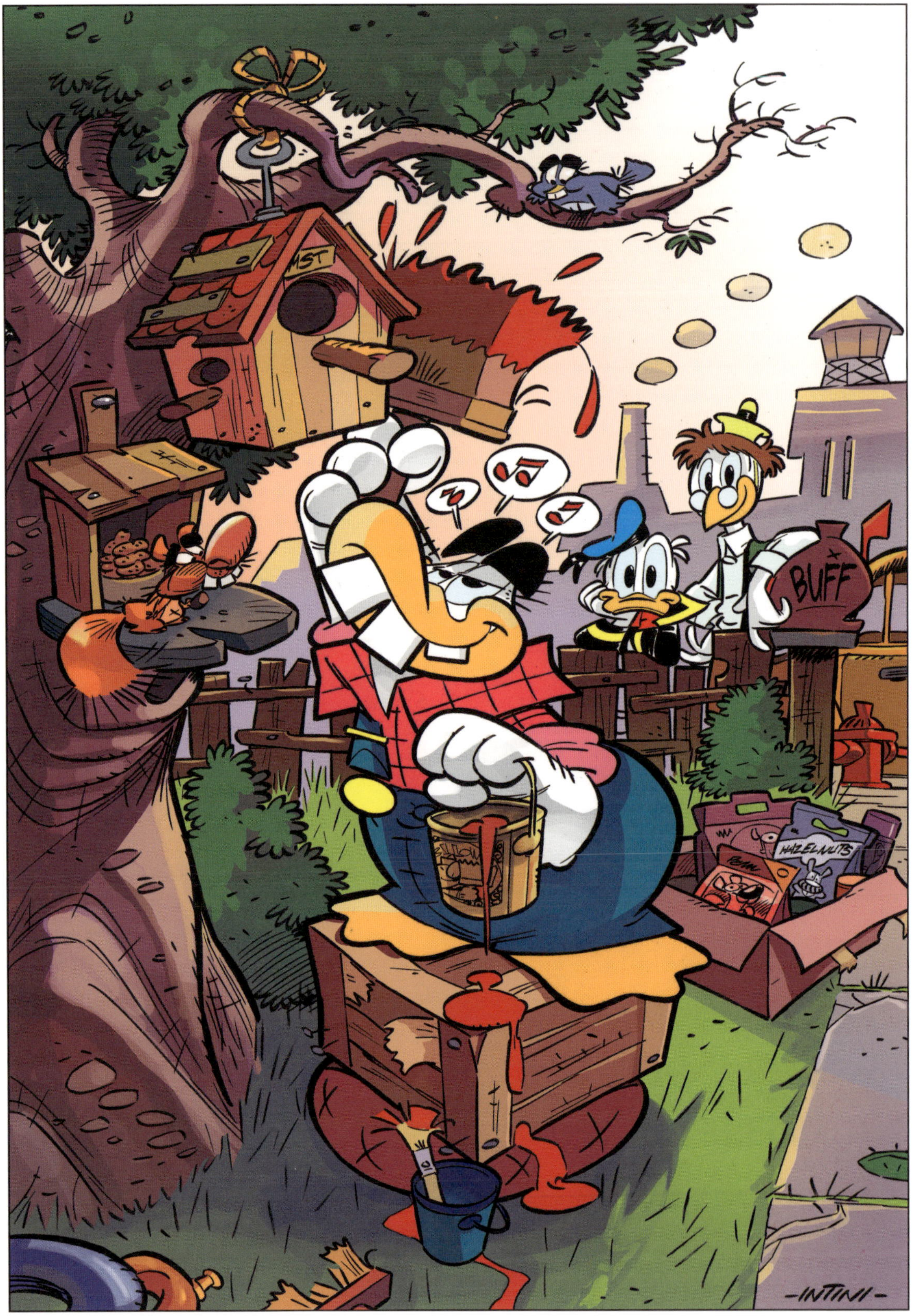
MST
BUFF
HAZELNUTS
-INTINI-

The creations of Corrado Mastantuono have proven inspirational to fellow Disney comics talents.
Finnish *Roope-setä* 2007-12 (December 5, 2007) featured this Boomer Buff pin-up page drawn and colored by Stefano Intini; the lovably annoying Boomer had long since become an ongoing co-star, beginning with the 1998 story opposite.

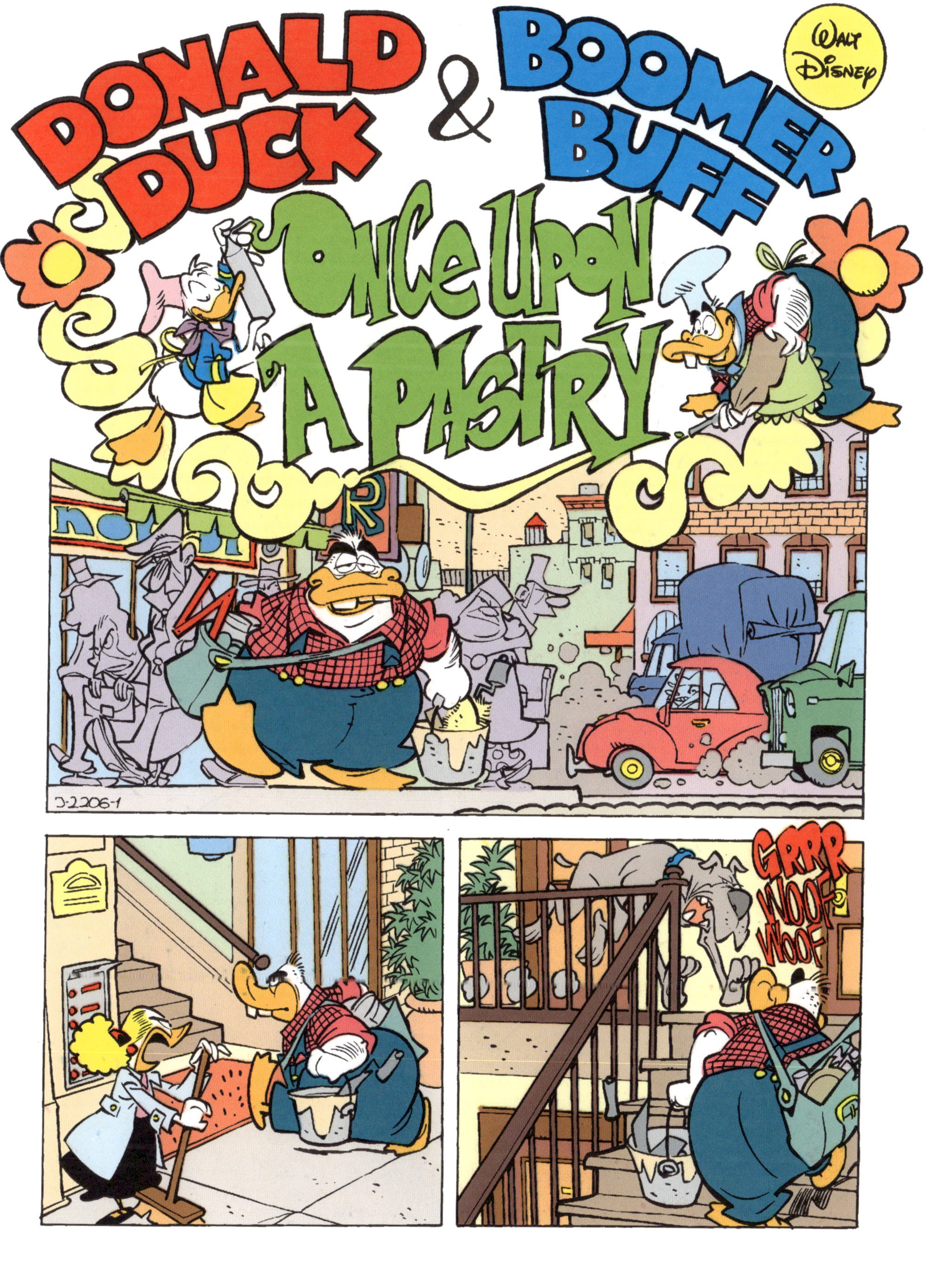
DONALD DUCK & BOOMER BUFF
WALT DISNEY
ONCE UPON A PASTRY
D-2206-1
GRRR
WOOF WOOF

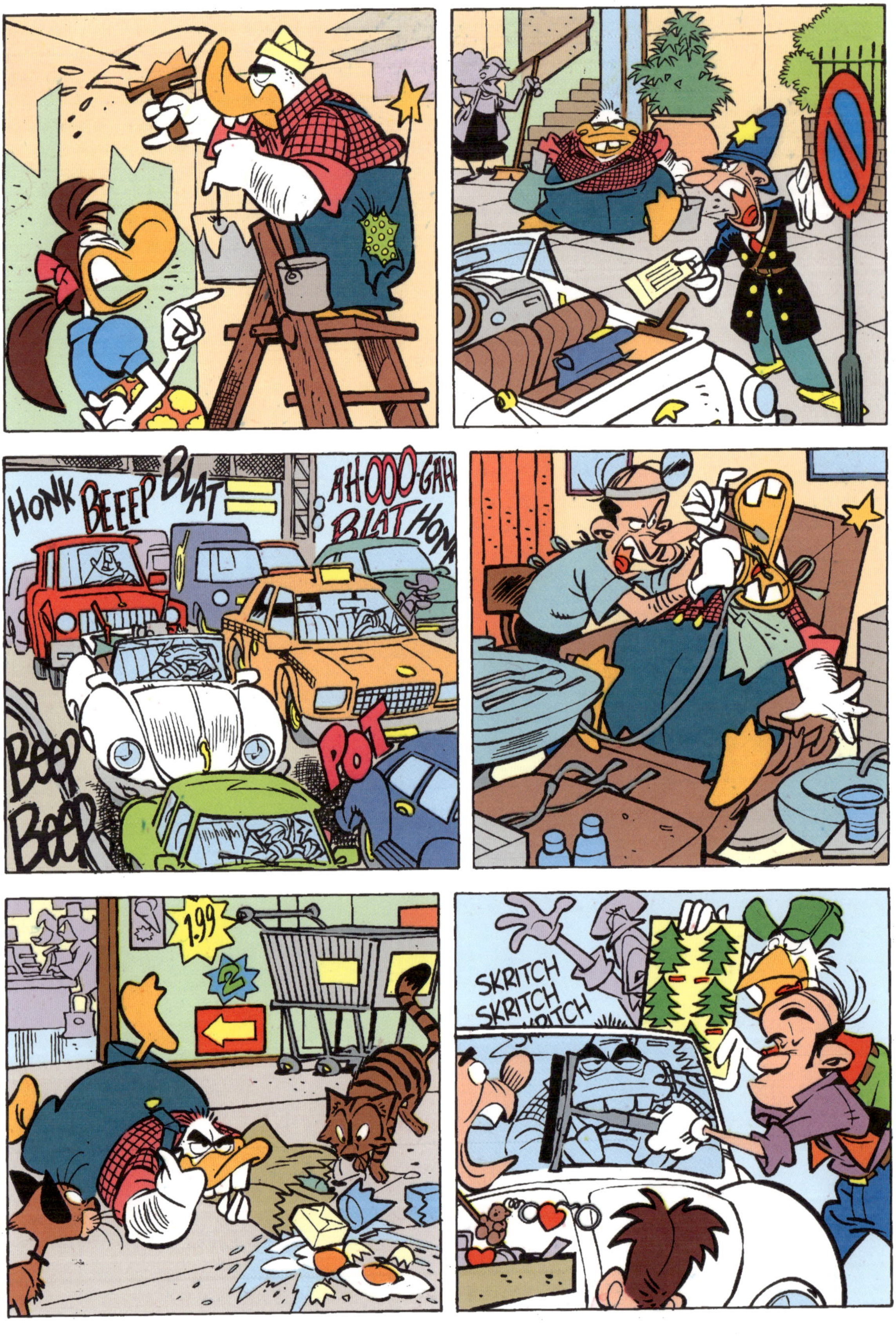
HONK
BEEEP
BLAT
AH-OOO-GAH
BLAT
HONK
BEEP
BEEP
POT
1.99
2
SKRITCH
SKRITCH

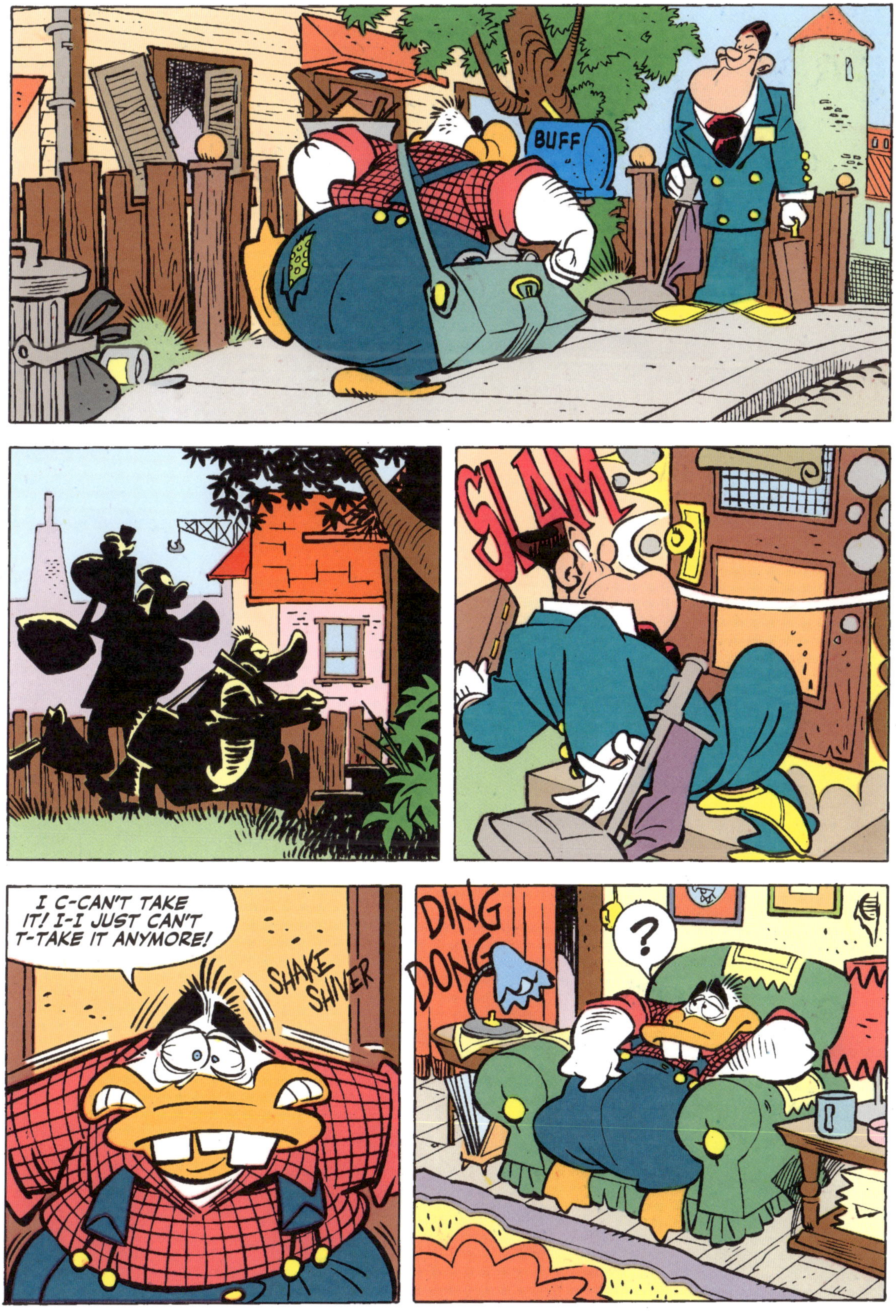
BUFF
SLAM
I C-CAN'T TAKE IT! I-I JUST CAN'T T-TAKE IT ANYMORE!
SHAKE SHIVER
DING DONG
?

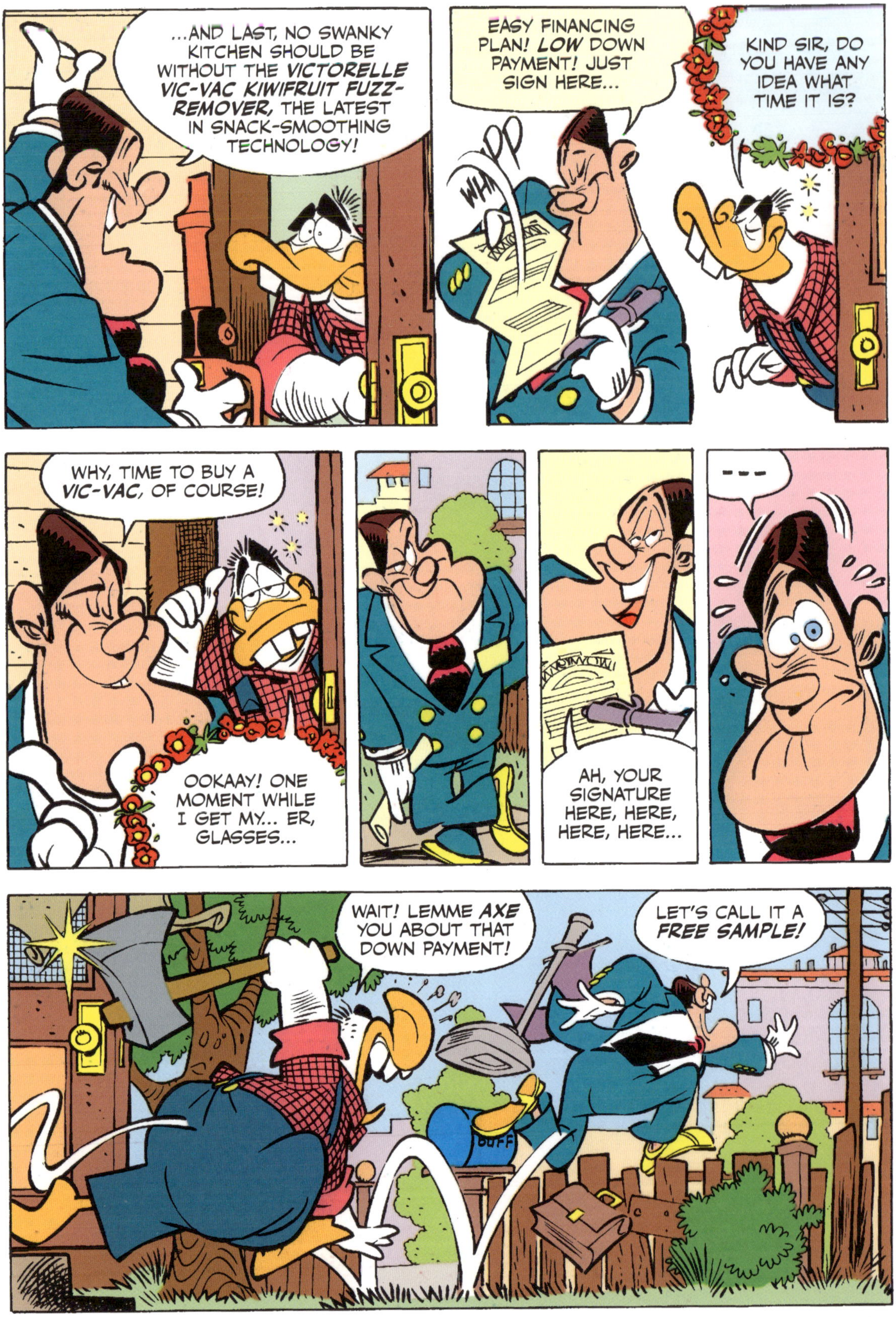
...AND LAST, NO SWANKY KITCHEN SHOULD BE WITHOUT THE VICTORELLE VIC-VAC KIWIFRUIT FUZZ-REMOVER, THE LATEST IN SNACK-SMOOTHING TECHNOLOGY!
EASY FINANCING PLAN! LOW DOWN PAYMENT! JUST SIGN HERE...
WHAPP
KIND SIR, DO YOU HAVE ANY IDEA WHAT TIME IT IS?
WHY, TIME TO BUY A VIC-VAC, OF COURSE!
OOKAAY! ONE MOMENT WHILE I GET MY... ER, GLASSES...
AH, YOUR SIGNATURE HERE, HERE, HERE, HERE...

WAIT! LEMME AXE YOU ABOUT THAT DOWN PAYMENT!
LET'S CALL IT A FREE SAMPLE!
BUFF

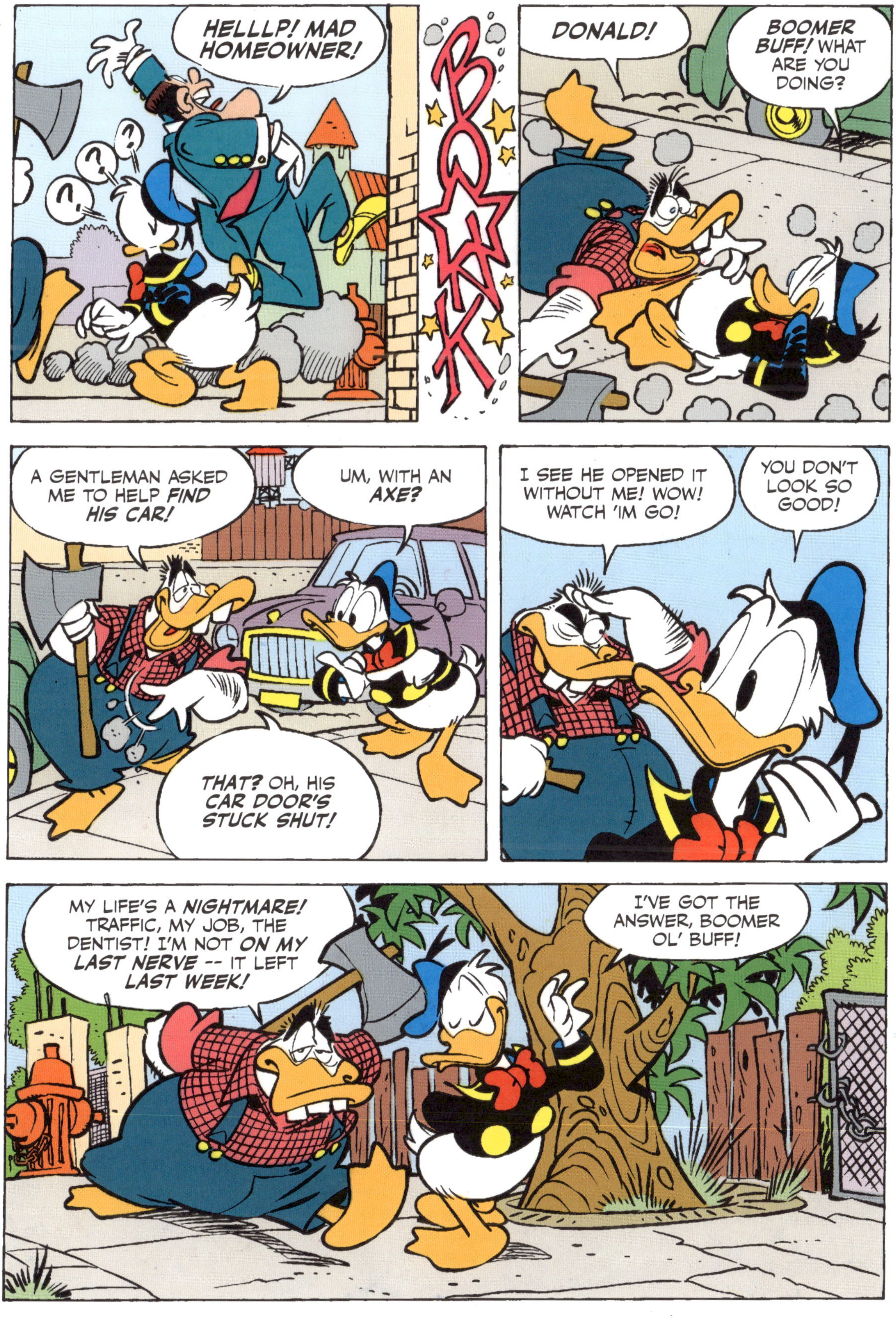
HELLLP! MAD HOMEOWNER!
BONK
DONALD!
BOOMER BUFF! WHAT ARE YOU DOING?
A GENTLEMAN ASKED ME TO HELP FIND HIS CAR!
UM, WITH AN AXE?
THAT? OH, HIS CAR DOOR'S STUCK SHUT!
I SEE HE OPENED IT WITHOUT ME! WOW! WATCH 'IM GO!
YOU DON'T LOOK SO GOOD!
MY LIFE'S A NIGHTMARE! TRAFFIC, MY JOB, THE DENTIST! I'M NOT ON MY LAST NERVE -- IT LEFT LAST WEEK!
I'VE GOT THE ANSWER, BOOMER OL' BUFF!

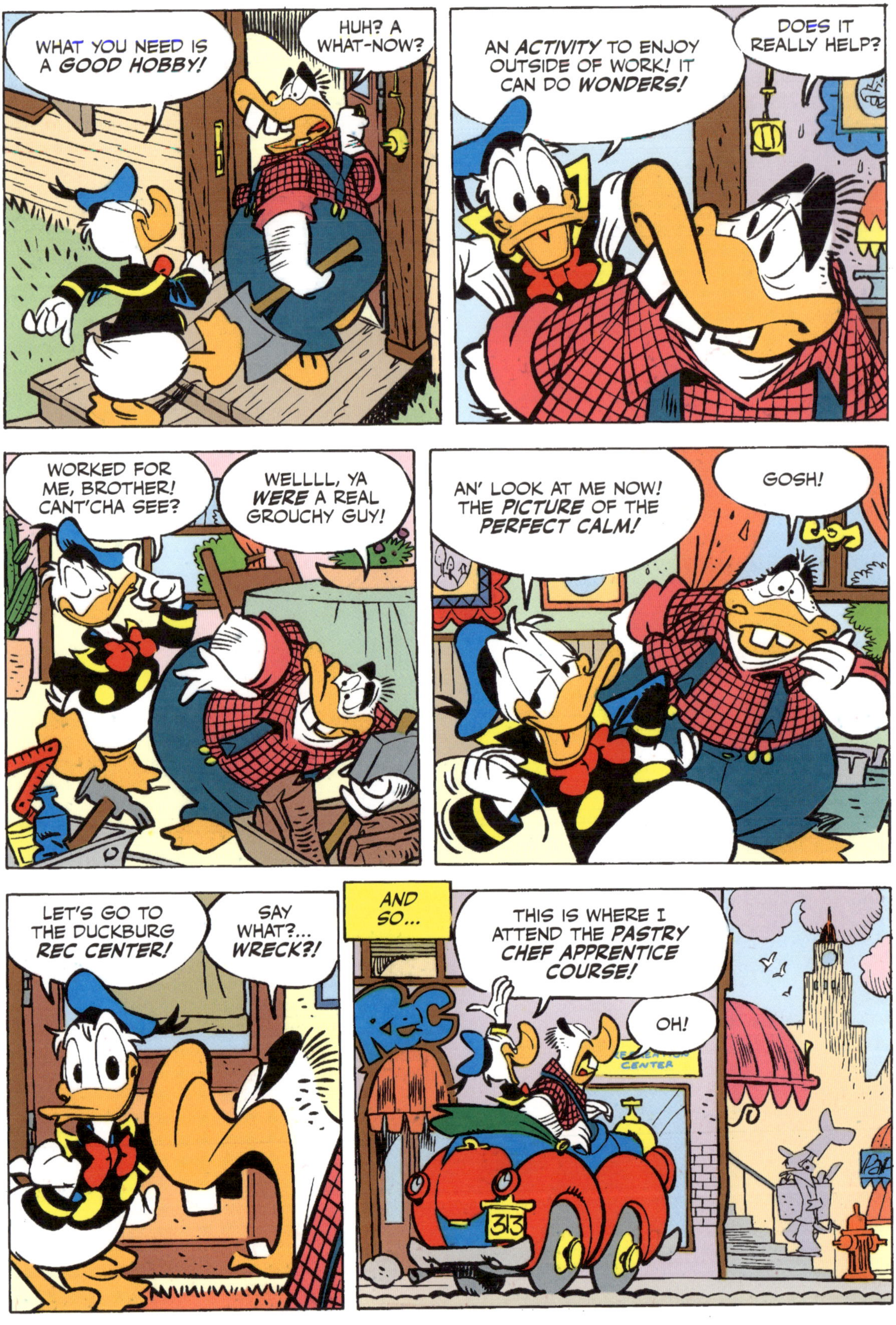
WHAT YOU NEED IS A *GOOD HOBBY!*
HUH? A WHAT-NOW?
AN *ACTIVITY* TO ENJOY OUTSIDE OF WORK! IT CAN DO *WONDERS!*
DOES IT REALLY HELP?
WORKED FOR ME, BROTHER! CANT'CHA SEE?
WELLLL, YA *WERE* A REAL GROUCHY GUY!
AN' LOOK AT ME NOW! THE *PICTURE* OF THE *PERFECT CALM!*
GOSH!
LET'S GO TO THE DUCKBURG *REC CENTER!*
SAY WHAT?... *WRECK?!*
AND SO...
THIS IS WHERE I ATTEND THE *PASTRY CHEF APPRENTICE COURSE!*
OH!
REC
CENTER
313

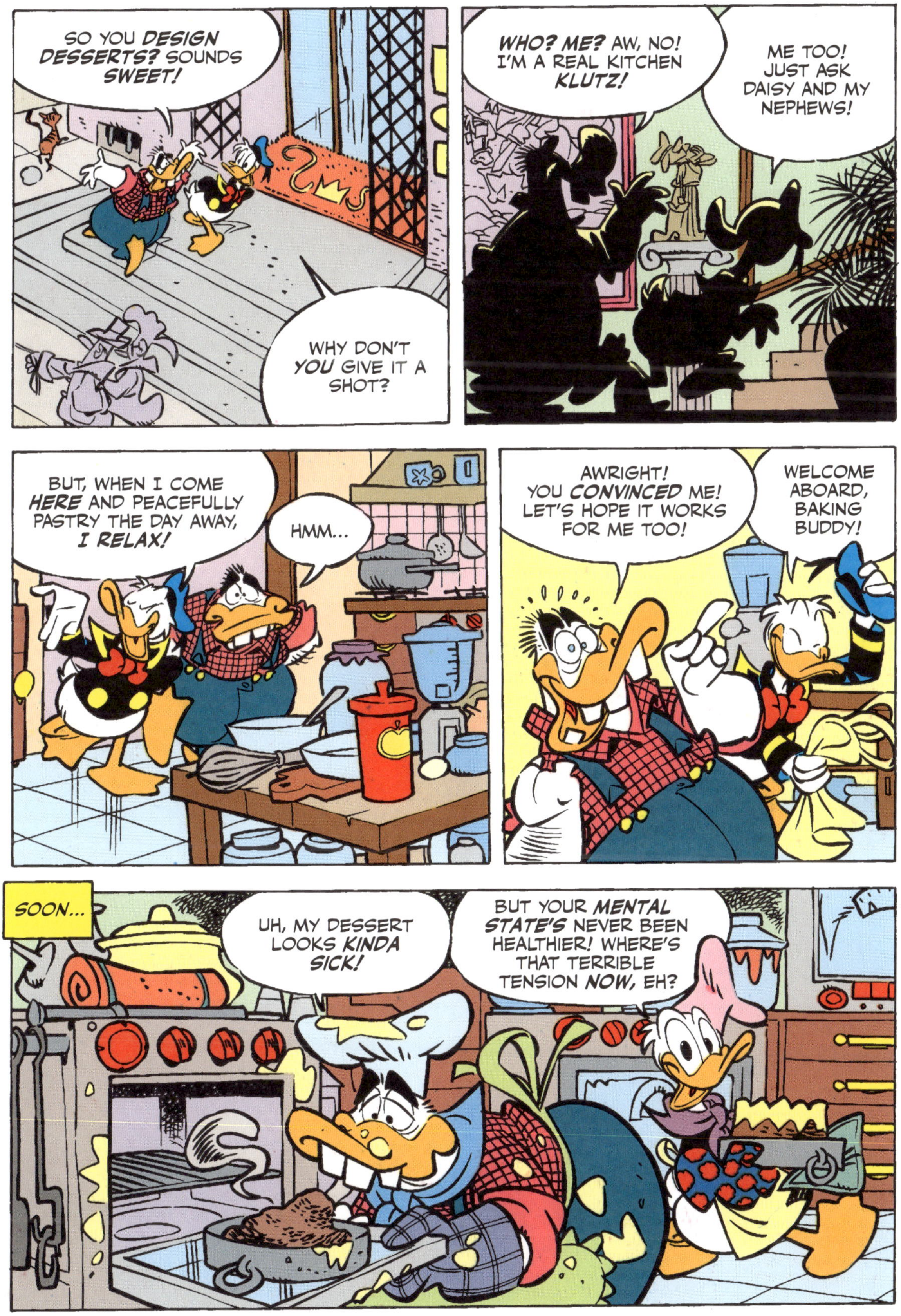
SO YOU DESIGN DESSERTS? SOUNDS SWEET!
WHY DON'T YOU GIVE IT A SHOT?
WHO? ME? AW, NO! I'M A REAL KITCHEN KLUTZ!
ME TOO! JUST ASK DAISY AND MY NEPHEWS!
BUT, WHEN I COME HERE AND PEACEFULLY PASTRY THE DAY AWAY, I RELAX!
HMM...
AWRIGHT! YOU CONVINCED ME! LET'S HOPE IT WORKS FOR ME TOO!
WELCOME ABOARD, BAKING BUDDY!
SOON...
UH, MY DESSERT LOOKS KINDA SICK!
BUT YOUR MENTAL STATE'S NEVER BEEN HEALTHIER! WHERE'S THAT TERRIBLE TENSION NOW, EH?

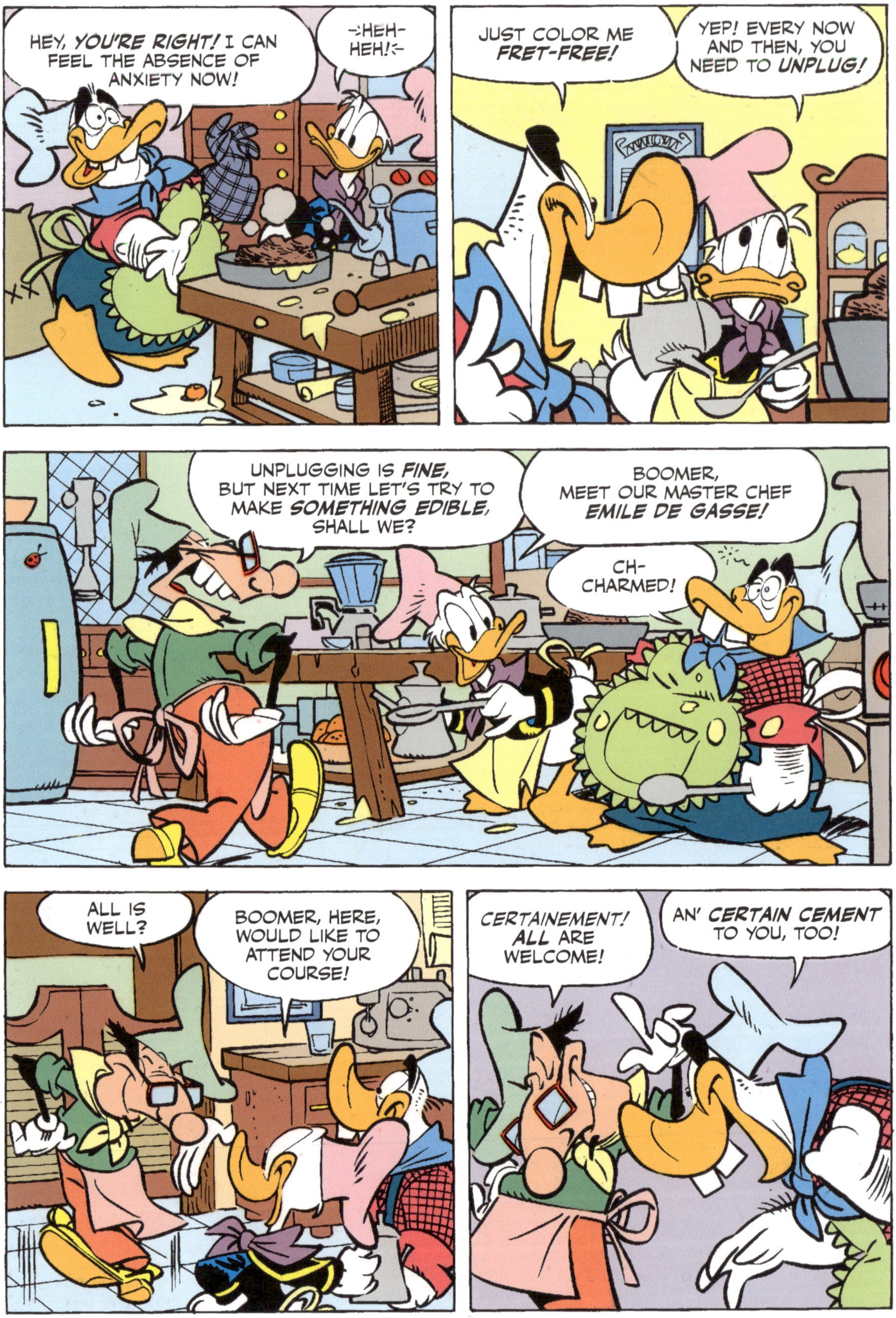
HEY, YOU'RE RIGHT! I CAN FEEL THE ABSENCE OF ANXIETY NOW!
-HEH-HEH!-
JUST COLOR ME FRET-FREE!
YEP! EVERY NOW AND THEN, YOU NEED TO UNPLUG!
UNPLUGGING IS FINE, BUT NEXT TIME LET'S TRY TO MAKE SOMETHING EDIBLE, SHALL WE?
BOOMER, MEET OUR MASTER CHEF EMILE DE GASSE!
CH-CHARMED!
ALL IS WELL?
BOOMER, HERE, WOULD LIKE TO ATTEND YOUR COURSE!
CERTAINEMENT! ALL ARE WELCOME!
AN' CERTAIN CEMENT TO YOU, TOO!

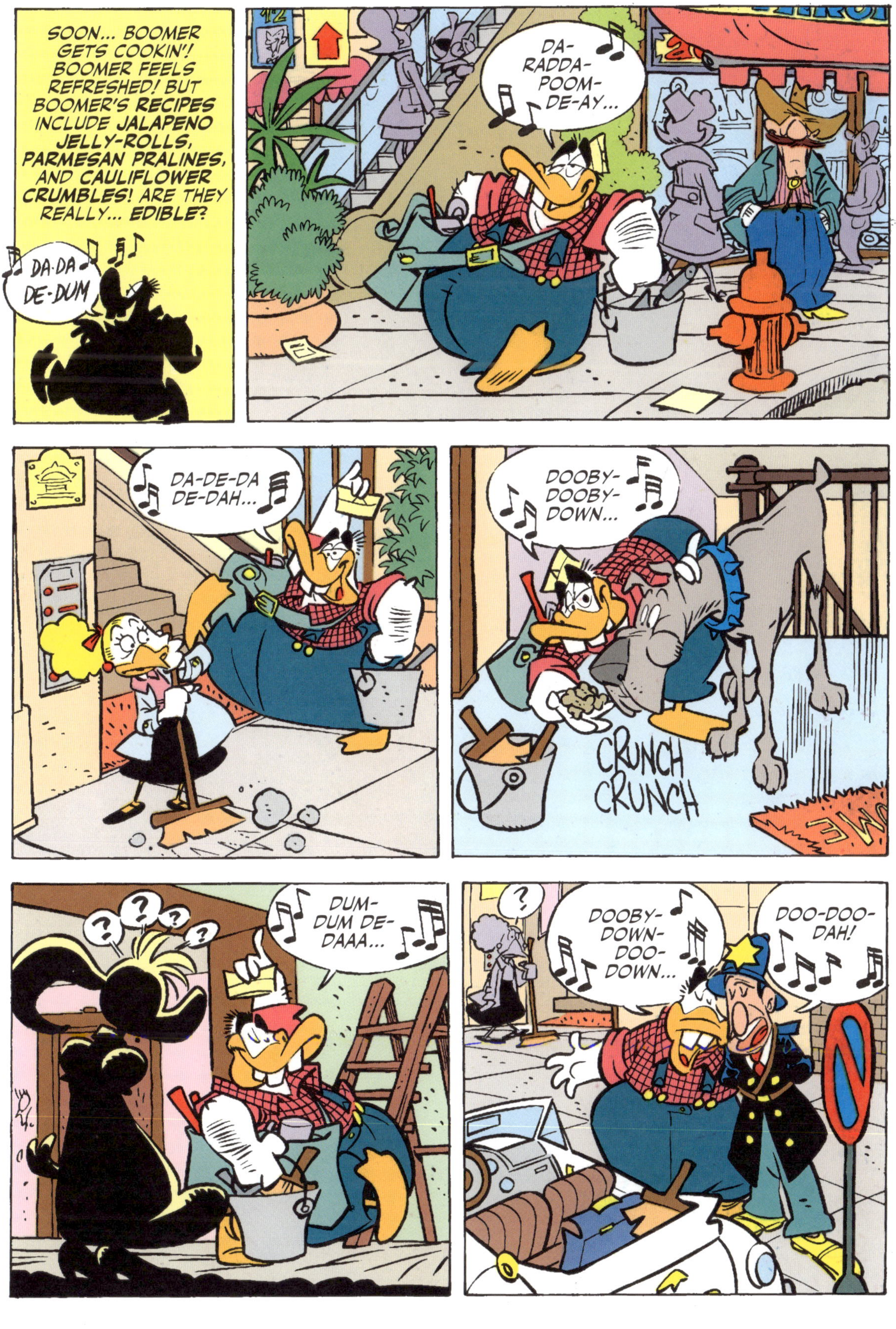

SOON... BOOMER GETS COOKIN'! BOOMER FEELS REFRESHED! BUT BOOMER'S **RECIPES** INCLUDE **JALAPENO JELLY-ROLLS, PARMESAN PRALINES,** AND **CAULIFLOWER CRUMBLES!** ARE THEY REALLY... **EDIBLE?**
DA-DA DE-DUM
DA-RADDA-POOM-DE-AY...
DA-DE-DA DE-DAH...
DOOBY-DOOBY-DOWN...
CRUNCH CRUNCH
DUM-DUM DE-DAAA...
DOOBY-DOWN-DOO-DOWN...
DOO-DOO-DAH!

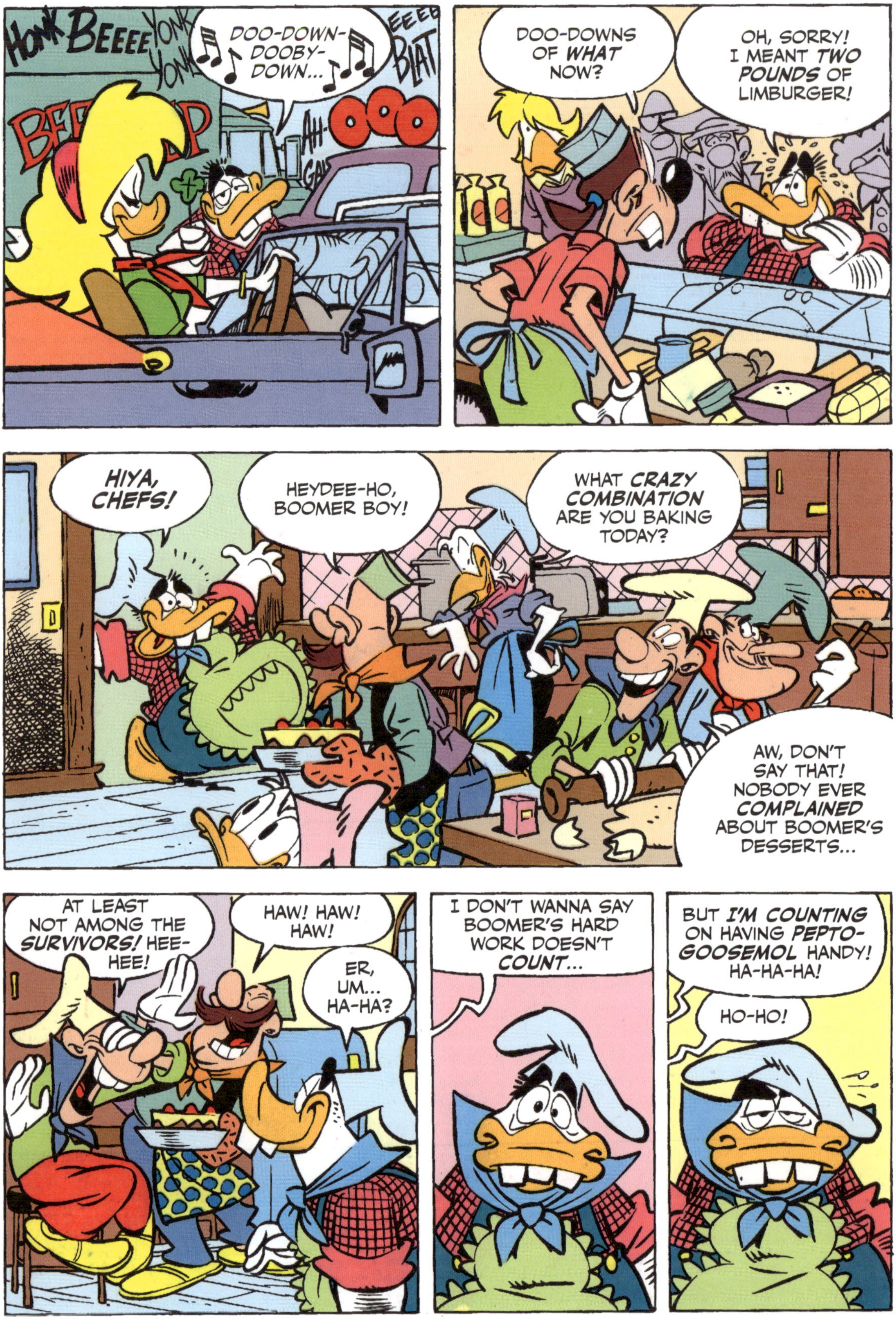
HONK BEEEEE YONK YONK
DOO-DOWN-DOOBY-DOWN...
EEEEE BLAT
AH-OOO
DOO-DOWNS OF WHAT NOW?
OH, SORRY! I MEANT TWO POUNDS OF LIMBURGER!
HIYA, CHEFS!
HEYDEE-HO, BOOMER BOY!
WHAT CRAZY COMBINATION ARE YOU BAKING TODAY?
AW, DON'T SAY THAT! NOBODY EVER COMPLAINED ABOUT BOOMER'S DESSERTS...
AT LEAST NOT AMONG THE SURVIVORS! HEE-HEE!
HAW! HAW! HAW!
ER, UM... HA-HA?
I DON'T WANNA SAY BOOMER'S HARD WORK DOESN'T COUNT...
BUT I'M COUNTING ON HAVING PEPTO-GOOSEMOL HANDY! HA-HA-HA!
HO-HO!

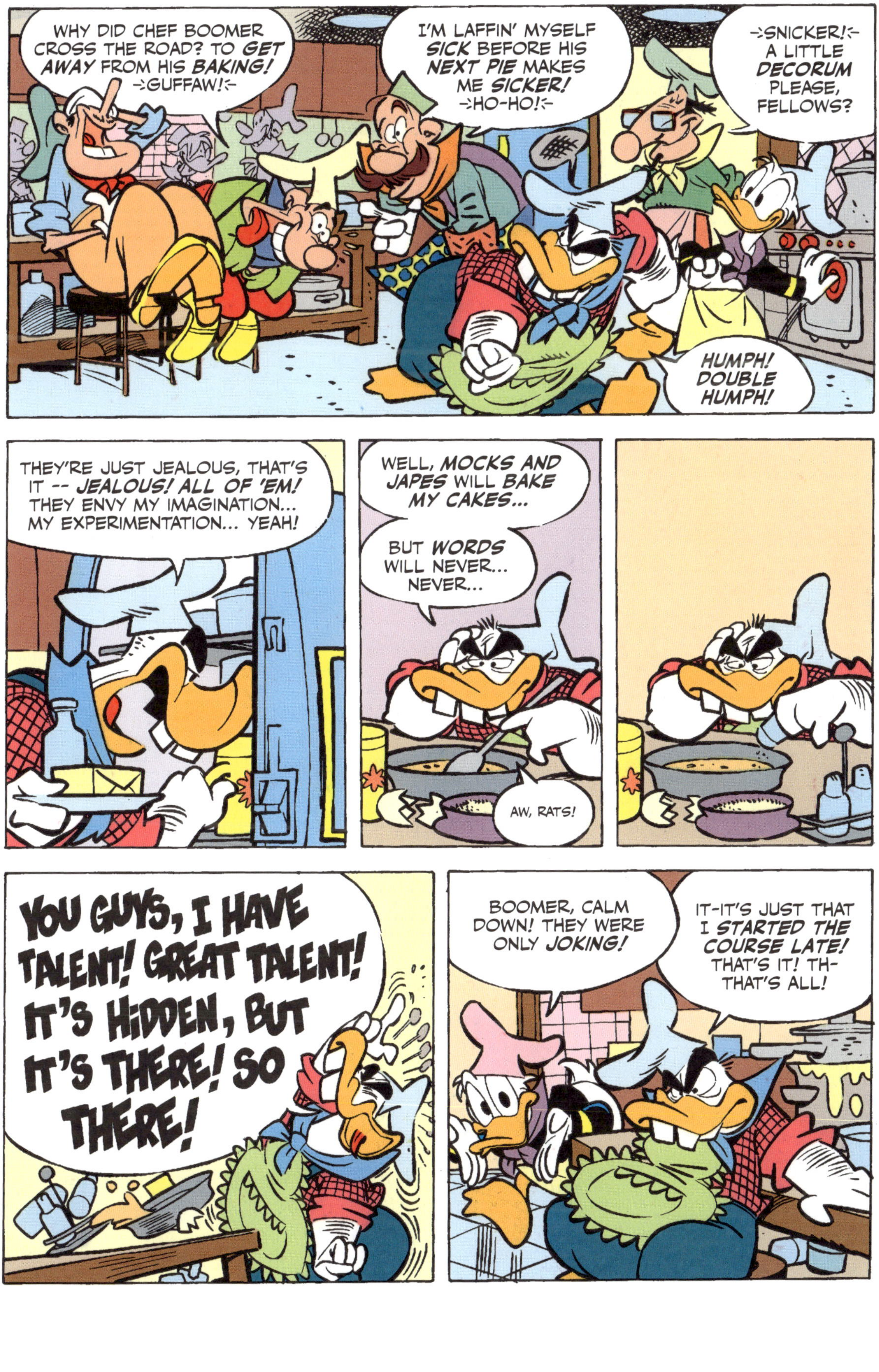
WHY DID CHEF BOOMER CROSS THE ROAD? TO GET AWAY FROM HIS BAKING! -GUFFAW!-
I'M LAFFIN' MYSELF SICK BEFORE HIS NEXT PIE MAKES ME SICKER! -HO-HO!-
-SNICKER!- A LITTLE DECORUM PLEASE, FELLOWS?
HUMPH! DOUBLE HUMPH!
THEY'RE JUST JEALOUS, THAT'S IT -- JEALOUS! ALL OF 'EM! THEY ENVY MY IMAGINATION... MY EXPERIMENTATION... YEAH!
WELL, MOCKS AND JAPES WILL BAKE MY CAKES...
BUT WORDS WILL NEVER... NEVER...
AW, RATS!
YOU GUYS, I HAVE TALENT! GREAT TALENT! IT'S HIDDEN, BUT IT'S THERE! SO THERE!
BOOMER, CALM DOWN! THEY WERE ONLY JOKING!
IT-IT'S JUST THAT I STARTED THE COURSE LATE! THAT'S IT! TH-THAT'S ALL!

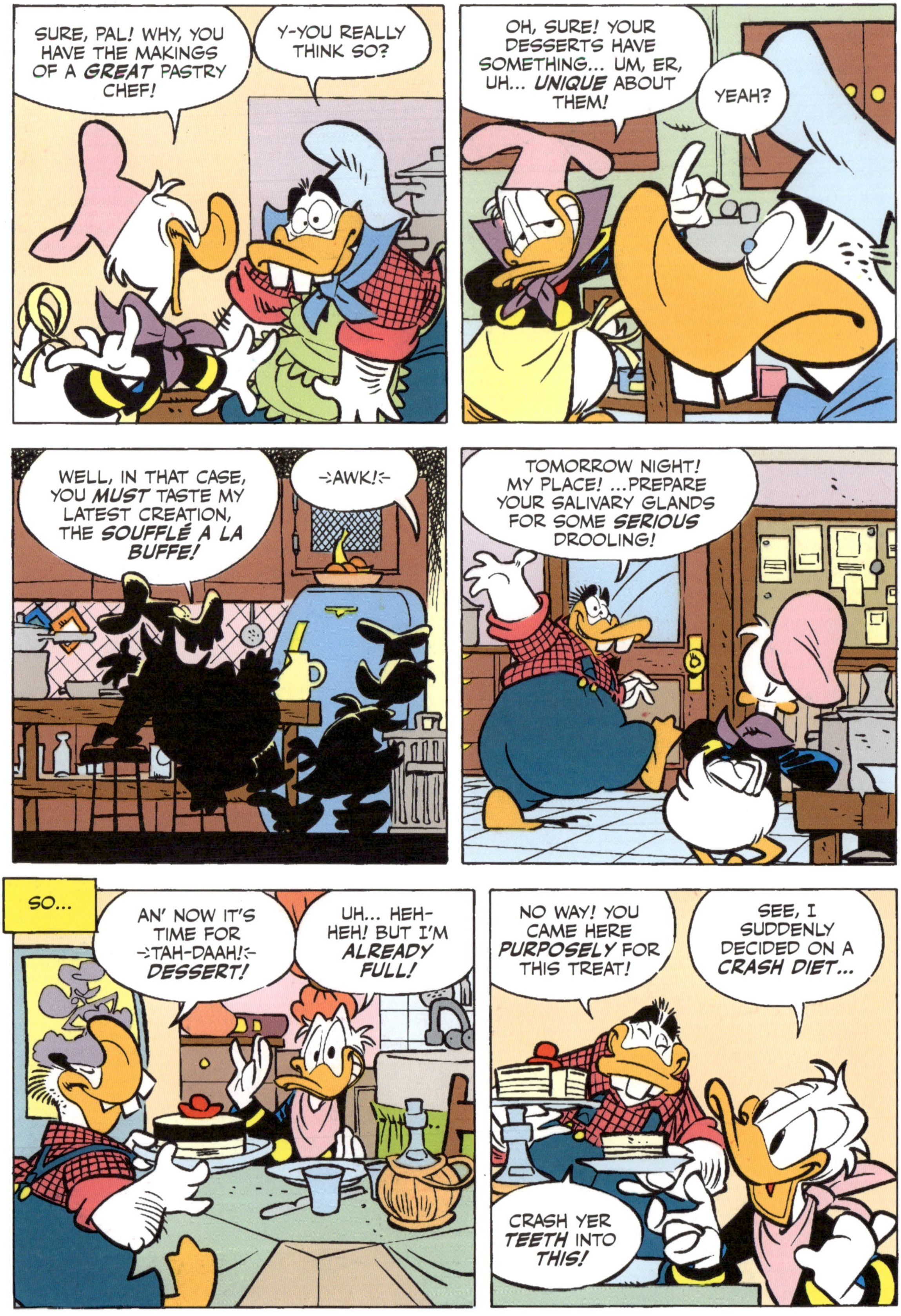
SURE, PAL! WHY, YOU HAVE THE MAKINGS OF A GREAT PASTRY CHEF!
Y-YOU REALLY THINK SO?
OH, SURE! YOUR DESSERTS HAVE SOMETHING... UM, ER, UH... UNIQUE ABOUT THEM!
YEAH?
WELL, IN THAT CASE, YOU MUST TASTE MY LATEST CREATION, THE SOUFFLÉ A LA BUFFE!
AWK!
TOMORROW NIGHT! MY PLACE! ...PREPARE YOUR SALIVARY GLANDS FOR SOME SERIOUS DROOLING!
SO...
AN' NOW IT'S TIME FOR TAH-DAAH! DESSERT!
UH... HEH-HEH! BUT I'M ALREADY FULL!
NO WAY! YOU CAME HERE PURPOSELY FOR THIS TREAT!
SEE, I SUDDENLY DECIDED ON A CRASH DIET...
CRASH YER TEETH INTO THIS!

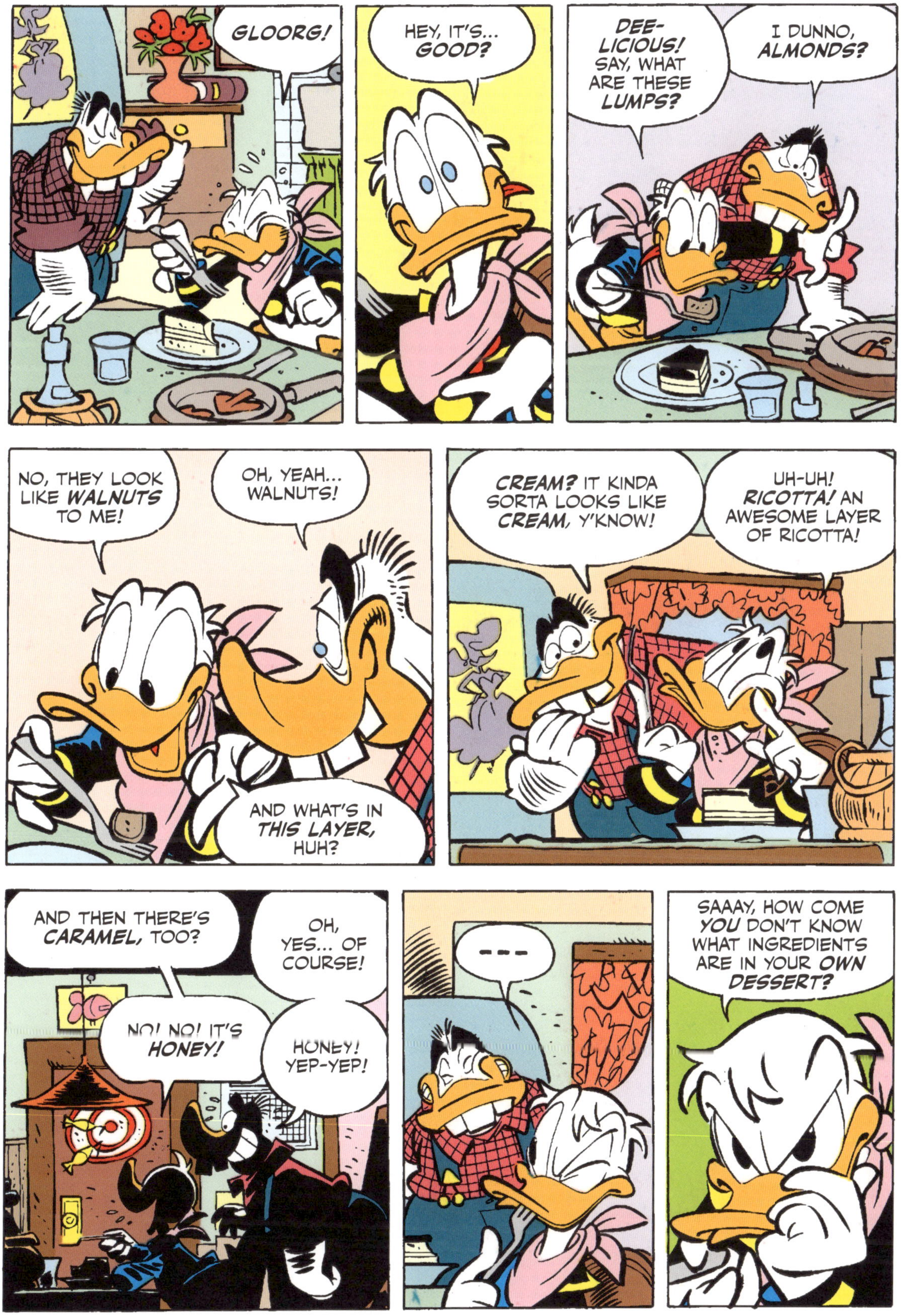

GLOORG!
HEY, IT'S... GOOD?
DEE-LICIOUS! SAY, WHAT ARE THESE LUMPS?
I DUNNO, ALMONDS?
NO, THEY LOOK LIKE WALNUTS TO ME!
OH, YEAH... WALNUTS!
AND WHAT'S IN THIS LAYER, HUH?
CREAM? IT KINDA SORTA LOOKS LIKE CREAM, Y'KNOW!
UH-UH! RICOTTA! AN AWESOME LAYER OF RICOTTA!
AND THEN THERE'S CARAMEL, TOO?
OH, YES... OF COURSE!
NO! NO! IT'S HONEY!
HONEY! YEP-YEP!

SAAAY, HOW COME YOU DON'T KNOW WHAT INGREDIENTS ARE IN YOUR OWN DESSERT?

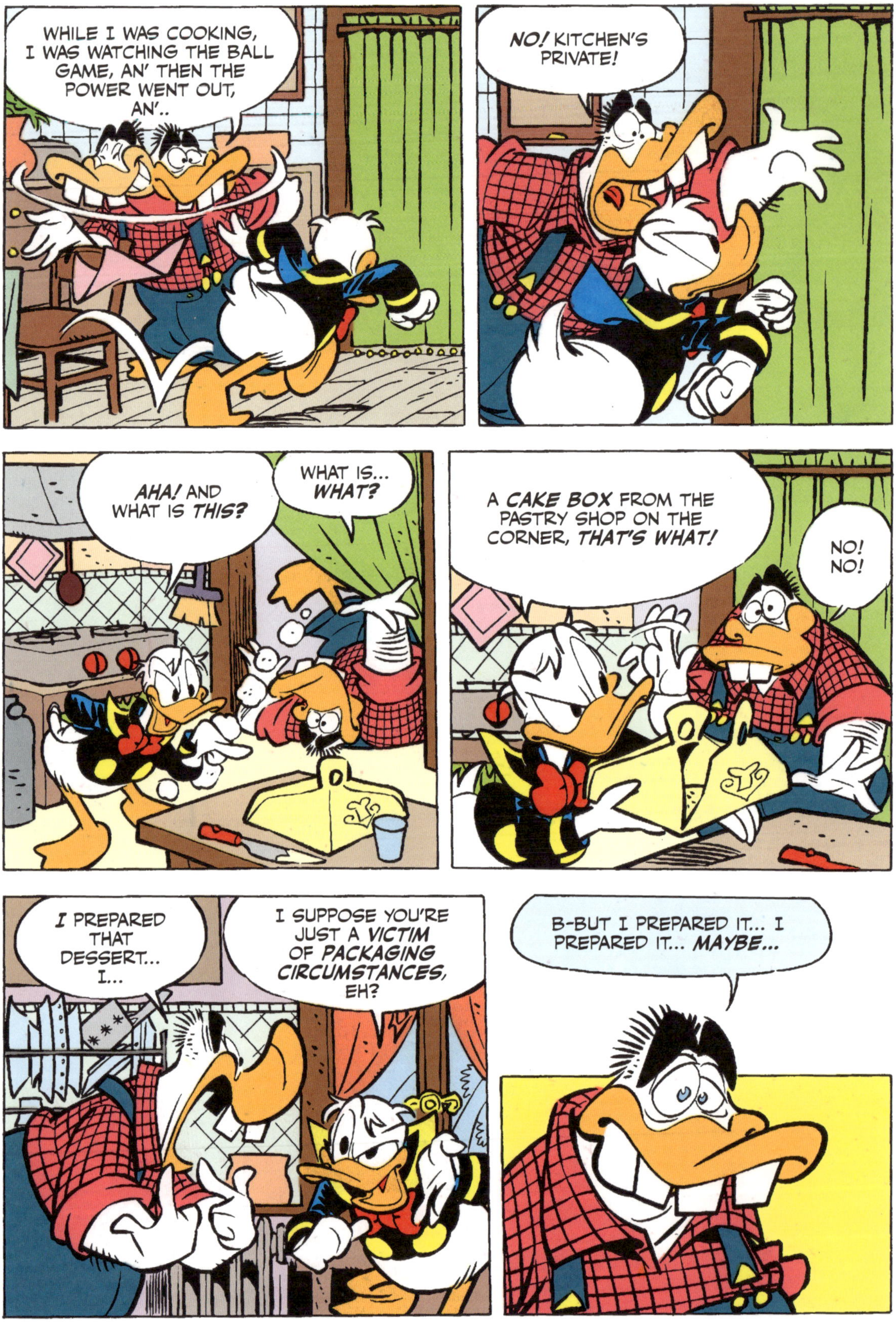
WHILE I WAS COOKING, I WAS WATCHING THE BALL GAME, AN' THEN THE POWER WENT OUT, AN'..
NO! KITCHEN'S PRIVATE!
AHA! AND WHAT IS *THIS?*
WHAT IS... *WHAT?*
A *CAKE BOX* FROM THE PASTRY SHOP ON THE CORNER, *THAT'S WHAT!*
NO! NO!
I PREPARED THAT DESSERT... I...
I SUPPOSE YOU'RE JUST A *VICTIM* OF *PACKAGING CIRCUMSTANCES,* EH?
B-BUT I PREPARED IT... I PREPARED IT... *MAYBE...*

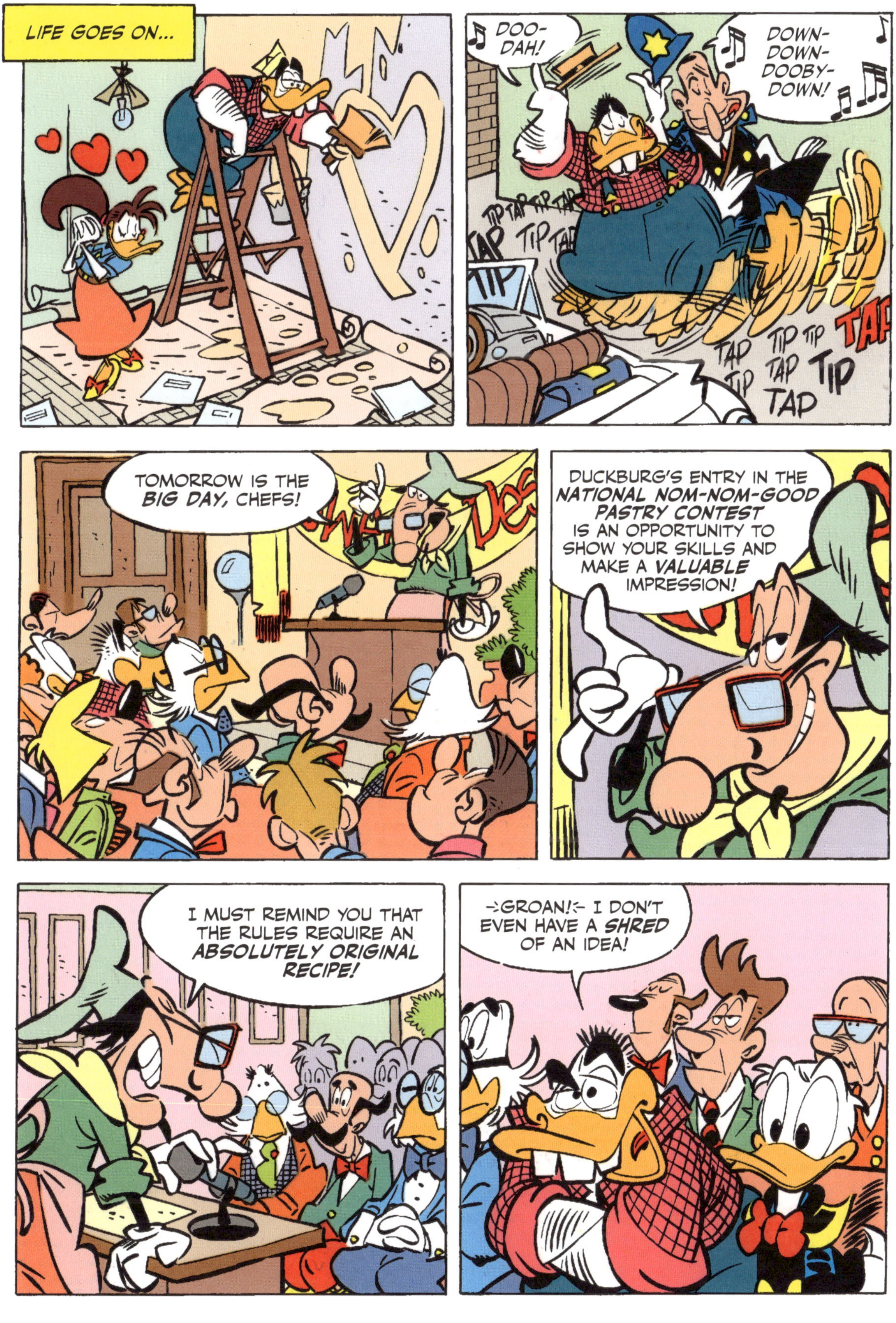

LIFE GOES ON...
DOO-DAH!
DOWN-DOWN-DOOBY-DOWN!
TIP TAP TIP TAP
TAP TIP
TIP
TAP TIP TIP TIP TAP
TIP TAP TIP TAP
TOMORROW IS THE BIG DAY, CHEFS!
DUCKBURG'S ENTRY IN THE NATIONAL NOM-NOM-GOOD PASTRY CONTEST IS AN OPPORTUNITY TO SHOW YOUR SKILLS AND MAKE A VALUABLE IMPRESSION!
I MUST REMIND YOU THAT THE RULES REQUIRE AN ABSOLUTELY ORIGINAL RECIPE!
-GROAN!- I DON'T EVEN HAVE A SHRED OF AN IDEA!

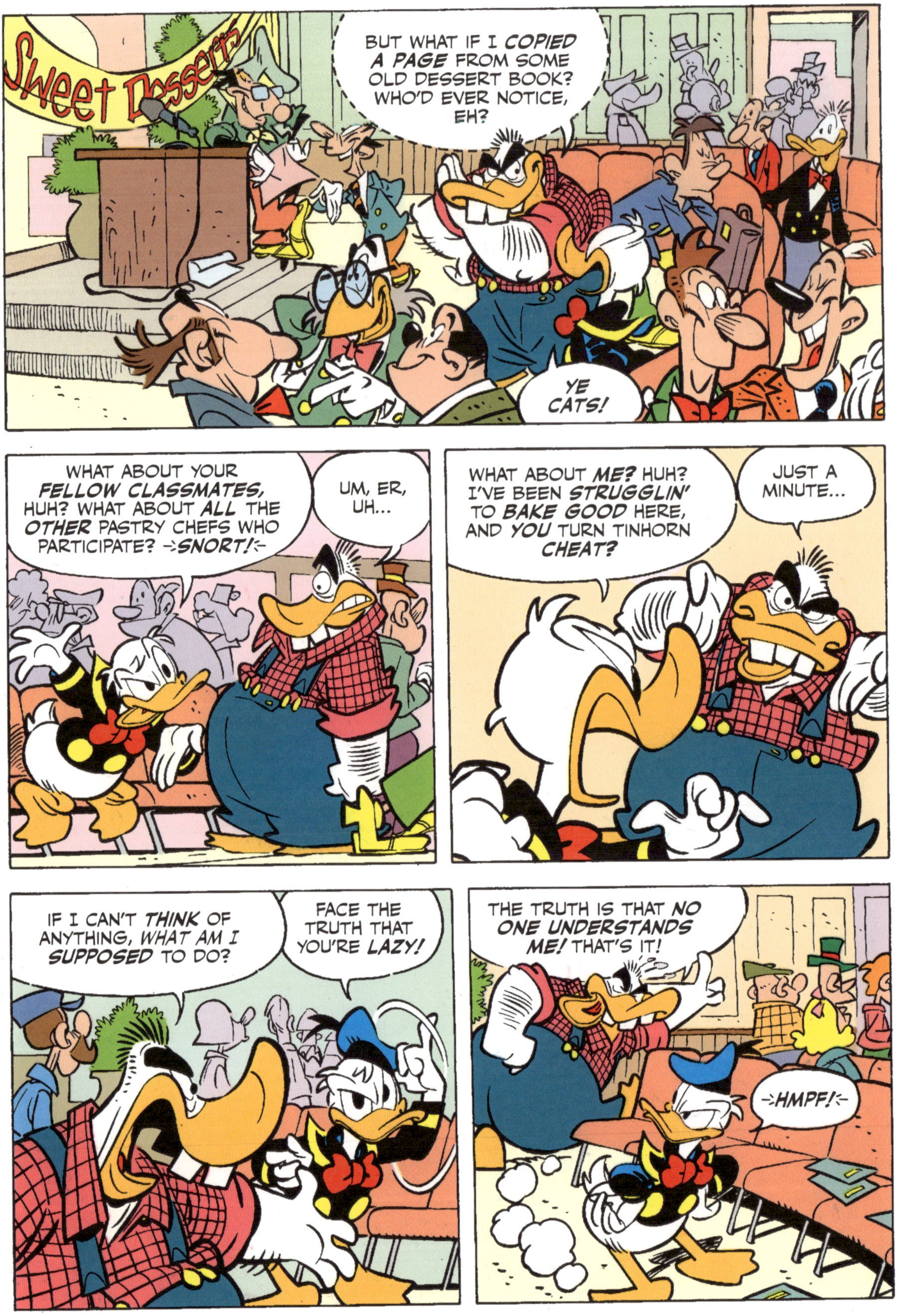

BUT WHAT IF I COPIED A PAGE FROM SOME OLD DESSERT BOOK? WHO'D EVER NOTICE, EH?
Sweet Desserts
YE CATS!
WHAT ABOUT YOUR FELLOW CLASSMATES, HUH? WHAT ABOUT ALL THE OTHER PASTRY CHEFS WHO PARTICIPATE? -SNORT!-
UM, ER, UH...
WHAT ABOUT ME? HUH? I'VE BEEN STRUGGLIN' TO BAKE GOOD HERE, AND YOU TURN TINHORN CHEAT?
JUST A MINUTE...
IF I CAN'T THINK OF ANYTHING, WHAT AM I SUPPOSED TO DO?
FACE THE TRUTH THAT YOU'RE LAZY!
THE TRUTH IS THAT NO ONE UNDERSTANDS ME! THAT'S IT!
-HMPF!-

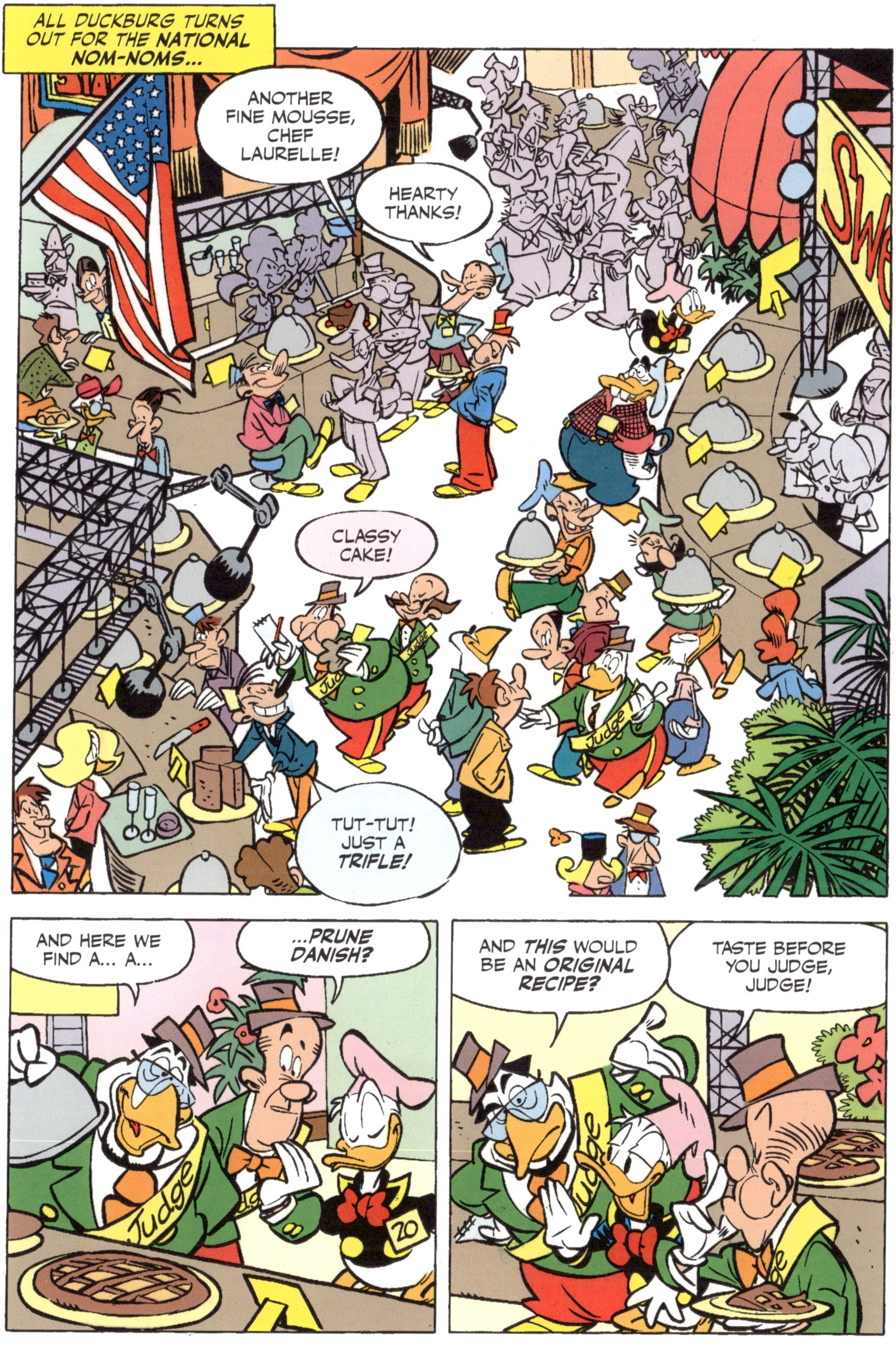
ALL DUCKBURG TURNS OUT FOR THE NATIONAL NOM-NOMS...
ANOTHER FINE MOUSSE, CHEF LAURELLE!
HEARTY THANKS!
CLASSY CAKE!
TUT-TUT! JUST A TRIFLE!
AND HERE WE FIND A... A...
...PRUNE DANISH?
AND THIS WOULD BE AN ORIGINAL RECIPE?
TASTE BEFORE YOU JUDGE, JUDGE!

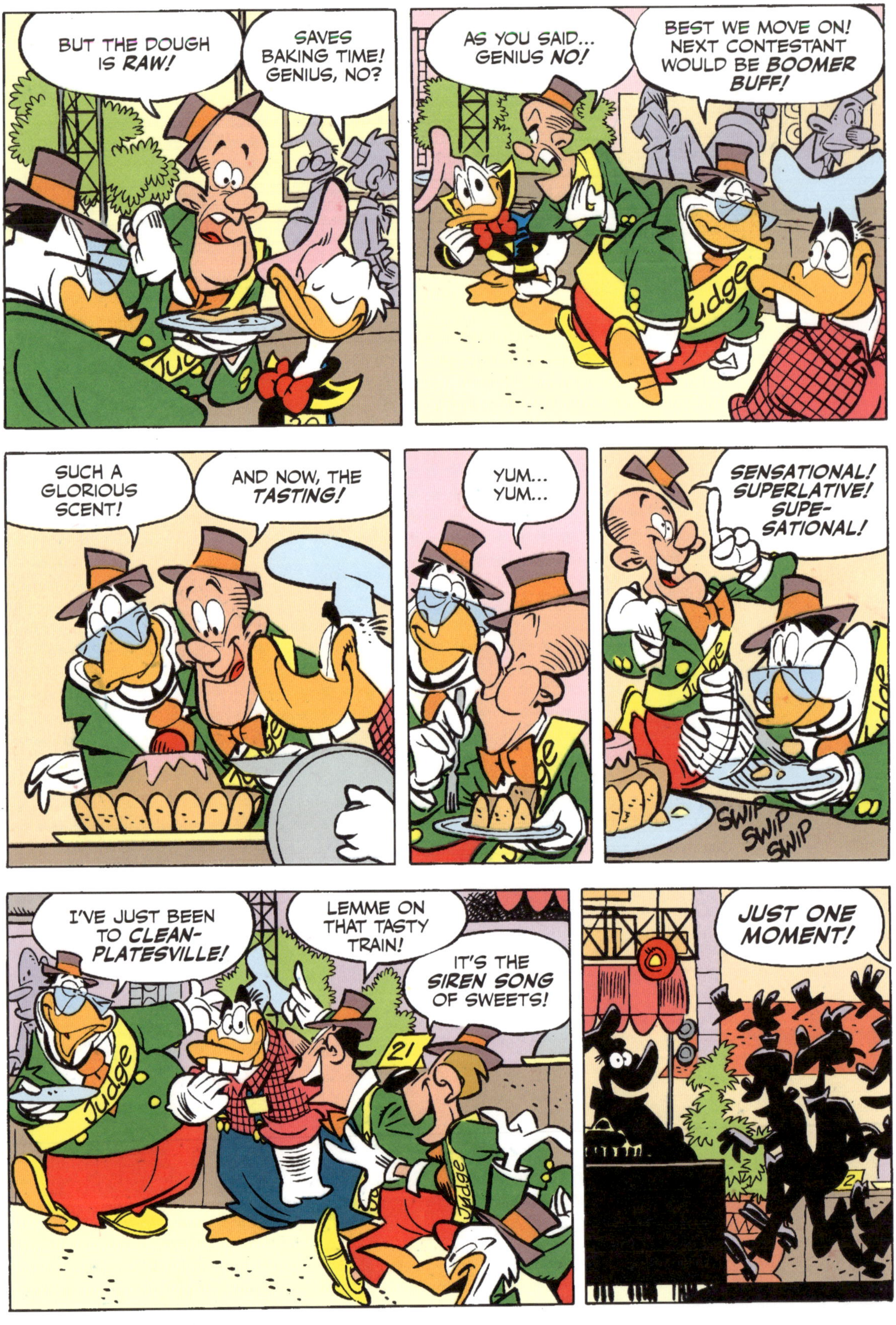

BUT THE DOUGH IS *RAW!*
SAVES BAKING TIME! GENIUS, NO?
AS YOU SAID... GENIUS *NO!*
BEST WE MOVE ON! NEXT CONTESTANT WOULD BE *BOOMER BUFF!*
Judge
SUCH A GLORIOUS SCENT!
AND NOW, THE *TASTING!*
YUM... YUM...
SENSATIONAL! SUPERLATIVE! SUPE-SATIONAL!
SWIP SWIP SWIP
I'VE JUST BEEN TO *CLEAN-PLATESVILLE!*
LEMME ON THAT TASTY TRAIN!
IT'S THE *SIREN SONG* OF SWEETS!
21
JUST ONE MOMENT!

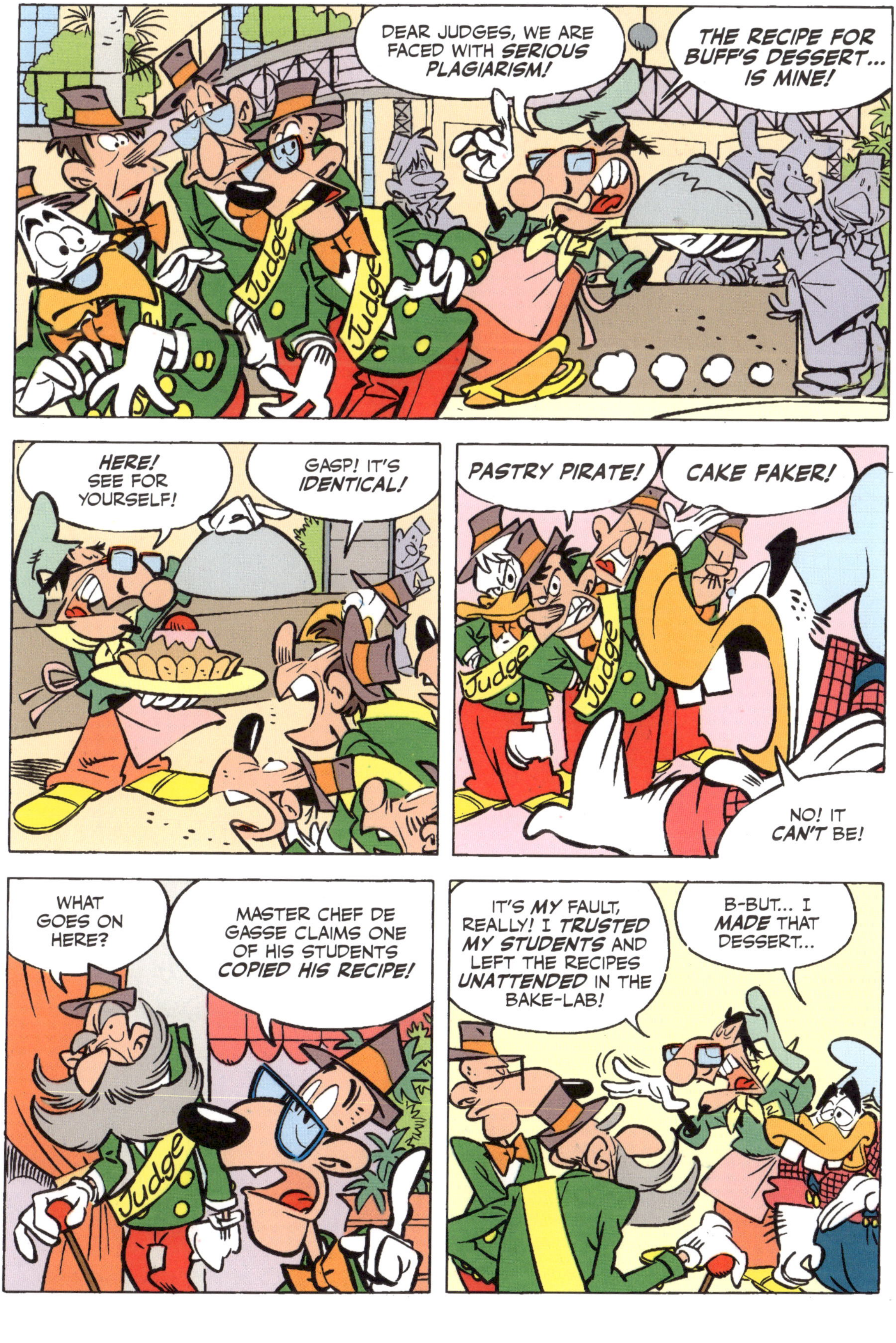

DEAR JUDGES, WE ARE FACED WITH SERIOUS PLAGIARISM!
THE RECIPE FOR BUFF'S DESSERT... IS MINE!
HERE! SEE FOR YOURSELF!
GASP! IT'S IDENTICAL!
PASTRY PIRATE!
CAKE FAKER!
NO! IT CAN'T BE!
WHAT GOES ON HERE?
MASTER CHEF DE GASSE CLAIMS ONE OF HIS STUDENTS COPIED HIS RECIPE!
IT'S MY FAULT, REALLY! I TRUSTED MY STUDENTS AND LEFT THE RECIPES UNATTENDED IN THE BAKE-LAB!
B-BUT... I MADE THAT DESSERT...

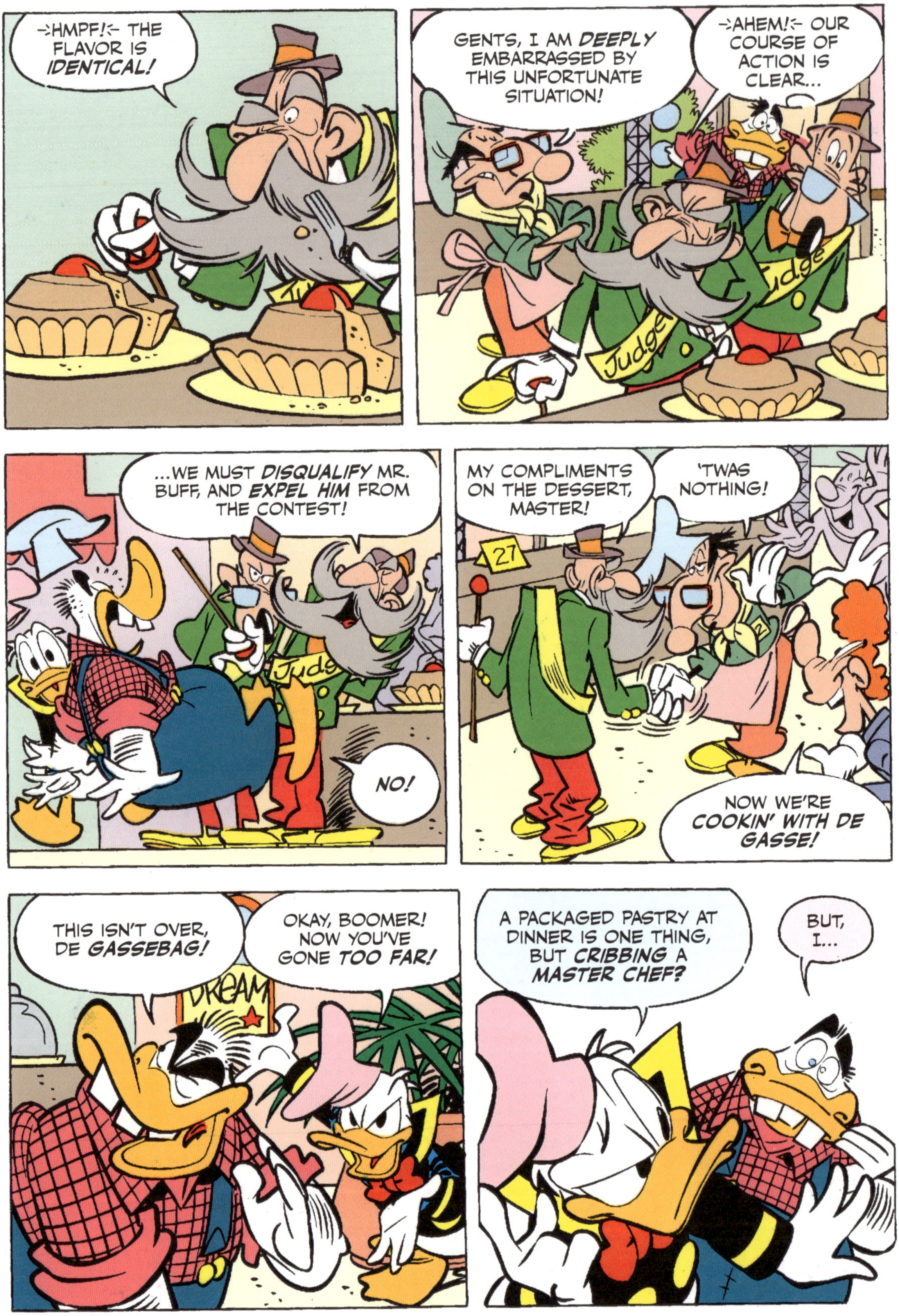
-HMPF!- THE FLAVOR IS IDENTICAL!
GENTS, I AM DEEPLY EMBARRASSED BY THIS UNFORTUNATE SITUATION!
-AHEM!- OUR COURSE OF ACTION IS CLEAR...
Judge
Judge
...WE MUST DISQUALIFY MR. BUFF, AND EXPEL HIM FROM THE CONTEST!
NO!
MY COMPLIMENTS ON THE DESSERT, MASTER!
'TWAS NOTHING!
27
NOW WE'RE COOKIN' WITH DE GASSE!
THIS ISN'T OVER, DE GASSEBAG!
OKAY, BOOMER! NOW YOU'VE GONE TOO FAR!
DREAM
A PACKAGED PASTRY AT DINNER IS ONE THING, BUT CRIBBING A MASTER CHEF?
BUT, I...

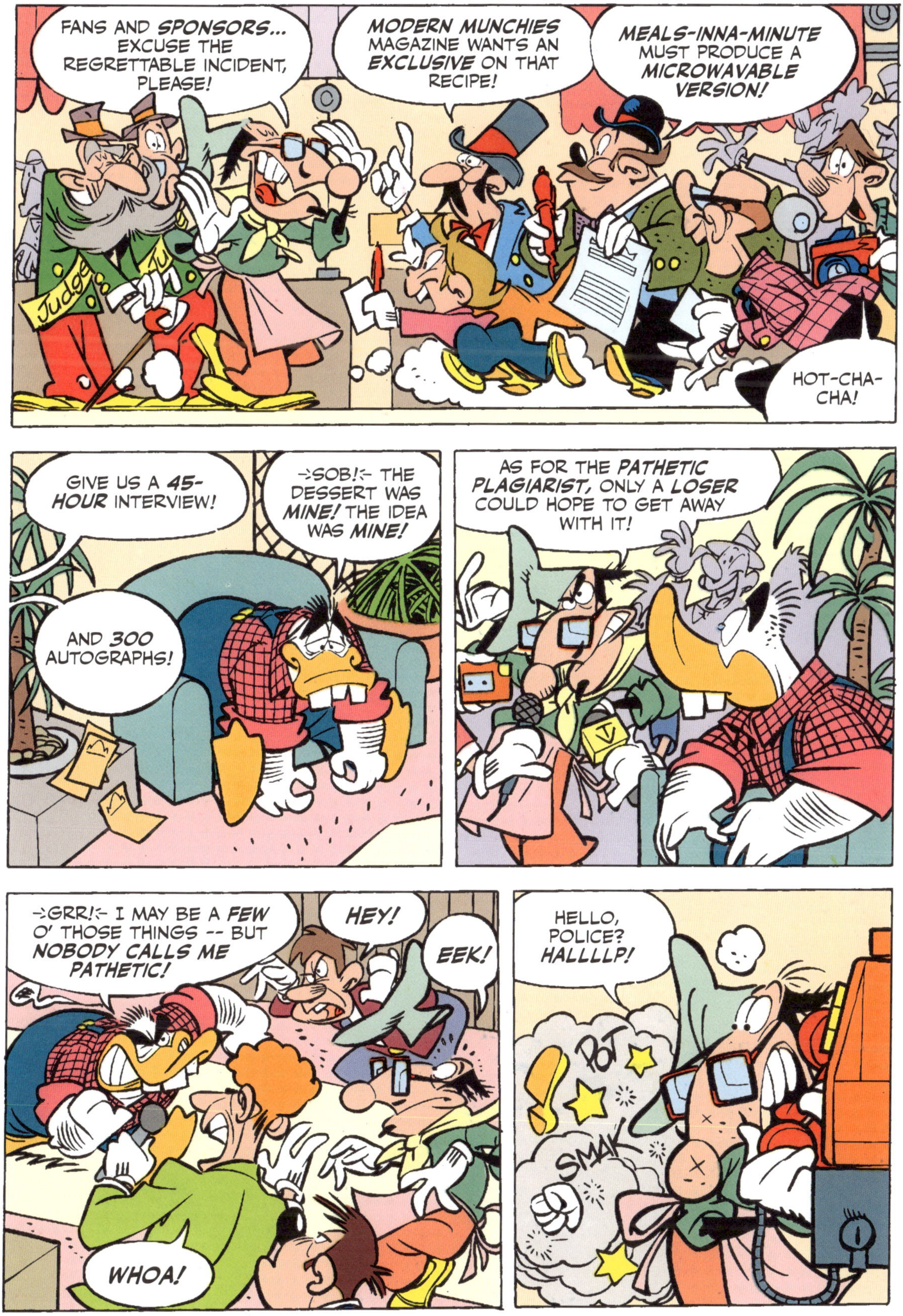
FANS AND SPONSORS... EXCUSE THE REGRETTABLE INCIDENT, PLEASE!
MODERN MUNCHIES MAGAZINE WANTS AN EXCLUSIVE ON THAT RECIPE!
MEALS-INNA-MINUTE MUST PRODUCE A MICROWAVABLE VERSION!
HOT-CHA-CHA!
Judge
GIVE US A 45-HOUR INTERVIEW!
AND 300 AUTOGRAPHS!
-SOB!- THE DESSERT WAS MINE! THE IDEA WAS MINE!
AS FOR THE PATHETIC PLAGIARIST, ONLY A LOSER COULD HOPE TO GET AWAY WITH IT!
-GRR!- I MAY BE A FEW O' THOSE THINGS -- BUT NOBODY CALLS ME PATHETIC!
HEY!
EEK!
WHOA!
HELLO, POLICE? HALLLLP!
POT
SMAK

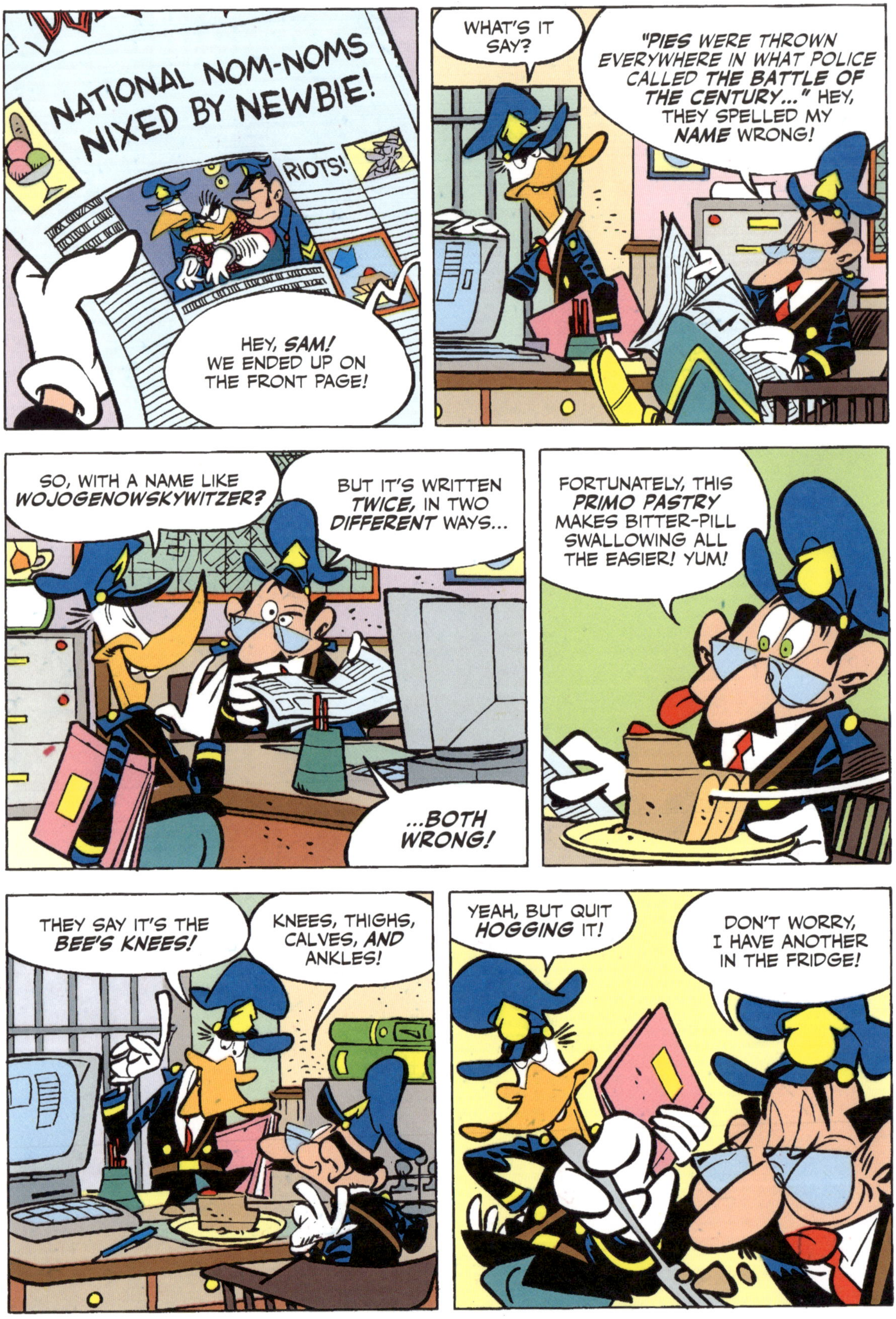
NATIONAL NOM-NOMS NIXED BY NEWBIE!
RIOTS!
HEY, SAM! WE ENDED UP ON THE FRONT PAGE!
WHAT'S IT SAY?
"PIES WERE THROWN EVERYWHERE IN WHAT POLICE CALLED THE BATTLE OF THE CENTURY..." HEY, THEY SPELLED MY NAME WRONG!
SO, WITH A NAME LIKE WOJOGENOWSKYWITZER?
BUT IT'S WRITTEN TWICE, IN TWO DIFFERENT WAYS...
...BOTH WRONG!
FORTUNATELY, THIS PRIMO PASTRY MAKES BITTER-PILL SWALLOWING ALL THE EASIER! YUM!
THEY SAY IT'S THE BEE'S KNEES!
KNEES, THIGHS, CALVES, AND ANKLES!
YEAH, BUT QUIT HOGGING IT!
DON'T WORRY, I HAVE ANOTHER IN THE FRIDGE!

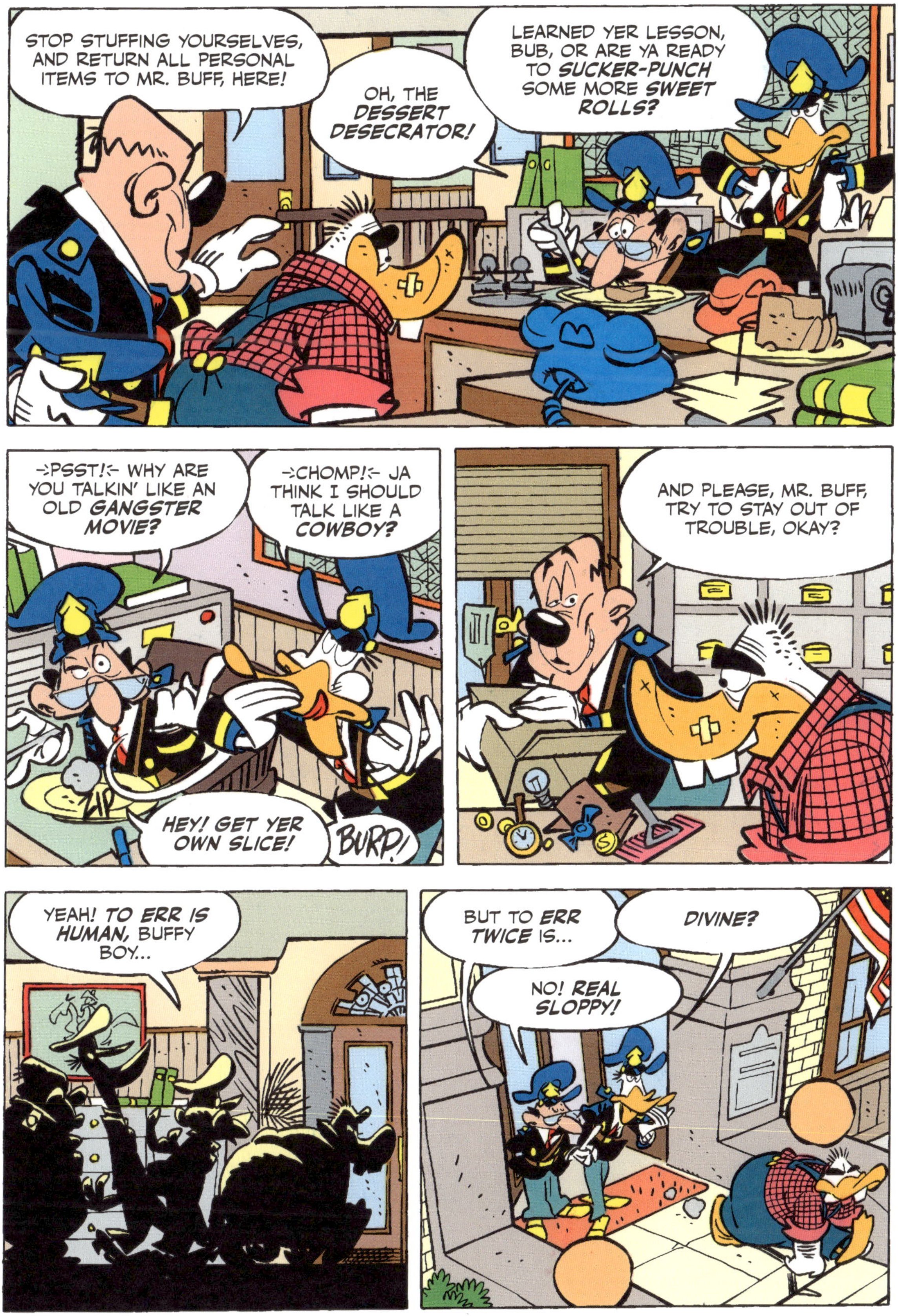
STOP STUFFING YOURSELVES, AND RETURN ALL PERSONAL ITEMS TO MR. BUFF, HERE!
OH, THE DESSERT DESECRATOR!
LEARNED YER LESSON, BUB, OR ARE YA READY TO SUCKER-PUNCH SOME MORE SWEET ROLLS?
-PSST!- WHY ARE YOU TALKIN' LIKE AN OLD GANGSTER MOVIE?
-CHOMP!- JA THINK I SHOULD TALK LIKE A COWBOY?
HEY! GET YER OWN SLICE!
BURP!
AND PLEASE, MR. BUFF, TRY TO STAY OUT OF TROUBLE, OKAY?
YEAH! TO ERR IS HUMAN, BUFFY BOY...
BUT TO ERR TWICE IS...
DIVINE?
NO! REAL SLOPPY!

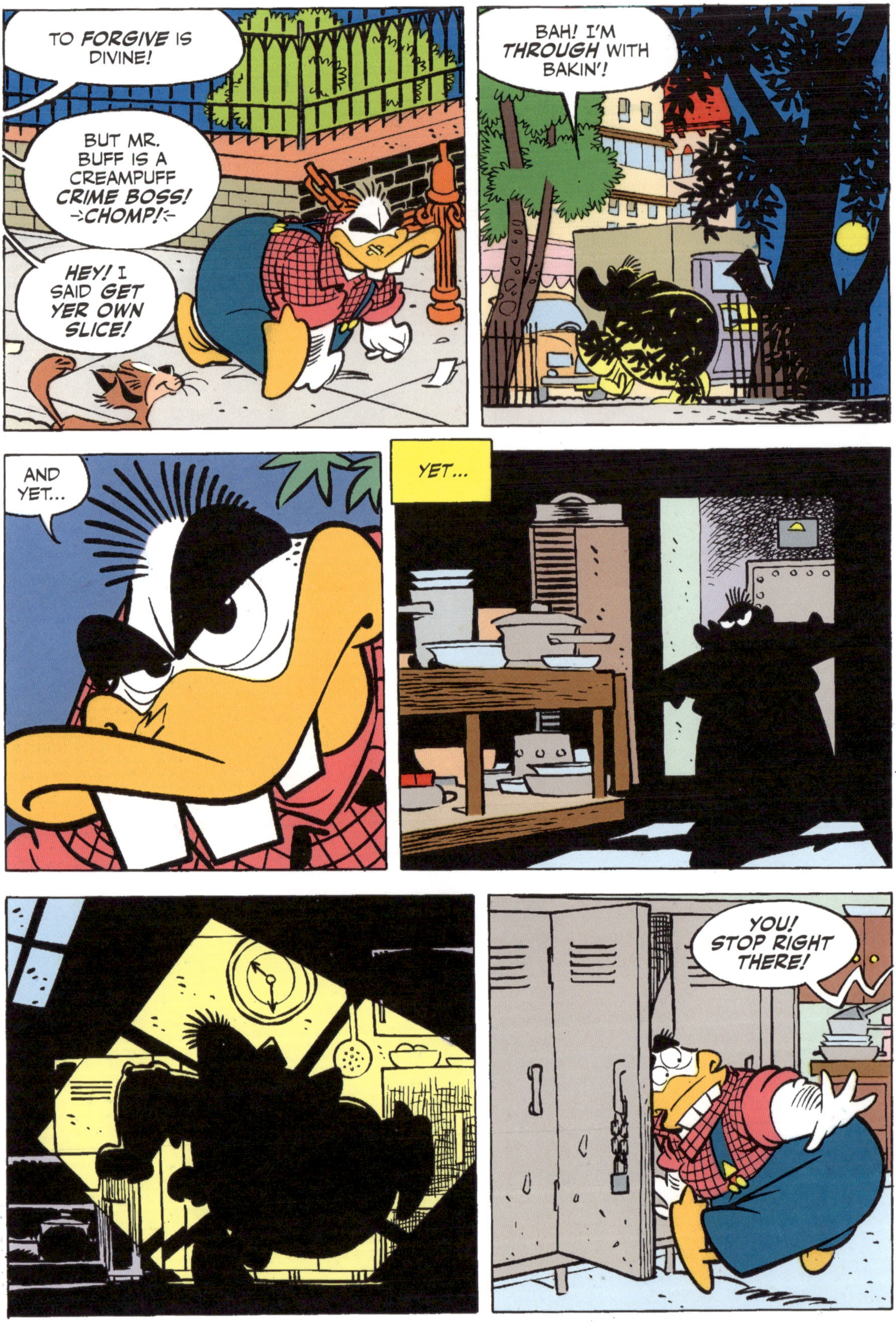
TO FORGIVE IS DIVINE!
BUT MR. BUFF IS A CREAMPUFF CRIME BOSS! -CHOMP!-
HEY! I SAID GET YER OWN SLICE!
BAH! I'M THROUGH WITH BAKIN'!
AND YET...
YET...
YOU! STOP RIGHT THERE!

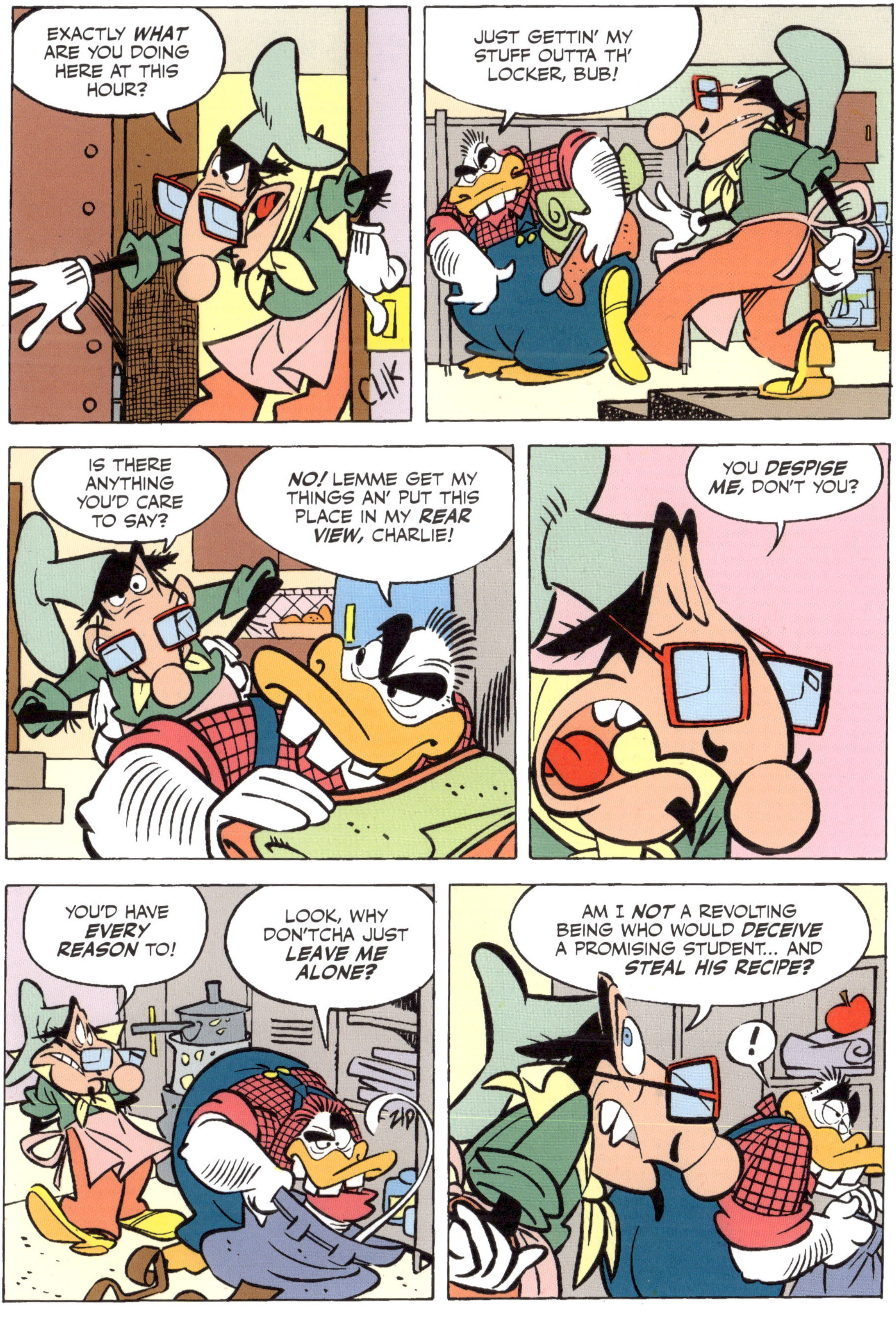
EXACTLY WHAT ARE YOU DOING HERE AT THIS HOUR?
CLIK
JUST GETTIN' MY STUFF OUTTA TH' LOCKER, BUB!
IS THERE ANYTHING YOU'D CARE TO SAY?
NO! LEMME GET MY THINGS AN' PUT THIS PLACE IN MY REAR VIEW, CHARLIE!
YOU DESPISE ME, DON'T YOU?
YOU'D HAVE EVERY REASON TO!
LOOK, WHY DON'TCHA JUST LEAVE ME ALONE?
ZIP
AM I NOT A REVOLTING BEING WHO WOULD DECEIVE A PROMISING STUDENT... AND STEAL HIS RECIPE?
!

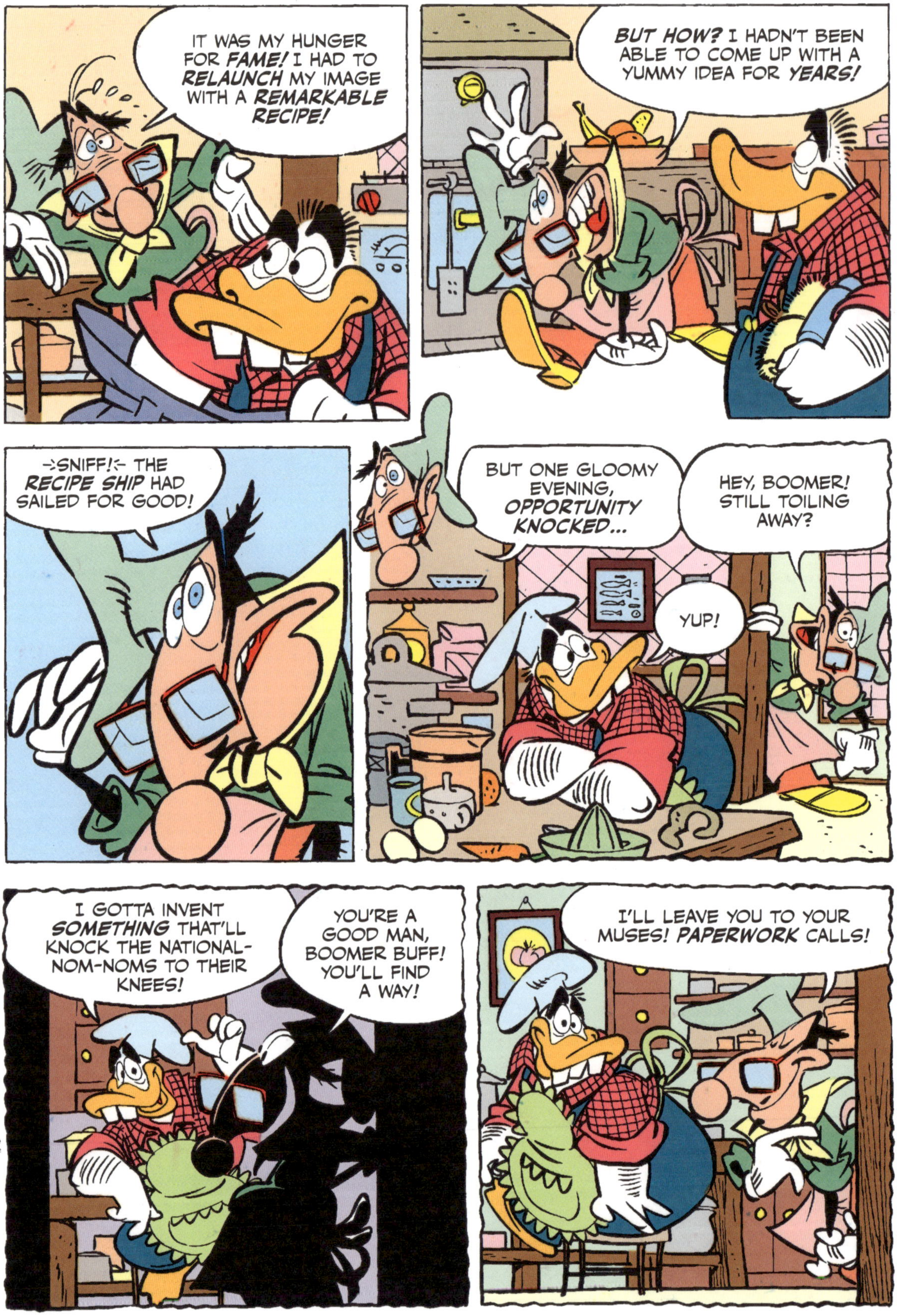
IT WAS MY HUNGER FOR FAME! I HAD TO RELAUNCH MY IMAGE WITH A REMARKABLE RECIPE!
BUT HOW? I HADN'T BEEN ABLE TO COME UP WITH A YUMMY IDEA FOR YEARS!
-SNIFF!- THE RECIPE SHIP HAD SAILED FOR GOOD!
BUT ONE GLOOMY EVENING, OPPORTUNITY KNOCKED...
HEY, BOOMER! STILL TOILING AWAY?
YUP!
I GOTTA INVENT SOMETHING THAT'LL KNOCK THE NATIONAL-NOM-NOMS TO THEIR KNEES!
YOU'RE A GOOD MAN, BOOMER BUFF! YOU'LL FIND A WAY!
I'LL LEAVE YOU TO YOUR MUSES! PAPERWORK CALLS!

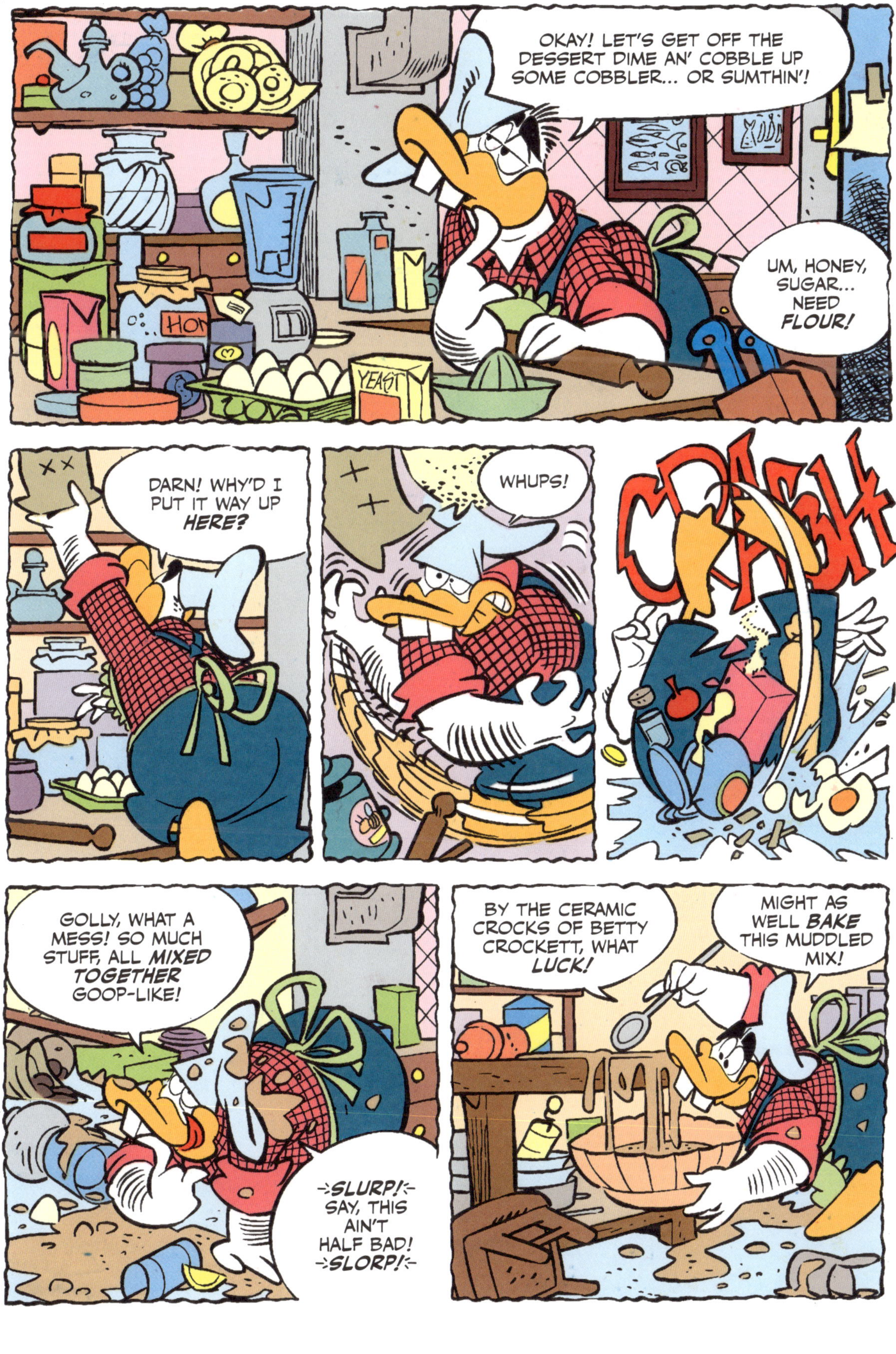
OKAY! LET'S GET OFF THE DESSERT DIME AN' COBBLE UP SOME COBBLER... OR SUMTHIN'!
UM, HONEY, SUGAR... NEED ***FLOUR!***
YEAST
DARN! WHY'D I PUT IT WAY UP ***HERE?***
WHUPS!
CRASH
GOLLY, WHAT A MESS! SO MUCH STUFF, ALL ***MIXED TOGETHER*** GOOP-LIKE!
-***SLURP!***- SAY, THIS AIN'T HALF BAD! -***SLORP!***-
BY THE CERAMIC CROCKS OF BETTY CROCKETT, WHAT ***LUCK!***
MIGHT AS WELL ***BAKE*** THIS MUDDLED MIX!

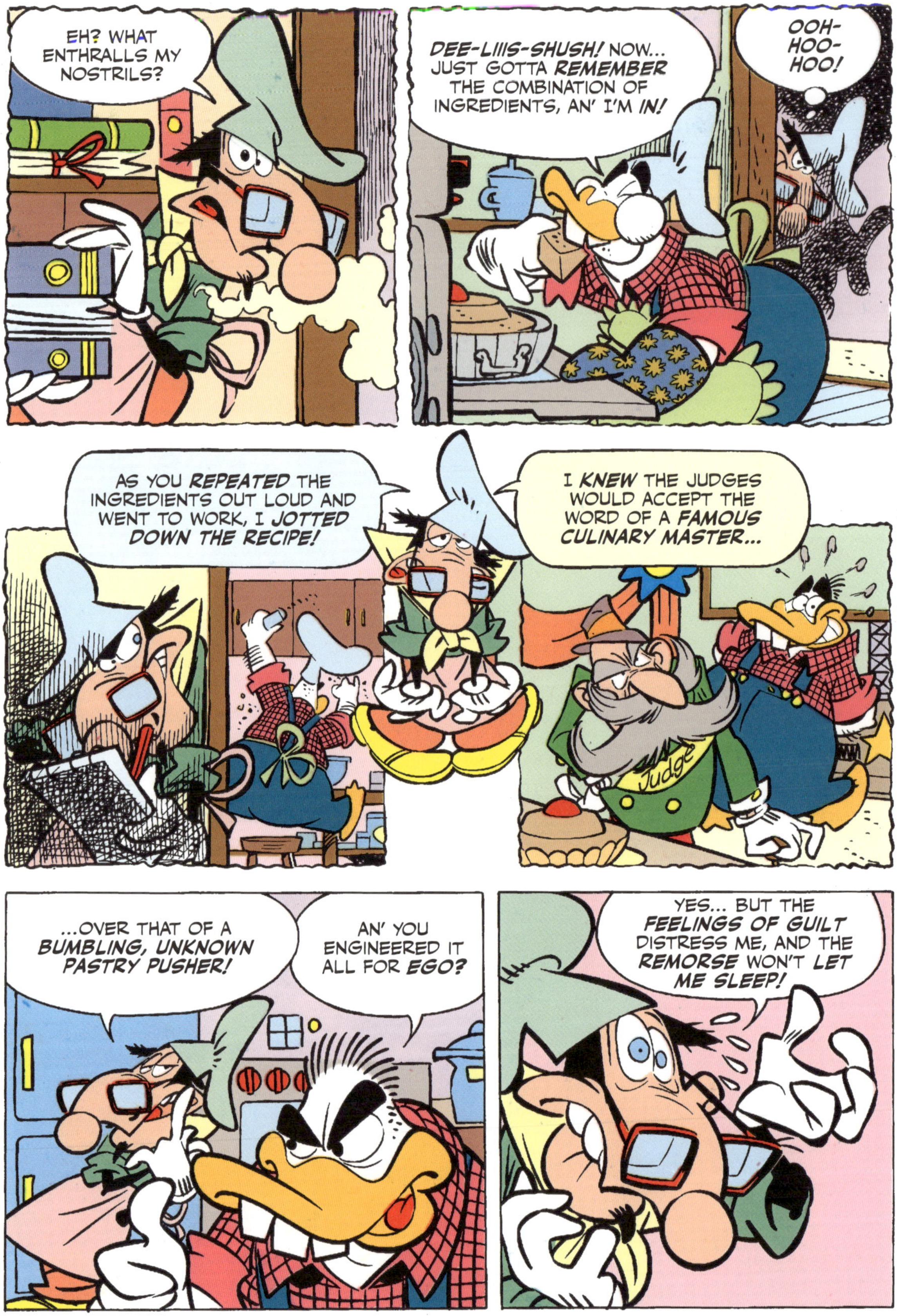
EH? WHAT ENTHRALLS MY NOSTRILS?
DEE-LIIIS-SHUSH! NOW... JUST GOTTA REMEMBER THE COMBINATION OF INGREDIENTS, AN' I'M IN!
OOH-HOO-HOO!
AS YOU REPEATED THE INGREDIENTS OUT LOUD AND WENT TO WORK, I JOTTED DOWN THE RECIPE!
I KNEW THE JUDGES WOULD ACCEPT THE WORD OF A FAMOUS CULINARY MASTER...
JUDGE
...OVER THAT OF A BUMBLING, UNKNOWN PASTRY PUSHER!
AN' YOU ENGINEERED IT ALL FOR EGO?
YES... BUT THE FEELINGS OF GUILT DISTRESS ME, AND THE REMORSE WON'T LET ME SLEEP!

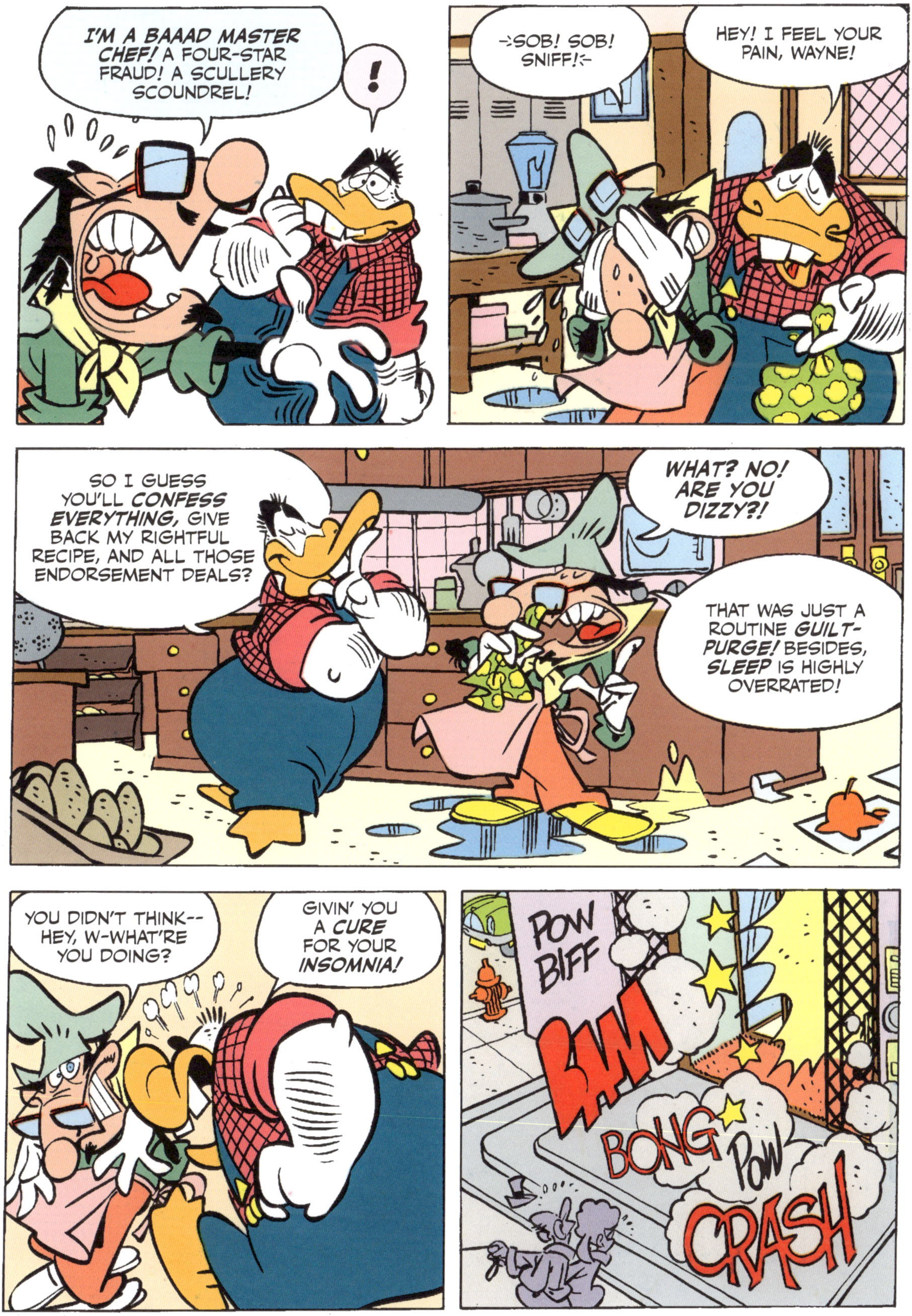
I'M A BAAAD MASTER CHEF! A FOUR-STAR FRAUD! A SCULLERY SCOUNDREL!
!
-SOB! SOB! SNIFF!-
HEY! I FEEL YOUR PAIN, WAYNE!
SO I GUESS YOU'LL CONFESS EVERYTHING, GIVE BACK MY RIGHTFUL RECIPE, AND ALL THOSE ENDORSEMENT DEALS?
WHAT? NO! ARE YOU DIZZY?!
THAT WAS JUST A ROUTINE GUILT-PURGE! BESIDES, SLEEP IS HIGHLY OVERRATED!
YOU DIDN'T THINK-- HEY, W-WHAT'RE YOU DOING?
GIVIN' YOU A CURE FOR YOUR INSOMNIA!
POW
BIFF
BAM
BONG
POW
CRASH

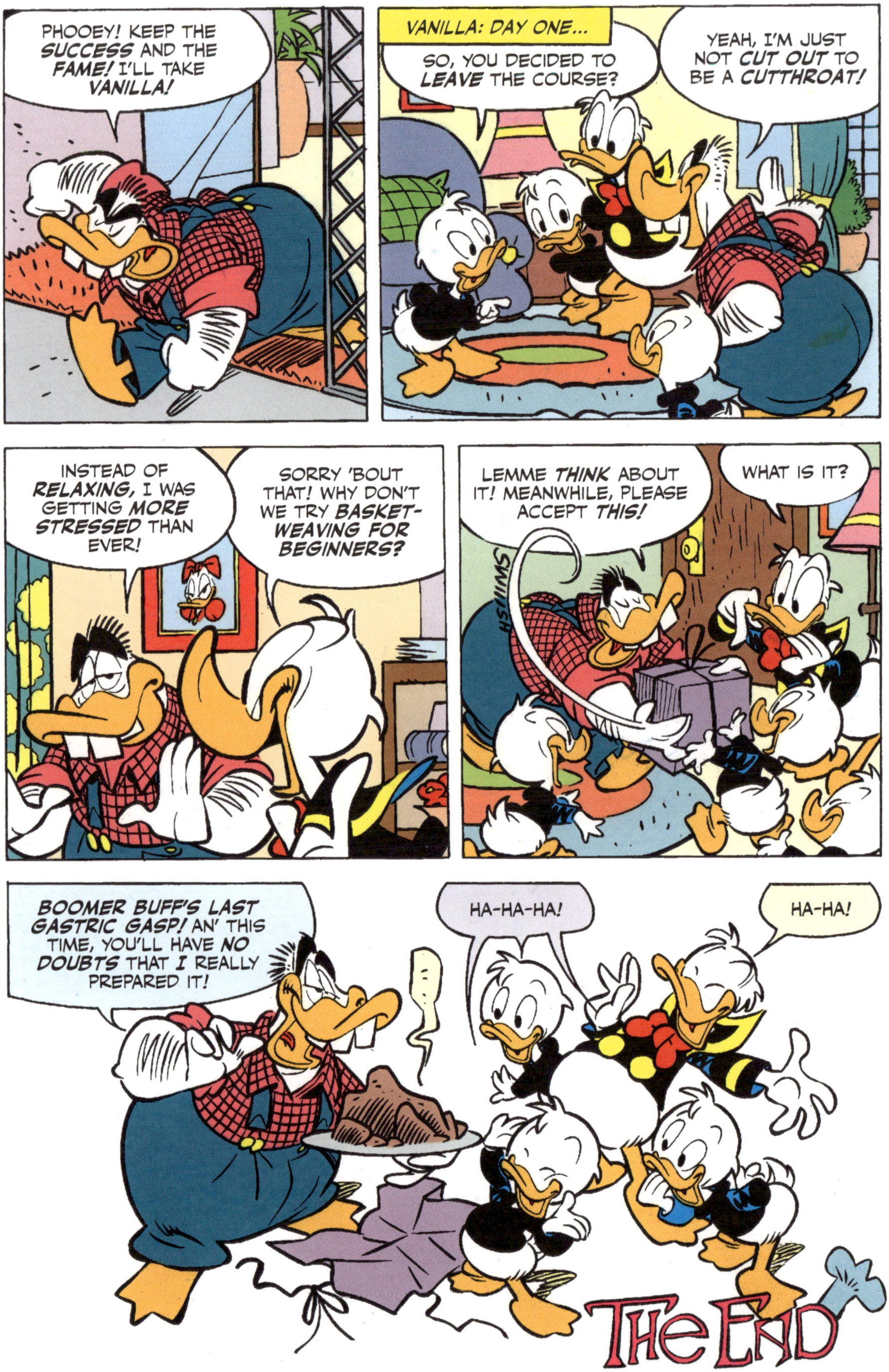
PHOOEY! KEEP THE SUCCESS AND THE FAME! I'LL TAKE VANILLA!
VANILLA: DAY ONE...
SO, YOU DECIDED TO LEAVE THE COURSE?
YEAH, I'M JUST NOT CUT OUT TO BE A CUTTHROAT!
INSTEAD OF RELAXING, I WAS GETTING MORE STRESSED THAN EVER!
SORRY 'BOUT THAT! WHY DON'T WE TRY BASKET-WEAVING FOR BEGINNERS?
LEMME THINK ABOUT IT! MEANWHILE, PLEASE ACCEPT THIS!
SWISH
WHAT IS IT?
BOOMER BUFF'S LAST GASTRIC GASP! AN' THIS TIME, YOU'LL HAVE NO DOUBTS THAT I REALLY PREPARED IT!
HA-HA-HA!
HA-HA!
THE END

Corrado Mastantuono

by ALBERTO BECATTINI

FEW COMICS ARTISTS IN ITALY are equally accomplished in both the humorous and realistic fields of illustration. Corrado Mastantuono is a member of this exclusive group.

Born in Rome on December 20, 1962, Mastantuono studied animation techniques in high school at the Roberto Rossellini State Institute for Cinema and Television, where his teachers included legendary comics artist Niso "Kremos" Ramponi. It was at Ramponi's recommendation that in 1980, the advertising firm Ital-Studio brought 17-year-old Mastantuono aboard as a full-time animator, illustrator, and set designer.

Mastantuono in 2012. Image courtesy Disney Publishing Worldwide.

Mastantuono also began producing independent animated films in 1985. "I was full of zest and enthusiasm then," he would later reminisce. "I could draw for 18 hours a day... I was a zombie!"[1]

Mastantuono's creative output caught the eye of Italian Disney comics artist Giovan Battista Carpi (*Uncle Scrooge and Donald Duck: Les Misérables and War and Peace*), who informed Mastantuono in 1989 that The Walt Disney Company Italia was looking for new comics artists. Just one year later, Mastantuono's *Topolino* career began with "Zio Paperone e l'unica giovialità" ("Scrooge's Lucky Star," 1990).

Mastantuono's Disney style was at first inspired by the bouncy "techno" artwork of Giorgio Cavazzano (*Donald Duck and Uncle Scrooge: World of the Dragonlords*), but he fast developed his own even bouncier look. In 1997, Mastantuono joined the talent pool on the fan-favorite *Paperinik New Adventures* series, where starting with "Two" (published in English in American *Duck Avenger* 4, 2017), futuristic Donald sci-fi tales proved a perfect match for his designs.

1997 was also the year in which Mastantuono began to write as well as draw, making the jump with "Boomer Buff's Big Boost," in which the raucous blue-collar Boomer was first unleashed. "I try to keep away from moralistic rhetoric and saccharine sweetness as much as I can," Mastantuono explained in 2004, "even though... my Boomer certainly has some positive traits... Before I realized what was happening, he'd become a star."

Mastantuono is also famed for his team-ups with scripter Francesco Artibani ("Scrooge's Last Adventure"). Beyond this volume's "The River of Time" and "The Explorers of Tomorrow," another prime collaboration was "Topolino e l'enigma di Cartunia" ("Crisis in Khartoun," 1995), featuring a caricature of beloved Disney animator Ward Kimball in mayhem at a cartoon studio.

Mastantuono's talent, however, goes beyond traditional Disney and even animation inspiration. Concurrent with Mastantuono's first *Topolino* work, the publisher Comic Art enlisted him to draw the hyper-realistic sci-fi series "Cargo Team" (1990-93), as well as the jailhouse saga "Buzzer and Todavia" (1992-93) and a new spin on Richard F. Outcault's historic *Yellow Kid* (1993-96). Mastantuono also created halftone illustrations for text stories, collected in *Il Teatro dell'assurdo* ("Theatre of the Absurd," 1995).

In 1994, Mastantuono joined up with publisher Sergio Bonelli Editore to draw a story for the detective comic *Nick Raider*. In 1996, Mastantuono became the series' regular cover artist. His Bonelli work has since entailed stories and covers for *Magico Vento* (1997-2001) and *Tex* (2009-present); other non-Disney collaborations have included a *Diabolik* special (2002) and the French fantasy graphic novel *Elias the Cursed*, scripted by Sylviane Corgiat (2009).

"I enjoy switching from one style to another," Mastantuono once opined. "It stirs my enthusiasm." With the energy of two talents in one—and, perhaps, Boomer Buff—Mastantuono forges on. ♣

---

[1] All quotes: Corrado Mastantuono to Edizioni il Penny editors, "A Conversation with Corrado," *Percorsi* 4, 2004.

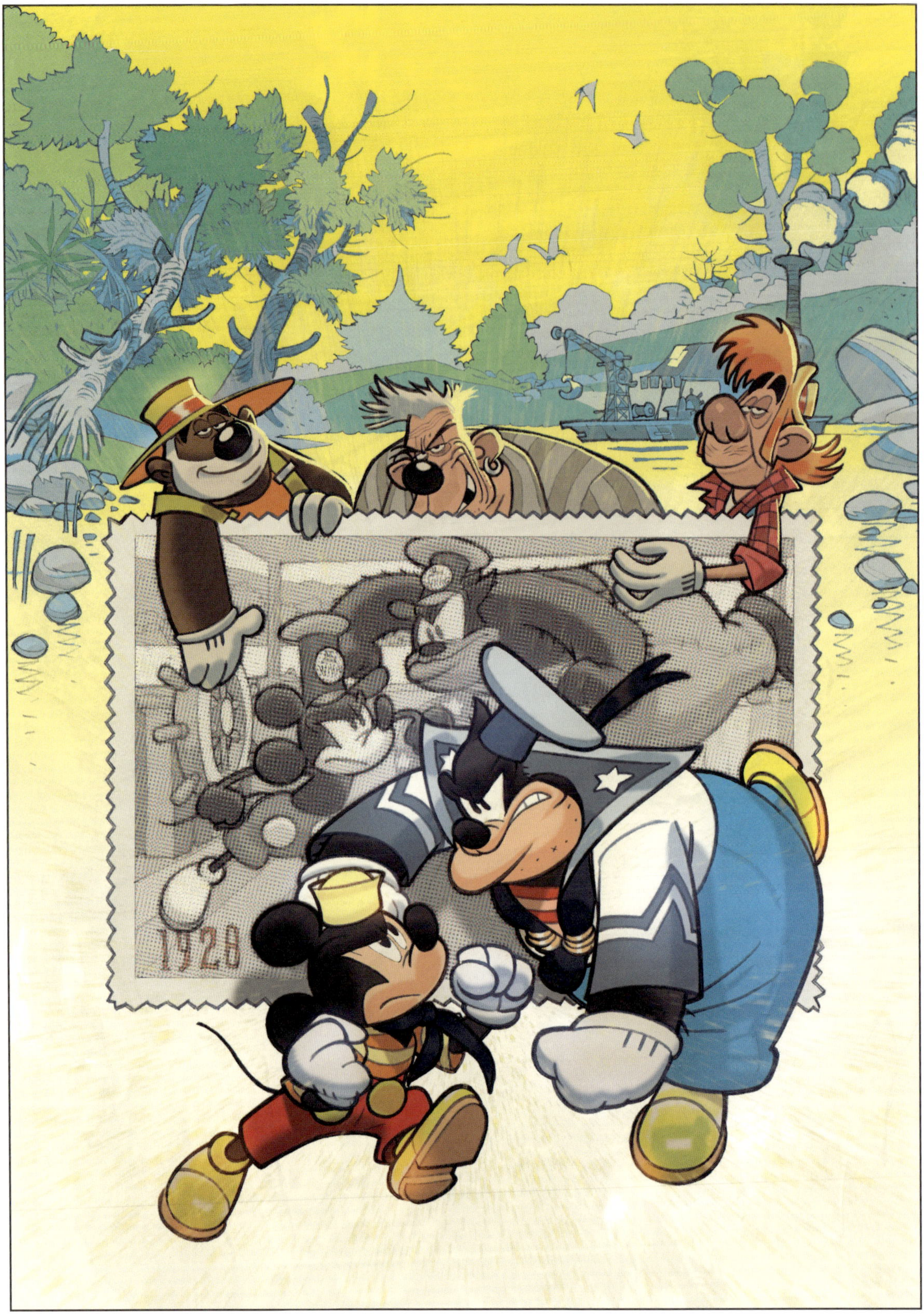
1928

Cover art illustrating "The River of Time," first published on Italian *Disney De Luxe Edition* 21 (November 2018). Art and color by Corrado Mastantuono.